CONGRESSIONAL POLICIES, PRACTICES AND PROCEDURES

THE FARM BILL

CURRENT LAW, BUDGET ISSUES AND LEGISLATIVE ACTIONS

CONGRESSIONAL POLICIES, PRACTICES AND PROCEDURES

Additional books and e-books in this series can be found on Nova's website under the Series tab.

CONGRESSIONAL POLICIES, PRACTICES AND PROCEDURES

THE FARM BILL

CURRENT LAW, BUDGET ISSUES AND LEGISLATIVE ACTIONS

BILLIE GRANT

EDITOR

nova science publishers

New York

Library of Congress Cataloging-in-Publication Data

ISBN: 978-1-53615-294-4

Published by Nova Science Publishers, Inc. † New York

CONTENTS

Preface

Congress has been active in establishing federal policy for the agricultural sector on an ongoing basis since the 1930s. Over the years, as economic conditions and technology have evolved, Congress has regularly revisited agricultural policy through periodic farm legislation. Over these decades, the breadth of policy areas addressed through such farm bills has expanded beyond providing support for a limited number of agricultural commodities to include establishing programs and policies that address a spectrum of related areas, such as agricultural conservation, credit, rural development, domestic nutrition assistance, trade and international food aid, organic agriculture, and support for beginning and veteran farmers and ranchers, among others.

Congress sets national food and agriculture policy through periodic omnibus farm bills. The 115th Congress has the opportunity to establish the future direction of farm and food policy because many of the provisions in the current farm bill expire in 2018. Chapter 1 provides a title-by-title summary of the policies and provisions in H.R. 2 and compares them with current law.

The Trump Administration released its first full budget request on May 23, 2017. It proposes specific amounts for the FY2018 Agriculture appropriation as well as legislative changes to various mandatory spending programs, including those in the farm bill. Chapter 2 separates the

President's budget request into proposed changes for agriculture based on congressional jurisdiction.

Over time, farm bills have tended to become more complicated and politically sensitive. As a result, the timeline for reauthorization has become less certain. Chapter 3 reports on the budget issues shaping the 2018 farm bill while chapter 4 examines the major legislative milestones for the last 12 farm bills covering 54 years.

Three farm bills have contained an energy title: the 2002 farm bill, the 2008 farm bill, and the 2014 farm bill. For all three farm bills, the major energy programs expire and lack baseline funding. Chapter 5 presents data on 2014 farm bill budgetary authority for energy provisions, as well as the original budget authority for Title IX programs under the previous 2008 farm bill.

The timing and consequences of expiration vary by program across the breadth of the farm bill. There are two principal expiration dates: September 30 and December 31. Chapter 6 reports on the possible consequences of expiration including minimal disruption (if the program is able to be continued via appropriations), ceasing new activity (if its authorization to use mandatory funding expires), or reverting to permanent laws enacted decades ago (for the farm commodity programs).

Chapter 1 - Congress sets national food and agriculture policy through periodic omnibus farm bills. The 115th Congress has the opportunity to establish the future direction of farm and food policy because many of the provisions in the current farm bill (the Agricultural Act of 2014, P.L. 113-79) expire in 2018. The 2014 farm bill addresses a broad range of farm and food programs and policies, including commodity support, crop insurance, conservation, domestic food assistance, trade and food aid, credit, rural development, research, horticulture, forestry, and bioenergy, among others. On June 21, 2018, the House voted 213-211 to approve H.R. 2, the Agriculture and Nutrition Act of 2018, an omnibus farm bill that would establish farm and food policy for the next five years, covering FY2019-FY2023. The vote to approve H.R. 2 followed a failed vote of 198-213 on the same bill on May 18, 2018. The final passage vote of June 21 occurred after a vote of 233-191 approving a motion to reconsider, which was made following the unsuccessful vote on final passage of May 18. In terms of cost, the most recent Congressional Budget Office (CBO) score of the programs in the bill with mandatory spending, such as nutrition programs, commodity support programs, major conservation programs, and crop insurance, amounts to $867 billion over a 10-year budget window (FY2019-FY2028). This amount is equivalent to CBO's baseline scenario in which existing farm bill programs would be extended with no changes. H.R. 2 would reauthorize most existing programs for five years through FY2023. Overall, the bill provides continuity with the existing framework of farm and food programs even as it modifies numerous programs, alters the amount and type of program funding certain programs receive, and exercises the committee's discretion not to reauthorize others. Among its many policy provisions, H.R. 2 would make changes to the eligibility requirements for individuals participating in the Supplemental Nutrition Assistance Program (SNAP), including expanding the population that is subject to work requirements, while requiring states to offer employment or training opportunities and increasing funding to the states for those purposes. Among the changes to commodity programs, an escalator provision could raise the effective reference price for crops enrolled in the Price Loss Coverage program (PLC) under certain market conditions. H.R. 2 would also amend payment limits and the adjusted gross income limit on eligibility for farm program payments to expand the list of producer exemptions from payment and income limits. Payment limits on certain disaster assistance programs would also be raised. The Dairy Margin Protection Program for milk producers is recast as the Dairy Risk Management Program, featuring an expanded range of coverage choices and lower premium rates on the first 5 million pounds of annual milk production. Within the conservation title, H.R. 2 would repeal the Conservation Stewardship Program (CSP), which has an enrollment of 70 million acres, and uses some of the savings to increase funding for the Environmental Quality Incentives Program (EQIP). It also raises the acreage enrollment limit under the Conservation Reserve Program (CRP). The bill further increases the loan limits for guaranteed farm ownership and operating loans. Bioenergy programs that comprise a separate title in the 2014 farm bill are included in a title on rural infrastructure and economic development. Also, while many of these bioenergy programs are currently authorized for mandatory funding in addition to being authorized for discretionary funds, H.R. 2 authorizes only discretionary funding. For rural communities, the bill authorizes the Secretary of Agriculture to reprioritize certain loan and grant programs to respond to specific health emergencies and to develop prevention, treatment, and recovery services. It would also require the Secretary to promulgate minimum acceptable standards for broadband service from the present day up to 30 years into the future.

Chapter 2 - Congress sets national food and agriculture policy through periodic omnibus farm bills. The 115th Congress has the opportunity to establish the future direction of farm and food policy because many of the provisions in the current farm bill (the Agricultural Act of 2014, P.L. 113-79) expire in 2018. The 2014 farm bill addresses a broad range of farm and food programs and policies, including commodity support, crop insurance, conservation, domestic food assistance, trade and food aid, credit, rural development, research, horticulture, forestry, and bioenergy, among others. On June 21, 2018, the House voted 213-211 to approve H.R. 2, the Agriculture and Nutrition Act of 2018, an omnibus farm bill that would establish farm and food policy for the next five years, covering FY2019-FY2023. The vote to approve H.R. 2 followed a failed vote of 198-213 on the same bill on May 18, 2018. The final passage vote of June 21 occurred after a vote of 233-191 approving a motion to reconsider, which was made following the unsuccessful vote on final passage of May 18. In terms of cost, the most recent Congressional Budget Office (CBO) score of the programs in the bill with mandatory spending, such as nutrition programs, commodity support programs, major conservation programs, and crop insurance, amounts to $867 billion over a 10-year budget window (FY2019-FY2028). This amount is equivalent to CBO's baseline scenario in which existing farm bill programs would be extended with no changes. H.R. 2 would reauthorize most existing programs for five years through FY2023. Overall, the bill provides continuity with the existing framework of farm and food programs even as it modifies numerous programs, alters the amount and type of program funding certain programs receive, and exercises the committee's discretion not to reauthorize others. Among its many policy provisions, H.R.

2 would make changes to the eligibility requirements for individuals participating in the Supplemental Nutrition Assistance Program (SNAP), including expanding the population that is subject to work requirements, while requiring states to offer employment or training opportunities and increasing funding to the states for those purposes. Among the changes to commodity programs, an escalator provision could raise the effective reference price for crops enrolled in the Price Loss Coverage program (PLC) under certain market conditions. H.R. 2 would also amend payment limits and the adjusted gross income limit on eligibility for farm program payments to expand the list of producer exemptions from payment and income limits. Payment limits on certain disaster assistance programs would also be raised. The Dairy Margin Protection Program for milk producers is recast as the Dairy Risk Management Program, featuring an expanded range of coverage choices and lower premium rates on the first 5 million pounds of annual milk production. Within the conservation title, H.R. 2 would repeal the Conservation Stewardship Program (CSP), which has an enrollment of 70 million acres, and uses some of the savings to increase funding for the Environmental Quality Incentives Program (EQIP). It also raises the acreage enrollment limit under the Conservation Reserve Program (CRP). The bill further increases the loan limits for guaranteed farm ownership and operating loans. Bioenergy programs that comprise a separate title in the 2014 farm bill are included in a title on rural infrastructure and economic development. Also, while many of these bioenergy programs are currently authorized for mandatory funding in addition to being authorized for discretionary funds, H.R. 2 authorizes only discretionary funding. For rural communities, the bill authorizes the Secretary of Agriculture to reprioritize certain loan and grant programs to respond to specific health emergencies and to develop prevention, treatment, and recovery services. It would also require the Secretary to promulgate minimum acceptable standards for broadband service from the present day up to 30 years into the future.

Chapter 3 - The farm bill is an omnibus, multi-year law that governs an array of agricultural and food programs. It provides an opportunity for policymakers to periodically address a broad range of agricultural and food issues. The farm bill has typically undergone reauthorization about every five years. The 115th Congress has considered a new farm bill but has not enacted one to date. Both the House and the Senate passed versions of a 2018 farm bill (H.R. 2) in June 2018. Conference proceedings officially began in September 2018 but have not reached agreement. The farm bill provides an opportunity for Congress to choose how much support, if any, to provide for various agriculture and nutrition programs and how to allocate it among competing constituencies. Under congressional budgeting rules, many programs are assumed to continue beyond the end of a farm bill. From a budgetary perspective, this provides funding to reauthorize programs, reallocate funding to other programs, or be taken for deficit reduction.

Chapter 4 - The farm bill provides an opportunity for Congress to address agricultural and food issues comprehensively about every five years. Over time, farm bills have tended to become more complicated and politically sensitive. As a result, the timeline for reauthorization has become less certain. With the exception of the 2018 farm bill, recent farm bills have taken longer to enact than in previous decades. Beginning in 2008, farm bills have been subject to various developments that have delayed enactment, such as insufficient votes to pass the House floor, presidential vetoes, or short-term extensions. The Agriculture Improvement Act of 2018 (P.L. 115-334), often called the "2018 farm bill," was enacted on December 20, 2018. In the House, the Agriculture Committee reported the bill on April 18, 2018. An initial floor vote on May 18 failed in the House 198-213, but floor procedures allowed that vote to be reconsidered (H.Res. 905). The House passed H.R. 2 in a second vote of 213-211 on June 21. In the Senate, the Agriculture Committee reported its bill (S. 3042) on June 13, 2018, by a vote of 20-1. The Senate passed its bill as an amendment to H.R. 2 by a vote of 86-11 on June 28. Conference proceedings officially began on September 5, 2018, and concluded in December with a Senate vote of 87-13 and a House vote of 369-47 (H.Rept. 115-1072). The 2018 farm bill took 8 months from introduction to passage. By comparison, the 2014 farm bill took more than 21 months from introduction to enactment, and spanned the 112th and 113th Congresses. The 2008 farm bill took more than a year to enact and was complicated by revenue provisions from another committee of jurisdiction, temporary extensions, and vetoes. Most farm bills have been introduced in the first session of a two-year Congress (the odd-numbered year). Three of the farm bills that were introduced in the second session—the 1970, 1990, and 2018 farm bills—were enacted during a lame duck Congress of the same year. The 2014 farm bill was the first farm bill to start in one Congress (2012), remain unfinished, and require reintroduction in a subsequent Congress. This chapter examines the major legislative milestones for the last 12 farm bills covering 54 years.

Chapter 5 - Title IX, the energy title of the 2014 farm bill (Agricultural Act of 2014; P.L. 113-79), contains authority for the energy programs administered by the U.S. Department of Agriculture (USDA). USDA energy programs have incentivized research, development, and adoption of renewable energy projects, including solar, wind, and anaerobic digesters. However, the primary focus of USDA energy programs has been to promote U.S. biofuels production and use—including corn starch-based ethanol (the predominant biofuel produced and consumed in the United States), cellulosic ethanol, and soybean-based biodiesel. The USDA energy programs via the farm bill are separate from the Renewable Fuel Standard (RFS) and tax incentives contained in separate energy and tax legislation. Three farm bills have contained an energy title: the 2002 farm bill, the 2008 farm bill, and the 2014 farm bill. For all three farm bills, the major energy programs expire and lack baseline funding. The enacted 2014 farm bill extended most of the energy provisions of the 2008 farm bill with new funding authority, with the exception of the Rural Energy Self-Sufficiency Initiative, the Forest Biomass for Energy Program, the Biofuels Infrastructure Study, and the Renewable Fertilizer Study, which were either omitted or repealed. At issue for Congress is what oversight, programs, and initiatives, if any, an energy title under the forthcoming farm bill might support. The 2014 farm bill energy title provisions may be of interest during the upcoming farm bill debate, as Congress may decide to modify or reauthorize many of the programs. The 2014 farm bill continued the attempt to refocus U.S. biofuels policy initiatives to favor non-corn feedstocks (e.g., cellulosic feedstocks). The most critical programs to this end are the Bioenergy Program for Advanced Biofuels, which pays producers for production of eligible advanced biofuels; the Biorefinery, Renewable

Chemical, and Biobased Product Manufacturing Assistance Program (formerly Biorefinery Assistance Program), which assists in the development of new and emerging technologies for advanced biofuels; the Biomass Crop Assistance Program (BCAP), which assists farmers in developing nontraditional crops for use as feedstocks for the eventual production of cellulosic biofuels; and the Renewable Energy for America Program (REAP), which has funded a variety of biofuels-related projects. In addition, the 2014 farm bill included a new provision that precludes the use of REAP funding for any mechanism for dispensing energy at the retail level (e.g., blender pumps). Also, despite several amendments to the contrary, and its explicit exclusion from all financial support in the House-passed version of the 2014 farm bill (H.R. 2642), BCAP funding for the collection, harvest, storage, and transportation (CHST) component was retained in the 2014 farm bill. Finally, the 2014 farm bill added a new reporting requirement on energy use and efficiency at USDA facilities. Over the five-year reauthorization period (FY2014-FY2018), the 2014 farm bill contained a total of $694 million in new mandatory funding and authorizes discretionary funding (i.e., subject to annual appropriations) of $765 million for the various farm bill renewable energy programs. This is a significant reduction from the 2008 farm bill, which had authorized slightly over $1 billion in mandatory funding over the five-year period of FY2008-FY2012, along with $1.7 billion in discretionary appropriations to Title IX energy programs. The mandatory funding has been the primary support for these programs, as appropriators have not provided funding for most of the discretionary authorizations.

Chapter 6 - The farm bill is an omnibus, multi-year law that governs an array of agricultural and food programs. It provides an opportunity for policymakers to periodically address a broad range of agricultural and food issues. The farm bill is typically reauthorized about every five years. Recent farm bills have been subject to various developments, such as insufficient votes to pass the House floor, presidential vetoes, or—as in the case of 2008 and 2014 farm bills—short-term extensions. The current farm bill (the Agricultural Act of 2014, P.L. 113-79) has many provisions that expire in 2018. The 115th Congress has begun but not finished a new farm bill. An initial House vote on H.R. 2 failed by vote of 198-213, but floor procedures allowed that vote to be reconsidered, and it passed by a second vote of 213-211. The Senate passed its bill as an amendment to H.R. 2 by a vote of 86-11. Conference proceedings officially began on September 5, 2018, but have not yet reached agreement. The timing and consequences of expiration vary by program across the breadth of the farm bill. There are two principal expiration dates: September 30 and December 31. The 2014 farm bill generally expires either at the end of FY2018 (September 30, 2018), or with the 2018 crop year. Crop years vary by commodity, but the first to be affected by a new crop year is dairy, whose 2018 crop year ends on December 31, 2018. The possible consequences of expiration include minimal disruption (if the program is able to be continued via appropriations), ceasing new activity (if its authorization to use mandatory funding expires), or reverting to permanent laws enacted decades ago (for the farm commodity programs). For example

- An appropriations act or a continuing resolution can continue some farm bill programs even though an authority has expired. Programs using discretionary funding—and programs using appropriated mandatory funding like those in the SNAP account—can continue to operate via appropriations action.
- Most farm bill programs with mandatory funding (except the Supplemental Nutrition Assistance Program (SNAP), the farm commodity programs, and crop insurance) generally cease new operations when they expire (e.g., the Conservation Reserve Program (CRP), and Market Assistance Program (MAP)).
- The mandatory farm commodity programs would begin reverting to permanent law beginning with the 2019 crop year, for which dairy is the first to be affected, beginning on January 1, 2019.
- Crop insurance is an example of a program with mandatory funding that is permanently authorized outside of the farm bill and does not expire.

"Permanent law" refers to non-expiring farm commodity programs that are generally from the 1938 and 1949 farm bills. A temporary suspension of permanent law has been included in all recent farm bills, but reverting to permanent law would occur if the suspension expires. The commodity support provisions of permanent law are commonly viewed as being fundamentally different from current policy—and inconsistent with today's farming practices, marketing system, and international trade agreements—as well as potentially costly to the federal government. Among the mandatory-funded programs that are usually the focus of the farm bill, there are two subcategories that may affect congressional action—some have baseline beyond FY2018 and some do not have baseline after FY2018. In an expiration, both categories of mandatory programs can face similar disruption when their authorizations expire. But the difference in having or not having a baseline is important if Congress considers an extension to deal with an expiration. Providing funding for those programs without baseline could make extension more difficult if budget offsets are needed to keep an extension budget-neutral.

In: The Farm Bill
Editor: Billie Grant

ISBN: 978-1-53615-294-4

Chapter 1

THE HOUSE AGRICULTURE COMMITTEE'S 2018 FARM BILL (H.R. 2): A SIDE-BY-SIDE COMPARISON WITH CURRENT LAW*

Mark A. McMinimy

ABSTRACT

Congress sets national food and agriculture policy through periodic omnibus farm bills. The 115th Congress has the opportunity to establish the future direction of farm and food policy because many of the provisions in the current farm bill (the Agricultural Act of 2014, P.L. 113-79) expire in 2018. The 2014 farm bill addresses a broad range of farm and food programs and policies, including commodity support, crop insurance, conservation, domestic food assistance, trade and food aid, credit, rural development, research, horticulture, forestry, and bioenergy, among others.

On June 21, 2018, the House voted 213-211 to approve H.R. 2, the Agriculture and Nutrition Act of 2018, an omnibus farm bill that would establish farm and food policy for the next five years, covering FY2019-

---

* This is an edited, reformatted and augmented version of Congressional Research Service, Publication No. R45197, dated June 29, 2018.

FY2023. The vote to approve H.R. 2 followed a failed vote of 198-213 on the same bill on May 18, 2018. The final passage vote of June 21 occurred after a vote of 233-191 approving a motion to reconsider, which was made following the unsuccessful vote on final passage of May 18.

In terms of cost, the most recent Congressional Budget Office (CBO) score of the programs in the bill with mandatory spending, such as nutrition programs, commodity support programs, major conservation programs, and crop insurance, amounts to $867 billion over a 10-year budget window (FY2019-FY2028). This amount is equivalent to CBO's baseline scenario in which existing farm bill programs would be extended with no changes.

H.R. 2 would reauthorize most existing programs for five years through FY2023. Overall, the bill provides continuity with the existing framework of farm and food programs even as it modifies numerous programs, alters the amount and type of program funding certain programs receive, and exercises the committee's discretion not to reauthorize others.

Among its many policy provisions, H.R. 2 would make changes to the eligibility requirements for individuals participating in the Supplemental Nutrition Assistance Program (SNAP), including expanding the population that is subject to work requirements, while requiring states to offer employment or training opportunities and increasing funding to the states for those purposes. Among the changes to commodity programs, an escalator provision could raise the effective reference price for crops enrolled in the Price Loss Coverage program (PLC) under certain market conditions. H.R. 2 would also amend payment limits and the adjusted gross income limit on eligibility for farm program payments to expand the list of producer exemptions from payment and income limits. Payment limits on certain disaster assistance programs would also be raised. The Dairy Margin Protection Program for milk producers is recast as the Dairy Risk Management Program, featuring an expanded range of coverage choices and lower premium rates on the first 5 million pounds of annual milk production.

Within the conservation title, H.R. 2 would repeal the Conservation Stewardship Program (CSP), which has an enrollment of 70 million acres, and uses some of the savings to increase funding for the Environmental Quality Incentives Program (EQIP). It also raises the acreage enrollment limit under the Conservation Reserve Program (CRP). The bill further increases the loan limits for guaranteed farm ownership and operating loans. Bioenergy programs that comprise a separate title in the 2014 farm bill are included in a title on rural infrastructure and economic development. Also, while many of these bioenergy programs are currently authorized for mandatory funding in addition to being authorized for discretionary funds, H.R. 2 authorizes only discretionary funding.

For rural communities, the bill authorizes the Secretary of Agriculture to reprioritize certain loan and grant programs to respond to specific health emergencies and to develop prevention, treatment, and recovery services.

It would also require the Secretary to promulgate minimum acceptable standards for broadband service from the present day up to 30 years into the future.

INTRODUCTION

Congress has been active in establishing federal policy for the agricultural sector on an ongoing basis since the 1930s. Over the years, as economic conditions and technology have evolved, Congress has regularly revisited agricultural policy through periodic farm legislation. Over these decades, the breadth of policy areas addressed through such farm bills has expanded beyond providing support for a limited number of agricultural commodities to include establishing programs and policies that address a spectrum of related areas, such as agricultural conservation, credit, rural development, domestic nutrition assistance, trade and international food aid, organic agriculture, and support for beginning and veteran farmers and ranchers, among others.

On June 21, 2018, the House voted 213-211 to approve H.R. 2, the Agriculture and Nutrition Act of 2018, an omnibus farm bill that would establish farm and food policy for the next five years, covering FY2019-FY2023. The vote to approve H.R. 2 followed a failed vote of 198-213 on the same bill on May 18, 2018. The final passage vote on June 21 followed a vote of 233-191 approving a motion to reconsider, which was made after the unsuccessful vote on final passage of May 18. The Committee on Agriculture marked up and ordered reported H.R. 2 on April 18, 2018.

The House-passed version of H.R. 2 continues the tradition of multi-year farm bills that would establish policy for farm programs and nutrition assistance. To this end, H.R. 2 addresses agriculture and food policy across 11 titles that cover commodity support programs, agricultural conservation, trade and international food aid, domestic nutrition assistance, credit, rural infrastructure and economic development, research and extension, forestry, horticulture, and a variety of other policies and initiatives. The Congressional Budget Office (CBO) projected that spending on mandatory programs under H.R. 2 would total $867 billion over the 10-year period FY2019-FY2028, which equals the cost of extending the current 2014 farm bill for 10 years.

H.R. 2 would supersede the current slate of farm programs and policies authorized by the 2014 farm bill, P.L. 113-79, many of which will expire in 2018 unless Congress acts to reauthorize them or to extend them. Certain programs, such as crop insurance, are permanently authorized and would continue to operate in the absence of new farm legislation or an extension of the current farm bill. But if the current farm law were to expire, many other programs—such as commodity support programs that provide a safety net for producers of major agricultural commodities, such as corn and wheat, milk, sugar, and others—would be governed by so-called permanent laws, which do not expire and date from the late 1930s and 1940s.

These permanent laws, including the Agricultural Adjustment Act of 1938 (P.L. 75-430) and Agricultural Act of 1949 (P.L. 81-439), emphasize supply controls to support price support regimes that would raise prices of these basic farm commodities well above existing market levels. A change in farm policy along these lines from the market-driven and export-oriented model that characterizes most existing commodity support programs could prove to be broadly disruptive for farmers, farm input suppliers, agricultural exporters, food manufacturers, and consumers. Many other programs, such as conservation programs and rural development programs, would cease to function. In the past, when Congress has faced the prospect of expiring farm legislation without enacting successor legislation, it has acted to extend the existing policies, as it did when the 2002 and 2008 acts expired.

This chapter provides a title-by-title summary of the policies and provisions in H.R. 2 and compares them with current law. Following an analysis of the budgetary implications of H.R. 2, summaries of major changes the bill would make in each of its 11 titles are provided. These summaries are followed by side-by-side comparison tables for each of the bill's 11 titles that briefly describe the provisions in H.R. 2 and compare them with current law. During the floor debate on H.R. 2, the House adopted a number of amendments to the bill, which are listed in Table A-1.

BUDGETARY IMPACT[1]

A farm bill authorizes funding in two ways. It authorizes and pays for mandatory outlays with multiyear budget estimates when the law is enacted. It also sets the parameters for discretionary programs and authorizes them to receive future appropriations but does not provide funding. Mandatory programs often dominate farm bill policy and the debate over the farm bill budget.

The budgetary impact of mandatory spending proposals is measured relative to an assumption that certain programs continue beyond the end of the farm bill. The benchmark is the CBO baseline—a projection at a particular point in time of future federal spending on mandatory programs under current law. The baseline provides funding for reauthorization, reallocation to other programs, or offsets for deficit reduction.[2]

When a new bill is proposed that would affect mandatory spending, the score (cost impact) is measured in relation to the baseline. Changes that increase spending relative to the baseline have a *positive* score; those that decrease spending relative to the baseline have a *negative* score. Budget enforcement uses these baselines and scores and may follow "PayGo" and other budget rules (that in part may require no increase to the federal deficit).[3]

In April 2018, CBO released a baseline for farm bill programs with mandatory spending that will be used for the rest of the legislative year.[4] It projects that, if current law were extended, farm bill programs would cost $867 billion over the next 10 years, FY2019-FY2028, 77% of which is in the nutrition title for the Supplemental Nutrition Assistance Program (SNAP). The remaining $203 billion baseline is for agricultural programs, mostly in crop insurance, farm commodity programs, and conservation.

---

[1] This section was written by Jim Monke, Specialist in Agricultural Policy.

[2] CRS In Focus IF10783, *Farm Bill Primer: Budget Issues.*

[3] CRS Report 98-560, *Baselines and Scorekeeping in the Federal Budget Process.*

[4] CBO, "Baseline Projections for Selected Programs," April 2018, https://www.cbo.gov/about/products/baseline- projections-selected-programs, and in table notes in "H.R. 2, Agriculture and Nutrition Act of 2018," May 2, 2018, https://www.cbo.gov/publication/53819.

Other titles of the farm bill contribute less than 1% of the baseline (Figure 1), some of which are funded primarily with discretionary spending.

Relative to this baseline, CBO released its score of H.R. 2 on April 13, 2018.[5] CBO estimates that H.R. 2 is essentially budget neutral over the procedural 10-year budget window (Table 2). The bill would increase mandatory (direct) spending by $458 million and is offset by increases in revenue of $465 million, reflecting fees paid by contractors in the SNAP electronic benefits transfer (EBT) program.

Under H.R. 2, the baseline of the three largest titles (nutrition, crop insurance, and commodities) is projected to remain within roughly 0.5% of current law. Within individual titles, the conservation and nutrition titles would experience larger shifts among programs within their respective titles. For example, the conservation title's 10-year baseline would be reduced by $795 million (-1.3%), reflecting a $12.6 billion reduction (21%) from repealing the Conservation Stewardship Program (CSP), which is the offset for increases in other conservation programs (Table 3). The nutrition title's 10-year baseline would increase by $463 million (+0.07%), although this includes reductions of $20 billion (3%) in benefits that are reallocated to other programs in the nutrition title. Moreover, the overall nutrition title increase, $463 million, is more than offset by the projected $465 million increase in revenue attributed to that title.

Bioenergy programs, which had their own title in recent farm bills, are addressed in the rural development title of H.R. 2, where their mandatory funding is eliminated (-$517 million over 10 years). Animal disease and preparedness programs, including a vaccine bank, receive new mandatory funding (+$450 million) in the miscellaneous title. Farm safety net program outlays would be essentially flat overall, with crop insurance title reductions (-$161 million over 10 years) nearly offsetting net increases in farm commodity title programs ($+193 million).[6]

---

[5] CBO, "Cost Estimate of H.R. 2, Agriculture and Nutrition Act of 2018," April 13, 2018, https://www.cbo.gov/publication/53760.

[6] The scoring of H.R. 2 assumes that changes in the Bipartisan Budget Act of 2018 (P.L. 115-141), particularly for the cotton and dairy programs, are already incorporated into the April 2018 CBO baseline projection. See CRS In Focus IF10829, *Agriculture Funding in the Bipartisan*

For several of the subset of programs in the 2014 farm bill that received mandatory funding but do not have a baseline beyond the end of FY2018,[7] H.R. 2 would provide new mandatory funding. Two research title programs would receive $250 million in mandatory funds, while trade title programs would receive $450 million and be provided with permanent baseline. A food insecurity program in the nutrition title would receive $472 million in mandatory funding and gain permanent baseline.

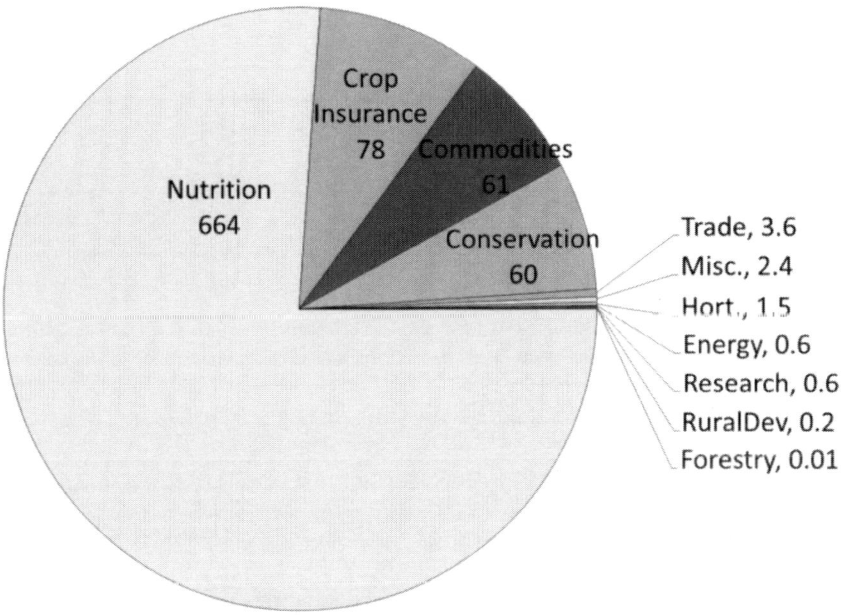

Source: CRS, using CBO April 2018 Baseline (unpublished).

Figure 1. CBO Baseline under Current Law, by Title; (10-year projected outlays, FY2019-FY2028, billions of dollars).

Budget Act of 2018; CRS In Focus IF10833, *Dairy Provisions in the Bipartisan Budget Act (P.L. 115-123)*; and CRS Report R45143, *Seed Cotton as a Farm Program Crop: In Brief*.

[7] CRS In Focus IF10780, *Farm Bill Primer: Programs Without Baseline Beyond FY2018*.

Table 1. Budget for a 2018 Farm Bill: Baseline and Scores, by Title (outlays in millions of dollars, 10-year total FY2019-FY2028)

House bill H.R. 2			
2014 Farm Bill Titles	**CBO Baseline**	**CBO Score**	**Baseline + Score**
Commodities	61,151	+193	61,344
Conservation	59,754	-795	58,959
Trade	3,624	+450	4,074
Nutrition	663,828	+463	664,291
Credit	-4,558	0	-4,558
Rural Development[a]	168	0[a]	168
Research	604	+250	854
Forestry	10	0	10
Energy[a]	612	-517[a]	95
Horticulture	1,547	+10	1,557
Crop Insurance	78,037	-161	77,876
Miscellaneous	2,423	+566	2,989
Subtotal	**867,200**	**+458**	**867,658**
Increases in Revenue	-	+465	465
Total	**867,200**	**-7**	**867,193**

Source: CRS, using the CBO baseline (April 2018) and CBO Cost Estimate of H.R. 2 (April 13, 2018).

[a] H.R. 2 combines rural development and energy into a Rural Infrastructure and Economic Development title.

This table retains the separate titles, consistent with the 2014 farm bill and CBO baseline.

Table 2. CBO Score of H.R. 2, by Section (Projected change in outlays relative to April 2018 baseline, FY2019-FY2028, millions of dollars)

Provision in H.R. 2	**FY 2019-28**	**Provision in H.R. 2**	**FY 2019-28**
Title I—Commodity Programs		Emergency Food Assistance	499
Agriculture Risk Coverage—Individual	-143	National Gateway	601
Agriculture Risk Coverage—County	-111	Nutrition Education	632
Dairy Program	-20	Transitional Benefits	895
Nonrecourse Marketing Assistance Loans	0	Retailer-Funded Incentives Pilot	1,204
Agriculture Disaster Assistance	11	Child Support; Cooperation with Agencies	3,494
Economic Assistance for Textile Mills	23	Earned Income Deduction	4,640
Implementation	25	Workforce Solutions: Administration	7,650

Provision in H.R. 2	**FY 2019-28**	**Provision in H.R. 2**	**FY 2019-28**
Price Loss Coverage	408	**Subtotal, Title IV**	463
Subtotal, Title I	193	**Title V—Credit**	0
Title II—Conservation		**Title VI—Rural Development, Energy**	
Repeal Conservation Stewardship Program	-12,618	Rural Energy for America Program	-435
Conservation Reserve Program	-23	Biorefinery Assistance	-82
Wetlands Mitigation Banking	10	**Subtotal, Title VI**	-517
Other Conservation Programs	614	**Title VII—Research**	
Regional Conservation Partnership Program	1,308	Beginning Farmer and Rancher Development	100
Agricultural Conservation Easement	2,221	Organic Agriculture Research and Extension	150
Environmental Quality Incentives Program	7,693	**Subtotal, Title VII**	250
Subtotal, Title II	-795	**Title VIII—Forestry**	0
Title III—Trade		**Title IX—Horticulture**	
International Development Program	450	National Organic Program Tech. Update	5
Subtotal, Title III	450	Organic Production and Market Data	5
Title IV—Nutrition		**Subtotal, Title IX**	10
Workforce Solutions: Benefits	-9,190	**Title X—Crop Insurance**	
Standard Utility Allowances Receipts	-5,250	Education and Risk Management Assistance	-125
Update to Categorical Eligibility	-5,035	Increase Cat. Coverage Fee to $500	-72
Duplicative Enrollment Database	-588	Research and Development Priorities	-45
State Performance Indicators	-432	Program Administration	-18
Benefit Recovery	<0.5	Whole Farm Applied to Beginning Farmers	9
Tolerance Level for Payment Errors	<0.5	Treatment of Forage and Grazing	90
Mobile Technologies	12	**Subtotal, Title X**	-161
SNAP Benefit Transfer Data Report	30	**Title XI—Miscellaneous**	
Interactions	30	Noninsured Assistance Program	-37
Simplified Homeless Housing Costs	76	Outreach to Socially Disadvantaged	50
Adjustment to Recovered Funds Retained	102	Textile Trust Fund	103
Basic Allowance for Housing	116	National Animal Disease Preparedness	450

Table 2. (Continued)

Provision in H.R. 2	FY 2019-28	Provision in H.R. 2	FY 2019-28
Implementation Funds	150	**Subtotal, Title XI**	566
Processing Fees	154	**Total Changes in Direct Spending**	458
Adjustment to Asset Limitations	201	Increases in Revenue	465
Food Insecurity Nutrition Incentive Program	472	**Net Effect on the Deficit**	-7

Source: CRS, sorted within titles using the CBO Score of H.R. 2, April 13, 2018,

TITLE-BY-TITLE SUMMARY

Title I, Commodity Program[8]

Title I commodity programs authorize support programs for dairy, sugar, and covered commodities—including major grain, oilseed, and pulse crops—as well as agricultural disaster assistance. Major field-crop programs include the Price Loss Coverage (PLC) and Agricultural Risk Coverage (ARC) programs and the Marketing Assistance Loan (MAL) program. The dairy program involves protecting a portion of the margin between milk and feed prices. The sugar program provides a combination of price support, border protection, and producer production allotments. Four disaster assistance programs that focus primarily on livestock and tree crops were permanently authorized in the 2014 farm bill. These disaster assistance programs provide federal assistance to help farmers recover financially from natural disasters, including drought and floods. Title I also includes several administrative provisions that suspend permanent farm law from 1938 and 1949; assign payment limits for individuals, joint ventures or partnerships, and corporations; specify the adjusted gross income (AGI) threshold for

[8] This section was written by Randy Schnepf (farm commodity support) and Mark McMinimy (sugar), Specialists in Agricultural Policy; Joel Greene (dairy) and Sahar Angadjivand (farm commodity support), Analysts in Agricultural Policy; and Megan Stubbs (disaster assistance), Specialist in Agricultural Conservation and Natural Resources Policy.

program payment eligibility; and identify other details regarding payment attribution and eligibility.

H.R. 2 extends authority for current commodity programs but with some modifications to programs for covered commodities and dairy as well as agricultural disaster assistance. The sugar program is extended but is otherwise unchanged. H.R. 2 also amends both payment limits and the AGI limit to expand the list of producer exemptions from payment and income limits under certain conditions.

In general, program changes affecting covered commodities under H.R. 2 make PLC a more attractive option for producers than ARC. In particular, H.R. 2 includes an escalator provision that would raise a covered commodity's effective reference price (used in the PLC payment formula) by as much as 115% of the statutory PLC reference price based on 85% of the five-year Olympic average[9] of farm prices. In addition, producers participating in PLC that experienced at least 20 consecutive weeks of severe drought during 2008-2012 would be allowed to update their program yields (used in the PLC payment formula). In contrast, producers enrolled in the county-level ARC program (or the stacked income protection plan for cotton) would be ineligible for crop insurance coverage under an area yield and loss basis or the supplemental coverage option. Furthermore, the individual, farm-level ARC program is eliminated.

The MAL program would be retained as is under H.R. 2, but any program benefits would be exempted from inclusion under both payment limits and the AGI limit. Payment limits would also be affected by H.R. 2's treatment of eligible payment entities. Under current law, partnerships and joint ventures are treated as collections of individuals, each with their own payment limits, whereas a corporation is treated as a single individual subject to a single payment limit. H.R. 2 would alter the treatment of certain corporations by defining a "qualified pass through entity" (QTPE) as including partnerships, joint ventures, limited liability corporations, and S corporations.[10] This would allow each separate owner of a QTPE (meeting all program eligibility criteria) to have an individual payment limit. Also,

---

[9] The Olympic average excludes the high- and low-price years from calculation of the average.

[10] S corporations meet the requirements of subchapter S of the Internal Revenue Code.

H.R. 2 would redefine *family farm* to include first cousins, nieces, and nephews, thus increasing the potential pool of individuals eligible for an individual payment limit on family farming operations.

With respect to agricultural disaster assistance programs, H.R. 2 amends the limits on payments received under the programs and waives the AGI requirement if more than 75% of the producer's income comes from farming, ranching, or silviculture. The bill also expands payments for livestock losses caused by disease.

H.R. 2 expands producer coverage choices under the current Margin Protection Program (MPP) and renames it the Dairy Risk Management Program (DRMP). Like MPP, the DRMP pays participating dairy producers the difference (when positive) between a producer-selected margin and the national milk margin (calculated as the all-milk price minus an average feed cost ration). Under H.R. 2, the U.S. Department of Agriculture (USDA) is required to conduct studies on whether the feed cost ration is representative of actual feed costs used in the margin calculation and on the cost of corn silage versus the feed cost of corn. The bill also directs USDA to report alfalfa hay prices in the top five milk producing states.

Under current law, for a $100 administrative fee, participating dairy producers automatically receive payments on 90% of their first 5 million pounds or less of milk production when the milk margin falls below $5.00 per hundredweight (cwt.). Under DRMP, the catastrophic margin is lowered to $4.00/cwt. Also, under current law dairy producers select a margin protection level in $0.50/cwt. increments from $4.00/cwt. to $8.00/cwt. and a percent coverage ranging from 25% to 90% of the farm's historical milk production. Premiums paid by producers vary with coverage levels selected and across two production tiers: Tier I is the first 5 million pounds of milk production; Tier II is milk production above 5 million pounds. Under DRMP, additional margin levels of $8.50/cwt. and $9.00/cwt. are available for Tier I. Premiums are reinstated for the $4.50/cwt. and $5.00/cwt. margins under Tier I, while premiums are reduced substantially for the other Tier I margins ranging from $5.50/cwt. to $8.00/cwt., and the percent coverage range is extended to 5% to 90% of a farm's milk production history. Premiums for Tier II would be left unchanged. A difference under DRMP from current law is that dairy producers would make a single one-time election of a margin coverage level and a percentage of milk production to cover. This election would last the duration of the farm bill.

H.R. 2 would also repeal the Dairy Product Donation Program; extend through FY2023 the Dairy Forward Pricing Program, the Dairy Indemnity Program, and the Dairy Promotion and Research Program; and eliminate the provision prohibiting dairy producers from participating in both the DRMP and the Livestock Gross Margin-Dairy insurance program, although dual coverage cannot be on the same milk production. Finally, H.R. 2 amends the formula for the Class I skim milk price used for calculating the Class I price under Federal Milk Marketing Orders.

Title II, Conservation[11]

USDA administers a number of agricultural conservation programs that assist private landowners with natural resource concerns. These can be broadly grouped into working land programs, land retirement and easement programs, watershed programs, emergency programs, technical assistance, and other programs. H.R. 2 amends portions of programs in all of these categories. However, the general focus is on the larger working lands, land retirement, and easement programs. All current conservation programs are reauthorized with the exception of the largest— CSP which is repealed. New spending on the conservation title is projected to increase by $656 million over five years but over 10 years would be reduced by nearly $800 million.

In general, working land programs provide technical and financial assistance to assist farmers to improve land management practices. The two largest working lands programs—Environmental Quality Incentives Program (EQIP) and CSP—account for more than half of all conservation

[11] This section was written by Megan Stubbs, Specialist in Agricultural Conservation and Natural Resources Policy.

program funding.[12] H.R. 2 repeals CSP, which currently has an enrollment of more than 70 million acres. CSP provides financial and technical assistance to producers to maintain and improve existing conservation systems and to adopt additional conservation activities in a comprehensive manner on a producer's entire operation. A more limited version of the CSP stewardship contract is included in EQIP with the proviso that no more than 50% of EQIP funding may be used for these contracts. Existing CSP contracts would remain active until completion. Repealing CSP is the primary driver behind the projected decline in spending under the conservation title over 10 years, since CSP contracts are five years in duration and would all be completed by FY2023. H.R. 2 also amends EQIP by expanding options for irrigation entities, removing a requirement that 60% of payments relate to livestock production, limiting the EQIP Conservation Innovation Grants to $25 million, and increasing the overall funding in annual increments through FY2023 to $3 billion from $1.75 billion in FY2018.

Land retirement and easement programs provide federal payments to private agricultural landowners for permanent or long-term land-use restrictions. The Conservation Reserve Program (CRP), the largest land retirement program, is reauthorized and amended by H.R. 2. CRP provides annual rental payments to producers to replace crops on highly erodible and environmentally sensitive land with long-term resource-conserving plantings. Total CRP enrollment would be authorized to increase incrementally through FY2023 to 29 million acres from the current limit of 24 million acres. In order to offset this increased enrollment level, the bill would reduce payments to participants, allow for a one-time early termination of select CRP contracts without penalty in FY2019, and reduce incentives for continuous contracts and reenrollment. A number of other changes are made to CRP that would further expand grazing and commercial uses on CRP acres. The Agricultural Conservation Easement Program (ACEP) USDA's easement program, is also reauthorized and amended by H.R. 2. ACEP provides financial and technical assistance through two types

[12] EQIP and CSP combined received approximately $2.6 billion in FY2017. Total mandatory spending in FY2017 was approximately $5.3 billion.

of easements: agricultural land easements that limit nonagricultural uses on productive farm or grasslands and wetland reserve easements that protect and restore wetlands. Most of the changes to ACEP focus on the agricultural land easements in which USDA enters into partnership agreements with eligible entities to purchase agricultural land easements from willing landowners. H.R. 2 would provide additional flexibilities to ACEP eligible entities. It would also remove planning requirements, waive the AGI requirement, allow for mineral development and participation in environmental markets, and increase overall funding to $500 million annually.

The 2014 farm bill created the Regional Conservation Partnership Program (RCPP), which enrolls land through existing conservation programs in partnership with eligible partners. Under RCPP, partners define the scope and location of the project, provide 50% or more of the project cost, and work with eligible landowners to enroll in existing conservation programs. H.R. 2 expands funding for the program as well as the existing set of conservation programs covered under program. H.R. 2 would also provide for longer partnership agreements and project renewal options.

Title III, Trade[13]

The trade title deals with statutes concerning U.S. international food aid and agricultural export programs. Under the farm bill authority, U.S. international food assistance is distributed through three main programs: (1) Food for Peace (emergency and nonemergency food aid); (2) Food for Progress (agricultural development programs); and (3) the McGovern-Dole International Food for Education and Child Nutrition program (school lunch and feeding programs). The largest of these, the Food for Peace (FFP) program, receives about $1.5 billion in annual appropriations. Traditionally, these three programs have relied on donated U.S. agricultural commodities as the basis for their activities. However, recent farm bills have increasingly

---

[13] This section was written by Jenny Hopkinson, Analyst in Agricultural Policy.

added flexibility to purchase food in local markets or to directly transfer cash or vouchers to needy recipients. FFP is administered by the U.S. Agency for International Development (USAID), while the other two programs are administered by the Foreign Agricultural Service of USDA.

H.R. 2 reauthorizes all of the international food aid programs along with several associated fellowship programs. FFP is amended to remove a minimum monetization requirement of 15% of FFP funds; raise the minimum requirement used for nonemergency programs to $365 million (up from $350 million) or not more than 30% of FFP funding; and require food vouchers, cash transfers, and local and regional procurement of non-U.S. foods to avoid market disruption in the recipient country. H.R. 2 also extends authority for several other related international programs— including the Farmer-to-Farmer program, Bill Emerson Humanitarian Trust, Cochran Fellowships, Borlaug Fellowships, and Global Crop Diversity Trust.

Current U.S. export promotion programs include the Market Access Program (MAP), the Foreign Market Development Program (FMDP), the Emerging Markets Program (EMP) and Technical Assistance for Specialty Crops (TASC). These programs are administered by the Foreign Agricultural Service. Under H.R. 2, all four export programs—MAP, FMDP, EMP, and TASC — are combined into a single program named the International Market Development Program (IMDP) while maintaining existing activities and eligibility requirements.[14] IMDP would be authorized to receive $255 million in annual mandatory Commodity Credit Corporation (CCC) funds for FY2019-FY2023. Of that, no less than $200 million shall be spent on promotional activities for both generic and branded U.S. agricultural products; no less than $35 million on promotional activities for generic commodities; no more than $9 million for technical assistance to specialty crop groups looking to export their crops; and no more than $10 million on promoting U.S. agricultural goods to emerging markets. These funding levels reflect current spending across MAP, FMDP, TASC and EMP. H.R. 2 further creates the Biotechnology and Agricultural Trade Program in Title III to assist with the removal of non-tariff and other trade

[14] A fifth existing export promotion program, the Quality Samples Program, is not included in the bill.

barriers to U.S. agricultural products produced with biotechnology and other agricultural technologies. Finally, H.R. 2 reauthorizes direct credits or export credit guarantees for the promotion of agricultural exports to emerging markets of not less than $1 billion in each fiscal year through 2023.

Title IV, Nutrition[15]

The Nutrition title in H.R. 2 proposes a number of policy changes to SNAP and related programs, while in some respects continuing current policy and operations. The bill would reauthorize SNAP and related programs for five years through the end of FY2023. Altogether, CBO estimates that the Nutrition title would increase spending by $463 million over 10 years (FY2019-FY2028). Certain individual policies are estimated to have large effects on SNAP spending, especially those expected to impact SNAP eligibility and benefit calculation.

H.R. 2 proposes a number of changes to the determination of households' financial and nonfinancial eligibility for SNAP benefits. Three of these policies were debated during committee markup:

1) Broad-based categorical eligibility. The bill proposes to place additional limits on households that are eligible for SNAP based on their receipt of Temporary Assistance for Needy Families benefits. CBO estimates that these changes would reduce SNAP spending by more than $5 billion over the 10-year window. CBO also estimates that in an average year about 400,000 households would lose SNAP eligibility. As SNAP recipients are also eligible for free school meals, CBO estimated that in an average year, 265,000 children would lose access to free meals.
2) Work-related requirements. The bill proposes to replace SNAP's general work requirements and able-bodied adults without dependents time limit with a work requirement for all states.

[15] This section was written by Randy A. Aussenberg, Specialist in Nutrition Assistance Policy.

Beginning with FY2021, the proposal would require a minimum of 20 hours of work per week for non-exempt able-bodied adults. Unlike the current-law time limit, which applies to 18- to 49-year-olds who do not have children, the proposed requirement would apply to 18- to 59-year-olds and would not exempt parents or caretakers of children six years old and older. The proposal continues to give states authority to exempt a portion of the caseload and to request geographic waivers based on labor-market measures, with some amendments to current law. Unlike the current law time limit, the proposal requires states to offer employment or training opportunities to those individuals subject to the requirements. The bill increases SNAP Employment and Training funding for the states, increasing mandatory funding in a formula grant for states from $110 million in current law to $270 million in FY2020 and to $1 billion in FY2021 and each year thereafter. CBO estimates that these work- related changes would reduce spending on SNAP benefits by approximately $9.2 billion over 10 years, and administration of the changes would increase spending by approximately $7.6 billion—a net reduction of $1.5 billion. In FY2028, CBO estimates that in an average month approximately 1.2 million recipients would no longer receive benefits, with each recipient losing an average annual SNAP benefit amount of $1,816. This provision was amended on the House floor (see Table A-1).

3) LIHEAP and benefit calculation. Under current law, an eligible household's receipt of a Low Income Home Energy Assistance Program (LIHEAP) payment over $20 has the potential to increase monthly benefit amounts, because this payment allows the household to have their benefits calculated using a standard utility allowance. For households without elderly members, under this bill (as amended on the House floor), LIHEAP, regardless of the amount provided, would no longer confer this advantage. CBO estimates that this provision would reduce 560,000 households' SNAP benefits by an average of $84 per month.

In addition to these three eligibility changes, the proposal increases asset limits and changes how vehicles and savings accounts are counted. It also amends the way certain income is counted or excluded, increases the deduction for earned income, and requires households' cooperation with child support enforcement.

The bill includes measures intended to address SNAP retailer and recipient fraud and to improve payment accuracy. This includes establishing a Duplicative Enrollment Database, making changes to the Quality Control system, and increasing USDA's oversight of state performance. The bill repeals funding for performance bonuses, which, under current law, financially rewards states' performance. The bill also proposes a number of policy changes for SNAP's EBT system and benefit redemption.

The bill proposes some changes to SNAP-related grants. It would make some amendments and increases funding for bonus incentives for fruits and vegetables under the (renamed) Gus Schumacher Food Insecurity Nutrition Incentive Program. It would also authorize and fund a pilot for retailers to receive federal funding for operating bonus incentive projects that incentivize fruit, vegetable, and milk purchases. It also proposes some changes to USDA's operations and funding of the Nutrition Education and Obesity Prevention Grant Program.

For many of the food distribution programs and other nutrition title programs and policies, the bill would extend them through FY2023 without substantive policy changes. The Emergency Food Assistance Program would receive an increase of approximately $45 million (adjusted annually for inflation) each year and would also include authority for a "Farm to Food Bank Fund." The Fresh Fruit and Vegetable Program would be renamed to "Fruit and Vegetable Program," and participating schools could serve fresh, canned, dried, frozen, or pureed fruits and vegetables.

The National School Lunch Program and School Breakfast Program are not reauthorized in this bill. However, an amendment incorporated on the House floor requires USDA to review and change its 2012 regulations updating school meal nutrition standards and 2016 regulations adding nutrition standards to foods sold outside the meals programs.

Title V, Credit[16]

H.R. 2 would make several permanent changes and reauthorize provisions in the Consolidated Farm and Rural Development Act that governs the USDA farm loan programs, make several permanent changes to the Farm Credit Act that governs the Farm Credit System, and reauthorize the State Agricultural Loan Mediation Program through FY2023.

For the farm loan programs of FSA, H.R. 2 would add specific conditions that the Secretary may use to reduce the requirement for three years of farming experience in order for beginning farmers to qualify for loans (e.g., coursework, military service, mentoring). It raises the maximum loan size for guaranteed farm ownership loans and guaranteed farm operating loans from a statutory base of $700,000 in FY1996 ($1.4 million in FY2018 after adjusting for inflation) to a higher base of $1.75 million per borrower, which inflation adjusts to an effective maximum guaranteed loan amount of about $3.5 million in FY2019. The bill also makes several technical corrections.

For the government-chartered, cooperative Farm Credit System (FCS), H.R. 2 would eliminate a host of obsolete references to outdated names and transition periods from the 1980s and 1990s. It adds clarification that FCS entities may share privileged information with the Farm Credit Administration (FCA) for regulatory purposes without altering the privileged status elsewhere. It expands FCA's jurisdiction to hold accountable "institution-affiliated parties" (e.g., including agents and independent contractors) and makes the scope retroactive for a six-year period. For the Federal Agricultural Mortgage Corporation (FarmerMac), it increases the acreage exception from 1,000 acres to 2,000 acres for the dollar limit to remain a qualified loan, subject to a study by FCA. It also directs FCA to study the risks and capitalization of loans in the FCS and FarmerMac portfolios. Finally, it deletes the compensation limit for FCS bank boards of directors.

---

[16] This section was written by Jim Monke, Specialist in Agricultural Policy.

For the State Agricultural Loan Mediation Program, H.R. 2 reauthorizes the program to FY2023 so that it may continue to provide matching grants for mediation of credit and certain other agricultural disputes.

Title VI, Rural Infrastructure and Economic Development[17]

The Rural Infrastructure and Economic Development title of H.R. 2 amends the Rural Development Act of 1972 (P.L. 92-419) to propose a new Subtitle A, Improving Health Outcomes in Rural Communities. The four sections of the proposed subtitle would permit the Secretary of Agriculture, after consultation with public health figures, to announce a temporary reprioritization of certain rural development loans and grants to assist rural communities in responding to a specific rural health emergency. The announced emergency would expire either when the Secretary has determined that the emergency has ended or 360 days after the announcement, whichever date is earlier. While the emergency is in effect, 10% of the funds available for the Distance Learning and Telemedicine Program would be made available to identify and treat individuals affected by the emergency. Under the Community Facilities program, priority would be given to entities providing prevention, treatment, and recovery services to those affected by the emergency. The subtitle would also reauthorize the Farm and Ranch Stress Assistance Network and authorize a new loan and grant program to help establish group health plans offered by agricultural associations.

Subtitle B of H.R. 2 makes changes to the Enhancing Broadband Telecommunications Services in Rural Areas Program. Provisions under this subtitle would establish minimum acceptable standards of broadband service of 25 megabits per second downstream transmission capacity and 3 megabits per second upstream transmission capacity and develop projections of broadband service 5, 10, 15, 20, and 30 years into the future. Other provisions would require broadband infrastructure loan guarantees,

---

[17] This section was written by Tadlock Cowan, Analyst in Natural Resources and Rural Development.

provide incentives to reach more isolated rural areas by establishing a residential density measure for loan guarantee applicants, permit the Rural Utility Service to obligate but not disburse broadband funding support, and give priority to applicants who would provide broadband service to areas not predominantly for business. Other provisions would authorize loans for middle-mile broadband infrastructure, modify build-out requirements for loan applicants from three to five years, and reduce reporting requirements for borrowers.

Subtitle C of the bill concerns provisions for rural communities, business development, and rural infrastructure. Its provisions would prioritize project applications that support implementation of strategic plans on a multi-jurisdictional basis and reserve a portion of funds for such projects, raise the maximum loan amount for water and waste water projects, increase funding for water and waste water technical assistance, and reauthorize a range of rural development programs authorized under the Consolidated Farm and Rural Development Act.

Subtitle D reauthorizes programs under the Rural Electrification Act of 1936 (P.L. 74-605), including expanding 911 access in rural areas and extending the rural economic development loan and grant program. Subtitle E amends and reauthorizes all of the agricultural energy programs in the 2014 farm bill that were previously in a separate title, extending most through FY2023. H.R. 2 also modifies the type of funding available for these programs. In prior farm bills, many of these programs were provided with mandatory funding, whereas H.R. 2 authorizes only discretionary funding.

Subtitle F reauthorizes the Value-Added Grants program and increases its discretionary funding authorization. The regional development commissions established in the 2008 farm bill are also reauthorized, and the current definition of *rural area* for the Rural Housing Service's programs is retained until the 2030 decennial census. Subtitle G repeals several unfunded programs, including the Rural Telephone Bank, the Rural Collaborative Investment Program, and the Delta Region Agricultural Development Grants Program. Subtitle H makes technical corrections to certain provisions of the Consolidated Farm and Rural Development Act (P.L. 92-419) and the Rural Electrification Act.

Title VII, Research[18]

USDA is authorized under four major laws to conduct agricultural research at the federal level and to provide support for cooperative research, extension, and postsecondary agricultural education programs in the states through formula funds and competitive grants to land-grant universities. H.R. 2 reauthorizes funding for these activities through FY2023, subject to annual appropriations.

With respect to the land-grant entities, H.R. 2 authorizes a new scholarship program for the 1890 land-grant institutions. A provision in the bill would also prohibit any further entities from being designated as eligible to receive formula funding under the Hatch Act (24 Stat. 440), Smith-Lever Act (P.L. 63-95), and McIntire-Stennis Act (P.L. 87-788). Permissible indirect cost recovery for federal funding of agricultural research and extension would increase to 30% from 22% of funding.

Several new research areas in the High Priority Research and Extension program are designated to be high priorities: macadamia tree health, national turfgrass research, fertilizer management, cattle fever ticks, and laying hen and turkey research. The bill also reauthorizes the Organic Agriculture Research and Extension Initiative and increases mandatory funding levels to $30 million annually for FY2019-FY2023. The Specialty Crop Research Initiative (SCRI) would be reauthorized through FY2023 and continues to include carve-out funding for the Emergency Citrus Disease Research and Extension Program. SCRI also expands program eligibility to include "size-controlling rootstock systems for perennial crops" and "emerging and invasive species," among other production practices and technologies.

---

[18] This section was written by Tadlock Cowan, Analyst in Natural Resources and Rural Development.

Title VIII, Forestry[19]

The Agriculture Committees have jurisdiction over forestry issues generally, as well as over some—but not all—National Forest System (NFS) lands managed by the USDA Forest Service (FS).[20] Previous farm bills have primarily addressed forestry research and assistance programs and have sometimes included provisions addressing management of federal forest land. The forestry title in H.R. 2 would reauthorize and modify several existing assistance programs and establish new assistance programs, and it also contains several provisions that would address management of the NFS and the public lands managed by the Bureau of Land Management (BLM) in the Department of the Interior.

Forestry assistance programs are authorized under two main laws: the Cooperative Forestry Assistance Act (CFAA)[21] and the Healthy Forests Restoration Act of 2003.[22] Most federal forestry assistance programs are permanently authorized to receive such sums as necessary in annual discretionary appropriations and thus do not require reauthorization in the farm bill. H.R. 2, however, would amend two forestry assistance programs by replacing their permanent authority to receive annual appropriations with an authorization limit through FY2023. H.R. 2 would also establish some new assistance programs—generally by providing explicit statutory authorization and congressional direction for current programs that are operating under existing, but broad, authorizations. The bill would also reauthorize funding for the National Forest Foundation.

H.R. 2 would also address federal and tribal forest management issues. For example, the bill would direct the Secretary of Agriculture to exempt unprocessed dead and dying trees on NFS lands in California from the export prohibition for 10 years. Subtitle B would amend the Secure Rural Schools

[19] This section was written by Katie Hoover, Specialist in Natural Resource Policy.

[20] The Agriculture Committees have jurisdiction over any national forest not reserved from the public domain. The House Committee on Natural Resources and the Senate Committee on Energy and Natural Resources have jurisdiction over public lands generally, including national forests reserved from the public domain.

[21] P.L. 95-313, 16 U.S.C. §§2101-2114.

[22] P.L. 108-148, 16 U.S.C. §§6501-6591c. For more information on these programs, see CRS Report R45219, *Forest Service Assistance Programs*.

and Self-Determination Act of 2000,[23] a program that authorizes payments to counties containing NFS lands and certain BLM lands.[24] The bill would also change how the FS and BLM comply with the requirements under the National Environmental Policy Act (NEPA)[25] and the consultation requirements under the Endangered Species Act[26] for specified management activities. For example, the bill would establish 10 categories of actions that would not be subject to the requirements to prepare an environmental assessment or environmental impact statement under NEPA. (Six apply to both FS and BLM actions; four apply to just FS actions.) H.R. 2 would also authorize federally recognized Indian tribes to enter into good neighbor agreements with the FS and BLM and to request to conduct forest management activities on NFS lands, among other provisions.

Title IX, Horticulture[27]

H.R. 2 reauthorizes many of the existing farm bill provisions supporting farming operations in the specialty crop, certified organic agriculture, and local foods sectors. These provisions cover several programs and provisions benefitting these sectors, including block grants to states, support for farmers markets, data and information collection, education on food safety and biotechnology, and organic certification, among other market development and promotion provisions. Other provisions in H.R. 2 would amend certain regulatory requirements under some federal statutes.

H.R. 2 makes changes to funding for farmers markets and local foods promotion. Whereas the 2014 farm bill provided $30 million in mandatory CCC funding for each of FY2014 through FY2018 for the Farmers Market Promotion Program and Local Food Promotion Program, H.R. 2

---

[23] P.L. 106-393, 16 U.S.C. §§7101-7153.

[24] For more information, see Reauthorizing the Secure Rural Schools and Community Self-Determination Act of 2000.

[25] P.L. 91-109, 42 U.S.C. §§4321-4347. For more information on NEPA, see CRS Report RL33152, *The National Environmental Policy Act (NEPA): Background and Implementation.*

[26] P.L. 93-205, 16 U.S.C. §1531 et seq. For more information, see CRS Report RL31654, *The Endangered Species Act: A Primer.*

[27] This section was written by Renée Johnson, Specialist in Agricultural Policy.

reauthorizes discretionary appropriations for these programs in the amount of $30 million annually for FY2019-FY2023. The bill does not provide any mandatory funding beyond FY2018.[28]

H.R. 2 also makes changes to USDA's National Organic Program (NOP). It would enact several provisions in H.R. 3871 (Organic Farmer and Consumer Protection Act of 2017), including limiting the types of operations excluded from NOP certification, requiring electronic import documentation, establishing mechanisms for collaborative investigations and enforcement, requiring increased documentation and reporting, and increasing USDA accreditation authority over certifying agents, among other changes. In addition, it requires USDA to establish procedures for expedited petitions under the NOP's "National List of Approved and Prohibited Substances" and amends the eligibility and consultation requirements of the National Organics Standards Board (NOSB). H.R. 2 reauthorizes NOP appropriations above current levels, increasing to $24 million by FY2023, and reauthorizes funding for the Organic Production and Market Data Initiatives. It also provides $5 million for technology upgrades to improve tracking and verification of organic imports. H.R. 2 does not reauthorize current mandatory funding for the National Organic Certification Cost Share Program, although the program remains authorized.

CBO estimates a total budget authority of $850 million (FY2019-FY2023) for programs in the Horticulture title. Under H.R. 2, CBO estimates an increase in mandatory spending of $10 million (FY2019-FY2023) for programs under this title, which would cover data collection and technology updates under NOP. Provisions affecting the specialty crop and certified organic sectors, however, are not limited to the Horticulture title but are contained within several other titles of the new law. These include programs in the research, nutrition, and trade titles, among others. For example, under H.R. 2, CBO estimates an increase in mandatory spending of $101 million (FY2019-FY2023) for the Organic Agriculture Research and Extension

---

[28] H.R. 2 takes a similar approach in Title VI with funding for the Value-Added Producer Grant (VAPG) program, which broadly benefits specialty crop and local food producers. The 2014 farm bill provided $63 million in mandatory funding for VAPG to remain available until expended. H.R. 2 amends authorizations for discretionary appropriation, providing $50 million in annual appropriations (FY2019-FY2023) with no additional mandatory funding.

Initiative in the bill's Research title. Other programs in the Research title, such as SCRI, would maintain current funding levels of more than $320 million (FY2019-FY2023). Budget estimates for other programs outside Title IX that benefit the specialty crop, certified organic agriculture, and local foods sectors—such as the Fresh Fruit and Vegetable Program (Snack Program) and Section 32 purchases for fruits and vegetables under the Nutrition title, among other farm bill programs—are not available.

Title IX includes several exemptions from certain regulatory requirements, amending existing provisions in the Federal Insecticide, Fungicide, and Rodenticide Act (FIFRA, 7 U.S.C. 136 *et seq.*), the Clean Water Act (33 U.S.C. §1251 *et seq.*), the Plant Protection Act (7 U.S.C. 7701 *et seq.*), and the Occupational Safety and Health Act (OSHA, 29 U.S.C. 651 *et seq.*). H.R. 2 amends FIFRA to clarify federal and state roles in the regulation of pesticides, to exempt certain pesticide discharges from point source discharge permitting requirements, and to not require that the Environmental Protection Agency consult with other federal agencies regarding pesticide registrations and their potential impact on endangered species. H.R. 2 would also enact into law H.R. 1029 (Pesticide Registration Improvement Enhancement Act of 2017), amending FIFRA to extend the authority to collect pesticide fees and other purposes. Finally, H.R. 2 amends the Plant Protection Act regarding the use of methyl bromide in response to an emergency event and also amends OSHA to exempt agricultural retailers from process safety management requirements.

Title X, Crop Insurance[29]

Crop insurance is designed cover economic losses from a variety of natural causes, as well as certain adverse market developments. The federal crop insurance program makes available subsidized crop insurance to producers who purchase policies to protect against losses in yield, crop revenue, margin, or whole farm revenue. The crop insurance title of H.R. 2

---

[29] This section was written by Isabel Rosa, Analyst in Agricultural Policy.

makes several modifications to the existing federal crop insurance program, which is permanently authorized by the Federal Crop Insurance Act. According to CBO, the crop insurance title of H.R. 2 would decrease authorized spending for crop insurance relative to baseline levels by $70 million during the FY2019-FY2023 period. The largest component for projected savings ($52 million) is attributed to eliminating the crop insurance education and information program for targeted states carried out by the Risk Management Agency and the Agricultural Management Assistance program. Up to $15 million per year of CCC funds could be saved from the elimination of the AMA program alone. Additional savings ($32 million) occur by increasing the administrative fee for catastrophic risk protection (commonly referred to as CAT fees) from $300 per crop per county to $500. CBO also projects another $23 million in savings from provisions that would eliminate several past research and development (R&D) priorities, discontinue R&D partnerships, and reduce CCC funding for R&D contracting from $12.5 million to no more than $8 million annually.

Among other adjustments, H.R. 2 expands coverage for forage and grazing by allowing separate crop insurance policies to be purchased for crops that can be both grazed and mechanically harvested on the same acres during the same growing season. Such separate policies can be independently indemnified for each intended use. CBO projects this expanded coverage to cost the government $40 million during the FY2019-FY2023 period. Similarly, by redefining "beginning farmer or rancher" as having actively operated and managed a farm or ranch for less than 10 years, the federal subsidy benefits available for the purposes of research, development, and implementation of whole farm insurance plans on such participating operations would result in a projected additional cost of $4 million during FY2019-FY2023.

Crops for which the producer has elected ARC or that are enrolled in stacked income protection would be ineligible for coverage based on an area yield and loss basis or for the supplemental coverage option. H.R. 2 also clarifies requirements for FCIC approval of reimbursement for the development of private submissions for modifying old plans of insurance or creating new plans of insurance.

Title XI, Miscellaneous[30]

The Miscellaneous title of H.R. 2 contains seven subtitles: Livestock; Beginning, Socially Disadvantaged, and Veteran Producers; Textiles; United States Grain Standards Act; Noninsured Crop Disaster Assistance Program; Protect Interstate Commerce; and Other Matters.

The Livestock subtitle would establish the National Animal Disease Preparedness and Response Program to address the risk of the spread of animal pests and diseases and the National Animal Health Vaccine Bank to prioritize the acquisition of foot-and-mouth disease vaccine. H.R. 2 would provide a combined $250 million in mandatory funding in FY2019 for these two new programs and to operate the National Animal Health Laboratory Network, as well as $50 million for the same purposes each year from FY2020 to FY2023. The livestock subtitle would also authorize appropriations for the National Aquatic Health Plan, amend a program for veterinarian training, and require USDA to conduct a study on the Food Safety and Inspection Service's guidance and outreach to small and very small meat processing plants.

The Beginning, Socially Disadvantaged, and Veteran Producers subtitle includes mandatory funding of $10 million each year from FY2019 to FY2023 for its outreach and assistance program for socially disadvantaged and veteran farmers and ranchers. H.R. 2 would prioritize youth agricultural employment and volunteer programs and establish an Agricultural Youth Organization Coordinator position to promote the role of youth-serving organizations and school- based agricultural education programs. The bill would also create a Commission on Farm Transition to study issues affecting the transition of farm operations from established farmers and ranchers to the next generation.

---

[30] This section was written by Joel Greene, Analyst in Agricultural Policy.

The Textile subtitle would repeal the trust funds for Pima Agriculture Cotton and Agriculture Wool Apparel Manufacturers. It would also repeal grant funding under the Wool Research and Promotion program. In place of these funds, H.R. 2 would establish the Textile Trust Fund to reduce injury for domestic users of imported pima cotton and wool fabric whose tariffs may exceed the tariffs on certain finished imported pima cotton and wool apparel. For each calendar year from 2019 to 2023, USDA would transfer $8 million and $15 million to the trust fund for domestic manufacturers who import pima cotton and wool fabric, respectively, and $2.25 million for grants for wool research and promotion. In addition, for FY2019, H.R. 2 would provide $2 million for strengthening and enhancing the U.S. sheep industry.

The United States Grain Standards Act (USGSA) would restore exceptions in grain inspection regulations that were implemented in 2003, and revoked in 2015, that allowed grain to be inspected by more than one designated official agency.

The Noninsured Crop Disaster Assistance Program (NAP) subtitle would amend NAP crop eligibility to include crops that may be covered by crop insurance but only under whole farm policies. It would also raise the service fees and reauthorize buy-up coverage through crop year 2023.

The Protect Interstate Commerce subtitle would prohibit a state or local government from setting standards or conditions on agricultural commodities produced in another state if the commodities are produced or manufactured in accordance with federal or state laws and regulations. The bill provides that producers, consumers, trade associations, governments, and other agents may bring an action against the standard or condition in the appropriate court.

The Other Matters subtitle would make technical amendments to various laws to account for USDA reorganizational changes that created the Under Secretary for Trade and Foreign Agricultural Affairs, the Under Secretary for Farm Production and Conservation, and the Assistant to the Secretary for Rural Development. H.R. 2 would also create a Food Loss and Waste Reduction Liaison within the Office of the Secretary, a Century Farms Program under the Secretary that recognizes farms in continuous operation for at least 100 years, and a National Agriculture Imagery Program within the Farm Service Agency. The subtitle would further prohibit the slaughter of dogs and cats for human consumption and would require a report on the importation of dogs.

In addition, the subtitle would require a report on including natural stone in a promotion and research program and a report on agriculture innovation in gene editing and precision plant breeding. It would amend the hiring authority for cotton classification employees to allow for non-competitive rehiring of qualified individuals and add South Carolina to the Virginia/Carolina region of the Peanut Standards Board.

PROVISIONS OF THE HOUSE PASSED BILL (H.R. 2), COMPARED WITH CURRENT LAW

Table 3. Title I: Commodities

Current Law/Policy	House Passed Bill (H.R. 2)
Commodity Program Terms	
Actual crop revenue. The amount determined by the Secretary under the Agriculture Risk Coverage (ARC) program for each covered commodity for a crop year. **(7 U.S.C. 9011(1))**	Same as current law. **(§1111(1)).**
ARC. Coverage provided under the ARC program. (7 U.S.C. 9011(2))	Same as current law. **(§1111(2)).**
ARC guarantee. The amount determined by the Secretary under the ARC program for each covered commodity for a crop year. **(7 U.S.C. 9011(3))**	Same as current law. **(§1111(3)).**
Base acres. For purposes of calculating farm program payments, base acres are the number of historical program acres of a specific covered commodity on a farm as established under the 2008 farm bill, as in effect on September 30, 2013 (except upland cotton), subject to adjustments (see 7 U.S.C. 90112 below).**(7 U.S.C. 9011(4))**	Individual crop-specific base acres are retained, as in effect as under the 2014 farm bill subject to any reallocation, adjustment, or reduction as described in Section 1112. **(§1111(4))**

Table 3. (Continued)

Current Law/Policy	House Passed Bill (H.R. 2)
County coverage. Type of coverage under the ARC program to be obtained by the producer at the county level. **(7 U.S.C. 9011(5))**	No comparable definition.
Covered commodities. Wheat, oats, and barley (including wheat, oats, and barley used for haying and grazing), corn, grain sorghum, long-grain rice, medium-grain rice, pulse crops, soybeans, other oilseeds, and peanuts. Effective beginning with the 2018 crop year, the term *covered commodity* includes seed cotton. **(7 U.S.C. 9011(6))**	Wheat, oats, and barley (including wheat, oats, and barley used for haying and grazing), corn, grain sorghum, long-grain rice, medium-grain rice, pulse crops, soybeans, other oilseeds, seed cotton, and peanuts. **(§1111(5))**
Effective price. The price calculated by the Secretary under the Price Loss Coverage (PLC) program for each covered commodity for a crop year to determine whether PLC payments are required to be provided for that crop year. **(7 U.S.C. 9011(7))**	Same as current law. **(§1111(6)).**
No comparable definition.	**Effective reference price.** The term *effective reference price*, with respect to a covered commodity for a crop year, means the lesser of the following: (A) 115% of the reference price for such covered commodity; or (B) the greater of (i) the reference price for such covered commodity or (ii) 85% of the average of the marketing year average price of the covered commodity for the most recent five crop years, excluding each of the crop years with the highest and lowest marketing year average price. **(§1111(7))**
Extra long staple (ELS) cotton. Cotton that (A) is produced from pure strain varieties of the Barbadense species or any hybrid of the species or other similar types of ELS cotton, designated by the Secretary, having characteristics needed for various end uses for which U.S. upland cotton is not suitable, and grown in irrigated or other designated U.S. cotton-growing regions; and (B) is ginned on a roller-type gin or other authorized gin for experimental purposes. **(7 U.S.C. 9011(8))**	Same as current law. **(§1111(8)).**
Generic base acres. The amount of cotton base acres in effect under the 2008 farm bill, as adjusted pursuant to Section 1101 of such act, as of September 30, 2013 **(7 U.S.C. 9011(9))**, subject to any adjustment or reduction. **(7 U.S.C. 9012(d)).**	No comparable provision. Generic base acres are indirectly retained via retention of base acres as under prior law by Section 1111(4). Base acres are discussed further in Section 1112.

Current Law/Policy	House Passed Bill (H.R. 2)
Individual coverage. Type of coverage selected by a producer under the ARC program at the farm (not county) level. **(7 U.S.C. 9011(10))**	No comparable definition.
No comparable definition. Instead, the full text "national average market price received by producers during the 12-month marketing year" for a covered commodity is used in the PLC and ARC programs.	**Marketing year average price (MYAP).** The national average market price received by producer during the 12-month marketing year for a covered commodity. **(§1111(9))**
Medium-grain rice. Includes short grain rice and temperate japonica rice. **(7 U.S.C. 9011(11))**	Same as current law. **(§1111(10))**
Other oilseed. A crop of sunflower seed, rapeseed, canola, safflower, flaxseed, mustard seed, crambe, sesame seed, or, if designated by the Secretary, another oilseed. **(7 U.S.C. 9011(12))**	Same as current law. **(§1111(11))**
Payment acres. The number of acres for a farm, as determined under 7 U.S.C. 9014, that are eligible for payments under the PLC or ARC programs. **(7 U.S.C. 9011(13))**	Same as current law. **(§1111(12))**
Payment yield. For a covered commodity, the yield used to make counter-cyclical payments under the 2008 farm bill as in effect on September 30, 2013, or the yield established under the PLC program. **(7 U.S.C.9011(14))**	For a covered commodity, the yield used to make PLC payments under the 2014 farm bill or the yield established in Section 1113. **(§1111(13))**
Price Loss Coverage (PLC). Coverage provided under the PLC program. **(7 U.S.C. 9011(15))**	Same as current law. **(§1111(14))**
Producer. Generally, an owner, operator, landlord, tenant, or sharecropper that shares in the risk of producing a crop and is entitled to share in the crop available for marketing from the farm or would have shared had the crop been produced. For a grower of hybrid seed, the existence of a hybrid seed contract and other program rules shall not adversely affect the ability to receive a payment. **(7 U.S.C. 9011(16))**	Same as current law. **(§1111(15))**
Pulse crop. Dry peas, lentils, small chickpeas, and large chickpeas. **(7 U.S.C. 9011(17))**	Same as current law. **(§1111(16))**

Table 3. (Continued)

Current Law/Policy	House Passed Bill (H.R. 2)
Reference prices: With respect to a covered commodity for a crop year: • For wheat, $5.50 per bushel (bu.). • For corn, $3.70 per bu. • For grain sorghum, $3.95 per bu. • For barley, $4.95 per bu. • For oats, $2.40 per bu. • For long-grain rice, $14.00 per hundredweight (cwt). • For medium-grain rice, $14.00 per cwt. • For soybeans, $8.40 per bu. • For other oilseeds, $20.15 per cwt. • For peanuts, $535.00 per ton. • For dry peas, $11.00 per cwt. • For lentils, $19.97 per cwt. • For small chickpeas, $19.04 per cwt. • For large chickpeas, $21.54 per cwt. • For seed cotton, $0.367 per lb. • **(7 U.S.C. 9011(18))**	Same as current law (Section 1111(17)) but with the following addition: **Reference price for temperate japonica rice.** To reflect price premiums, the reference price for temperate japonica rice equals $14.00 per cwt., as adjusted by the formula for calculating the effective reference price (Section 1111(17)) multiplied by the ratio of the simple average of the MYAP of medium-grain rice from crop years 2012-2016 divided by the simple average of the MYAP of all rice from crop years 2012-2016. **(§1116(g))**
Secretary. The Secretary of Agriculture. **(7 U.S.C. 9011(19))**	Same as current law. **(§1111(18))**
Seed cotton. Unginned upland cotton that includes both lint and seed. **(7 U.S.C. 9011(20))**	Same as current law. **(§1111(19))**
State. Each of the U.S. states, the District of Columbia, the Commonwealth of Puerto Rico, and any other U.S. territory or possession. **(7 U.S.C. 9011(21))**	Same as current law. **(§1111(20))**
Temperate japonica rice. Rice that is grown in high altitudes or temperate regions of high latitudes with cooler climate conditions in the Western United States, as determined by the Secretary, for the purpose of the reallocation of base acres, the establishment of a reference price and an effective price, and the determination of the actual crop revenue and ARC guarantee. **(7 U.S.C. 9011(22))**	Same as current law. **(§1111(21))**
Transitional yield. Defined in Section 502(b) of the Federal Crop Insurance Act **(7 U.S.C. 1502(b)(11))** as the maximum average production per acre or equivalent measure that is assigned to acreage for a crop year by the Federal Crop	Same as current law. **(§1111(22))**

Current Law/Policy	**House Passed Bill (H.R. 2)**
Insurance Corporation (FCIC) whenever the producer fails to certify that acceptable documentation of production and acreage for the crop year is in the possession of the producer or present the acceptable documentation. **(7 U.S.C. 9011(23))**	
United States. When used in a geographical sense, all of the states. **(7 U.S.C. 9011(24))**	Same as current law. **(§1111(23))**
United States premium factor. The percentage by which the difference in the U.S. loan schedule premiums for Strict Middling 1 1/8-inch upland cotton and for Middling 1 3/32-inch upland cotton exceeds the difference in the applicable premiums for comparable international qualities. **(7 U.S.C. 9011(25))**	Same as current law. **(§1111(24))**
PLC and ARC Programs	
Base Acres	
One-time reallocation of base acres among covered commodities. Crop-specific base acres were subject to a producer's one-time choice to retain base acres or undertake a reallocation of total farm base acres among covered commodities based on average shares of planted base by commodity during the 2009-2012 period. Generic base acres are retained and may not be reallocated. **(7 U.S.C. 9012(a))**	No comparable provision. Base acres (subject to the previous one-time reallocation choice) are included through the retention of crop-specific base acres under prior law. **(§1114(a))**
Seed cotton base acres. Not later than May 10, 2018, the Secretary shall require the owner of a farm to allocate all generic base acres based on whether the farm has a recent history of covered commodities (including seed cotton) being planted or prevented from being planted during the 2009-2016 crop years. If a farm has no such recent history, then the farm owner allocates the farm's generic base to unassigned crop base for which no ARC or PLC payments may be made. If a farm has such a recent history, then the farm owner allocates the farm's generic base among seed cotton and other covered commodities as (A) to seed cotton base acres in a quantity equal to the greater of 80% of generic base acres or the average of seed cotton acres planted or prevented from being planted on the farm during the 2009-2012	No comparable provision. Seed cotton base acres are included indirectly through the retention of crop-specific base acres under prior law. **(§1114(a))**

Table 3. (Continued)

Current Law/Policy	House Passed Bill (H.R. 2)
crop years (not to exceed the farm's total generic base acres) or (B) to commodity-specific base acres in proportion to each crop's share of planted (or prevented from being planted) acreage during 2009 to 2012. Following the base allocation under either (A) or (B), any residual generic base acres shall be allocated to unassigned crop base for which no ARC or PLC payments may be made. If a farm owner fails to make an election for generic base, then the farm owner shall be deemed to have elected to allocate all generic base acres in accordance with formulation (A) above. **(7 U.S.C. 9014(b)(4))**	
Adjustments to base. Base acres are increased/decreased when land leaves/enters conservation programs **(7 U.S.C. 9012(b))**.	The same as current law. **(§1112(a))**
Prevention of excess base acres. Base is reduced if the sum of the base acres for the farm (including any new oilseed acreage and generic base acres) plus any acreage in the Conservation Reserve Program or the Wetlands Reserve Program (or any other federal conservation program that makes payments in exchange for not producing a crop) exceeds the actual cropland acreage on the farm. An exception shall be made in the case of certain double-cropped acreage as determined by the Secretary. The owner of the farm shall be given an opportunity to select the base acres that will be reduced. **(7 U.S.C. 9012(c))**	The same as current law. **(§1112(b))**
Reduction of base acres. The farm owner may reduce, at any time, base acres for any covered commodity. Such reduction shall be permanent. Base is reduced proportionately when acreage has been subdivided and developed for multiple residential units or other non-farming uses. **(7 U.S.C. 9012(d))**	Reduction of base acres is the same as current law **(§1112(c)(1-2))** but with two additional provisions under Section 1112(c)(3) and Section 1112(c)(4).
No comparable provision.	**Treatment of unplanted base.** If no base acres are planted to a covered commodity during the period January 1, 2009, to December 31, 2017, then all the base acres on that farm are allocated to unassigned crop

Current Law/Policy	**House Passed Bill (H.R. 2)**
	base for which no payment shall be made. **(§1112(c)(3))**
No comparable provision.	**Reconstitution of farm to expand base.** The Secretary shall ensure that a farm may not be reconstituted after the date of enactment of this section to alter the treatment of base acres. **(§1112(c)(4))**
Payment Yields	
Payment yields. For making PLC program payments, all covered commodities must use a program yield to derive a per- acre payment rate. In this regard, the Secretary shall establish a program yield for each farm for any designated oilseed for which a payment yield was not established under Section 1102 of the 2008 farm bill **(7 U.S.C. 9013(a))**; for designated oilseeds, such a payment yield on a farm equals the product of the average yield per planted acre for the 1998-2001 crop years (excluding years in which acreage planted was zero) and the ratio of the national average yield for the 1981-1985 crops and the national average yield for the 1998-2001 crops. If the yield per planted acre for a designated oilseed for any of the 1998-2001 crop years was less than 75% of the county yield for that designated oil-seed, the Secretary shall assign a yield "plug" for that crop year equal to 75% of the county yield. **(7 U.S.C. 9013(b))** For other covered commodities, see the discussion under 7 U.S.C. 9013 (c)-(e).	To make PLC payments, this provision continues the Secretary's authority to establish payment yields for each farm for any designated oilseed that does not have a payment yield under the 2014 farm bill. The payment yield is calculated as 90% of the most recent five-year- average yield (excluding any year in which the yield was zero). Provides that this subsection only applies to oilseeds designated after the date of enactment of the Agriculture and Nutrition Act of 2018. **(§1113(a))**
Absence of payment yield. In the case of a covered commodity on a farm for which base acres have been established or that is planted on generic base acres, if no payment yield has been established, the Secretary shall establish an appropriate payment yield by taking into consideration the farm program payment yields applicable to that covered commodity for similarly situated farms. The use of such data in an appeal, by the Secretary or by the producer, shall not be subject to any other provision of law. **(7 U.S.C. 9013(c))**	Authorizes the Secretary to establish a payment yield if no payment yield is otherwise established for a covered commodity using the program payment yields of similarly situated farms. **(§1113(b))**

Table 3. (Continued)

Current Law/Policy	House Passed Bill (H.R. 2)
Updating payment yields. The owner of a farm was given a one-time opportunity to update, on a covered commodity-by- covered-commodity basis, the payment yield used in calculating PLC payments for each covered commodity for which the PLC election was made. The election shall be made at a time and manner to be in effect beginning with the 2014 crop year as determined by the Secretary. The PLC payment yield update was equal to 90% of the average of the yield per planted acre for the covered commodity for the 2008-2012 crop years, excluding any crop year in which the acreage planted to the covered commodity was zero. If the yield for any of the 2008-2012 crop years was less than 75% of the average county yield, a "plug" yield was used for that crop year equal to 75% of the county average for 2008 to 2012. **(7 U.S.C. 9013(d))**	**Yield update for drought-affected counties.** Provides a one-time opportunity for a farm owner to update yields where the farm is located in a county that experienced 20 or more consecutive weeks of exceptional drought (rated D4 by the U.S. Drought Monitor) between January 1, 2008, and December 31, 2012. On a covered-commodity by covered- commodity basis, yields may be updated as 90% of average yield per planted acre for 2013-2017 crop years. If the farm-level yield is less than 75% of the average county yield for a covered commodity for any of the years (excluding any year in which the yield was zero), then the Secretary shall assign 75% of the 2013-2017 average county yield for the covered commodity for that crop year. The election must be made prior to the 2019 crop year. **(§1113(c))**
Payment yield for seed cotton. The payment yield for seed cotton for a farm shall be equal to 2.4 times the payment yield for upland cotton for the farm established under the 2008 farm bill, as in effect on September 30, 2013. At the sole discretion of the owner of a farm with an established yield for upland cotton, the owner shall have a one-time opportunity to update the payment yield for upland cotton, as provided in 7 U.S.C. 9013(d), for the purpose of calculating the payment yield for seed cotton. **(7 U.S.C. 9013(e))**	The average yield for seed cotton per planted acre equals 2.4 times the average yield for upland cotton per planted acre. At the discretion of the owner of a farm that meets the drought criteria described in this section, the owner may update the payment yield for upland cotton, using the same method as described in this section. **(§1113(c))**
Payment Acres	
Payment acres. With respect to PLC and county-level ARC payments, payment acres are 85% of the base acres of a covered commodity on a farm. For individual (farm-level) ARC, the payment acres equal 65% of the base acres for all of the covered commodities on the farm. Generic base is eligible for payments if a covered crop is planted on the farm. Specifically, for each crop year, generic base acres are attributed (i.e.,)	Continues the establishment of payment acres for PLC and county-level ARC payments for each covered commodity on the farm at 85% of the base acres. **(§1114(a))** No reference is made to the individual farm-level ARC program or its associated payment acres.
Payment Acres	

Current Law/Policy	House Passed Bill (H.R. 2)
temporarily designated as) base acres to a particular covered commodity base in proportion to that crop's share of total plantings of all covered commodities in that year. The amount of generic base attributed for a particular year cannot exceed the acreage planted to covered crops in that year (use of double-cropping for payment calculations is not allowed unless the practice is approved by the Secretary). **(7 U.S.C. 9014)**	
Exclusion from payment acres. Payment acres may not include any crop subsequently planted during the same crop year on the same land for which the first crop is eligible for PLC or ARC payments unless the crop was approved for double cropping as determined by the Secretary. **(7 U.S.C. 9014(c))**	No comparable provision.
Minimal payment acres. A producer on a farm may not receive PLC payments or ARC payments if the sum of the base acres on the farm is 10 acres or less except for socially disadvantaged farmers/ ranchers or limited resource farmers/ ranchers. **(7 U.S.C. 9014(d))**	Same as current law. **(§1114(b))**
Effect of planting fruits and vegetables on payment acres. Any crop may be planted without effect on base acres. However, payment acres on a farm are reduced in any crop year in which fruits, vegetables (other than mung beans and pulse crops), or wild rice (FVWR) have been planted on base acres. The reduction to payment acres is one-for-one for each acre planted to these crops in excess of 15% of base acres for either the PLC or county coverage under the ARC program and in excess of 35% of base acres for ARC individual coverage. **(7 U.S.C. 9014(e)(1-3))** No reduction to payment acres shall be made under this subsection, as determined by the Secretary, if FVWR are grown solely for conservation purposes and not harvested for use or sale or if a region has a history of double-cropping covered commodities with FVWR and the FVWR were so double- cropped on the base acres. **(7 U.S.C. 9014(e)(4))**	Same as current law. **(§1114(c))**
Unassigned crop base. Requires the Secretary to maintain information on generic base acres on a farm allocated as unassigned crop base under the	Requires the Secretary to maintain information on unassigned crop base acres on a farm under the one-time reallocation of base acres under

Table 3. (Continued)

Current Law/Policy	House Passed Bill (H.R. 2)
formulation for seed cotton base acres. **(7 U.S.C. 9014(b)(4)(B,D); 7 U.S.C. 9014(f))**	the 2014 farm bill and prevention of excess base acres. **(§1114(d))**
Producer Election	
Producer election. For the 2014-2018 crop years, all producers involved in a single farm operation had to unanimously make a one-time, irrevocable election to obtain either (1) PLC or county-level ARC on a covered-commodity-by-covered- commodity basis or (2) ARC individual coverage applicable to all of the covered commodities on the farm. Failure to make a unanimous election for the 2014 crop year results in no program payments to the farm for the 2014 crop year, and the producers on the farm are deemed to have elected PLC for all covered commodities on the farm for the 2015-2018 crop years. If all the producers on a farm selected ARC county coverage for a covered commodity, the Secretary could not make PLC payments to the producers on the farm with respect to that covered commodity. If all the producers on a farm selected individual coverage, payment calculations included the producer's share of all farms in the same state in which the producer has an interest and for which individual coverage was selected. Producers on a farm cannot reconstitute the farm to void or change a program election. **(7 U.S.C. 9015)**	For the 2019-2023 crop years, all producers involved in a single farm operation must unanimously make a one-time, irrevocable election to obtain either PLC or county-level ARC on a covered-commodity-by-covered-commodity basis. **(§1115(a))** Failure to make a unanimous election for the 2019 crop year results in no program payments to the farm for the 2019 crop year, and producers on the farm are deemed to have elected PLC for all covered commodities on the farm for the 2020-2023 crop years. **(§1115(b))** Prohibits farm reconstitution to void or change an election made under this section. **(§1115(c))**
Price Loss Coverage (PLC) Program	
PLC. Establishes the PLC program for crop years 2014-2018. PLC payments are made on a farm where the owners have unanimously elected to participate in PLC on a covered commodity-by-covered-commodity basis if the effective price is less than the reference price. **(7 U.S.C. 9016(a))**	Requires the Secretary to make PLC payments on a covered-commodity-by-covered-commodity basis where all of the producers on a farm have elected PLC for crop years 2019-2023 when the effective price for a crop year is less than the effective reference price. **(§1116(a))**
PLC Effective Price	
Effective price. The higher of (1) the "national average market price received by producers during the 12-month marketing year" for the covered commodity, as determined by the Secretary, or (2) the national average loan rate for a marketing assistance loan. **(7 U.S.C. 9016(b))**	Same as current law. **(§1116(b))**

Current Law/Policy	House Passed Bill (H.R. 2)
Effective price for barley. The all-barley price. **(7 U.S.C. 9016(f))**	Same as current law. **(§1116(f))**
Effective price for seed cotton. The MYAP for seed cotton, calculated as the quotient obtained by dividing (A) the sum obtained by adding (i) the product of the upland cotton lint MYAP and total U.S. upland cotton lint production, measured in pounds, and (ii) the product of the cottonseed MYAP and total U.S. cottonseed production, measured in pounds; by (B) the sum of total U.S. upland cotton lint production and total U.S. cottonseed production, both measured in pounds. **(7 U.S.C. 9016(h)).**	Same as current law.
PLC Payment Rate and Payment Amount	
PLC payment rate. The difference between the reference price in statute and the MYAP or loan rate, if higher. **(7 U.S.C. 9016(c))**	Same as current law. **(§1116(c))**
PLC payment amount. If PLC payments for a covered commodity are triggered for any of crop years 2014-2018, the payment amount equals the payment rate times payment acres times payment yield. **(7 U.S.C. 9016(d))**	If PLC payments for a covered commodity are triggered for any of crop years 2019-2023, the payment amount equals the payment rate times payment acres times payment yield. **(§1116(d))**
Timing of PLC payment. Payments shall be made beginning October 1, or as soon as practicable thereafter, after the end of the applicable marketing year for the covered commodity. **(7 U.S.C. 9016(e))**	Same as current law. **(§1116(e))**
Agricultural Risk Coverage (ARC) Program	
ARC. Establishes the ARC program as either a county-level, commodity-specific ARC or an individual whole-farm ARC. Under the "producer election" (7 U.S.C. 9015), producers may select county-level ARC or PLC on a commodity-by-commodity basis for each farm or select individual farm-level ARC for all covered commodities on the farm. ARC payments for a crop year are triggered if the actual crop revenue is less than its ARC guarantee. Both the actual crop revenue and ARC guarantee are calculated differently based on the producer's election choice: either county- or farm-level ARC. **(7 U.S.C. 9017(a))**	Requires the Secretary to make ARC payments if all of the producers on a farm have elected ARC for crop years 2019-2023 if a covered commodity's crop-year actual crop revenue is less than its ARC guarantee. **(§1117(a))** (Refers only to the county-level ARC. Does not include the individual ARC coverage option.)

Table 3. (Continued)

Current Law/Policy	House Passed Bill (H.R. 2)
Actual crop revenue. The actual crop revenue varies with the choice of county-level or farm-level ARC. County coverage for a crop year of a covered commodity: actual crop revenue per acre equals the actual average county yield per planted acre for a covered commodity times the higher of the MYAP, or the national average marketing assistance loan rate. **Individual (farm-level) coverage.** Actual crop revenue per acre is the producer's share of the aggregated revenue per acre for all covered commodities planted on all farms for which individual coverage has been selected. Actual crop revenue per acre equals the sum of covered commodity revenue (total production of each covered commodity on such farms times the higher of (i) the MYAP or (ii) the national average loan rate) divided by the total planted acres of all covered commodities on such farms. **(7 U.S.C. 9017(b))**	Defines actual crop revenue specific to county- level ARC for a crop year for a covered commodity as the product of the actual average county yield per planted acre for a covered commodity times the higher of the MYAP or the national average marketing assistance loan rate. **(§1117(b))** By omission, individual (farm-level) ARC expires at the end of the 2018 crop year.
ARC revenue guarantee. ARC guarantee per acre equals 86% times the benchmark revenue. The benchmark revenue varies with the choice of county-level or individual (farm-level) ARC. For county ARC coverage for a covered commodity for a crop year, benchmark revenue per acre equals the recent five-year average county yield (excluding the years with the highest and lowest yields, or "Olympic average") times the covered commodity's Olympic MYAP for the most recent five crop years. For individual ARC coverage for a crop year, benchmark revenue is based on the producer's share of all covered commodities planted on all farms for which individual coverage has been selected and in which the producer has an interest. Benchmark revenue is the summation of Olympic five-year average revenue for each covered commodity aggregated across all farms with individual coverage, adjusted to reflect current-year planted acreage shares by covered commodity. **(7 U.S.C. 9017(c))**	Same as current law. **(§1117(c))** By omission, individual (farm-level) ARC expires at the end of the 2018 crop year.

Current Law/Policy	House Passed Bill (H.R. 2)
Yield conditions in ARC actual revenue and revenue guarantee calculations. If, for the covered commodity for any of the five most recent crop years, the yield per planted acre or historical county yield per planted acre is less than 70% of the transitional yield, then 70% of the transitional yield shall be used for those years. **(7 U.S.C. 9017(c)(4))**	Same as current law. **(§1117(c)(3))**
Reference price in ARC revenue guarantee. The reference price is used if the MYAP for any of the five most recent crop years is lower than the reference price. **(7 U.S.C. 9017(c)(5))**	Same as current law. **(§1117(c)(4))**
ARC payment rate. The payment rate for a covered commodity, in the case of either county coverage or individual coverage, is equal to the lesser of (1) the amount that the ARC guarantee exceeds the actual crop revenue for the crop year or (2) 10% of the benchmark revenue for the crop year. **(7 U.S.C. 9017(d))**	The payment rate for a covered commodity is equal to the lesser of (1) the amount that the ARC guarantee exceeds the actual crop revenue for the crop year or (2) 10% of the benchmark revenue for the crop year. **(§1117(d))**
ARC payment amount. If ARC payments are required to be paid for any of the 2014-2018 crop years, then the payment amount equals the payment rate times the payment acres. **(7 U.S.C. 9017(e))**	If ARC payments are required to be paid for any of the 2019-2023 crop years, then the payment amount equals the payment rate times the payment acres. **(§1117(e))**
Timing of ARC payments. Payments shall be made beginning October 1, or as soon as practicable thereafter, after the end of the applicable marketing year for the covered commodity. **(7 U.S.C. 9017(f))**	Same as current law. **(§1117(f))**
Additional duties of the Secretary. In providing ARC, the Secretary shall use all available inform-ation and analysis, including data mining, to check for anomalies in the determination of ARC pay-ments, calculating a separate actual crop revenue and ARC guarantee for irrigated and nonirrigated covered commodities, and, if necessary, assist with yield determinations as follows: For individual coverage, if the Secretary determines that the farm has planted acreage in a quantity that is insufficient to calculate a representative average yield for the farm, then the Secretary will assign an average yield for a farm on the basis of the yield history of representative farms in the state, region, or crop reporting	Sets forth additional duties of the Secretary, including using available information and analysis to check for anomalies in the determination of ARC payments; calculating a separate actual crop revenue and agriculture risk coverage guarantee for irrigated and nonirrigated covered commodities; assigning an actual or benchmark county yield for planted acres for a covered commodity for a crop year using first Risk Management Agency data, if sufficient, or, second, other sources of data as determined by the Secretary, or, third, the yield history of representative farms in the state, region, or crop reporting district; and making payments

Table 3. (Continued)

Current Law/Policy	House Passed Bill (H.R. 2)
district, as determined by the Secretary; and For county coverage, if the Secretary cannot establish the actual or benchmark county yield for each planted acre for a crop year for a covered commodity in the county, or the yield is an unrepresentative average yield for the county, then the Secretary will assign an actual or benchmark county yield for each planted acre for the crop year for the covered commodity on the basis of the yield history of representative farms in the state, region, or crop reporting district, as determined by the Secretary. **(7 U.S.C. 9017(g))**	using the payment rate of the county of the physical location of the base acres of a farm. **(§1117(g))**
Producer Agreements	
Producer agreements. The Secretary may require producers agree to comply with certain provisions in exchange for receiving payments, issue rules to ensure compliance, and modify compliance requirements. Eligibility for PLC and ARC payments and marketing loans requires producers to comply with conservation and wetland protection, control noxious weeds, maintain sound agricultural practices, and use the farm's land attributable to base acres for agricultural or conserving use and not for nonagricultural commercial, industrial, or residential use as determined by the Secretary. **(7 U.S.C. 9018(a))**	Same as current law. **(§1118(a))**
Termination of payments. A transfer of or change in the interest of the producers on a farm will result in the termination of payments unless the transferee or owner agrees to assume all compliance obligations. An exception to payment termination is made for producers who die or become incapacitated. **(7 U.S.C. 9018(b))**	Same as current law. **(§1118(b))**
Annual acreage reports. Eligibility for PLC and ARC payments and marketing loans requires producers to submit annual acreage reports. **(7 U.S. Annual Crop Production reports. C. 9018(c))**	Same as current law. **(§1118(c))**
Eligibility for ARC payments for individual (i.e., the whole-farm, farm-level) coverage (as opposed to the crop-specific, county- level ARC program) requires a producer to submit annual production	No comparable provision.

Current Law/Policy	House Passed Bill (H.R. 2)
reports for each covered commodity that is covered by the farm's ARC individual program—as produced on all farms in the same State. **[7 U.S.C. 9018(d)]**	
Effect of inaccurate reports. No penalties (with respect to benefits under PLC, ARC, or marketing loans) can be assessed against a producer for an inaccurate acreage or production report unless the Secretary determines that the producer knowingly and willfully falsified the report. **(7 U.S.C. 9018(e))**	Same as current law. **(§1118(d))**
The Secretary shall provide adequate safeguards to protect the interests of tenants and sharecroppers and shall provide for the sharing of payments among producers on a farm. **(7 U.S.C. 9018(f-g))**	Same as in current law. **(§1118(e-f))**
Nonrecourse Marketing Assistance Loan Program	
Nonrecourse marketing loans are available for any amount of loan of a loan commodity (see list below) produced in crop years 2014-2018. To receive a marketing assistance loan, a producer must comply with applicable conservation and wetland protection requirements during the term of the loan. **(7 U.S.C. 9031)**	Authorizes nonrecourse loans for loan commodities for 2019-2023 crop years in the same manner as current law. Retains the requirement that producers must comply with applicable conservation and wetland protection requirements. **(§1201)**
Peanuts nonrecourse marketing loans, authorized separately, may be obtained through a marketing cooperative or association approved by USDA. Storage to be provided on a non-discriminatory basis and under any additional requirements. USDA shall pay storage, handling, and other associated costs incurred for peanuts placed under loan. Such costs must be repaid if the peanuts under loan are redeemed but not if forfeited. **(7 U.S.C. 9031(e))**	Same as current law. **(§1201(e))**

Table 3. (Continued)

Current Law/Policy	House Passed Bill (H.R. 2)
Loan commodities and loan rates. For crop years 2014-2018, the loan rate for a nonrecourse marketing assistance loan for each loan commodity is as follows: • Wheat, $2.94 per bu. • Corn, $1.95 per bu. • Grain sorghum, $1.95 per bu. • Barley, $1.95 per bu. • Oats, $1.39 per bu. • ELS cotton, $0.7977 per lb. • Long-grain rice, $6.50 per cwt. • Medium-grain rice, $6.50 per cwt. • Soybeans, $5.00 per bu. • Other oilseeds, $10.09 per cwt. for sunflower seed, rapeseed, canola, safflower, flaxseed, mustard seed, crambe, sesame seed, or any other oilseeds designated by the Secretary. • Dry peas, $5.40 per cwt. • Lentils, $11.28 per cwt. • Small chickpeas, $7.43 per cwt. • Large chickpeas, $11.28 per cwt. • Graded wool, $1.15 per lb. • Nongraded wool, $0.40 per lb. • Mohair, $4.20 per lb. • Honey, $0.69 per lb. • Peanuts, $355 per ton. **(7 U.S.C. 90321)**	Continues the loan rates for commodities in current law for the 2019-2023 crop years, except (as described in Section 1202(a)(6))d for an adjustment to upland cotton and establishing a loan rate for seed cotton of $0.25 per lb. **(§1202)**
Upland cotton loan rate. The simple average of the adjusted prevailing world price for the two immediately preceding marketing years but in no case less than $0.45 per lb. or more than $0.52 per lb. (announced October 1 preceding the next domestic plantings). **(7 U.S.C. 9032(a)(6))**	The simple average of the adjusted prevailing world price for the two immediately preceding marketing years but in no case more than $0.52 per lb. nor less than $0.45 per lb. or an amount equal to 98% of the loan rate for the preceding year (announced October 1 preceding the next domestic plantings). **(§1202(a)(6))**
Single county loan rate for other oilseeds is established in each county for each other kind of oilseed. **(7 U.S.C. 9032(b))**	Same as current law. **(§1202(b))**
Seed cotton loan rate. Only for implementation of the PLC and ARC programs, the loan rate for seed cotton is deemed to be $0.25 per lb. This does not	Same as in current law. **(§1202(c))**

Current Law/Policy	House Passed Bill (H.R. 2)
authorize a seed cotton nonrecourse marketing loan. **(7 U.S.C. 9032(c))**	
Term of loans. Nine months after the day the loan is made. Extensions prohibited. **(7 U.S.C. 9033)**	Same as current law. **(§1203)**
Repayment of loans. Loans may be repaid at the lesser of (1) the loan rate plus interest, (2) a rate based on average market prices during the preceding 30-day period, or (3) a rate determined by USDA that will minimize forfeitures, accumulation of stocks, storage costs, market impediments, and discrepancies in benefits across states and counties. Excludes upland cotton, rice, ELS cotton, confectionery, and each kind of sunflower seed (other than oil sunflower seed). **(7 U.S.C. 9034(a))**	Same as current law. **(§1204(a))**
Special repayment rates. For upland cotton, long-grain rice, and medium-grain rice, repayment may be at the lesser of the loan rate plus interest or the prevailing world price for the commodity adjusted to U.S. quality and location. **(7 U.S.C. 9034(b))** ELS cotton repayment rate is the loan rate plus interest. **(7 U.S.C. 9034(c))** For confectionery and each kind of sunflower seed (other than oil sunflower seed), loans must be repaid at the lesser of the loan rate plus interest or the repayment rate for oil sunflower seed. **(7 U.S.C. 9034(f))**	Same as current law. **(§1204(b,c,f))**
Prevailing world market price. The Secretary shall prescribe by regulation a formula to determine the prevailing world market price for each of upland cotton, long-grain rice, and medium- grain rice and a mechanism to announce periodically prevailing world market prices. **(7 U.S.C. 9034(d))** Provides explicit market conditions to USDA for adjustments to the prevailing world market price for quality and location (both rice and upland cotton) and additionally the potential for loan forfeitures (upland cotton). **(7 U.S.C. 9034(e))**	Same as current law. **(§1204(d,e))**
Payment of cotton storage costs. For each of crop years 2014-2018, the Secretary shall make cotton storage payments available in the same manner and at the same rates as the Secretary provided storage payments for the 2006 crop of cotton,	Extends current law for crop years 2019-2023. **(§1204(g))**

Table 3. (Continued)

Current Law/Policy	House Passed Bill (H.R. 2)
except that the rates shall be reduced by 10%. **(7 U.S.C. 9034(g))**	
Repayment rate for peanuts. Loans may be repaid at the lesser of (1) the loan rate plus interest or (2) a rate determined by USDA that will minimize forfeitures, accumulation of stocks, storage costs, market impediments, and discrepancies in benefits across states and counties. **(7 U.S.C. 9034(h))**	Same as current law. **(§1204(h))**
Authority to temporarily adjust repayment rates. USDA may temporarily, and on a short term basis only, adjust the repayment rates in the event of a severe disruption to marketing, transportation, or related infrastructure. **(7 U.S.C. 9034(i))**	Same as current law. **(§1204(i))**
Loan deficiency payments (LDPs). For the crop years 2014-2018, USDA makes available LDPs to producers who agree to forego marketing loans. An LDP is computed by multiplying the payment rate (the amount that the loan rate exceeds the rate at which a marketing loan may be repaid) for the commodity times the quantity of the commodity produced. LDPs are available for unshorn pelts or hay and silage, even though they are not eligible for marketing loans. ELS cotton is not eligible. Payment rates determined using the rate in effect as of the date that producers request payment. (Producers do not need to lose beneficial interest.) **(7 U.S.C. 9035)**	Extends current law for crop years 2019-2023. **(§1205)**
Payments in lieu of LDPs are available for grazed acreage of wheat, barley, oats, or triticale if a producer forgoes harvesting any crop from that acreage. Crop production on the grazed acreage is not eligible for crop insurance or noninsured crop assistance. **(7 U.S.C. 9036)**	Extends current law for crop years 2019-2023. **(§1206)**
Special marketing loan provisions for upland cotton. Imposes a special import quota on upland cotton without an expiration date beginning on August 1, 2014, when price of U.S. cotton, delivered to a definable and significant international market, exceeds the prevailing world market price for four weeks. **(7 U.S.C. 9037(b))** Limited global import quota is imposed on upland	Continues both provisions in the same manner as current law without an expiration date beginning on August 1, 2019. **(§1207(a,b))**

Current Law/Policy	House Passed Bill (H.R. 2)
cotton when U.S. prices average 130% of the previous three-year average of U.S. prices. **(7 U.S.C. 9037(b))**	
Economic adjustment assistance to users of upland cotton provides assistance to domestic users of upland cotton for uses of all cotton regardless of origin to acquire, construct, install, modernize, develop, convert, or expand land, plant, buildings, equipment, facilities, or machinery. Rate is $0.03 per lb. effective beginning August 1, 2013. **(7 U.S.C. 9037(c`)).**	Extends without an expiration date the economic adjustment assistance to users of upland cotton at the rate of $0.0315 per lb. **(§1207(c))**
Special competitive provisions for ELS cotton. Payments to domestic users and exporters are triggered whenever the world market price for the lowest priced ELS cotton is below the prevailing U.S. price for a competing growth of ELS cotton for a four-week period and the lowest priced competing growth of ELS cotton is less than 134% of the loan rate for ELS cotton. Effective through July 31, 2019.	Continues the authorization through July 31, 2024, of the special competitive provisions for ELS cotton but adjusts the payment trigger to whenever the world market price for the lowest priced ELS cotton is below the prevailing U.S. price for a competing growth of ELS cotton for a four-week period and the lowest priced competing growth of ELS cotton is less than 113% of the loan rate for ELS cotton.
Payments equal the difference between the trigger prices (above) times the amount purchased by domestic users or exported by exporters in the week following the four-week trigger period. **(7 U.S.C. 9038)**	This adjustment, in turn, alters the value of assistance available to domestic users of upland cotton. **(§1208)**
Availability of recourse loan. For crop years 2014-2018, recourse loans for high-moisture feed grains and seed cotton are available for farms that normally harvest corn or sorghum in a high-moisture condition at rates set by the USDA. For recourse loans for seed cotton, repayment is at loan rate plus interest. **(7 U.S.C. 9039)**	Continues the authorization for recourse loans for certain crops for the 2019-2023 crop years in same manner as current law except for the addition of a provision providing for recourse loans for commodities that are contaminated but still merchantable. **(§1209)**
Adjustment of loans. Adjustments are authorized for any commodity (other than cotton) based on differences in grade, type, quality, location, and other factors. Allows county loan rates as low as 95% of the U.S. average if it does not increase outlays. Prohibits adjustments that would increase the national average loan rate. For cotton, loan rates may be adjusted for differences in quality factors (made after consultation with the U.S. cotton industry). For rice, loan rates may be adjusted for differences in grade and quality (including milling yields). **(7 U.S.C. 9040)**	Continues the authorization to adjust loan rates in the same manner as current law except for the inclusion of cost-saving option authority for the Secretary that requires the consideration of methods that minimize the potential for loan forfeitures. **(§1210)**

Table 3. (Continued)

Current Law/Policy	House Passed Bill (H.R. 2)
Sugar Program	
Price support program. Requires USDA to the maximum extent practicable to operate the sugar nonrecourse loan program at no net cost by avoiding loan forfeitures to the CCC (i.e., no outlays recorded). **(7 U.S.C. 7272 (f))** Directs USDA to maintain market prices above loan rates by (1) limiting amount of sugar that processors of sugar beets and sugarcane sell into the U.S. market under marketing allotments (see Flexible Marketing Allotments below), (2) restricting imports under a quota (see Import Quotas below), and (3) operating the feedstock flexibility program for bioenergy producers (i.e., sugar- to-ethanol program) under specified conditions. **(7 U.S.C. 1359aa *et seq.*, 7 U.S.C. 8110)** Maintains sugar loan rates through the 2018 crop year at $0.1875 per lb. for raw cane sugar and $0.2409 per lb. for refined beet sugar. Continues other provisions found in prior law. **(7 U.S.C. 7272 (a, b, c, d, e, g, h, i))**	Same as current law except that all price-support-related provisions are extended through the 2023 crop year. **(§1301)** Extends the feedstock flexibility program (i.e., sugar-to- ethanol program) through 2023 crops.
Flexible marketing allotments for sugar. Limits amount of sugar for food that processors can sell into the domestic market for human consumption each year (equal to a national "overall allotment quantity," divided between sugarcane and sugar beet sectors, and then allocated to individual processors). Requires USDA each year to set the overall allotment quantity at not less than 85% of estimated U.S. human consumption. **(7 U.S.C. 1359aa-1359jj, 1359ll)**	Same as current law except that all provisions are extended through the 2023 crop year. **(§1301)**.
Import quotas. For each marketing year, requires USDA by October 1 to set the initial sugar import quota at 1.256 million short tons—the minimum spelled out in a U.S. multilateral trade commitment to other World Trade Organization member countries. Stipulates that this quota can be raised only before the midpoint of the year (April 1) in case of an emergency sugar shortage caused by a weather disaster, war, or a similar event determined by the Secretary. Specifies steps to be followed to increase imports in the event of such a shortage. For each marketing year, grants USDA	Same as current law except that all provisions are extended through the 2023 crop year. **(§1301)**.

Current Law/Policy	House Passed Bill (H.R. 2)
discretionary authority to increase the sugar quota beginning on April 1 in order to allow for reassignment of imports and to address any domestic shortages so long as additional quota imports will not result in sugar loan forfeitures. **(7 U.S.C. 1359 kk)**	
Dairy Programs	
Repeal or Reauthorization of Dairy Programs	
Dairy Product Donation Program (DPDP). Requires USDA to purchase dairy products at prevailing market prices when the dairy margin (milk price-feed costs) is $4.00 per cwt. or lower for two-consecutive months. DPDP purchases end when certain conditions occur, such as three-consecutive months of purchases, or the margin moves higher than $4.00/cwt. Purchased dairy products are to be given to low-income populations utilizing the services of public and private nonprofit groups. DPDP is funded through the CCC. Expires December 31, 2018. **(7 U.S.C. 9071)**	Repeals DPDP. **(§1406)**
Dairy Forward Pricing Program. Authorizes a dairy forward pricing program. Prices paid by milk handlers under forward contracts are deemed to satisfy the minimum price requirements of federal milk marketing orders. Forward contracts apply only to milk purchased for manufactured products (Classes II, III, and IV) and excludes milk purchased for fluid consumption (Class I). Expires on September 30, 2018. **(7 U.S.C. 8772)**	Extends program through FY2023. Allows for new contracts until September 30, 2023, but no contract can extend beyond September 30, 2026. **(§1403)**
Dairy Indemnity Program. Authorizes payments to dairy farmers when a public regulatory agency directs removal of raw milk from the market because of contamination by pesticides, nuclear radiation or fallout, or toxic substances and other chemical residues. Expires September 30, 2018. **(7 U.S.C. 4551)**	Extends program through FY2023. **(§1404)**
Dairy Promotion and Research Program. The Dairy Production Stabilization Act of 1983 authorized a generic dairy product promotion, research, and nutrition education program, funded by a mandatory $0.15 per cwt. assessment on milk produced/marketed in the 48 contiguous states. Importers in all 50 states, the District of Columbia, and Puerto Rico must also pay an assessment rate	Extends program through FY2023. **(§1405)**

Table 3. (Continued)

Current Law/Policy	House Passed Bill (H.R. 2)
of $0.075 per cwt. on imported products. Expires September 30, 2018. **(7 U.S.C. 4504)**	
Dairy Risk Management Program (DRMP) for Dairy Producers	
No comparable provision.	**Review of data used in calculation of average feed cost.** No later than 60 days from enactment, USDA is to provide the House Committee on Agriculture and the Senate Committee on Agriculture, Nutrition, and Forestry a report that evaluates whether the average feed costs used to calculate dairy margins are representative of actual feed costs. **(§1401(a))**
No comparable provision.	**Corn silage report.** No later than one year from enactment, USDA is to provide the committees a detailed report on the cost for dairies to use corn silage as feed and the difference between the feed cost of corn silage and corn. **(§1401(b))**
No comparable provision.	**Collection of alfalfa hay data.** Not later than 120 days from enactment, the USDA National Agricultural Statistics Service is to revise monthly price survey reports to include the prices for high-quality alfalfa hay for the top five milk producing states, by volume, in the month prior to the reported monthly price. **(§1401(c))**
Treatment of multi-producer dairy operations. In dairy operations with more than one producer, all of the producers are treated as a single dairy operation for the purposes of participating in the dairy Margin Protection Program (MPP). **(7 U.S.C. 9054(b)(3))**	In multi-producer dairy operations, registration information may be excluded for producers with less than 5% ownership or who are entitled to less than 5% of income, revenue, profit, gain, loss, expenditure, deduction, or credit in a multi-producer operation. The dairy risk management payment to the multi-producer operation is reduced by the ownership share of the excluded owner(s) or the percentage of income, revenue, profit, gain, loss, expenditure, deduction, or credit of the excluded owner(s), whichever is greater. **(§1401(d))**

Current Law/Policy	House Passed Bill (H.R. 2)
Relation to livestock gross margin for dairy program. Dairy producers may participate in MPP or Livestock Gross Margin-Dairy (LGM-D) but not both programs. **(7 U.S.C. 9054(d))**	Amends the provision to allow dairy producers to participate in the renamed DRMP, and the LGM-D. The dual coverage cannot be on the same milk production. **(§1401(e))**
Production history. For MPP, the production history is equal to the highest annual milk marketings of dairy operations during any one of the three calendar years 2011, 2012, or 2013. In subsequent years, USDA shall adjust the production history to reflect any increase in the national average milk production. **(7 U.S.C. 9055(a))**	The DRMP uses the highest annual milk marketings during calendar years 2011, 2012, or 2013 for production history for participation through 2023. USDA is to adjust production history to reflect increases in national average milk production for calendar years ending before January 1, 2019. **(§1401(f))**
No comparable provision.	**Limitation on changes to business structure.** Amends 7 U.S.C. 9055 by adding a subsection that limits changes to business structure of participating dairy operations. USDA may not make payments to dairy operations that reorganize for the sole purpose of qualifying as new dairy operations. **(§1401(f))**
Margin protection payments. Participating dairy operations annually elect coverage level thresholds and coverage percentage of milk production. **(7 U.S.C. 9056)**	Amends subsection (a) by deleting *annually* and inserting a new subsection. **Deadline for election; duration.** Not later than 90 days after enactment of DRMP, participating dairies are to elect a coverage level threshold and a coverage percentage. This election remains in effect for the duration of the DRMP. **(§1401(g)(1))**
Margin protection payments. Participating dairy operations may elect a coverage level threshold from $4.00 to $8.00 in $0.50 increments. **(7 U.S.C. 9056(a)(1))**	Amends the section by adding $8.50 and $9.00 thresholds for the first 5 million pounds of milk production. **(§1401(g)(2))**
Margin protection payments. Participating dairy operations may elect a coverage percentage, in 5% increments, from 25% to 90% of production history. **(7 U.S.C. 9056(a)(2))**	Amends the section by striking 25%. Dairy operations may elect a coverage percentage, in 5% increments, not to exceed 90% of production history. **(§1401(g)(3))**
Premiums for MPP. For the first 5 million pounds of milk production, producer premiums for coverage level thresholds per cwt. are $0 for $4.00, $4.50, and $5.00; $0.009 for $5.50; $0.016 for $6.00; $0.040 for $6.50; $0.063 for $7.00; $0.087 for $7.50; and $0.142 for $8.00. **(7 U.S.C.**	Amends the producer coverage threshold premiums, per cwt., for the first 5 million pounds of milk production to $0 for $4.00, $0.002 for $4.50, $0.005 for $5.00, $0.008 for $5.50, $0.010 for $6.00, $0.017 for $6.50, $0.041 for $7.00, $0.057 for $7.50, $0.090

Table 3. (Continued)

Current Law/Policy	House Passed Bill (H.R. 2)
9057(b)(2)) as amended by the Bipartisan Budget Act (P.L. 115-123).	for $8.00, $0.120 for $8.50, and $0.170 for $9.00. **(§1401(h)(1))**
Time for payment of premiums. Requires USDA to provide more than one method for participating dairies to pay premiums to maximize payment flexibility and program integrity. **(7 U.S.C. 9057(d))**	In a technical correction, the subsection title is amended to **Method of Payment of Premiums. (§1401(h)(2))**
No comparable provision.	**Effective date.** The amendments establishing the DRMP take effect 60 days after the date of enactment. **(§1401(j))**
Duration. The margin protection program ends on December 31, 2018. **(7 U.S.C. 9059)**	Deletes *margin protection* and inserts *dairy risk management.* Amends the end date to December 31, 2023. **(§1401(k))**
Conforming Amendments Related to Program Name	
Subtitle D—Dairy, Part I—Margin Protection Program for Dairy Producers. (Agricultural Act of 2014 (P.L. 113-79))	Amends the heading to read "Part I—Dairy Risk Management Program for Dairy Producers." **(§1401(i)(1))**
Definitions. Section 1401 of the Agricultural Act of 2014 (P.L. 113-79) defines certain terms of the dairy MPP. **(7 U.S.C. 9051)**	Deletes paragraphs 5 and 6 of 7 U.S.C. 9051 and inserts new paragraphs that define the DRMP as the program required in Sections 1403 and 1406 of P.L. 113-79. Deletes the term *margin protection* in paragraphs 7 and 8 of the section. **(§1401(i)(2))**
Calculation of actual dairy production margin. Calculates the margin for the MPP as the difference between the feed cost and all-milk price. **(7 U.S.C. 9052(b)(1))**	Amends the section by striking *margin protection* and inserting *dairy risk management.* **(§1401(i)(3))**
Establishment of MPP for dairy producers. Requires USDA to establish and administer the MPP no later than September 1, 2014. **(7 U.S.C. 9053)**	The section heading is amended by deleting *Establishing Margin Protection* and inserting *Dairy Risk Management.* The September 1, 2014, date is struck and replaced with *The Secretary shall continue to administer a dairy risk management program. Margin protection payment* is replaced with *dairy management payment* where it appears. **(§1401(i)(4))**
Participation of dairy operations in MPP. Describes eligibility, the registration process, and the annual administrative fee to participate in MPP. **(7 U.S.C. 9054)**	Strikes *Margin Protection* from section heading. Replaces *margin protection* with *dairy risk management* in subsections (a), (b), and (c). **(§1401(i)(5))**
Production history. Describes production history in general, adjustments to production history,	*Margin protection program* is replaced with *dairy risk management program* in

Current Law/Policy	House Passed Bill (H.R. 2)
elections for new dairy operations, and required information to establish production history in the MPP. **(7 U.S.C. 9055)**	subsection (a)(1) of the section. Strikes *margin protection* where it appears in other parts of the section. **(§1401(i)(6))**
Margin protection payments. Describes coverage level thresholds, coverage percentage for margin payments, and the amount of payments. **(7 U.S.C. 9056)**	*Dairy Risk Management* replaces *Margin Protection* in the section heading. Strikes *margin protection* in each place it appears. Strikes *Margin Protection* from the heading of subsection (c). **(§1401(i)(7))**
Premiums for MPP. Describes premium calculations, lists premiums for different coverage level thresholds and coverage percentages, and premium obligations. **(7 U.S.C. 9057)**	*Dairy Risk Management* replaces *Margin Protection* in the section heading. In subsection (a), *dairy risk management program* replaces *margin protection program*. Strikes *margin protection* where it appears in subsection (e). **(§1401(i)(8))**
Effect of failure to pay administrative fees or premiums. Dairy operations that participate in MPP are legally obligated to pay administrative fees and premiums. They may not receive MPP payments if payments are in arrears. **(7 U.S.C. 9058)**	Strikes *margin protection* where it appears and replaces it with *dairy risk management.* **(§1401(i)(9))**
Administration and enforcement. The Secretary will promulgate regulations for (1) the MPP, (2) prohibiting reconstituting dairies to receive MPP payments, and (3) administrative appeals. **(7 U.S.C. 9060)**	Strikes *margin protection* where it appears and replaces it with *dairy risk management.* **(§1401(i)(10))**
Federal Milk Marketing Orders	
Terms—milk and its products. Sets terms of classifying milk by its use and setting a minimum price for each classified use (Class I, II, III, and IV) that handlers pay producers or cooperatives. The prices are uniform to handlers subject to adjustments for (1) volume, market, and production differentials; (2) grade or quality of milk; and (3) location for delivery of milk to handlers. The section sets minimum dollar amounts of adjustments to Class I milk by	**Class I skim milk price.** Amends the section by striking the minimum adjustments to Class I milk, the table of marketing area adjustments, and the effective period. The amended Class I skim milk price per cwt. is to be calculated as the simple average of the USDA reported advanced Class III and Class IV skim milk pricing factors plus applicable differential adjustments as specified in regulation plus $0.74. **(§1402(a))** The amen-ded pricing takes effect on the first day of the first month beginning more than 120 days after enactment. **(§1402(b))** The amen-dment is not subject to (1) the notice and comment provisions of 5 U.S.C. 553, (2) the notice and hearing requirements of 7 U.S.C. 608c, (3)

Table 3. (Continued)

Current Law/Policy	House Passed Bill (H.R. 2)
marketing areas for a hundredweight of milk at 3.5% milkfat. The minimum adjustments went into effect on December 23, 1985, and are included in a table. **(7 U.S.C. 608c(5)(A))**	the order amendment requirements of 7 U.S.C. 608c(17), or (4) the referendum section of 7 U.S.C. 608c(19). **(§1402(c))**
Agricultural Disaster Assistance Programs	
The **Livestock Indemnity Program** compensates producers at a rate of 75% of market value for livestock mortality or livestock sold at a loss caused by adverse weather or reintroduced animal attacks. **(7 U.S.C. 9081(b))**	Expands payments to include losses from disease that is caused or transmitted by a vector and is not controlled by vaccination or other acceptable management practices. **(§1501(a))**
Total payments received under the **Livestock Forage Disaster Program (LFP)** and **Emergency Assistance for Livestock, Honey Bees, and Farm-Raised Fish Program (ELAP)** are limited to $125,000 for any crop year. **(7 U.S.C. 9081(f))**	Excludes ELAP from the $125,000 per crop year payment limit. LFP remains subject to a $125,000 per crop year payment limit. **(§1501(b)(1))**
No comparable provision.	Adds exclusion to the adjusted gross income limit (§1604) for participants under the Supplemental Agricultural Disaster Assistance Programs who receive more than 75% of their income from farming, ranching, or silviculture. **(§1501(b)(2))**
Payment Limits	
Payment limitations. Establishes the maximum amount of payments per year to a person or legal entity from PLC and ARC payments, marketing loan gains, and LDPs for the sum of all covered commodities, except peanuts, at $125,000. Any benefits arising from forfeiture of crops held under marketing assistance loans is not subject to a payment limit. Peanuts has a separate payment limit of $125,000 for those same programs. **(7 U.S.C. 1308(a)-(d))** Payments made to a legal entity are reduced proportionately by the ownership share of any person or legal entity that has otherwise exceeded the applicable payment limitation. **(7 U.S.C. 1308(e)(3)(B)(iii))**	Retains the payment limit of $125,000 per year for all covered commodities (with a separate limit for peanuts) to a person or legal entity but applies it only to the sum of PLC and ARC payments. **(§1603(a)(2))** Any benefits arising from marketing loan gains, LDPs, and forfeiture of crops held under marketing assistance loans are not subject to a payment limit. **(§1603(a)(3))** Amends the definition of *family member* (see below) **(§1603(a)(1)(B))** and adds *qualified pass through entity* as a payment recipient subject to specific treatment (see below). **(§1603(a)(1)(D))** All changes made to payment limits shall apply starting with the 2019 crop year. **(§1603(d))**
Family member. A person to whom a member in the farming operation is related as lineal ancestor,	Revises the definition of family member to include first cousins, nieces, and nephews. **(§1603(a)(1)(B))**

Current Law/Policy	**House Passed Bill (H.R. 2)**
lineal descendant, sibling, spouse, or otherwise by marriage. **(7 U.S.C. 1308(a)(2))**	
No comparable provision.	**Defines a qualified pass-through entity (QPTE).** Based on the Internal Revenue Code definition (subchapter K, chapter 1), QPTE includes partnerships, limited liability companies, S corporations, and joint ventures. **(§1603(a)(1)(D))**
Treatment of joint ventures and partnerships. Payment limit for joint ventures and general partnerships equals the payment limit for a person or legal entity of $125,000 times the number of eligible persons or legal entities that comprise the businesses ownership. **(7 U.S.C. 1308(e)(3)(B)(ii))**	**Treatment of QPTE.** The payment limit for joint ventures and partnerships is replaced with a broader payment limit for QPTEs that encompasses joint ventures, partnerships, limited liability companies, and S corporations. The payment limit equals the individual payment limit times the number of eligible persons or legal entities that comprise the QTPE. Thus, the payment passes through the QTPE and is attributed to its owners (either individuals or entities) depending on where taxable revenue is recognized. **(§1603(b))**
Adjusted Gross Income (AGI) Limitation.	
AGI limitation. Prohibits farm commodity program benefits (including benefits under PLC, ARC, MAL, agricultural disaster assistance, or conservation programs) to an individual or entity if AGI exceeds $900,000. The AGI limit is calculated as the average AGI or comparable measure of the person or legal entity over the three taxable years prior to the most immediately complete taxable year. **(7 U.S.C. 1308-3a)**	Amends AGI limitation to no longer apply to any benefits under the MAL program **(§1604(a))**. Exempts QPTEs from the AGI limitation. **(§1604(b))** Provides authority to Secretary to waive AGI limitation, on case-by-case basis, to protect environmentally sensitive land of special significance. **(§1604 (b)(1)(B)** Applies the Section 1604 (a-b) changes starting with the 2018 crop, fiscal, or program year as appropriate. **(§1604(c))**
Administrative Programs	
General administration. The Secretary may use the funds and facilities of the CCC to carry out this title **(7 U.S.C. 9091(a))**. Provides that a determination made by the Secretary under this title shall be final and conclusive **(7 U.S.C. 9091(b))**. Provides for an expedited implementation of this title: Not later than 90 days after February 7, 2014, USDA and the CCC shall promulgate such regulations as necessary **(7 U.S.C. 9091(c))**.	Continues these provisions as current law, noting that promulgation of implementing regulations shall occur not later than 90 days after enactment. **(§1601(a,b,c))**

Table 3. (Continued)

Current Law/Policy	House Passed Bill (H.R. 2)
Adjustment authority to comply with trade agreements. Provides the Secretary authority to adjust expenditures under this title to ensure that the United States remains in compliance with domestic support levels allowed under the World Trade Organization. **(7 U.S.C. 9091(d))**	Same as current law. **(§1601(d))**
Suspension of permanent price support authority. Suspends the permanent price support authority of the Agricultural Adjustment Act of 1938 and the Agricultural Adjustment Act of 1949 for the 2014-2018 crop years (covered commodities, cotton, and sugar) and for milk through December 31, 2018. **(7 U.S.C. 9092)**	Extends the suspension of permanent price authority in the Agriculture Marketing Adjustment Act of 1938 and the Agricultural Act of 1949 for the 2019-2023 crop years for covered commodities, cotton, and sugar and for milk through December 31, 2023. **(§1602)**
Prevention of deceased individuals receiving payments under farm commodity programs. at least twice each year, the secretary shall reconcile Social Security numbers of all individuals who receive payments under this chapter, whether directly or indirectly, with the commissioner of Social Security to determine if the individuals are alive. The Secretary shall preclude the issuance of payments to, and on behalf of, deceased individuals that were not eligible for payments. **(7 U.S.C. 9003)**	Same as current law. **(§1605)**
Assignment of payments. Provides the authority for a producer who receives a payment under this title to assign the payment to someone else after proper notice to the Secretary. **(7 U.S.C. 9003)**	Same as current law. **(§1606)**
Tracking of benefits. Authorizes the Secretary to track the benefits provided to individuals getting payments under Titles I and II programs. **(7 U.S.C. 9003)**	Same as current law. **(§1607)**
Signature authority. In carrying out a Title I or II program, if the Secretary approves a document, then the Secretary may not subsequently (or retroactively) determine that the document is inadequate or invalid due to the lack of authority of any person signing on behalf of another individual, entity, general partnership, or joint venture unless the person knowingly and willfully falsified the signature. **(7 U.S.C. 9003)**	Same as current law but with the addition of a QPTE to the list of potential represented groups. **(§1608)**
Personal liability of producers for deficiencies. No producer shall be personally liable for any	Extends current law to include the provisions of this bill. **(§1609)**

Current Law/Policy	House Passed Bill (H.R. 2)
deficiency arising from the sale of the collateral securing any nonrecourse loan unless the loan was obtained through a fraudulent representation by the producer. However, USDA may require a producer to assume liability for a deficiency in the grade, quality, or quantity of a commodity stored on a farm or delivered by the producer; failure to properly care for and preserve a commodity; or failure or refusal to deliver a commodity in accordance with a program. **(7 U.S.C. 7284)**	
Implementation. Requires the Secretary to maintain base acres and payment yields for each covered commodity. **(7 U.S.C. 9097(a))** Requires the Secretary to continue to streamline administrative burdens and costs; to improve coordination, information sharing, and administrative work within USDA; and to use new technologies to enhance efficiency and effectiveness of program delivery.	Same as current law for all provisions except: • The Secretary is required to make $25 million available to implement this title **(§1610(c))**; and
(7 U.S.C. 9097(b)) The Secretary shall make $100 million available to implement this title. Additional funds are made available upon notification to House and Senate Agriculture Committees of significant progress by September 20, 2014 ($10 million) and full implementation by September 30, 2015 ($10 million). Also $3 million is available for state extension services to educate farmers and ranchers of their options under this title and $3 million to support qualified universities to develop and train producers on web-based decision aids. **(7 U.S.C. 9097(c))**. USDA shall use CCC funds to ensure that the MAL program and benefits are fully functional in any year that discretionary spending limits are enforced via sequestration or other means. **(7 U.S.C. 9097(d))**	• USDA shall use CCC funds to ensure that PLC and ARC payments are fully made prior to enforcing in any year where discretionary spending limits are enforced via sequestration or other budgetary means. **(§1603(a)(4))**
Exemption from certain reporting requirements for certain producers. Section 1244(m) of the Food Security Act of 1985, as amended by Section 766 of the Consolidated Appropriations Act of 2018 (P.L. 115-124), stipulates that select federal grant financial reporting requirements for producers (defined as producers and landowners	Expands the federal grant financial reporting requirement exemption for NRCS conservation programs to all USDA commodity and conservation programs administered by the Farm Service Agency

Table 3. (Continued)

Current Law/Policy	House Passed Bill (H.R. 2)
eligible to participate in any USDA conservation program) should not apply to Natural Resources Conservation Service (NRCS) conservation programs. **(16 U.S.C. 3844(m))**	and the NRCS. As written, the applicability of the exemption is unclear given that the exemption was provided for regulations directed at federal agencies in administering grant programs rather than for specific grant program regulations. **(§1611)**

Table 4. Title II: Conservation

Current Law/Policy	House Passed Bill (H.R. 2)
Wetland Conservation	
Program ineligibility. The wetland conservation or "swampbuster" provision denies various USDA program benefits to producers who plant program crops on wetlands converted after December 23, 1985, or who convert wetlands, making agri-cultural commodity production possible, after November 28, 1990. For a producer to be found out of compliance, crop production does not actually have to occur; production only needs to be made possible through activities such as draining, dredging, filling, or leveling the wetland. Exemptions for compliance violators may be granted following a review. **(16 U.S.C. 3821 *et seq.*)**	Requires the Secretary to consider all possible exemptions before denying program benefits to producers found to be out of compliance. **(§2101)**
Minimal effect. The Secretary is required to exempt producers that are found in violation of the wetland conservation requirements if the action is determined to have a "minimal effect" on the functional hydrological and biological value of the wetland area, including wildlife. USDA has identified categorical minimal effect exemptions for activities that are routinely determined to have a minimal effect on wetland functions. **(16 U.S.C. 3822(d) and (f))**	Requires that categorical minimal effect exemptions be published no later than 180 days after the date of enactment. **(§2102(a))**

Current Law/Policy	House Passed Bill (H.R. 2)
Wetland mitigation banking program. One option violators of wetland conservation have to mitigate the violation is through wetland mitigation banking. Wetland mitigation banking is a type of wetlands mitigation whereby a wetland is created, enhanced, or restored, and "credit" for those efforts is sold to others as compensation for the loss of impacted wetlands elsewhere. The 2014 farm bill created a permanent wetland mitigation banking program exclusively for farmers to comply with swampbuster. The program has a onetime authorization for $10 million in mandatory funding. **(16 U.S.C. 3822(k))**	Provides the wetland mitigation banking program with an additional $10 million in mandatory funding authority for FY2019 and authorizes the appropriation of $5 million for each of FY2019 through FY2023. **(§2102(b))**
Conservation Reserve Program (CRP)	
Authority. CRP is authorized through FY2018 to provide annual rental payments to producers to replace crops on highly erodible and environmentally sensitive land with long-term resource conserving plantings. **(16 U.S.C. 3831(a))**	Reauthorizes CRP through FY2023. **(§2201(a))**
Enrollment. CRP is authorized to enroll up to 27.5 million acres in FY2014, 26 million acres in FY2015, 25 million acres in FY2016, and 24 million acres in both FY2017 and FY2018. **(16 U.S.C. 3831(d)(1))**	Increases enrollment limits to 25 million acres in FY2019, 26 million acres in FY2020, 27 million acres in FY2021, 28 million acres in FY2022, and 29 million acres in FY2023. **(§2201(b)(1))**
CRP grassland enrollment is capped at 2 million acres between FY2014 and FY2018. **(16 U.S.C. 3831(d)(2)(A))**	Creates a minimum CRP grassland enrollment level of 3 million acres by the end of FY2023. Incrementally increases the enrollment of grassland acres to 1 million acres in FY2019, 1.5 million acres in FY2020, 2 million acres in FY2021, 2.5 million acres in FY2022, and 3 million acres in FY2023. If USDA cannot enroll grassland acres according to the defined schedule, the unenrolled acres may not be used to enroll other eligible land into the program. **(§2201(b)(2))**
No comparable provision. CRP acres are enrolled based on the relative environmental benefits of the land offered.	**Minimum enrollment by state.** Requires a minimum enrollment rate per state based on historical enrollment. Enrollment rates must consider the average total number of acres enrolled in each state during FY2007 through FY2016, average number of acres enrolled in CRP during FY2007 through FY2016, and the acres available for enrollment for FY2019

Table 4. (Continued)

Current Law/Policy	House Passed Bill (H.R. 2)
	through FY2023. Also requires that a general sign-up be held every year. **(§2201(b)(3))**
CRP contracts are 10-15 years in duration. In the case of land devoted to hardwood trees, shelterbelts, windbreaks, or wildlife corridors, the landowner may specify the duration of the contract between 10 and 15 years. **(16 U.S.C. 3831(e))**	Amends the duration for CRP contracts by requiring select continuous enrollment contracts to enroll for 15-30 years. **(§2201(c))**
All expiring CRP land is eligible for reenrollment in the program. **(16 U.S.C. 3831(h))**	Limits reenrollment for land devoted to hardwood trees to only one reenrollment. **(§2201(d))**
Farmable Wetlands Program (FWP). A subprogram under CRP authorized through FY2018 to enroll up to 750,000 acres of wetland and buffer acreage in CRP. USDA may, after a	Reauthorizes FWP through FY2023. Amends buffer acreage enrollment and reduces total enrollment to not more than 500,000 acres. Deletes a provision allowing
review, increase the number of acres enrolled in FWP by 200,000 additional acres. **(16 U.S.C. 3831b(a)-(c))**	buffer acres and Conservation Reserve Enhancement Program (CREP) acres to be considered separate from the total enrollment cap. Deletes USDA's authority to increase acreage enrollment. **(§2202(a)-(c))**
Owners and operators of FWP land must agree to (1) restore the hydrology of the wetland, (2) establish vegetative cover, (3) prohibit commercial use, and (4) carry out the other duties required of all CRP contracts. **(16 U.S.C. 3831b(e))**	Deletes the prohibition on commercial use. **(§2202(d))**
Under FWP, the Secretary is required to make rental payments and cost-share payments in accordance with CRP. Additional incentives are authorized to enroll filter strips. **(16 U.S.C. 3831b(f))**	Reduces the annual rental rate and deletes the additional incentives for filter strips. **(§2202(e))**
Duties of owners and operators. In exchange for payments under CRP, owners and operators agree to a number of requirements and restrictions on the land under contract. These requirements are outlined in the CRP contract and conservation plan. **(16 U.S.C. 3832)**	Adds grazing as a management activity that may be undertaken to implement a conservation plan. Allows for a conservation plan to include permitted commercial uses. Adds a requirement for hardwood and other trees, excluding windbreaks and shelterbelts, to carry out thinning and forest management practices. **(§2203)**

Current Law/Policy	House Passed Bill (H.R. 2)
Duties of the Secretary. Certain specified activities are permitted on CRP land. Managed harvesting is allowed if it is consistent with soil conservation, water quality, and wildlife habitat (including primary nesting seasons) and in exchange for not less than a 25% reduction in annual rental rates for acres covered by the activity. Managed harvesting may occur at least every five years but not more than once every three years. Routine grazing is also permitted in exchange for not less than a 25% reduction in annual rental rate, subject to nesting season restrictions, vegetation management requirements and stocking rates, and limited to not more than once every two years (accounting for regional differences). **(16 U.S.C. 3833(b))**	Expands permitted harvesting and grazing activities on CRP land. Caps the reduction in annual rental rate for managed harvesting at 25% and does not allow vegetative cover to be harvested for seed. Amends the frequency of harvesting to not more than once every three years and not more than 75 percent of the covered acres in accordance with a conservation plan. *Routine grazing* is amended to allow for grazing during periods of primary nesting season if the stocking rates are reduced by 50% in accordance with a conservation plan. Requires the frequency and duration of routine grazing to be limited to the health of established cover rather than a specific time frame. Adds a provision allowing grazing conducted as a management activity under a conservation plan to occur without a rental rate reduction. Adds a new provision that allows for grazing on CRP land during the FSA determined "normal grazing period" under the **Livestock Forage Disaster Program (LFP)** without regard to primary nesting season if there is a 50% reduction of the normal carrying capacity determined under LFP. **(§2204(b))**
No comparable provision.	Adds a new provision providing that when a natural disaster or adverse weather event has the same effect as a management practice required under a conservation plan, USDA cannot require a similar management practice if the natural disaster or adverse weather event achieved the same effect. **(§2204(c))**
Payments. Land enrolled in CRP is eligible to receive cost- share assistance for practices implemented. Cost-share payments are limited to 50% of the actual or average cost of establishing the practice and no more than 100% of the total cost. Hardwood trees, windbreaks, shelterbelts, and wildlife corridors are eligible for additional cost-share payments. **(16 U.S.C. 3834)**	Reduces cost-share assistance. Cost-share payments are limited to 40% of the actual or average cost of establishing the practice except for seed, which is limited to 25% of the cost. No cost- share is available for contract management activities. No incentive payments, except those described below, are allowed beyond the cost of installing the practices. Removes the additional cost-share assistance for hardwood trees, windbreaks, shelterbelts, and wildlife corridors. **(§2205(a))**

Table 4. (Continued)

Current Law/Policy	House Passed Bill (H.R. 2)
Incentive payments are allowed for up to 150% of the total cost of thinning and other practices to promote forest management or enhance wildlife habitat. **(16 U.S.C. 3834(c))**	Reduces incentive payments to not more than 100% of the total cost of thinning and other practices to promote forest management or enhance wildlife habitat. **(§2205(b))**
Land enrolled in CRP is eligible to receive an annual rental payment. In determining the amount to be paid, the Secretary has discretion in determining the amount necessary to encourage enrollment. **(16 U.S.C. 3834(d)(1))**	Adds a requirement that when determining the amount of annual rental payments the Secretary must consider the impact on the local farmland rental market. **(§2205(c)(1))**
CRP enrollment is conducted through the submission of bids by owners and operators of eligible land. Annual rental payments under CRP contracts are determined by the Secretary in accordance with the rental rate criteria (see below). **(16 U.S.C. 3834(d)(2))**	Reduces annual rental payments based on enrollment type. Newly enrolled acres receive not more than 80% of the average county rental rate (described below). Reenrolled land receives not more than a percentage of the average county rental rate for the year of reenrollment subject to the following schedule: • First reenrollment: not more than 65%, • Second reenrollment: not more than 55%, • Third reenrollment: not more than 45%, and • Fourth reenrollment: not more than 35%. **(§2205(c)(2))**
Enrollment of hardwood tree acres are to be considered on a continuous basis. **(16 U.S.C. 3834(d)(4))**	Deletes provision. **(§2205(c)(3))**
CRP rental rates are based on soil productivity and the county average rental rate. USDA may use the National Agricultural Statistics Service's (NASS) survey estimates relating to dryland cash rental rates when determining annual rental rates. NASS is required to conduct a survey no less than once a year on county average market dryland and irrigated cash rental rates. **(16 U.S.C. 3834(d)(5))**	Requires NASS to conduct a county average rental rate survey annually and publish the survey estimate not later than September 15 each year. Requires the Secretary to use the NASS survey estimates relating to dryland rental rates when determining annual rental rates. Deletes references to "cash" rental rates. **(§2205(c)(4))**
No comparable provision.	**CREP.** Limits payments to states under CREP to 50% of the cost of activities carried out under the CREP agreement. **(§2205(d))**

Current Law/Policy	House Passed Bill (H.R. 2)
Contracts. Owners and operators were allowed to terminate their CRP contracts in FY2015 without penalty if the contract had been in place for at least five years. Land not eligible for early release includes filterstrips, waterways, strips adjacent to riparian areas, windbreaks, shelterbelts, erodibility index of more than 15, hardwood trees, wildlife habitat, duck nesting habitat, pollinator habitat, upland bird habitat buffer, wildlife food plots, State Acres for Wildlife Enhancement, shallow water areas for wildlife, rare and declining habitat, farmable wetlands, restored wetlands, diversions, erosion control structures, flood control structures, contour grass strips, living snow fences, salinity reducing vegetation, cross wind trap strips, sediment retention structures, federally designated wellhead protection areas, an easement under CRP, an average width of a perennial stream or permanent water body, and a CREP contract. Terminations become effective upon approval and payments are prorated. Land is still eligible for future CRP contracts and, if returned to production, is subject to conservation compliance requirements. **(16 U.S.C. 3835(e))**	Amends the early termination provisions to allow producers with a CRP contract in place for five or more years to terminate the contract in FY2019. **(§2206(a))**
Transition Incentives Program. The transition option under CRP facilitates the transfer of CRP acres from a retiring owner to a beginning/socially disadvantaged/veteran producer to return land to production, and it allows the new owner to begin land improvements or start the organic certification process one year before the CRP contract expires. In exchange, the retiring owner receives up to two additional years of annual CRP rental payments following the expiration of the CRP contract. **(16 U.S.C. 3835(f))**	Amends the CRP transition option to allow new owners to start the organic certification process up to three years before the CRP contract expires. Requires that financial and technical assistance be provided to the new owner to carry out a conservation plan. **(§2206(b))**
Landowners may enroll in Conservation Stewardship Program (CSP) and conduct activities required under CSP in the final year of the CRP contract without violating the terms of the contract. **(16 U.S.C. 3835(g))**	Amends the provision to allow for enrollment in EQIP and conduct EQIP practices in the final year of the CRP contract without violating the terms of the contract. **(§2206(c))**
Environmental Quality Incentives Program (EQIP)	
Definitions. Five terms are defined under EQIP: *eligible land*, *organic system plan*, *payment*,	Amends the definition of *practice* by adding precision conservation management planning

Table 4. (Continued)

Current Law/Policy	House Passed Bill (H.R. 2)
practice, and *program*. *Practice* is defined as one or more improvements (e.g., structural, land management, or vegetative practice; forest management; and other practices defined by USDA) or conservation activities (e.g., comprehensive nutrient management plans and other plans as determined by USDA). **(16 U.S.C. 3839aa-1)** Under CSP, priority resource concern is defined as a resource concerned that is identified at the national, state, or local level as a priority, is significant in a state or region, and could be addressed successfully under the program. Stewardship threshold is defined as a level of management required to conserve or improve the quality and condition of a natural resource. **(16 U.S.C. 3838d(5) and (7))**	and the use of cover crops and resource conserving crop rotations as eligible conservation activities. Adds definitions for *priority resource concerns* and *stewardship practice*. Both new definitions are similar but not identical to the definitions for priority resource concern and stewardship threshold that are repealed under CSP. **(§2301)**
Establishment and administration. EQIP is authorized through FY2019. **(16 U.S.C. 3839aa-2(a))**	Reauthorizes EQIP through FY2023. **(§2302(a))**
Requires that 60% of payments go to practices related to livestock production and that a minimum of 5% of annual funds go to payments benefiting wildlife habitat through FY2018. **(16 U.S.C. 3839aa-2(f))**	Deletes carve-out for livestock related practices. Reauthorizes wildlife habitat payment minimum (5%) through FY2023. **(§2302(b))**
EQIP may fund irrigation efficiency practices. Priority is given for applications that reduce water use on the operation or those in which the producer agrees not to use the water savings to bring new land into irrigation. **(16 U.S.C. 3839aa-2(h))**	Amends the provision by specifying that payments may be provided for water conservation scheduling technology or management, irrigation-related structural practices, or transition to water- conservation crops or rotations. Adds a new provision allowing USDA to contract with irrigation districts, irrigation associations, and acequias if the watershed-wide project will effectively conserve water. Only eligible land or land owned by the irrigation entity is eligible. USDA may waive income and payment limits and impose additional limits. Priority is amended to include the new irrigation entity land. **(§2302(c))**

Current Law/Policy	House Passed Bill (H.R. 2)
No directly comparable provision. Under CSP, contracts (five years in length with the option of renewal) are based on meeting or exceeding a stewardship threshold on the entire agricultural operation. Participants must meet two priority resource concerns upon entry and meet or exceed one additional priority resource concern by the end of the contract. Contract renewal participants must meet the threshold for two additional priority resources concerns or exceed the threshold for two existing priority resource concerns. CSP provides two possible payments: (1) an annual payment for installing new conservation activities and maintaining existing activities and (2) a supplemental payment for adopting a resource-conserving crop rotation. Enrollment is offered through a continuous sign-up and applications are accepted year-round. CSP payments are limited to not more than $200,000 total between FY2014 and FY2018. **(16 U.S.C. 3838d-3838g)**	**Stewardship contracts.** Establishes a new stewardship contract based on priority resource concerns within a state. No more than three priority resource concerns are identified in each state. Contracts are for five to 10 years and provide annual payments to incentivize increased conservation stewardship and the adoption, installation, management, and maintenance of conservation practices. Payment amounts are to consider the level and extent of the practice, cost, income forgone, and longevity of the practice. Payments are limited to $50,000 per fiscal year. Not more than 50% of total EQIP funds may be used for stewardship contracts. **(§2302(d))**
Limitation on payments. An EQIP participant's payments are limit to an aggregate of $450,000 between FY2014-FY2018. **(16 U.S.C. 3839aa-7)**	Extends the EQIP payment limit ($450,000) for FY2019-FY2023 **(§2303)**
Conservation Innovation Grants (CIG) and payments. CIG is a competitive grant program within EQIP. Grants are provided, on a matching basis, to implement innovative conservation practices. **(16 U.S.C. 3839aa-8(a))**	Limits CIG to no more than $25 million annually. Amends eligible uses to include persons participating in an educational activity through an institution of higher education. (§2304(a))
Requires that $25 million of EQIP funds annually (through FY2018) be used to address air quality concerns. **(16 U.S.C. 3839aa-8(b))**	Reauthorizes and increases the air quality funding carve-out to $37 million of EQIP annually between FY2019 and FY2023. **(§2304(b))**
No comparable provision.	Requires up to $25 million of EQIP funds for FY2019-FY2023 be used for on-farm conservation innovation trials to test new or innovative conservation approaches either directly with producers or with eligible entities. **(§2304(c))**
Report. A report is required no later than December 31, 2014, and every two years thereafter, to Congress regarding CIG funding, project results, and technology transfer efforts. **(16 U.S.C. 3839aa-8(c))**	Adds a requirement that USDA use the required CIG reports to establish and maintain a public conservation practice database. **(§2304(c))**

Table 4. (Continued)

Current Law/Policy	House Passed Bill (H.R. 2)
Other Conservation Programs	
Conservation of Private Grazing Land Program. Authorizes appropriations of $60 million annually through FY2018. **(16 U.S.C. 3839bb(e))**	Extends authorization of appropriations at $60 million annually through FY2023. **(§2401)**
Grassroots Source Water Protection Program. Authorizes appropriations of $20 million annually through FY2018 and a one-time authorization for $5 million in mandatory funding to remain available until expended. **(16 U.S.C. 3839bb-2(b))**	Extends authorization of appropriations at $20 million annually through FY2023 and authorizes an additional $5 million in mandatory funding in FY2019 to remain available until expended. **(§2402)**
Voluntary Public Access and Habitat Incentive Program. Authorizes $50 million in mandatory funds for FY2009-FY2012 and $40 million in mandatory funds for FY2014-2018. **(16 U.S.C. 3839bb-5(f))**	Adds authorization for $50 million in mandatory funding for FY2019-FY2023. **(§2403)**
Small Watershed Rehabilitation Program. Authorizes appropriations of up to $85 million annually for FY2008-FY2018 and $250 million in mandatory funding for FY2014 to remain available until expended. **(16 U.S.C. 1012(h)(2)(E))**	Extends annual authorization of appropriations of $85 million annually through FY2023. **(§2404(a))**
Watershed Protection and Flood Prevention (Watershed Operations). Provides technical and financial assistance to states and local organizations to plan and install watershed projects. Such sums as necessary are authorized to be appropriated for the program. **(16 U.S.C. 1001 et seq.)**	Adds a new section authorizing $100 million annually in mandatory funding between FY2019 and FY2023 to remain available until expended. (§2404(b))

Current Law/Policy	**House Passed Bill (H.R. 2)**
No directly comparable provision. **National Feral Swine Damage Management Program.** APHIS administers the program to manage damage caused by feral swine in the United States. APHIS works with states, tribes, federal agencies, universities, organizations, and the public and coordinates with Mexico and Canada on feral swine disease monitoring and control activities. **Feral Swine Initiative.** Administered by NRCS in select states through EQIP. The initiative offers planning and management practice implementation to affected landowners.	Creates a new **Feral Swine Eradication and Control Pilot Program**. USDA is required to study the extent of damage from feral swine, develop eradication and control measures and restoration methods, and provide cost-share funding to agricultural producers in established pilot areas. NRCS and APHIS must coordinate the pilot through NRCS State Technical Committees. Cost-share assistance is limited to 75% of the cost of eradication and control measures or restoration. Authorizes $100 million in mandatory funding for the period FY2019-FY2023. Requires funding to be split equally between NRCS and APHIS with no more than 10% for administrative expenses. **(§2405)**
Emergency Conservation Program. Provides emergency funding and technical assistance to producers to rehabilitate farmland damaged by natural disasters. **(16 U.S.C. 2201)** Payments are made to individual producers based on a share of the cost of completing the practice. This can be up to 75% of the cost or up to 90% of the cost if the producer is considered to be a limited-resources producer. Total payments may not exceed 50% of the agricultural value of the affected land. Payments are made following completion and inspection of the practice. **(7 C.F.R. 701.126)**	Adds a reference to wildfires in a list of natural disasters. Adds a new provision allowing producers repairing or replacing damaged fences the option of accepting payment (percentage of the fair market value of the cost) before repairing or replacing the fence rather than following the completion and inspection of the practice. Adds a new section similar to existing regulations limiting the cost-share to 75% of the total allowable cost or up to 90% of the total allowable cost if the producer is considered limited resource, socially disadvantaged, or beginning farmer or rancher. Requires that total payments for a single event may not exceed 50% the agricultural; value of the land. **(§2406)**
Funding and Administration	
Commodity Credit Corporation (CCC). Authorizes the use of funds (mandatory), facilities, and authorities of the CCC to carry out conservation programs between FY2014 and FY2018 and through FY2019 for EQIP. **(16 U.S.C. 3841(a))**	Extends the CCC authority between FY2014 and FY2023. Specific funding levels for programs are outlined below. **(§2501(a)(1))**
CRP funding. Authorizes $10 million for thinning activities and $33 million for transition contracts between FY2014 and FY2018. Total	Extends the specific authorizations of $10 million for thinning incentive payments and

Table 4. (Continued)

Current Law/Policy	House Passed Bill (H.R. 2)
funding for CRP is limited by enrolled acres, not total dollars. See above. **(16 U.S.C. 3841(a)(1))**	$33 million for transition contracts between FY2014 and FY2023. **(§2501(a)(1) & (a)(2))**
ACEP funding. Authorizes $400 million in FY2014, $425 million in FY2015, $450 million in FY2016, $500 million in FY2017, and $250 million in FY2018. **(16 U.S.C. 3841(a)(2))**	Reauthorizes the authority for the CCC to fund ACEP for $500 million annually between FY2019 and FY2023. **(§2501(a)(3))**
Conservation Security Program funding. Authorizes contracts (enrolled prior to FY2009) with such sums as necessary. **(16 U.S.C. 3841(a)(3))**	Deletes provision. **(§2501(a)(4))**
CSP funding. Total funding for CSP is limited by enrolled acres, not total dollars between FY2014 and FY2018. **(16 U.S.C. 3841(a)(4))**	Authorizes the CCC to carry out CSP contracts enrolled prior to enactment. **(§2501(a)(5))**
EQIP funding. Authorizes $1.35 billion in FY2014, $1.6 billion in FY2015, $1.65 billion in each FY2016 and FY2017, and $1.75 billion in each FY2018 and FY2019. **(16 U.S.C. 3841(a)(5))**	Reauthorizes the authority for the CCC to fund EQIP, including: $2 billion in FY2019, $2.5 billion in FY2020, $2.75 billion in FY2021, $2.935 billion in FY2022, and $3 billion in FY2023. **(§2501(a)(6))**
Availability of funds. Mandatory funding made available for CRP, ACEP, CSP, and EQIP between FY2014 and FY2018 (FY2019 for EQIP) are authorized to remain available until expended. **(16 U.S.C. 3841(b))**	Reauthorizes mandatory funding made available for CRP, ACEP, CSP, and EQIP between FY2019 and FY2023 to remain available until expended. **(§2501(b))**
Technical assistance. USDA is required to give priority to producers who request technical assistance to comply with highly erodible land conservation (sodbuster) and wetland conservation (swampbuster) for the first time because of the changes made in the 2014 farm bill that tied crop insurance subsidies to compliance requirements. Requires reports to Congress related to the effect of conservation compliance on specialty crop producers and requested technical assistance. **(16 U.S.C. 3841(c))**	Deletes reporting requirements. **(§2501(c))**
Regional equity. Requires regional equity through proportional distribution of conservation program funds based on historical funding levels. Allows states in the first quarter of the fiscal year to establish that they can use a total of 0.6% of certain conservation funds. If established, those	Deletes provision. **(§2501(d))**

Current Law/Policy	House Passed Bill (H.R. 2)
states may receive 0.6% of funds. **(16 U.S.C. 3841(d))**	
Assistance to certain farmers or ranchers for conservation access. Establishes an annual set aside in EQIP and CSP from FY2014 to FY2018—5% to beginning farmers or ranchers and 5% to socially disadvantaged farmers or ranchers. Unobligated funds for EQIP and unobligated acres for CSP under this provision may be repooled and obligated in accordance with the respective program. Preference is provided for veteran farmers or ranchers eligible under the provision. **(16 U.S.C. 3841(h))**	Reauthorizes the EQIP set-aside through FY2023 and deletes the reference to CSP **(§2501(e))**
Report on program enrollments and assistance. Reports are required for program enrollments and assistance under conservation programs, including significant payments, waivers, and exceptions. **(16 U.S.C. 3841(i))**	Reauthorizes reporting requirements through FY2023, adds reports on annual and current enrollment statistics, and removes references to CSP. **(§2501(f))**
Delivery of technical assistance. All producers participating in conservation programs must be provided technical assistance either by USDA or through an approved third party. **(16 U.S.C. 3842(a))**	Adds a definition of third-party provider: a commercial entity, nonprofit entity, state or local government, or federal agency that has expertise in the technical aspect of conservation planning. **(§2502(a))**
Technical service providers (TSP). TSPs are third-party providers (individuals or businesses) that have technical expertise in conservation planning and design for a variety of conservation activities. Farmers, ranchers, private businesses, nonprofit organizations, or public agencies hire TSPs to provide these services on behalf of NRCS. NRCS certifies and approves TSPs. **(16 U.S.C. 3842(e))**	Adds an alternative certification process for TSPs requiring the acceptance of other professional certification criteria that meets or exceeds the TSP certification criteria. **(§2502(b))**
Administrative requirements for conservation programs. Stipulates that select federal grant financial reporting requirements for producers (defined as producers and landowners eligible to participate in any USDA conservation program) should not apply to NRCS conservation programs. **(16 U.S.C. 3844(m)).**	Deletes provision and adds a similar provision to Section 1611 of the Commo-dities title, which expands the federal grant financial reporting requirement exemption for NRCS conservation programs to all US DA commodity and conservation programs administered by the Farm Service Agency and the NRCS. As written, the applicability of the exemption is unclear given that the exemption was provided for regulations directed at federal agencies in administering grant

Table 4. (Continued)

Current Law/Policy	House Passed Bill (H.R. 2)
	programs rather than for specific grant program regulations. **(§2503(1))**
No comparable provision.	**Source water protection carve-out.** Requires USDA to encourage conservation practices related to water quality and quan-tity that protect source waters for drinking. Producers can receive incentives and high payments for such practices. USDA must collaborate with community water systems and NRCS state technical committees to identify local priority areas. Requires 10% of all funding for conserveation programs (except CRP) be used annually between FY2019 and FY2023. **(§2503(2))**
Establishment of state technical committees. Requires each state technical committee be composed of representatives from: NRCS, FSA, Forest Service, the National Institute of Food and Agriculture (NIFA), state fish and wildlife agency, state forester, state water resources agency, state department of agriculture, state soil and water conservation district, agriculture producers, nonindustrial private forest landowners, nonprofit organizations working with producers, and agribusinesses. **(16 U.S.C. 3861(c))**	Adds land-grant colleges to the list of required representatives. **(§2504)**
Agricultural Conservation Easement Program (ACEP)	
Establishment and purpose. ACEP provides financial and technical assistance through two types of easements: agricultural land easements that limit nonagricultural uses on productive farm or grasslands and wetland reserve easements that protect and restore wetlands. **(16 U.S.C. 3865)**	Amends the purpose of ACEP agricultural land easements by adding that the purpose of protecting agricultural use by limiting nonagricultural uses applies specifically for those uses that negatively affect agricultural uses and conservation values. For grasslands, the purpose is amended from protecting grasslands by restoring *and* conserving land to restoring *or* conserving land. **(§2601)**
Definitions. Five terms are defined under ACEP: *agricultural land easement*, *eligible entity*, *eligible land*, *program*, and *wetland reserve easement*. *Agricultural land easement* is defined as an easement that protects the natural resources and	Amends the definition of *agricultural land easement* by removing the requirement that landowners farm according to an approved agricultural easement plan. Amends the definition of *eligible land.* Increases the percentage of nonindustrial private forest land that may be enrolled in an

Current Law/Policy	House Passed Bill (H.R. 2)
the agricultural nature of the land while maintaining production. *Eligible land* is defined separately for agricultural land easements and wetland reserve easements. Agricultural land easements include land with a pending easement offer; with prime, unique, or productive soils; that contains historical or archaeological resources; that would protect grazing uses; that furthers a similar state or local policy; that is cropland, rangeland, grassland, area historically dominated by grassland, pastureland, or nonindustrial private forest land. Wetland reserve easements include farmed or converted wetlands; cropland or grassland that has prior flooding from a closed basin lake or pothole if the state or other entity is willing to provide a 50% cost-share of the easement; wetlands that are enrolled in the CRP, have high wetland functions, and are likely to return to production after CRP; riparian areas that link protected wetlands; and wetlands determined by USDA to be significant. **(16 U.S.C. 3865a)**	agricultural land easement to 100%. Removes the requirement under wetland reserve easements that USDA consult with the Department of the Interior on the wildlife benefits and wetland functions and values. Adds a definition for monitoring report for agricultural land easements. **(§2602)**
Agricultural land easements. ACEP funds are provided for the purchase of agricultural land easements by eligible entities and for technical assistance pursuant to an agricultural land easement plan. **(16 U.S.C. 3565b(a))**	Deletes the requirement that technical assistance be used pursuant to an agricultural land easement plan and instead be used to implement the program. **(§2603(a))**
Eligible entities are required to provide contributions equivalent to the federal share or at least 50% of the federal share if the entity includes contributions from the private landowner.	Amends the nonfederal share of agricultural land easements. Removes the requirement that an eligible entity's contribution be equal to the federal share or at least 50% of the federal share if the entity includes contributions from the private landowner.
Grasslands of special environmental significance are allowed up to 75% of the fair market for the federal share. USDA is authorized to waive any portion of the eligible entity cash contribution requirement for projects of special significance subject to an increase of private landowner donation equal to the amount of the waiver if donation is voluntary. **(16 U.S.C. 3865b(b)(2)(B), (b)(2)(C))**	Allows the eligible entity to use cash contributions, landowner contributions, or other non-USDA federal funding. Deletes the authority for USDA to waive an eligible entity's cash contribution for projects of special significance. **(§2603(b)(1))**
The evaluation and ranking criteria for agricultural land easement applications is required to maximize the benefit of federal	Adds a requirement that USDA adjust the evaluation and ranking criteria for geographic differences among states. **(§2603(b)(2))**

Table 4. (Continued)

Current Law/Policy	House Passed Bill (H.R. 2)
investment under ACEP. **(16 U.S.C. 3865b(b)(3))**	
ACEP agricultural land easement enrollment is through eligible entities that enter into cooperative agreement of three to five years in length with USDA. The entities acquire easements and hold, monitor, manage, and enforce the easements. Entities agree to a minimum level of terms and conditions for agricultural land easements including the effect of a violation. **(16 U.S.C. 3865b(b)(4))**	Amends the minimum terms and conditions by limiting the right of enforcement for USDA and removing the requirement that an agricultural land easement be subject to an agricultural land easement plan unless the land is highly erodible. Adds new provisions allowing mineral development and preventing USDA from limiting participation in environmental services markets. **(§2603(b)(3))**
USDA certifies eligible entities through a certification process and according to a criterion. **(16 U.S.C. 3865b(b)(5))**	Amends the certification process to allow certified entities to use their own terms and conditions for agricultural land easements. Amends the certification criteria to automatically certify land trusts accredited by the Land Trust Accreditation Commission with more than five agricultural land easements under ACEP. **(§2603(b)(4))**
USDA, if requested, may provide technical assistance for compliance with the terms and conditions of the easements and to implement an agricultural land easement plan. **(16 U.S.C. 3865b(d))**	Deletes reference to the agricultural land easement plan. **(§2603(c))**
Wetland reserve easements. ACEP wetland reserve easements may include grazing rights if it complies with the wetland reserve easement plan. **(16 U.S.C. 3865c(b)(5)(D)(III))**	Adds that a grazing management plan may be used if consistent with the wetland reserve easement plan and is reviewed at least every five years. **(§2604)**
Administration. Certain land is ineligible for ACEP easements, including land owned by the federal government, land owned by a state, land subject to an easement or deed restriction, or land where an ACEP easement would be undermined due to on- and off-site conditions (e.g., hazardous substances, proposed or existing rights of way, infrastructure development, or adjacent land use). **(16 U.S.C. 3865d(a))**	Amends ineligible land where an ACEP easement would be undermined to consider only on-site conditions. **(§2605(a))**
USDA may subordinate, exchange, modify, or terminate any ACEP easement if it is in the federal government's interest, will address a compelling public need where there is no alternative or further the administration of ACEP, and will result in a comparable conservation	Amends the subordination, exchange, modification, and termination requirements by providing separate criteria for modifications and terminations. Modifications may be made if they would have a neutral or increased conservation effect

Current Law/Policy	House Passed Bill (H.R. 2)
value and greater or equivalent economic value to the United States. **(16 U.S.C. 3865d(c))**	and are consistent with the original intent of the easement and purposes of ACEP. Terminations may be made if the current land owner and easement holder agree and the termination would be in the public interest. **(§2605(b))**
No comparable provision.	Waives the AGI limitation for ACEP landowners. **(§2605(c))**
Regional Conservation Partnership Program (RCPP)	
Definitions. Six terms are defined under RCPP: *covered program*, *eligible activity*, *eligible land*, *eligible partner*, *partnership agreement*, and *program*. *Covered program* is defined as ACEP, EQIP, CSP, and the Healthy Forests Reserve Program. *Eligible activity* is defined as activities for water quality and quantity improvement, drought mitigation, flood prevention, water retention, air quality improvement, habitat conservation, erosion control and sediment reduction, forest restoration, and others defined by USDA. **(16 U.S.C. 3871a)**	Amends the definition of *covered program* by adding CRP and Watershed Protection and Flood Prevention operations and removing CSP. Amends the definition of *eligible activity* by adding resource-conserving crop rotations and protection of source waters for drinking water. **(§2701)**
Regional conservation partnerships. Under RCPP, USDA enters into partnership agreements with eligible partners for a period not to exceed five years with a possible one-year extension. Partners define the scope of projects, conduct outreach, act on behalf of producers to apply for assistance, leverage financial and technical assistance, conduct assessments, and report results. Partners must provide a "significant portion" of the overall cost of the project.	Amends the length of partnership agreements to include agreements longer than five years. Amends the project assessments to require partners to quantify the project's environmental outcomes. Adds a renewal option for projects that have met or exceeded the project's objectives. **(§2702)**
Applications are competitive, and the selection criteria are publicly available. Priority is given to applications that assist producers meeting or avoiding the need for regulation, include a large percentage of producers in the project area, provide significant resource leverage, deliver a high percentage of applied conservation to priorities or conservation initiatives, or provide innovative conservation methods and delivery. **(16 U.S.C. 3871b)**	
Assistance to producers. Five-year payments may be made for conversion to dryland farming and nutrient management. AGI limits may be	Extends the payments for dryland farming conversion and nutrient management to match the extended partnership agreements. Expands

Table 4. (Continued)

Current Law/Policy	House Passed Bill (H.R. 2)
waived to fulfill the objectives of the program. **(16 U.S.C. 3871c(c)(2) and (c)(3))**	the AGI waiver to also waive a covered program's payment limitation. **(§2703)**
Funding. Authorized to receive $100 million in mandatory funding annually for FY2014-FY2018. **(16 U.S.C. 3871d(a))**	Increases mandatory funding authority to $250 million annually for FY2019-FY2023. **(§2704)**
No comparable provision.	**Report.** Adds a requirement for USDA to provide partners and producers guidance on how to quantify and report environmental outcomes associated with conservation practice adoption. Requires a report on the progress of quantification. **(§2705)**
Critical conservation areas. The authorities granted under the Watershed Protection and Flood Prevention program may be used in critical conservation areas. **(16 U.S.C. 3871f(c)(3))**	Deletes provision. **(§2706)**
Repeals and Transitional Provisions; Technical Amendments	
Conservation Security Program. Authorized in the 2002 farm bill and replaced by the Conservation Stewardship Program in the 2014 farm bill. The program enrolled acres in five- to 10-year stewardship contracts, the last of which will expire in FY2018. **(16 U.S.C. 3838 – 16 U.S.C. 3838c)**	Repeals the Conservation Security Program. **(§2801)**
Conservation Stewardship Program (CSP). Provides financial and technical assistance to producers to maintain and improve existing conservation systems, and adopt additional conservation activities. Under CSP, participants must meet a "stewardship threshold" for a set number of priority resource concerns when they apply for the program and then must agree to meet or exceed the stewardship threshold for additional priority resource concerns by the end of the five-year contract. In exchange, participants receive annual payments that are based, in part, on conservation performance. The program is limited by the number of acres available for enrollment each fiscal year (10 million), not total funding. Enrollment is offered through a continuous sign-up, and applications are accepted year-round. **(16 U.S.C. 3838d-16 U.S.C. 3838g)**	Repeals CSP with transition provisions for current contracts to receive CCC funding until expiration with no option for renewal. **(§2801)**

Current Law/Policy	House Passed Bill (H.R. 2)
Desert terminal lakes. Authorizes USDA to transfer $150 million of CCC funds to the Bureau of Reclamation to purchase water for at-risk desert terminal lakes. Includes a voluntary land purchase grant program authorized to receive $25 million through appropriations and to remain available until expended. **(16 U.S.C. 3839bb-6)**	Repeals the Desert Terminal Lakes program. **(§2802)**
No comparable provision.	Provides technical amendments and spelling corrections. **(§2803)**

Table 5. Title III: Trade

Current Law/Policy	House Passed Bill (H.R. 2)
Food for Peace Act (All section references in this subsection are to this act.)	
Labeling. Commodity donations shall, to the extent practicable, be clearly identified with appropriate markings on the package or container of such commodity in the language of the locality in which such commodities are distributed as being furnished by the people of the United States of America. **(7 U.S.C. 1722(g))**	Extends the labeling requirement to commodities and food procured outside of the United States or on printed material that accompanies other assistance. **(§3002)**
Food aid quality assurance. The administrator of USAID shall use the funds made available annually from FY2014 onwards to carry out Food for Peace programs to assess types and quality of agricultural commodities donated as food aid, adjust products and formulation as necessary to meet nutrient needs of target populations, test	Extends authority to fund this section through FY2023. **(§3003)**
prototypes, adopt new specifications or improve existing specifications for micronutrient food aid products based on latest development in food and nutrition science, develop new program guidance for cooperators to facilitate improved matching of products to purposes, develop improved guidance on how to address nutritional efficiencies among long-term food-aid recipients, and evaluate the performance and cost-effectiveness of new/modified food products and program approaches to meet nutritional needs of vulnerable groups. Authorizes not more than $4.5 million of funds be made available for FY2014-FY2018 to carry out this section. **(7 U.S.C. 1722(h)(3))**	

Table 5. (Continued)

Current Law/Policy	House Passed Bill (H.R. 2)
Local sale and barter of commodities. An agreement between the administrator of USAID and a private voluntary organization or cooperative (i.e., nongovernmental organization) to provide U.S.-donated commodities for sale or barter in recipient countries, or a neighboring region, to generate proceeds for use as provided in this section. Such an agreement must involve a minimum level of local sales equal to not less than 15% of all commodities distributed under non-emergency Food for Peace programs for each fiscal year. **(7 U.S.C. 1723)**	Amends this section to provide for administrator discretion in the levels of local sales and to remove the requirement for a minimum level of monetization for non-emergency programs in recipient country or neighboring regional markets. **(§3004)**
Minimum levels of assistance. The Administrator of USAID shall make available not less than 2.5 million metric tons (mt) of agricultural commodities for food distribution each fiscal year through FY2018, including not less than 1,875,000 mt for non- emergency food distribution through eligible organizations. The Administrator may waive this requirement if sufficient quantities of donated commodities are not available. **(7 U.S.C. 1724(a))**	Extends authority, with waiver authority, for requiring minimum levels of food quantities be available for emergency and non-emergency assistance through FY2023. **(§3005)**
Food Aid Consultative Group. Establishes a Food Aid Consultative Group to review and address issues concerning the effectiveness of the regulations and procedures that govern food assistance programs established and implemented under Title II of the Food for Peace Act. The group shall terminate on December 31, 2018. **(7 U.S.C. 1725(f))**	Extends the authority for the Food Aid Consultative Group through FY2023. **(§3006)**
Regulations and guidance. Not later than 270 days after enactment of the Agricultural Act of 2014, the administrator shall issue all necessary regulations and revisions to agency guidelines with respect to changes in the operation or implementation of the U.S. food assistance programs. **(7 U.S.C. 1726a(c)(1))**	Requires that the Administrator shall issue all necessary regulations and revisions to agency guidelines with respect to changes in the operation or implementation of the U.S. food assistance programs not later than 270 days after enactment of the Agricultural and Nutrition Act of 2018. **(§3007)**
Program oversight, monitoring, and evaluation. The Administrator shall establish systems and carry out activities to determine the need for food assistance and to improve, monitor, and evaluate the effectiveness and efficiency of the assistance provided so as to maximize its impact. The	Extends authority to fund this section through FY2023. Amends this section by replacing the $17 million cap on funds with a maximum of 1.5% of the funds made available under Title II of the Food for Peace Act for each of FY2019-FY2023 for

Current Law/Policy	**House Passed Bill (H.R. 2)**
Administrator may contract with cooperators for such services to be performed in recipient countries or regions. In addition to other funds made available for monitoring of emergency food assistance, the Administrator may use up to $17 million of the funds made available under Title II of the Food for Peace Act for each of FY2014 through FY2018, subject to an annual $500,000 maximum for maintenance of information technology systems, and an annual maximum of $8 million for early warning assessments and systems to help prevent famines (provided at least $8 million are available under chapter 1 of part I of the Foreign Assistance Act of 1961). **(7 U.S.C. 1726a(f)(4))**	monitoring of emergency food assistance subject to an annual $500,000 maximum for maintenance of information technology systems and an annual maximum of $8 million for early warning assessments and systems to help prevent famines (provided at least $8 million is available under the Foreign Assistance Act of 1961). **(§3008)**
Assistance for stockpiling and rapid transportation, delivery, and distribution of shelf-stable pre-packaged foods. The administrator may provide grants to qualifying cooperators for preparation of shelf-stable prepackaged foods and establishment and maintenance of stockpiles of the foods in the United States and for the rapid transportation, delivery, and distribution of shelf-stable prepackaged foods to needy individuals in foreign countries. **(7 U.S.C. 1726b)**	Changes the heading of this section to "International Food Relief Partnership" and extends the program authority to FY2023. **(§3009)**
Impact on local farmers and economy. Under general provisions governing the implementation of Title II of the Food for Peace Act, no agricultural commodity shall be made available unless it is determined that (1) adequate storage facilities will be available in the recipient country at the time of the arrival of the commodity to prevent the spoilage or waste of the commodity; and (2) the distribution of the commodity in the recipient country will not result in a substantial disincentive to, or interference with, domestic production or marketing in that country. Also, the Secretary or the administrator, as appropriate, shall ensure that the donation of U.S. agricultural commodities and the use of local currencies for development purposes will not have a disruptive impact on the farmers or local economy of the recipient country. **(7 U.S.C. 1733(a))**	Amends this section to ensure that no modalities of assistance—importation of donated commodities or food vouchers, cash transfers, or local and regional procurement of food outside of the United States—are distributed in a recipient country where adequate storage facilities are not available or where distribution would create a substantial disincentive to, or interference with, domestic production or marketing or where it would have a disruptive impact on the farmers or local economy of a recipient country. **(§3010)**

Table 5. (Continued)

Current Law/Policy	House Passed Bill (H.R. 2)
Prepositioning of agricultural commodities. The administrator may use funds made available for FY2001-FY2018 to carry out Title II (subchapter III) and Title III (subchapter III-A) of the Food for Peace Act to procure, transport, and store agricultural commodities for prepositioning within the United States and in foreign countries, except that for each of FY2014- FY2018 not more than $15 million of such funds may be used to store agricultural commodities for prepositioning in foreign countries. **(7 U.S.C. 1736a)**	Extends authority for prepositioning of donated agricultural commodities through FY2023. **(§3011)**
Annual report on food aid programs and activities. The administrator and the Secretary shall jointly prepare and submit to the appropriate committees of Congress, by April 1 of each fiscal year, a report regarding each program and activity carried out under U.S. international food assistance programs—Food for Peace, Section 416(b), Food for Progress, and McGovern-Dole programs—during the prior fiscal year including funds spent, quantities distributed, number of beneficiaries, progress made in reducing food insecurity in recipient populations, description of the Food Aid Consultative Group efforts, an assessment of progress made as relates to food assistance quality, and finally an assessment of the program oversight, monitoring, and evaluation system and its impact on program effectiveness. **(7 U.S.C. 1736a(f)(1))**	Amends Section 407(f) of the Food for Peace Act to allow the administrator and the Secretary to file the annual report either jointly or separately. In addition, this section requires that, where the annual report is not filed by the April 1 deadline, the administrator and the Secretary notify the relevant congressional committees of any delay and the reasons for such delay. In addition, Section 407(f) is updated to combine an existing annual report with more detailed information about the utilization of funds by cooperators and recipient countries under each program and the rate of return for each commodity monetized (sold to generate cash to fund cooperator projects) in recipient countries. The rate of return is defined as the ratio of the proceeds generated from monetization and the cost to procure and ship a commodity to the recipient country for monetization. **(§3012)**
Agreements to finance sales or to provide other assistance. No agreements to finance sales or to provide other assistance under the Food for Peace Act shall be entered into after December 31, 2018. **(7 U.S.C. 1736b)**	Extends the deadline for agreements to finance sales or to provide other assistance until December 31, 2023. **(§3013)**
Minimum level of nonemergency food assistance. In general, of the amounts made available to carry out emergency and nonemergency food assistance programs under Title II (subchapter III) of the Food for Peace Act, not less than 20% nor more than 30% for each of	Amends the Food for Peace Act to provide a minimum annual outlay for nonemergency food assistance of not less than $365 million nor more than 30% of the amounts made available to carry out Title II (subchapter III) of the act. Further, certain community

Current Law/Policy	**House Passed Bill (H.R. 2)**
FY2014-FY2018 shall be expended for nonemergency food assistance programs but subject to a minimum level of not less than $350 million for any fiscal year that shall be made available to carry out nonemergency food assistance programs. **(7 U.S.C. 1736f(e))**	development funds that are made available through grants or cooperative agreements and that assist in implementing certain activities—income-generating, community development, health, nutrition, cooperative development, agricultural and other development—may be deemed to have been expended on nonemergency food assistance programs for the purposes of this section. **(§3014)**
Micronutritient fortification programs. The administrator shall establish micronutrient fortification programs to assist developing countries in correcting micronutrient dietary deficiencies among segments of the populations of the countries and to assess and apply technologies and systems to improve and ensure the quality, shelf life, bioavailability, and safety of fortified food aid agricultural commodities and products of those agricultural commodities. Under the program, grains and other commodities made available to a participating developing country may be fortified with micronutrients (such as vitamin A, iron, iodine, and folic acid) with respect to which a substantial portion of the population in the country is deficient. The commodity may be fortified in the United States or in the developing country. The authority to carry out programs established under this section shall terminate on September 30, 2018. **(7 U.S.C. 1736g-2)**	Extends authority for the micronutrient fortification program through FY2023. **(§3015)**
John Ogonowski and Doug Bereuter Farmer-to-Farmer (F2F) Program. The F2F program is established to implement assistance between the United States and qualifying countries—developing and middle income countries, emerging markets, and in Sub-Saharan Africa (SSA) and the Caribbean Basin (CB)—to increase farm production and farmer incomes. The F2F program may use U.S. agricultural producers, agriculturalists, colleges and universities, private agribusinesses, private organizations, private corporations, and nonprofit farm organizations to work in conjunction with agricultural producers and farm organizations in those countries on a	Clarifies that the nature of assistance provided by the F2F program is technical assistance. Includes retired extension staff of USDA in the list of entities that may work in conjunction with agricultural producers and farm organizations on a voluntary basis. Includes explicit language to reinforce that longer-term and sequenced assignments and partnerships are allowed within the F2F program. Continues minimum fiscal year funding of not less than the greater of $15 million or 0.6% of amounts made available to carry out

Table 5. (Continued)

Current Law/Policy	House Passed Bill (H.R. 2)
voluntary basis. Not less than the greater of $15 million or 0.6% of total Food for Peace program funds available for each of FY2014-FY2018, shall be used to carry out F2F programs with not less than 0.2% for programs in developing countries and not less than 0.1% for programs in SSA and CB countries. There are authorized to be appropriated for each of FY2008-FY2018 $10 million for SSA and CB countries and $5 million for other developing or middle-income countries or emerging markets not included in SSA or CB countries. **(7 U.S.C. 1737)**	the Food for Peace Act—with continued set-asides for certain geographic locations—through FY2023. Provides that funds used to carry out F2F programs shall be counted toward the minimum level of nonemergency food assistance of the Food for Peace Act. Reauthorizes the authorization of appropriations until 2023. **(§3016)**
Other Food Aid Programs	
Local and Regional Food Aid Procurement Program. Establishes a local and regional procurement program with appropriations of $80 million authorized for each of FY2014- FY2018. Preference in carrying out this program may be given to eligible organizations that have, or are working toward, projects under the McGovern-Dole International Food for Education and Child Nutrition Program. Requires an annual report to Congress on the program's implementation time frame, costs, and impact on local and regional) producers, markets, and consumers. **(7 U.S.C. 1736c**	Extends authority to fund this section through **3201)**
Bill Emerson Humanitarian Trust. Establishes a reserve of commodities and cash to meet emergency food needs in developing countries when there are unanticipated needs or when U.S. domestic supplies are short. The trust can be held as a combination of cash and commodities. The commodities in the trust may be exchanged for funds available under Title II or the McGovern-Dole Program or for sale in the market. The funds in the trust can be invested in low-risk short-term securities or instruments**. (7 U.S.C. 1736f-1 note)**	Amends Section 302 of the Bill Emerson Humanitarian Trust to reauthorize the trust through 2023. **(§3203)**
Food for Progress Program. Provides donated commodities to participating cooperators (under agreement with the U.S. government and subject to presidential approval) to support countries that have made commitments to expand free	Expands eligible program cooperators to include a college or university as defined in 7 U.S.C. 3103(4). Extends authority to implement and fund the Food for Progress program through FY2023. **(§3204)**

Current Law/Policy	**House Passed Bill (H.R. 2)**
enterprise in their agricultural economies. Authorized through FY2018. **(7 U.S.C. 1736o)**	
McGovern-Dole International Food for Education and Child Nutrition. Makes available U.S. agricultural commodities and financial and technical assistance to carry out food for education and child nutrition programs in foreign countries. Authorizes such sums as may be necessary during FY2008- FY2013. **(7 U.S.C. 1736o-1 note)**	Amends this section to ensure, to the extent practicable, that assistance will be provided on a timely basis so as to coincide with the beginning of the school year and when needed during the relevant school year. Extends authority to fund this program through FY2023. **(§3205)**
Other International Agricultural Programs	
Cochran Fellowship Program. As established by the Secretary of Agriculture, the Cochran Fellowship Program provides a fellowships to individuals from eligible countries—(1) middle-income countries that are not receiving U.S. bilateral foreign aid assistance, (2) middle-income countries that have never received U.S. bilateral assistance but where a mutual relationship with the United States would be beneficial, or (3) a country that is transitioning to a representative type of government—who specialize in agriculture for study in the United States. Appropriations are authorized, by country category, as (1) $3 million, (2) $2 million, and (3) $5 million. **(7 U.S.C. 3293)**	Amends this section to permit study in foreign colleges or universities that have met certain criteria: have sufficient scientific and technical facilities, have established a partnership with at least one college or university in the United States, and have substantial participation by U.S. faculty in the design of the fellowship curriculum and classroom instruction under the fellowship. Also amends this section to clarify that the purpose of the fellowship includes trade linkages involving regulatory systems governing sanitary and phytosanitary standards for agricultural products. **(§3206)**
Borlaug Fellowship Program. As established by the Secretary of Agriculture, the Borlaug Fellowship Program provides fellowships for scientific training and study in the United States to individuals from eligible countries (i.e., developing country, as determined by the Secretary using a gross national income per capita test) that specialize in agricultural education, research, and extension. The Secretary shall—directly or via collaborating universities—manage, coordinate, evaluate, and monitor the fellowship program. There are authorized to be appropriated such sums as are necessary to carry out this section to remain available until expended. **(7 U.S.C. 3319j)**	Amends current law to permit U.S. citizens to receive Borlaug fellowships in order to assist eligible countries in developing school-based agriculture and youth extension programs and to permit study in foreign colleges or universities that have met certain criteria. Further, Section 3207 clarifies that training or study of fellowship recipients from eligible countries outside of the United States shall occur in the United States or at a qualified college or university outside of the United States. Finally, Section 3207 authorizes appropriations of $6 million for the Borlaug fellowship program with $2.8 million set aside for participants from eligible foreign countries. **(§3207)**
Global Crop Diversity Trust. The administrator of USAID shall contribute funds to endow the Global Crop Diversity Trust to assist in the	Amends this section to limit the aggregate contribution of U.S. funds to the trust to 33% of the total funds contributed from all sources

Current Law/Policy	House Passed Bill (H.R. 2)
conservation of genetic diversity in food crops through the collection and storage of germ plasm to provide for (1) maintenance and storage of seed collections; (2) documentation and cataloguing of genetics and characteristics of conserved seeds for researchers, plant breeders, and the public; (3) building the capacity of seed collection in developing countries; (4) making information regarding crop genetic data publicly available for researchers, plant breeders, and the public; (5) operation and maintenance of a backup facility in which are stored duplicate samples of seeds in the case of natural or man-made disasters; and (6) oversight to ensure international coordination of those actions and efficient, public accessibility to that diversity through a cost-effective system. U.S. fund contributions to the trust shall not exceed 25% of the total funds contributed from all sources. There is authorized to be appropriated $60 million for FY2014-FY2018. **(22 U.S.C. 2220a note)**	and authorizes appropriations through 2023. **(§3208)**
Export Promotion and Market Development	
Market development and export assistance programs. Provides funds and assistance to U.S. farmers and commodity exporters through the Market Access Program (MAP) **(7 U.S.C. 5623),** Foreign Market Development Cooperator Program (FMDP) **(7 U.S.C. 5721)**, Emerging Markets Program (EMP) **(7 U.S.C. 5622 note)**, and Technical Assistance for Specialty Crops Program (TASC) **(7 U.S.C. 5680).** Authorizes mandatory CCC funds totaling $253.5 million annually (FY2014- FY2018) across all programs.	**International Market Development Program.** Merges USDA's four market development and export promotion programs into one program. Maintains requirements for spending for components of MAP, FMDP, EMP, and TASC. Authorizes mandatory CCC funds of $255 million annually (FY2019-FY2023). Repeals individual statutes for MAP, FMDP, EMP, and TASC. **(§3102)**
Promotion of agricultural exports to emerging markets. Authorizes direct credits or export credit guarantees of not less than $1 billion each fiscal year through 2018 for exports to emerging markets. Requires export credit guarantees be made available to establish or improve facilities and services for U.S. products. **(7 U.S.C. 5622 note)**	Reauthorizes program and funding through FY2023. **(§3202)**
No comparable provision.	**Biotechnology and Agricultural Trade Program.** Establishes a program to assist with the removal of non-tariff and other trade

Current Law/Policy	House Passed Bill (H.R. 2)
	barriers to U.S. agricultural products produced with biotechnology and other agricultural technologies. **(§1543A)**

Table 6. Title IV: Nutrition

Current Law/Policy	House Passed Bill (H.R. 2)
Supplemental Nutrition Assistance Program (SNAP)—Appropriations, Implementation Funding	
Authorizes appropriations for SNAP and related programs through FY2017. **(7 U.S.C. 2027(a))**	Reauthorizes appropriations through FY2023. **(§4031)**
Implementation funds. No comparable provision.	Provides $150 million in mandatory funding in FY2019, available until expended, to be used by the Secretary to carry out the amendments made by Subtitle A, which consists of Sections 4001 to 4036. **(§4036)**
SNAP—Eligibility, Benefit Calculation	
Thrifty Food Plan (TFP). Maximum monthly benefit allotments are tied to the cost of purchasing a nutritionally adequate low-cost diet, as measured by the USDA-created and -calculated TFP. Allotments are adjusted for food price inflation annually, each October, to reflect the cost of the TFP in the immediately previous June. Although USDA calculates the *cost* of the TFP each year to account for food price inflation, the *contents* of the TFP—often thought of as its own market basket of goods—were last revised in 2006. Maximum allotments are standard across the 48 contiguous states and the District of Columbia, but they are higher—reflecting substantially different food costs—in Alaska, Hawaii, Guam, and the Virgin Islands. **(7 U.S.C. 2012(u), 2017(a))**	Requires the Secretary to re-evaluate the current TFP market basket and publish findings by 2022. Requires subsequent re-evaluations every five years. **(§4004)**
Broad-based categorical eligibility. In addition to regular eligibility rules of 130% of the federal poverty line and an asset limit of $2,000/3,000 (inflation indexed), states may opt to implement broad-based categorical eligibility. Under this option, a SNAP applicant that receives Temporary Assistance for Needy Families (TANF) cash assistance, Supplemental Security Income, state-funded general assistance cash benefits, or any TANF-funded benefit may be deemed eligible for	Limits categorical eligibility to TANF cash assistance, Supplemental Security Income, state- funded general assistance cash benefits, or "ongoing and substantial" TANF-funded services. Limits categorical eligibility for households without elderly or disabled members to at or below 130% of the federal poverty line. Households with elderly or disabled members must be at or below

Table 6. (Continued)

Current Law/Policy	House Passed Bill (H.R. 2)
SNAP benefits and potentially not subject to asset limits. By regulation, the TANF-funded benefit must be for households at or below 200% of the federal poverty line. **(7 U.S.C. 2014(a), 7 C.F.R. 273.2(j))**	200% of the federal poverty line. **(§4006) (see also Table A-1)**
Basic allowance for housing. Some active military members receive a "Basic Allowance for Housing" (BAH) within their pay **(37 U.S.C. 403)** in lieu of on-base or other in-kind housing. This payment is not excluded (and therefore counted) in income for SNAP eligibility determination. **(7 U.S.C. 2014(d))** Among SNAP deductions from gross income is an "excess shelter deduction" for which a household is eligible if housing expenses exceed a certain threshold. **(7 U.S.C. 2014(e)(5))**	Amends law to exclude from income up to $500 of BAH. Amends excess shelter deduction to include a household's BAH above $500. **(§4007)**
Earned income deduction. Applicants with earned income (i.e., from a job) have 20% of that income deducted from their gross income for net income eligibility and benefit calculations. **(7 U.S.C. 2014(e)(2))**	Increases earned income deduction to 22%. **(§4008)**
Simplified homeless housing costs. For households where all members are homeless, but the household has some housing costs and does not claim the "excess shelter deduction," states have an option to simplify SNAP's calculation of housing costs with a standard deduction of $143. **(7 U.S.C. 2014(e)(2))**	Requires states to include a deduction of $143 (indexed for inflation) for households where all members are homeless, free shelter has not been provided, and the household has not opted to use the excess shelter deduction. **(§4009)**
Standard utility allowances. A SNAP household can use a Low Income Home Energy Assistance Program (LIHEAP) payment (so long as it is greater than $20) as evidence that the household has incurred heating and cooling costs. This documentation triggers a standard utility allowance, a figure that enters into the SNAP benefit calculation equation. Unless the household is already receiving the maximum SNAP benefit, a household's monthly benefit can increase if the standard utility allowance calculation results in an excess shelter deduction. LIHEAP payments are excluded from counted income. **(7 U.S.C. 2014(e)(6)(C))**	For households without elderly members, a LIHEAP payment (of any amount) would no longer suffice for the standard utility allowance. **(§4010)** Does not change the law for households with elderly members. **(see also Table A-1)**

Current Law/Policy	House Passed Bill (H.R. 2)
Child support. For non-custodial parents applying for SNAP, it is a state option to treat child support paid as an income exclusion (impacting eligibility and benefit calculation) or as a deduction (impacting only benefit calculation). For SNAP eligibility, states may choose to require custodial parent and/or non-custodial parent cooperation with child support enforcement. States may choose not to require either. States may also choose to disqualify applicants based on child support arrears. **(7 U.S.C. 2014(e), 2016(l)-(n))**	Requires all states to treat child support paid as an income exclusion, not a deduction. Requires all states to require child support cooperation for custodial and non-custodial parents. Eliminates disqualification for child support arrears. **(§4011)**
Asset/resource limits. Households *without* elderly or disabled members cannot have counted liquid assets above $2,000. Households *with* elderly or disabled members cannot have counted liquid assets above $3,000. Limits are adjusted annually for inflation and rounded down to the nearest $250. For FY2018, these limits are $2,250 and $3,500, respectively. **(7 U.S.C. 2014(g)(1))**	Increases asset limits to $7,000 and $12,000, respectively. Continues inflation adjustment. **(§4012)**
In calculating assets for asset limit, excludes up to $4,650 of the fair market value of any household vehicle. This amount is not adjusted for inflation. States have the option to conform how they count vehicles in SNAP with how they count vehicles in TANF. TANF frequently excludes the value of a vehicle. **(7 U.S.C. 2014(g)(2))**	Excludes up to $12,000 of the fair market value of one vehicle per licensed driver and adds inflation adjustment. Deletes the state option to use an alternative vehicle allowance that conforms with how vehicles are counted in TANF. **(§4013)**
Any savings account—regardless of whether there is a penalty for early withdrawal—is included in a household's counted assets in eligibility. **(7 U.S.C. 2014(g)(2))**	Excludes up to $2,000 (adjusted annually for inflation) of a household's savings from assets counted in eligibility determination. **(§4014)**
Work-related requirements. *General work requirements and E&T.* Able-bodied, non-elderly (ages 16-60) SNAP applicants that are not working are required to register for work opportunities. Certain individuals, such as students and those with children under six, are exempt. Each state is required to operate a SNAP Employment and Training (E&T) program. States design their respective programs' services and capacity and may offer workfare. States have the option to require SNAP participants to participate in E&T and may require a *maximum* of 120 hours per month of participation or the household's benefit amount divided by the applicable minimum wage. Individuals that do not comply with general	Amends work-related rules to combine aspects of general work requirements and time limit to create one work requirement for all states. Includes changes to states' E&T requirements and funding. Beginning in FY2021, able-bodied adults (ages 18-59) with no children or with children six years of age or older are required to work, participate in E&T, or combine work and E&T for a *minimum* of 20 hours per week (increased to 25 hours in FY2026). Certain individuals are exempt from the work requirement, including pregnant women. Non-exempt individuals that do not comply with work requirement are, subject to

Table 6. (Continued)

Current Law/Policy	House Passed Bill (H.R. 2)
requirements (including state-specific requirements) are, subject to exceptions for good cause, ineligible for benefits anywhere from one month to indefinitely, depending on number of occurrences and state option. In some cases, sanction may apply to entire household. Program requirements, uptake of these funds, and activities designed vary by state. **(7 U.S.C. 2015(d)(4), 7 U.S.C. 2025(h))** *Able-bodied adults without dependents (ABAWDs) time limit and available waivers and exemptions.* ABAWDs (ages 18-50) who do not meet specified work requirements (20 hours per week of work or comparable workfare) are limited to receiving three months of SNAP benefits in a 36-month period. Some are exempt from time limit, including pregnant women. States are permitted to exempt a portion of the population from this time limit based on the number of ABAWDs who received benefits prior to the enactment of the 1996 welfare reform law. Some individuals may be subject to general work requirements but not time limit. States are not required to provide E&T or work opportunities for individuals subject to the time limit. **(7 U.S.C. 2015(o); 7 C.F.R. 273.24)**	exceptions for good cause, ineligible for 12 months for first violation and 36 months for subsequent violations. Eligibility reinstates if individual obtains employment sufficient enough to meet hourly requirements or becomes exempt. For geographic or labor-market-based waivers to the work requirement, includes but modifies the requirements in ABAWD time limit regulations, limiting the combining of areas and making a more stringent unemployment rate standard.
E&T funding. The federal government funds SNAP E&T in four ways: (1) $90 million in mandatory funds that are allocated and reallocated to states based on a formula, (2) $20 million in mandatory funding allocated to states that pledge to provide E&T to all ABAWDs, (3) open-ended matching funds for states' administrative costs for E&T, and (4) open-ended matching funds for states' reimbursement of E&T participants' dependent care and transportation costs. **(7 U.S.C. 2025(h))** *2014 farm bill E&T pilots.* USDA selected 10 states to pilot projects to test a variety of work and job readiness strategies for SNAP participants, including mandatory and voluntary strategies. Those pilots and their independent longitudinal evaluation are ongoing. Progress reports are available, but evaluation is not complete. Mandatory funding of $200 million was	Requires states to offer E&T services for individuals subject to the work requirement to get to 20 hours or otherwise reach compliance. Requires all state E&T programs to provide case management services. Modifies allowable E&T activities. Eliminates authority to operate workfare. For FY2020, increases to $270 million mandatory funds that are allocated and reallocated to states based on a formula. Increases to $1 billion annually in FY2021 and each fiscal year thereafter. In FY2021 and each year thereafter, reserves not more than $150 million of E&T funding for allocation to states to provide training services through providers on the state's eligible training provider list (defined in the Workforce Innovation and Opportunity Act)

Current Law/Policy	**House Passed Bill (H.R. 2)**
provided and is available until end of FY2018. **(7 U.S.C. 2025(h)(1)(F))**	for SNAP participants subject to hourly requirements. **§4015(a),(b),(d),(e),(f)(g),(h)) (see also Table A-1)**
College students. For the most part, college students (attending higher education courses half-time or more) between ages 18 and 50 are ineligible for SNAP. A student enrolled in an institution of higher education more than half- time is eligible for SNAP benefits only if the individual is (1) under 18 years old or age 50 or older, (2) disabled, (3) enrolled in school because of participation in certain programs, (4) employed at least 20 hours per week or participates in a work-study program during the school year, (5) a certain category of parent *or* (6) receiving TANF cash assistance benefits. Eligible parent circumstances are a single parent enrolled in school full-time caring for a dependent under the age of 12, a parent caring for a dependent under age six, or a parent caring for a child between the ages of five and 12 for whom child care is not available to enable the parent to both attend class and work 20 or more hours per week. **(7 U.S.C. 2015(e))**	Amends the exception for parents of children under six years to also include a parent with responsibility for the care of an incapacitated person. **(§4015(c)) (see also Table A-1)**
Transitional benefits. States have the option to provide not more than five months of SNAP benefits to households that have had their cash assistance from TANF terminated. The benefit amount for these months is to equal the amount received before TANF assistance was terminated. **(7 U.S.C. 2020(s))**	Requires states to provide five months of SNAP benefits to such households. **(§4024)**
SNAP—Fraud, Errors, Quality Control System	
Duplicative enrollment database. Individuals are not allowed to apply for or receive benefits from more than one state agency at a time. **(7 U.S.C. 2015(j))** Some state agencies detect duplicate enrollment through exchanging enrollment data with neighboring states. Since 2013, the National Accuracy Clearinghouse, a five-state pilot, uses a database to detect and prevent duplicate enrollment. Periodically, USDA publishes a report that uses data from the U.S. Census Bureau's Survey of Income and Program Participation to analyze participants' duration of participation. The last report was published in 2014 and uses data from 2008 to 2012.	Requires the Secretary to establish a Duplicative Enrollment Database. Requires the states to use the database in eligibility determinations to prevent participants from receiving benefits concurrently in multiple states. The Secretary is to establish a uniform method and format for collection and submission of data, and states are required to collect from each household member a Social Security number (or substitute), employment status, specified income, benefits, and asset information. Requires the Secretary to use the database to publish an -

Table 6. (Continued)

Current Law/Policy	House Passed Bill (H.R. 2)
	annual report on participants' duration of participation in the program. **(§4001)**
Access to state systems. States are required to keep such records as may be necessary to determine compliance with SNAP law. The law requires that these records be available for audit and inspection. **(7 U.S.C. 2020(a)(3)(B))** States participate in a federally run Quality Control (QC) system. **(7 U.S.C. 2025(c))** USDA pays half of states' computer system costs, as allowed. **(7 U.S.C. 2025(g))**	Amends to specify that records and information systems that contain records are to be made available for inspection and audit by the Secretary, subject to security protocols agreed to by the state and the Secretary. QC system reporting requirements are also amended to reflect the availability of these records and systems. Computer systems must be accessible by the Secretary for program oversight in order to receive federal cost- share funding for computer systems. **(§4023)**
Adjustment to percentage of recovered funds retained by states. State agencies establish and collect claims against recipients who traffic SNAP benefits. If a state agency collects on a claim resulting from fraud, such as recipient trafficking or recipient application fraud, the state agency is entitled to retain 35% of the amount collected. **(7 U.S.C. §2025(a))**	Increases to 50% the amount of collected claims the state agency is entitled to retain. Allows states to use amounts collected only for SNAP, including investments in technology and other actions to prevent fraud. **(§4027)**
The SNAP QC system measures improper payments in SNAP, comparing the amounts of overpayments and underpayments that exceed the error tolerance level or threshold to total benefits issued. Error rates are used as a basis for calculating state award and liability amounts depending on high or low performance. Via statute and regulation, the threshold amount has changed over the years. Since FY2014, the quality control error threshold has been set in statute at $37 (with annual inflation adjustment). **(7 U.S.C. 2025(c))**	For FY2018 and subsequent years, reduces QC tolerance level to $0. Makes related amendments in the calculation of liability amounts in light of the changed tolerance level. **(§4028)**
State performance indicators. Based on QC system error rates and other data, USDA measures state performance and provides financial awards to highest performing and most improved states. Performance awards total $48 million in mandatory funding each fiscal year. **(7 U.S.C. 2025(d); 7 C.F.R. 275.24)**	Repeals authority and funding for bonus awards. Beginning FY2018, requires Secretary to establish, by regulation, performance criteria relating to actions taken to correct errors, reduce rates of error, and improve eligibility determinations and other indicators of effective administration as determined by the Secretary. **(§4029)**

Current Law/Policy	House Passed Bill (H.R. 2)
	annual report on participants' duration of participation in the program. **(§4001)**
Retail food store and recipient trafficking. Authorizes civil penalties and SNAP disqualification penalties for retailers that engage in SNAP trafficking (the sale of SNAP benefits for money or ineligible items). USDA enforces those penalties through a variety of activities and funds from the SNAP account. Additional grant funding provided to track and prevent SNAP trafficking: $15 million in mandatory funding in FY2014, which was available until expended; authorizes up to $5 million, subject to appropriations, for each year from FY2014 through FY2018. **(7 U.S.C. 2036b)**	Extends authorization of $5 million annual funding through FY2023. **(§4034)**
SNAP—Electronic Benefit Transfer (EBT) Systems	
Required state agencies to implement EBT systems by October 1, 2002, unless Secretary provides a waiver. Requires Secretary to issue final regulations that establish standards for the approval of such systems. **(7 U.S.C. 2016(h)(1)-(2))**	Requires Secretary to periodically update EBT system regulations. Requires Secretary to include "risk-based measures" to maximize system security based on what the state agency considers appropriate and cost effective balanced against recipients' program access. **(§4016)**
Mobile technologies. Depending on results of an authorized demonstration project, retailers are authorized to conduct EBT transactions using mobile technologies (defined as "electronic means other than wired point of sale devices") if retailers meet certain requirements. **(7 U.S.C. 2016(h)(14))**	Amends this provision to create a different pilot to test SNAP recipients' use of mobile technology (e.g., smartphones) to redeem their SNAP benefits. Authorizes up to five states to pilot. States are to submit a plan to the Secretary that meets certain requirements including recipient privacy, access protections, and retailers (with some exemptions) bearing the costs of implementation. States are to be selected by January 1, 2020. By January 1, 2020, the Secretary is required to determine whether to implement in all states and/or whether more study is required. **(§4017) (see also Table A-1)**
Processing fees. No "interchange fees" shall apply to EBT transactions. No bar on "switching" fees in Food and Nutrition Act, the statute authorizing SNAP. **(7 U.S.C. 2016(f)(13))** In recent years, third-party processors have been charging retailers such fees. FY2018 appropriations law provision bars charging of	Bars a state, or an agent or contractor of the state, from charging any fee for switching or routing SNAP benefits. *Switching* is defined as "routing of an intrastate or interstate transaction that consists of transmitting the details of a transaction electronically recorded through the use of an [EBT] card in one State

Table 6. (Continued)

Current Law/Policy	House Passed Bill (H.R. 2)
"switching fees" through FY2019. **(P.L. 115-141, §750)**	to the issuer of the card that may be in the same or different State." **(§4018)**
Replacement of EBT cards. Secretary has the authority to require states to decline, unless an explanation is provided, to issue a replacement card to a household that has made "excessive requests" for replacement cards. **(7 U.S.C. 2016(h)(8))** Current regulations require a state to contact a household after they have made four replacement requests in a 12-month period. **(7 C.F.R. §274.6(b)(6))** In December 2017, USDA's Food and Nutrition Service (FNS) granted a waiver for one state to contact recipients who request a replacement card more than two times in a 12-month period.	Amends statute to specify that "2 lost cards in a 12-month period" is an excessive number. **(§4019)**
Benefit recovery. States must store offline benefits a household has not accessed in a six-month period. States must expunge from participants' EBT cards benefits that have not been accessed after a 12-month period. **(7 U.S.C. 2016(h)(12))**	Requires benefit storage after a household has not accessed SNAP account for three months. Requires benefit expunging if the benefits have not been accessed by a household for six months or upon verification that all members of the household are deceased. **(§4020)**
Online acceptance of benefits. Requires, depending on results of a demonstration project, that USDA authorize retailers to accept benefits online. **(7 U.S.C. 2016(k))** Demonstration is ongoing.	Amends definition of *retail food store* to include "online entity." Amends pilot provision to require nationwide implementation of online benefit redemption. **(§4021)**
National gateway. USDA is required to set procedures for the delivery of benefits to benefit issuers (i.e., state-contracted EBT processors). **(7 U.S.C. 2016(d))** To connect to the state's EBT processor and accept SNAP, most SNAP-authorized retailers are required pay for their own EBT equipment and services. **(7 U.S.C. 2016(f)(2))** These retailers purchase equipment and processing services from a variety of private entities. Between the retailer and EBT processor, transactions are technologically routed through third-party processors and sometimes "gateways." A variety of third parties can hinder USDA access to and analysis of SNAP data.	Expands the Secretary's EBT authority to set procedures for independent sales organizations, third-party processors, and web service providers (each defined in provision) in addition to benefit issuers. Requires, pending the completion of a feasibility study, the Secretary to establish a centralized "national gateway" through which all SNAP transactions are required to route. States are required to ensure that benefit issuers connect to the national gateway. The Secretary is required to set and collect fees, paid by benefit issuers and third-party processors, to sustain the national gateway. Provision includes additional specifications for study and gateway. Authorizes funding of $10.5 million for FY2019 and $9.5 million for each

Current Law/Policy	House Passed Bill (H.R. 2)
	of FY2020-FY2023 and allows no more than $1 million from these funds to be used for the study. **(§4022)**
SNAP benefit transfer transaction data report. No comparable provision. USDA undertook research on SNAP recipients' purchases using 2011 transaction data and published a report in November 2016.	Requires the Secretary to, not more often than every two years, collect a statistically significant sample of retailer food store transaction data, including cost and description of items purchased with SNAP, and to summarize and report that data in a manner that prevents identification of individual retailer food store chains and SNAP recipients. Provision requires specified data protections. **(§4026)**
SNAP—Other SNAP-Related Grants	
Food Insecurity Nutrition Incentive (FINI). Grant program provides grants to governmental agencies and nonprofit organizations for projects that "increase the purchase of fruits and vegetables by low-income consumers participating in [SNAP] by providing incentives at the point of purchase." Retailers often partner with grantees, and retailers financially benefit from incentives, but for-profit retailers are not eligible grantees. Mandatory funding through a transfer from the CCC: $35 million for FY2014 and FY2015, $20 million for each of FY2016 and FY2017, $25 million for FY2018. FINI evaluation is ongoing. **(7 U.S.C. 7517(b))**	Renames the program Gus Schumacher Food Insecurity Nutrition Incentive Program. Adds new priority criteria for the awarding of grants: Secretary is required to prioritize projects that coordinate with multiple stakeholders (example listed) and have the capacity to generate sufficient data and analysis. Certain other additional priority criteria are at the Secretary's discretion. Limits program incentives to financial incentives. Requires Secretary to consult with the director of NIFA to establish a training, evaluation, and information center for use by program grantees. Increases funding, providing $45 million for FY2019, $50 million for FY2020, $55 million for FY2021, $60 million for FY2022, and $65 million for FY2023 and each year thereafter. **(§4003)** Establishes a pilot project through which authorized retail food stores may receive federal funding to provide bonus incentives to SNAP households for purchases of fruits, vegetables, and milk. Funding may not exceed 25% of bonuses earned by households. Retailers participating in FINI are not eligible. Aggregate value of reimbursements in a pilot project shall not exceed $120 million each fiscal year. Mandatory funding from SNAP account provided. **(§4002)**

Table 6. (Continued)

Current Law/Policy	House Passed Bill (H.R. 2)
Nutrition Education and Obesity Prevention Grant Program. Formerly SNAP Nutrition Education and formerly an open-ended federal match to state funding, this program, administered by FNS, provides formula grant funding to SNAP state agencies to provide programs for SNAP (and other domestic food assistance program) participants as well as other low-income households. Annual mandatory funding provided, most recently $421 million in FY2018. For FY2018 and each fiscal year thereafter, 50% of funding is allocated based on states'	Makes 1862 and 1890 institutions eligible institutions for carrying out this program. Requires Secretary to act through NIFA to implement the program and to consult with FNS. Requires eligible institutions, to the extent practicable, to employ and train professional and paraprofessional aides from the target population to engage in direct nutrition education and to partner with other entities to optimize program delivery. Increases mandatory funding to $485 million beginning in FY2019.
SNAP population, and 50% of funding is allocated based on states' funding received during FY2009 (when funding for the program was an open-ended federal match). **(7 U.S.C. 2036a, P.L. 115-141)**	This amount is adjusted for inflation in FY2020 and subsequent years. Authorizes additional discretionary funding of $65 million for FY2019 through FY2023. Funds are allocated based solely on states' SNAP populations. Limits administrative costs for eligible institutions to 10%. **(§4033)** **(see also Table A-1)**
Mandatory funding of $5 million provided for Grants for Simple Application and Eligibility Determination Systems and Improved Access to Benefits. **(7 U.S.C. 2020(s))**	Retitles to "Grants for Simple Application and Eligibility Determination Systems." Amends law to exclude projects with the purposes of reducing barriers to participation or improving methods for informing and enrolling eligible households. **(§4025)**
No comparable provision.	**Food insecurity pilot project grants.** Authorizes grants for up to 10 pilot projects that support public-private partnerships addressing food insecurity and poverty. Projects are to last no more than two years and address specified objectives. Grantees shall report annually to Secretary, who shall report to congressional committees. Authorizes $5 million in discretionary funding for grants to eligible entities. **(§4030)**
Food Distribution Programs	
Food Distribution Program on Indian Reservations (FDPIR). Commodity distribution program established to distribute commodities, in lieu of SNAP benefits, at the request of a tribal organization. $5 million in mandatory funding	Amends locally grown and traditional food fund to include "regionally grown" foods. Reauthorizes fund's authorization of appropriations through FY2023. Requires that

Current Law/Policy	House Passed Bill (H.R. 2)
authorized for a traditional and locally grown food fund. **(7 U.S.C. (2014)(b))** Annual appropriations language provides FDPIR funding to be spent in one fiscal year. **(e.g., P.L. 115-141)**	FDPIR funding be available for spending for a two-year period. **(§4005)**
The Emergency Food Assistance Program (TEFAP). For FY2018, for USDA-purchased commodity foods, provides $250 million in TEFAP commodity purchases plus the addition of $15 million, each adjusted for inflation according to changes to the Thrifty Food Plan.	Increases annual mandatory funding by $45 million (plus inflation adjustment), for FY2019 and each fiscal year thereafter, by amending the additional funds from $15 million to $60 million. Establishes a "Farm to Food Bank Fund," where, of TEFAP
USDA is to distribute the foods to states for distribution to emergency feeding organizations. **(7 U.S.C. 2036)**	commodity funds provided, Secretary is required to distribute $20 million to states to procure, or for states to enter into agreements with food banks to procure, excess fresh fruits and vegetables grown in the state or surrounding regions to be provided to emergency feeding organizations. **(§4032)**
Commodity Distribution Program. Authority to purchase and distribute agricultural commodities expires at the end of FY2018. **(7 U.S.C. 612c note)**	Reauthorizes through FY2023. **(§4101)**
Commodity Supplemental Food Program. Various authorities expire at the end of FY2018.	Reauthorizes through FY2023. **(§4102)**
Distribution of surplus commodities to special nutrition projects. Secretary required to encourage consumption of surplus commodities by contracting with private companies to process such commodities into end-food products. Authority expires at the end of FY2018. **(7 U.S.C. 1431e(a))**	Reauthorizes through FY2023. **(§4103)**
Other Nutrition Programs and Policies	
Purchase of fresh fruits and vegetables for distribution to schools and service institutions. In addition to the minimum ($200 million per year) acquisitions required by the 2002 farm bill, USDA is required to purchase additional fruits, vegetables, and tree nuts for use in domestic nutrition assistance programs using Section 32 funds. The added purchases required include $206 million (FY2012 and each year thereafter). Of this money for additional purchases, at least $50 million annually (for each of FY2008 through FY2018) is required for USDA fresh fruit and	Extends $50 million requirement through FY2023. **(§4201)**

Table 6. (Continued)

Current Law/Policy	House Passed Bill (H.R. 2)
vegetable acquisitions for schools. **(7 U.S.C. 612c-4)**	
Senior Farmers' Market Nutrition Program. Authorizes and provides CCC mandatory funding of $20.6 million annually for the Senior Farmers' Market Nutrition Program through FY2018. **(7 U.S.C. 612c-4(b))**	Reauthorizes funding through FY2023. **(§4202)**
Authorizes up to $125 million to be appropriated for a **"Healthy Food Financing Initiative"** to remain available until expended. USDA is authorized to approve a community development financial institution as "national fund manager" that would administer these funds by supporting food retail projects that would "expand or preserve access to staple foods" (as defined within this section) and accept SNAP benefits. **(7 U.S.C. 6953)**	Reauthorizes authorization for appropriations through October 1, 2023. **(§4203)**
Amendments to the Fresh Fruit and Vegetable Program. Provides grants to states for children at low- income elementary schools to receive fruit and vegetable snacks throughout the day. Purchases are limited to fresh fruits and vegetables. Program is permanently authorized and permanently funded. **(42 U.S.C. 1769a)** The 2014 farm bill required USDA to administer a pilot project to implement and evaluate at least five states providing frozen, canned, and dried fruits and vegetables through this program and provided $5 million. **(42 U.S.C. 1769a note)**	Amends program to provide fresh, canned, dried, frozen, or pureed fruits and vegetables. Renames program Fruit and Vegetable Program. **(§4204)**

Table 7. Title V: Credit

Current Law/Policy	House Passed Bill (H.R. 2)
Subtitle A—USDA Farm Ownership Loans	
Eligibility. Requires, for eligibility for direct loans, at least three years of farming experience or other acceptable experience as determined by the Secretary. The applicant must also be a beginning farmer, not have received prior direct farm ownership loans, or have not received a	Specifies conditions under which the Secretary may reduce the three-year farming experience requirement for beginning farmers and ranchers as follows: (A) To two years if the borrower (1) has 16 credit hours of postsecondary education in

Current Law/Policy	House Passed Bill (H.R. 2)
direct farm ownership loan more than 10 years ago. **(7 U.S.C. 1922(b)(1))**	agriculture, (2) has one-year of substantive management experience in a business, (3) was honorably discharged from the military, (4) has successfully repaid an FSA youth loan, or (5) has a mentoring relationship with Service Corps Retired Executives or a local farmer, rancher, or organization approved by the Secretary. (B) To one year with military leadership or management experience from completing a military leadership course.
	(C) Waived entirely if the beginning farmer meets two of the options (1)-(5) above, including mentoring in (5). **(§5101)**
Funding. Authorizes appropriations of $150 million annually for a conservation loan and loan guarantee program for FY2014- FY2018. **(7 U.S.C. 1924(h))**	Extends the authorization of appropriation to FY2023 and reduces it to $75 million annually. **(§5102)**
Loan Limit. Sets the loan limit per borrower for guaranteed farm ownership loans at $700,000, increased beginning with FY2000 by the inflation percentage since 1996 in the NASS Index of Prices Paid by Farmers. In FY2018, USDA announced the inflation-adjusted limit at $1,399,000. **(7 U.S.C. 1925)**	Raises the loan limit for guaranteed farm ownership loans to $1.75 million per borrower and adjusts it in FY2019 and thereafter for inflation. The calculation of the inflation percentage remains the same using a 1996 base year. Thus, the inflation-adjusted limit in FY2019 may be about $3.5 million. **(§5103)**
Subtitle B—USDA Farm Operating Loans	
Loan limit. Sets the loan limit per borrower for guaranteed farm operating loans at $700,000, increased beginning with FY2000 by the inflation percentage since 1996 in the NASS Index of Prices Paid by Farmers. In FY2018, USDA announced the inflation-adjusted limit at $1,399,000. **(7 U.S.C. 1943(a))**	Raises the loan limit for guaranteed farm operating loans to $1.75 million per borrower and adjusts it in FY2019 and thereafter for inflation. The calculation of the inflation percentage remains the same using a 1996 base year; thus, the inflation-adjusted limit in FY2019 may be about $3.5 million. **(§5201)**
Authorizes a microloan program for loans less than $50,000. **(7 U.S.C. 1943(c))**	Changes *title* to *subsection* to clarify technical references within the statute. **(§5202)**
Subtitle C—Administrative Provisions	
Funding. Authorizes appropriations for the Beginning Farmer and Rancher Individual Development Account Program at $5 million per year through FY2018. **(7 U.S.C. 1983b)**	Reauthorizes appropriations of the same amount per year through FY2023. **(§5301)**
Authorizes specific loan levels for direct and guaranteed farm ownership and farm operating loans through FY2018. **(7 U.S.C. 1994(b)(1))**	Reauthorizes the same loan levels through FY2023. **(§5302)**

Table 7. (Continued)

Current Law/Policy	House Passed Bill (H.R. 2)
Carve-out for beginning farmers and ranchers. Reserves 50% of each year's direct farm operating loan authority to be used for beginning farmers and ranchers for 11 months through September 1 of each fiscal year from FY2008 to FY2018. **(7 U.S.C. 1994(b)(2)(A)(ii)(III))**	Reauthorizes the same set-aside preference for beginning farmers and ranchers through FY2023. **(§5303)**
Subtitle D—Technical Corrections to the ConAct	
The **Down Payment Loan Program** encourages retiring farmers and ranchers to sell their property to beginning farmers and ranchers with seller financing. The 2008 farm bill added *and socially disadvantaged farmers and ranchers* but did not specify the location and was executed with a note in Section 310E(d)(3) of the Consolidated Farm and Rural Development Act (ConAct) about placement to reflect the probable intent of Congress. **(7 U.S.C. 1935(d)(3))**	Clarifies the location for the addition of *and socially disadvantaged farmers and ranchers* in the statute about encouraging retiring farmers and ranchers to offer seller financing Retroactive to the 2008 farm bill. **(§5401(a))**
For eligibility in the **Emergency Loan Program**, the 2014 farm bill added *and such other legal entities* to the first sentence. It was executed in Section 321(a) of the ConAct in the second sentence to reflect the probable intent of Congress. **(7 U.S.C. 1961(a))**	Clarifies the location in the second sentence for the addition of *and such other legal entities* to the eligibility for the Emergency Loan Program. Retroactive to the 2014 farm bill. **(§5401(b))**
The Agricultural Credit Improvement Act of 1992 attempted to add flexibility for a state director to extend a 60-day period for a borrower to respond to notice of loan delinquency that was sent by the Secretary. The 1992 revision of Section 331D(e) of the ConAct could not be executed. **(7 U.S.C. 1981d(e))**	Clarifies that a state director may add flexibility to the time period allowed for a borrower to respond to a notice sent by the Secretary about a loan becoming delinquent. Retroactive to 1992. **(§5401(c))**
Approved lender. The definition of *approved lender* in Section 333A(f)(1)(A) of the ConAct references Section 114. Notes in the act suggest that the probable intent of Congress was likely Section 339. **(7 U.S.C. 1983a(f)(1)(A))**	Clarifies the definition of *approved lender* with reference to Section 339 of the ConAct. Retroactive to 1992. **(§5401(d))**
In the guaranteed loan program, the classification of "preferred certified lender" has authority to make certain decisions about loans that are not granted to all lenders that receive guarantees. **(7 U.S.C. 1989(d)(3))**	Capitalizes the spelling of Preferred Certified Lender. **(§5401(e))**
An instruction in the 2014 farm bill attempted to change the reference to *or joint operators* in Section 343(a)(11)(C) of the ConAct to *joint*	Clarifies in the definition of *qualified beginning farmer or rancher* that flexibility was added with the addition of *or owners* to

Current Law/Policy	House Passed Bill (H.R. 2)
operator, or owners, as noted in its execution. **(7 U.S.C. 1991(a)(11)(C))**	the phrase about alternative legal entities. Retroactive to the 2014 farm bill. **(§5401(f))**
To apply certain definitions, Section 343(b) of the ConAct references Section "307(c)." Notes for the execution suggest that the intent may have been Section 307(d). **(7 U.S.C. 1991(b))**	Deletes reference to Section 307(e), and inserts reference to Section 307(d). Retroactive to the 2014 farm bill. **(§5401(g))**
A paragraph in statute ended in an extra comma after an amendment was made in the 1996 farm bill. **(7 U.S.C. 1994(a))**	Deletes the extra comma at the end of the paragraph. **(§5401(h))**
Subtitle E: Amendments to the Farm Credit Act of 1971 (Farm Credit System)	
Update definition of Farm Credit System (FCS) entities. Defines the entities that comprise the FCS, all of which are regulated by FCA. **(12 U.S.C. 2002(a))**	Revises the definition of entities that comprise the FCS to include more specific identification of the current types of entities and includes the Federal Farm Credit Banks Funding Corporation, FarmerMac, and service corporations, all of which shall continue to be regulated by FCA. **(§5501(a))**
Allows a production credit association in a district with two such associations to serve borrowers who are denied credit by the other association if FCA determines that the denying association was "unduly restrictive" in granting credit. **(12 U.S.C. 2075(d))**	Deletes this section, which is no longer applicable. **(§5501(b))**
Establishes a system of banks for cooperatives in the FCS. **(12 U.S.C. 2121, 2123, 2128, 2130, 2131(c), 2132, 2141, 2142, 2149)**	Deletes various references to a Central Bank for Cooperatives, United Bank of Cooperatives, and/or a National Bank of Cooperatives while continuing to recognize the existence of a bank for cooperatives. **(§5501(c), (d), (e), (f), (h), (j), (k), (m), (n), (o), (p), (q), (r), (s))**
Establishes provisions relating to the funding and governance of the Farm Credit Banks through referring to district banks. **(12 U.S.C. 2126, 2131(d))**	Deletes the obsolete word *district* in reference to the Farm Credit Banks, as that is no longer used following years of consolidation. **(§5501(g), (l))**
Allows a bank for cooperatives to make loans to the Rural Electrification Administration. **(12 U.S.C. 2129(b)(1)(A))**	Inserts language recognizing a successor agency to the Rural Electrification Administration after the latter was absorbed into the USDA Rural Utilities Service. **(§5501(i))**
Establishes, and sets conditions for an Assistance Board, a Financial Assistance Corporation, and related funding to remediate losses within the FCS during the 1980s. **(12 U.S.C. 2278a-2278b-11, 2151, 2159, 2277a-9(b), 2162(c), 2202c, 2219c, 2254(b), 2271 (4), 2277a-7(2), 2279d(a)(4))**	Deletes references to the now-obsolete Assistance Board, Financial Assistance Corporation, and funding. Terminates the Financial Assistance Corporation after December 31, 2018. **(§5501(t), (u), (x), (bb), (ee), (ii), (jj), (mm), (nn), (oo), (qq))**

Table 7. (Continued)

Current Law/Policy	House Passed Bill (H.R. 2)
During the tenure of the Assistance Board, a member of the Assistance Board shall be a non-voting member of the board of the Farm Credit System Funding Corporation. After termination of the Assistance Board, its successor, the Farm Credit System Insurance Corporation, shall not have a member on the Funding Corporation board. **(12 U.S.C. 2160(d)(2))**	Deletes reference to the now-obsolete Assistance Board and retains language that the Insurance Corporation shall not have a member on the board of the Funding Corporation. **(§5501(v))**
Establishes provisions and conditions for the transition of various parts of the FCS as it is created, especially from the 1980s and 1990s for FarmerMac. **(12 U.S.C. 2160(e), 2202a(h), 2252(a)(2), 2253, 2275, 2279c-2(c), 2279aa(2), 2279aa(6), 2279aa(8), 2279aa-2(b), 2279aa-4(a)(1), 2279aa-6(d), 2279bb-1(a), 2279bb-4(e))**	Deletes provisions that are transitional in nature now that the FCS is established. **(§5501(w), (aa), (ff), (gg), (ll), (pp), (rr), (ss), (tt), (uu), (vv), (ww), (xx))**
Lists the FCS institutions that are applicable to various requirements. **(12 U.S.C. 2184(a)(1), 2205, 2207(a), 2254 (a), 2274)**	Revises the lists to more generically refer to FCS banks or associations and its current structure. **(§5501(y), (cc), (dd), (hh), (kk))**
Defines terms relating to the restructuring of distressed loans. **(12 U.S.C.2202a(a))**	Applies the definitions that are used for distressed loans to the section about the "right of first refusal" for borrowers' rights. (12 U.S.C. 2219). **(§5501(z))**
Provides for the establishment and administration of FCA and certain of its powers to regulate entities of FCS. **(12 U.S.C. 1141b, 1141c, 1141d, 1141e, 1141f, 1141i, 1141j, 1141d-1, 1148, 1148a-4, 1148b, 1148c, 1148d, 1401-1404)**	**Conforming repeals.** Repeals sections about FCA that have been superseded by newer statutes for FCA that are in 12 U.S.C. 2241 *et seq*. and that are part of the Farm Credit Act of 1971, as amended. **(§5502)**
Headquarters. Provides for the provision of headquarters and other facilities for FCA. **(12 U.S.C. 2251)**	Directs that the principal office of FCA shall be in the Washington, DC, metropolitan area, with other offices throughout the United States as necessary. **(§5503)**
Privileged information. Instructs FCA to examine the banks and associations of the FCS, and to report on the condition of the System. Empowers FCA to share confidentially with the Farm Credit Insurance Corporation information about examinations. **(12 U.S.C. 2254)**	Provides authority for FCS institutions to provide privileged communications that they have (e.g., with attorneys and accountants) to FCA, pursuant to its supervision and regulatory authority, without losing the ability to assert this privilege with respect to others. **(§5504)**
Scope of FCA jurisdiction. Provides various enforcement powers to FCA against FCS entities, directors, officers, employees, and agents that	Adds a provision that the scope of FCA's jurisdiction shall include "institution-affiliated parties" (as defined in Section 5506) and that the parties may be held

Current Law/Policy	**House Passed Bill (H.R. 2)**
engage in unsafe or unsound practices or violate the regulations of the FCS. **(12 U.S.C. 2261-2274)**	accountable to laws and regulations. This jurisdiction is retroactive and shall continue to apply for six years after the party ceases to be affiliated with the FCS. **(§5505)**
Defines various terms for the enforcement powers of FCA. **(12 U.S.C. 2271)**	Adds a definition for *institution-affiliated party* (as used in Section 5505) to include the directors, officers, employees, shareholders, and agents of system institutions, including independent contractors (such as attorneys, appraisers, or accountants) and any others who participate in system affairs. **(§5506)**
FarmerMac qualified loans. Defines that the maximum size of a "qualified loan" that FarmerMac may finance is $2.5 million adjusted for inflation ($12.6 million in FY2018), except if the loan is secured by less than 1,000 acres. **(12 U.S.C. 2279aa-8(c)(2))**	Increases the acreage exception to the dollar limit to be a "qualified loan" for FarmerMac from 1,000 acres to 2,000 acres. Effective one year after the study by FCA (ordered in Section 5602(a)(2)) indicates that it is feasible to increase the limit. **(§5507)**
Compensation of bank directors. Establishes a limit for compensation of members of the boards of directors of FCS banks as $20,000 per year, adjusted for inflation. **(12 U.S.C. 2209)**	Deletes the section that establishes the limit on compensation of FCS bank boards of directors. **(§5508)**
Use of funds. Specifies various prohibitions and limitations about the Farm Credit System Insurance Corporation. **(12 U.S.C. 2277a-14)**	Adds a paragraph that no funds of the Farm Credit System Insurance Corporation may be used to assist FarmerMac. **(§5509)**
Subtitle F: Miscellaneous	
State mediation program funding. Authorizes appropriations for a matching grant program for states that provide third-party mediation services for agricultural credit disputes. Appropriations authorized at $7.5 million annually through FY2018. **(7 U.S.C. 5106)**	Reauthorizes appropriations of $7.5 million annually through FY2023. **(§5601)**
No comparable provision.	**FCA study.** Directs FCA to conduct a study that (1) analyzes and compares financial risks of loans in the FCS and by FarmerMac and how such risks are capitalized and (2) assesses the feasibility of increasing to 2,000 acres the 1,000 acre exception in the definition for *qualified loans* for FarmerMac (see 12 U.S.C. 2279aa-8). The study is to be submitted to Congress 180 days after enactment. **(§5602)**

Table 8. Title VI: Rural Infrastructure and Economic Development

Current Law/Policy	House Passed Bill (H.R.2)
Improving Health Outcomes in Rural Communities	
Project prioritization. The Secretary is authorized to coordinate a nationwide rural development program using the services of executive branch departments and agencies. **(7 U.S.C. 2204a-2204b)**	Authorizes the Secretary to announce a reprioritization of certain loan and grant programs to assist rural communities in responding to specific health emergencies (e.g., opioid abuse). Authorizes not less than 10% of the distance learning/telemedicine appropriation for telemedicine services to individuals affected by the emergency. Prioritizes the community facilities loan and grant program for developing prevention, treatment, and recovery services for individuals affected by the emergency. **(§6001)**
Distance learning and telemedicine program. Provides grants to rural hospitals, clinics, schools, and libraries to develop and improve their telecommunications infrastructure. Authorizes funding of $75 million annually FY2014-FY2018, subject to appropriations. **(7 U.S.C. 950aaa)**	Authorizes appropriations of $82 million annually FY2019-FY2023 for the distance learning and telemedicine program. **(§6002)**
Farm and Ranch Stress Assistance Network. In coordination with the Secretary of Health and Human Services, the Secretary is authorized to make competitive grants to establish a Farm and Ranch Stress Assistance Network to provide stress assistance programs for those engaged in agriculture-related occupations. Such sums as necessary authorized FY2008-FY2012. **(7 U.S.C. 5936)**	Reauthorizes such sums as necessary for FY2019-FY2023. Requires a review of the program within two years after the first grant is awarded. **(§6003)**
No comparable provision.	**Agricultural association group health plans.** Authorizes a loan and grant program to assist in the establishment of agricultural association group health plans for rural areas. In coordination with the Secretary of Labor, the Secretary is authorized to make no more than 10 loans to establish agricultural association group health plans to qualified agricultural associations. Authorizes $65 million for the period FY2019-FY2022. **(§6004)**
Connecting Rural Americans to High-Speed Broadband	
No comparable provision.	**Establishing forward-looking broadband standards. amends Section 601 of the**

Current Law/Policy	House Passed Bill (H.R.2)
	Rural Electrification Act of 1936. Directs the Secretary to establish minimum acceptable standards of broadband service of 25 megabits per second downstream transmission capacity and three megabits per second upstream transmission capacity and projections of broadband service five, 10, 15, 20, and 30 years into the future. Loans are conditioned on meeting the acceptable minimum standards. Requires a report to the House and Senate Agriculture Committees on the effectiveness of broadband loans for expanding broadband to rural areas. **(§6101)**
No comparable provision.	**Incentives to reach hard-to-reach communities.** Amends Title VI of the Rural Electrification Act of 1936. Establishes a method for calculating service points per road mile as a density measure. Eligible applicants are those areas with a density of 12 or fewer homes, businesses, or institutions in a proposed service area. Authorizes appropriations of $350 million for each of FY2019-FY2023. **(§6102)**
Access to broadband telecommunications services in rural areas. Title VI of the Rural Electrification Act of 1936. States that the Secretary "shall make or guarantee" loans to provide funds for the costs of the construction, improvement, and acquisition of facilities and equipment for broadband service in rural areas. **(7 U.S.C. 950bb(c)(1))**	Amends Section 601 of the Rural Electrification Act to state that the Secretary "shall make loans and shall guarantee loans" for expanding broadband services. **(§6103)**
No comparable provision	**Smart utility authority for broadband.** Amends the ConAct to permit any recipient of a loan or grant from USDA Rural Development to use up to 10% of the amount provided for any activity provided under the Access to Broadband Telecommunications Services in Rural Areas and to construct other broadband infrastructure in areas not served by minimum acceptable standards of broadband service. **(§6104)**
Rural gigabit network. A rural, ultra-high-speed gigabit pilot program is authorized in the 2014 farm bill (P.L. 113-79). Authorized appropriation	Renames the Rural Gigabit Program Innovative Broadband Advancement. Authorizes loans and grants for the purpose of demonstrating innovative broadband)

Table 8. (Continued)

Current Law/Policy	House Passed Bill (H.R.2)
of $10 million each of FY2014-FY2018. **(7 U.S.C. 950bb-2)**	technologies or methods of broadband deployment that significantly decrease the costs of broadband deployment. Gives priority to projects involving multiple entities and would provide service to the greatest number of rural residents at or above the minimum broadband speed. **(§6105**
Unified broadband reporting requirements. Authorizes loans and loan guarantees to provide funds for the costs of the construction, improvement, and acquisition of facilities and equipment for broadband service in rural areas. **(7 U.S.C. 950bb)**	Directs the Secretary to report annually to Congress on the extent of participation in the broadband loan and grant program. **(§6106)**
Rural Electrification Act's Telephone Loan Program. The Secretary is authorized to make loans to persons now providing or who may hereinafter provide telephone service in rural areas; to public bodies now providing telephone service in rural areas; and to cooperative, nonprofit, limited dividend, or mutual associations. **(7 U.S.C. 922-928)**	Authorizes the Secretary to obligate but not disburse funds for broadband projects before completion of otherwise required environmental, historical, or other reviews of the project. The Secretary is also authorized to de-obligate funds for projects if any such review will not be completed in a reasonable period of time. **(§6107)**
Evaluation period. Establishes not less than two evaluation periods for each fiscal year to compare loan and loan guarantee applications and to prioritize loans and loan guarantees to all or part of rural communities that do not have residential broadband service that meets the minimum acceptable level of broadband service. **(7 U.S.C. 950bb(c)(2)(A))**	Reduces the evaluation period from two evaluation periods to one. **(§6108)**
Priority to certain applicants. Gives priority to applicants that offer to provide broadband service not predominantly for business service if at least 25 percent of the customers in the proposed service territory are commercial. **(7 U.S.C. 950bb(c)(2))**	Removes priority for applicants that provide broadband service not predominantly for business service if at least 25% of the customers in the proposed service territory are commercial interests. **(§6109)**
Buildout requirement. Eligible applicants agree to complete buildout of the broadband service described in the loan application by not later than three years after the initial date on which proceeds from the loan made or guaranteed under this section are made available. **(7 U.S.C. 950bb(d)(1)(A)(iii))**	Amends requirements to have a broadband loan applicant agree to the buildout of the service in no later than five years rather than three years. **(§6110)**

Current Law/Policy	**House Passed Bill (H.R.2)**
Borrower refinancing options. The Secretary is authorized and empowered to make loans to persons now providing or who may hereinafter provide telephone service in rural areas; to public bodies now providing telephone service in rural areas; and to cooperative, nonprofit, limited dividend, or mutual associations. **(7 U.S.C. 922)**	Adds refinancing of loans for broadband services and other loans provided to purposes of telecommunications. **(§6111)**
Reporting requirements. Requires reporting that provides the progress toward fulfilling the objectives for which the assistance was granted, including (I) the number and location of residences and businesses that will receive new broadband service, existing network service improvements, and facility upgrades resulting from the federal assistance; (II) the speed of broadband service; (III) the average price of broadband service in a proposed service area; (IV) any changes in broadband service adoption rates, including new subscribers generated from demand-side projects; and (V) any metrics the Secretary determines to be appropriate. **(7 U.S.C. 950bb(d)(8)(A)(ii))**	Removes a reporting requirement that borrowers report the location of residences and businesses that will receive new broadband service, existing network service improvements, and facility upgrades. **(§6112)**
Authorization of appropriations. There is authorized to be appropriated to the Secretary to carry out this section $25 million for each of FY2008-FY2018 to remain available until expended. **(7 U.S.C. 950bb(k))**	Authorizes appropriations for loans and loan guarantees at $150 million each of FY2019-FY2023. **(§6113)**
No comparable provision.	**Middle mile broadband infrastructure.** Authorizes loans for development of middle mile broadband infrastructure, defined as infrastructure that does not directly connect to end user locations. Loans and loan guarantees for middle mile infrastructure are limited to no more than 20% of the amounts made available under Section 601 of the Rural Electrification Act of 1936. **(§6114)**
No comparable provision.	**Outdated broadband systems.** Amends Section 601 of the Rural Electrification to Act of 1936 to require the Secretary to consider any portion of a broadband service area subject to an outstanding grant agreement where service is not at least 10 megabits per second and one megabit per second upstream as "unserved" for purposes of broadband loans, unless the broadband

Table 8. (Continued)

Current Law/Policy	House Passed Bill (H.R.2)
	provider has constructed or begun to construct service that meets minimal acceptable of standards as established under Section 601(e)(1) of the Rural Electrification Act of 1936. **(§6115)**
No comparable provision.	**Effective date.** Requires that the Secretary issue final rules before any amendments in this Subtitle take effect. **(§6116)**
Rural Community, Business Development, and Infrastructure Programs	
No comparable provision.	**Regional economic development incentives.** Amends the ConAct to prioritize project applications that support implementation of strategic investment plans on a multi-sectoral and multi-jurisdictional basis by reserving a portion of funds available in a fiscal year for such projects. Also authorizes assistance for developing strategic community investment plans. Authorizes an appropriation of $5 million for each of FY2019-FY2023 for developing investment plans. **(§6201)**
No comparable provision.	**Expanding access to credit for rural communities.** Amends the ConAct to exclude guaranteed water and waste disposal loans from the requirement of an eligible rural area being one of 10,000 or less population. **(§6202)**
Access to broadband telecommunications services in rural areas. Defines an eligible rural area as any area other than a city, town, or incorporated area that has a population of greater than 20,000 inhabitants. **(7 U.S.C. 950bb(b)(3)(A)(ii))**	Makes a rural area with a city of 20,000 or more ineligible for direct broadband loans. **(§6202)**
Special conditions and limitations on loans. Establishes various standards on borrowers. **(7 U.S.C. 1983)**	Authorizes the collection of loan fees for guaranteed loans in a fiscal year to equal the total subsidy costs for loan guarantees in that fiscal year. **(§6203)**
Collection of fees. Authorizes loans and loan guarantees to provide funds for the costs of the construction, improvement, and acquisition of facilities and equipment for broadband service in rural areas. **(7 U.S.C. 950bb(c))**	Authorizes the collection of loan fees for broadband guaranteed loans in a fiscal year to equal the total subsidy costs for loan guarantees in that fiscal year. **(§6203)**

Current Law/Policy	House Passed Bill (H.R.2)
Water, waste disposal, and wastewater facility grants. Authorizes grants to capitalize revolving loan funds of nonprofit association to support water and waste water projects in rural areas. Authorizes $30 million in grants annually for FY2008- FY2018, subject to annual appropriations. **(7 U.S.C. 1926(a)(2)(B))**	Raises the maximum amount of project financing from $100,000 to $200,000. Authorizes $15 million annually for FY2019-FY2023. **(§6204)**
Rural water and wastewater technical assistance and training programs. Provides grants to private nonprofit organizations to provide technical assistance to rural water systems. **(7 U.S.C. 1926(a)(2)(B))**	Directs technical assistance toward identifying options to enhance long-term sustainability of rural water systems. Increases appropriations for technical assistance grants from no less than 1% or more than 3% of the water, waste disposal, and wastewater facility grant appropriation to no less than 3% or more than 5%. **(§6205)**
Rural Water and Waste Water Circuit Rider Program. Provides funding to support technical assistance to water rural water systems. Authorizes funding of $20 million annually in FY2014 and each fiscal year thereafter. **(7 U.S.C. 1926(a)(22))**	Authorizes funding at $25 million in FY2018 and for each fiscal year thereafter. **(§6206)**
Tribal college and university essential community facilities. Provides grant funding to entities that are tribal colleges to provide the federal share of the cost of developing specific tribal college or university essential community facilities. Authorizes funding of $10 million each of FY2008-FY2018. **(7 U.S.C. 1926(a)(25)(C))**	Amends the provision by authorizing funding of $5 million for each of FY2019-FY2023. **(§6207)**
Emergency and Imminent Community Water Assistance Program. Provides assistance to water systems in rural communities of 10,000 or less where there is a threat to potable water supplies. Authorizes funding of $35 million for each of FY2008-FY2018. **(7 U.S.C. 1926a(i)(2))**	Amends the program to limit any until July 1 of the fiscal year except where a natural disaster has threatened potable water supplies. Authorizes funding at $27 million annually for FY2019-FY2023. **(§6208)**
Current Law/Policy	**House Passed Bill (H.R.2)**
Grants for water systems for rural and Native Villages in Alaska. Funding for water projects to improve sanitation and potable water in rural Alaska. Authorizes $30 million annually for FY2008-FY2013, subject to appropriations. **(7 U.S.C. 1926d)**	Reauthorizes appropriations at $30 million annually for FY2019-FY2023. **(§6209)**
Household water well systems. Provides funding to third- party organizations with expertise in residential well-water systems to construct, refurbish, and service individually owned household water well systems in rural areas for	Reauthorizes appropriations at $5 million annually for FY2019-FY2023. **(§6210)**

Table 8. (Continued)

Current Law/Policy	House Passed Bill (H.R.2)
individuals with low or moderate incomes. Authorizes $10 million annually for FY2008-FY2018, subject to appropriations. **(7 U.S.C. 1926(e))**	
Solid waste management grants. Provides grant assistance for communities to establish or improve solid waste management facilities. Authorizes $10 million annually for FY2008-FY2018, subject to annual appropriations. **(7 U.S.C. 1932(b))**	Reauthorizes appropriations at $10 million for each of FY2019-FY2023. **(§6211)**
Rural business development grants. Provides grants in rural areas for business opportunities and for support of business enterprises that finance small and emerging private enterprises. Authorizes $65 million for each fiscal year 2014-2018. **(7 U.S.C. 1932 (c)(4)(A))**	Reauthorizes the program at $65 million for each of FY2019-FY2023. **(§6212)**
Rural cooperative development grants. Authorizes the creation of jobs in rural areas through the development of new rural cooperatives, value-added processing, and rural businesses. Authorizes $40 million annually for FY2008-FY2013, subject to appropriations. **(7 U.S.C. 1932(e)(5))**	Reauthorizes the program at $40 million for each of FY2019-FY2023. **(§6213)**
Locally or regionally produced agricultural food products. Provides funding to increase domestic consumption of locally and regionally produced agricultural products and to provide affordable food products in underserved rural and urban areas. Reserves not less than 5% of the funds of the Business and Industry Loan Guarantee program for support of locally and regionally produced food. Requires an annual report to Congress on the program. **(7 U.S.C. 1932(g)(9)(B)(v)(I))**	Reauthorizes the program for FY2019-FY2023. **(§6214)**
Appropriate technology transfer for rural areas. Provides grant support at an agricultural institution (e.g., universities) for information activities to agricultural producers. Authorizes $5 million annually for FY2008-FY2018, subject to appropriations. **(7 U.S.C. 1932(i)(4))**	Reauthorizes the program at $5 million for each of FY2019-FY2023. **(§6215)**
Rural Economic Area Partnership. The program assists communities dealing with geographic and economic isolation, low- density population, absence of nearby metropolitan centers, and	Reauthorizes the program for FY2019-FY2023. **(§6216)**

Current Law/Policy	House Passed Bill (H.R.2)
historical dependence on agribusiness, out-migration, and economic upheaval to develop strategies for revitalization zones. **(7 U.S.C. 1932j)**	
Intermediary Relending Program. Provides direct loans at 1% interest to intermediaries to finance business facilities and community development projects in rural areas with populations of 25,000 or less. The Rural Business Service loan to an intermediary is used to establish or fund a revolving loan program to provide financial assistance to ultimate recipients for community development projects, establishment of new businesses or expansion of existing businesses. Authorizes appropriations of $25 million for each of FY2014-FY2018, subject to annual appropriations. **(7 U.S.C 1936b(e))**	Reauthorizes the program at $10 million for each of FY2019-FY2023. **(§6217)**
No comparable provision.	**Prison populations in the definition of *rural area*.** Excludes incarcerated prison populations in determining whether an area is "rural" or a "rural area." **(§6218)**
National Rural Development Partnership. A state-federal rural economic development coordinating entity operating through State Rural Development Councils and a National Rural Development Coordinating Committee. Authorizes appropriations of $10 million annually for FY2014-FY2018. **(7 U.S.C. 2008m)**	Reauthorizes the program at $10 million for each of FY2019-FY2023. **(§6219)**
Grants for weather radio transmitters. Provides grant funding to public and nonprofit entities for the federal share of the cost of acquiring radio transmitters to increase coverage in rural areas by the all hazards weather radio broadcast system of the National Oceanic and Atmospheric Administration. Authorizes $1 million for each of FY2014-FY2018, subject to annual appropriations. **(7 U.S.C. 2008p)**	Reauthorizes the program at $1 million for each of FY2019-FY2023. **(§6220)**
Rural Microentrepreneur Assistance Program. Provides grant support to third-party entities that assist rural entrepreneurs in establishing microenterprises in rural areas. Authorizes $40 million annually in discretionary spending for each of FY2009- FY2018, subject to appropriations, and $3 million in mandatory spending annually for FY2014-FY2018. **(7 U.S.C. 2008s)**	Reauthorizes the program at $4 million in discretionary funding for each of FY2019-FY2023. **(§6221)**

Table 8. (Continued)

Current Law/Policy	House Passed Bill (H.R.2)
Health care services. Addresses unmet health needs in the Mississippi Delta region through grants awarded to health care services and health care education programs. Authorizes $3 million in appropriations for each of FY2008-FY2018. **(7 U.S.C. 2008u)**	Reauthorizes the program at $3 million for each of FY2019-FY2023. **(§6222)**
Delta Regional Authority. An eight-state and federal regional planning and development entity that provides loan and grant support for economic development projects in rural counties in the Mississippi Delta area. Authorizes $30 million annually for FY2008-FY2018, subject to appropriations. **(7 U.S.C. 2009aa *et seq.*)**	Reauthorizes the program at $12 million for each of FY2019-FY2023. **(§6223)**
Northern Great Plains Regional Authority. Authorizes an economic development commission that develops regional plans and makes loans and grants for infrastructure and economic development in five Great Plains states. Authorizes $30 million annually for FY2008-FY2018, subject to appropriations. **(7 U.S.C. 2009bb *et seq.*)**	Reauthorizes the program at $2 million for each of FY2019-FY2023. **(§6224)**
Rural Business Investment Program. Modeled on the Small Business Administration's Small Business Investment Companies, the Rural Business Investment Program provides funding to help capitalize Rural Business Companies that, in turn, provide loans to rural businesses. Authorizes $20 million for each of FY2014- FY2018, subject to appropriations. **(7 U.S.C. 2009cc *et seq.*)**	Reauthorizes the program at $20 million for each of FY2019-FY2023. **(§6225)**
Rural Electrification Act of 1936	
Guarantees for bonds and notes issued for electrification or telephone purposes. Provides for federal guarantees for bonds and notes that finance rural electrification and telephone infrastructure. **(7 U.S.C. 940c-1(f))**	Reauthorizes the program through FY2023. **(§6301)**
Expansion of 911access. Authorizes expanding the emergency telephone service of 911 in rural areas by using any funds otherwise made available for telephone loans for each of FY2008- FY2013. **(7 U.S.C. 940(e)d)**	Reauthorizes the program through FY2023. **(§6302)**
Improvements to the Guarantees Underwriter Program. States that a lender receiving a guarantee on a bond or note shall pay a fee to the Secretary. **(7 U.S.C. 940c-1)**	Amends the Rural Electrification Act of 1936 to authorize guaranteed payments on bonds or notes issued by cooperatives or other lenders on a not-for-profit basis if the

Current Law/Policy	House Passed Bill (H.R.2)
	bonds are used to make utility infrastructure loans or to refinance bonds or notes issued for such purposes. Defines the terms of such bonds or notes. **(§6303)**
Extension of time for repayment of loans. Permits any borrower to defer the payment of principal and interest on any insured or direct loan made under this chapter under circumstances described in this subsection. **(7 U.S.C. 912(b)(3)(D))**	Inserts a new section that authorizes grants and no-interest loans for purposes of supporting rural economic development projects. In addition to other funds available for the program, the provision also authorizes $10 million for each of FY2019-FY2023. **(§6304)**
Farm Security and Rural Investment Act of 2002 (Bio-Energy Provisions)	
Authorized Programs	
Rural Energy Savings Program. Extends program through FY2018. Provides loans to rural families and small businesses to implement durable cost-effective energy efficiency measures. Authorized to be appropriated $75 million annually for FY2014- FY2018. **(7 U.S.C. 8107a)**	Adds two requirements to the loans for eligible entities section—eligibility for other loans and accounting. Increases the loan interest to not exceed 5 percent. Authorizes to be appropriated $75 million annually for FY2019- FY2023. **(§6401)**
Biobased Markets Program. Extends program through FY2018. Requires federal agencies to purchase products with maximum biobased content (explicitly including forest products) subject to availability, flexibility, and performance standards. Minimum biobased content standards applied to federal contracts on case-by-case basis. Continued voluntary labeling. Authorized mandatory funding of $3 million annually for FY2014-FY2018 for biobased products testing and labeling. Authorized to be appropriated $2 million annually for FY2014-FY2018. **(7 U.S.C. 8102)**	Extends program through FY2023. Authorizes to be appropriated $2 million annually for FY2014-FY2023. No mandatory funding is authorized. Prohibits federal agencies from placing limitations on the procurement of wood and wood-based products. **(§6402)**
Biorefinery, Renewable Chemical, and Biobased Product Manufacturing Assistance Program. Extends program through FY2018. Assists in development of new and emerging technologies for advanced biofuels, renewable chemicals, and biobased products by providing loan guarantees—not to exceed 80% of project costs—for development, construction, and/or retrofitting of commercial-scale biorefineries. Authorizes mandatory funding of $100 million in FY2014 and $50 million each for FY2015 and FY2016. Authorizes to be appropriated $75	Extends program through FY2023. Expands the definition of *eligible technology*. Authorizes to be appropriated $75 million annually for FY2019- FY2023. No mandatory funding is authorized. **(§6403)**

Table 8. (Continued)

Current Law/Policy	House Passed Bill (H.R.2)
million annually for FY2014-FY2018. **(7 U.S.C. 8103)**	
Repowering Assistance Program. Extends program through FY2018. Provides funds to replace the use of fossil fuels used to produce heat or power to operate biorefineries in existence as of the 2008 farm bill enactment date. Authorizes mandatory funding of $12 million for FY2014, available until expended. Authorizes to be appropriated $10 million annually for FY2014-FY2018. **(7 U.S.C. 8104)**	Extends program through FY2023. Authorizes to be appropriated $10 million annually for FY2019-FY2023. No mandatory funding is authorized. **(§6404)**
Bioenergy Program for Advanced Biofuels. Extends program through FY2018. Provides payments to producers to support and expand production of advanced biofuels by entering into contracts to pay producers for production of eligible advanced biofuels. Provides mandatory funding of $15 million annually for FY2014- FY 2018. Authorizes to be appropriated $20 million annually (FY20014-FY2018) **(7 U.S.C. 8105)**	Extends program through FY2023. Modifies the equitable distribution portion of the program by limiting the amount of payments for advanced biofuel produced from a single eligible commodity to not exceed one-third of the total program funding available in a fiscal year. Authorizes to be appropriated $50 million annually for FY2019-FY2023. No mandatory funding is authorized. **(§6405)**
Biodiesel Fuel Education Program. Extends program through FY2018. Awards competitive grants to nonprofit organizations that educate fleet operators and the public on biodiesel benefits. Provides mandatory funding of $1 million annually (FY2008- FY2018). Authorizes to be appropriated $1 million annually for FY2014-FY2018. **(7 U.S.C. 8106)**	Extends program through FY2023. Authorizes to be appropriated $2 million annually for FY2019-FY2023. No mandatory funding is authorized. **(§6406)**
Rural Energy for America Program. Exists in perpetuity. Provides grants to conduct energy audits and for renewable energy development assistance and provides loan guarantees and grants for energy efficiency improvement projects and renewable energy systems. Provides mandatory funds of $50 million in FY2014 and each fiscal year thereafter. Authorizes to be appropriated $20 million annually for FY2014-FY2018. **(7 U.S.C. 8107)**	Extends program through FY2023. Limits mandatory funding to FY2014-FY2018. Authorizes to be appropriated $20 million annually for FY2014-FY2023. No mandatory funding is authorized. Provides a categorical exclusion for electric generating facilities with a capacity of 10 megawatts or less in the program from having to prepare an environmental assessments or an environmental impact statement. **(§6407)**
Rural Energy Self-Sufficiency Initiative. Not included in the 2014 farm bill—funding authority expired after FY2013. Established in the 2008 farm bill to provide financial assistance to	Repeals the initiative. **(§6408)**

Current Law/Policy	House Passed Bill (H.R.2)
increase the energy self-sufficiency of such communities. **(7 U.S.C. 8109)**	
Feedstock Flexibility Program. Extends program through FY2018. Allows the CCC to purchase surplus sugar from processors for resale to ethanol producers for fuel ethanol. **(7 U.S.C. 8110)**	Extends program through FY2023. **(§6409)**
Biomass Crop Assistance Program. Extends program through FY2018. Provides payments to owners and operators of agricultural land and nonindustrial private forest land that establish, produce, and deliver biomass feedstocks to eligible processing plants. Modifies enrolled land eligibility requirements, limits one- time establishment payments, reduces the matching payment rate, and stipulates how much funding—10-50%—may be used for collection, harvest, storage, and transportation. **(7 U.S.C. 8111)**	Extends program through FY2023. Authorizes to be appropriated $25 million annually for FY2019-FY2023. No mandatory funding is authorized. **(§6410)**
Miscellaneous	
Value-added agricultural product market development grants. Provides grant support to agricultural producers to undertake projects that add value to commodities and thereby increase producer income. Also supports planning and business development for value-added projects. Authorizes $40 million annually for FY2008-FY2018, subject to annual appropriations, in addition to $63 million in mandatory spending to remain available until expended. **(7 U.S.C. 1632a(b)(7))**	Eliminates mandatory funding and increases discretionary funding to $50 million annually FY2019-FY2023. **(§6501)**
Agriculture Innovation Center Demonstration Program. Provides grant funding to producers for technical assistance in developing agricultural-based businesses based on value-added production. Authorizes funding of $1 million annually for FY2014- FY2018, subject to annual appropriations. **(7 U.S.C. 1632(b)(i))**	Reauthorizes the program through FY2023 at the current appropriation. **(§6502)**
Regional economic and infrastructure development commissions. Consists of three regional development authorities: a Northern Border Regional Commission, a Southeast Crescent Regional Commission, and a Southwest Border Regional Commission. These commissions develop regional development plans and then make infrastructure loans and grants to	Reauthorizes the commissions through FY2023 at the current appropriation. **(§6503)**

Table 8. (Continued)

Current Law/Policy	House Passed Bill (H.R.2)
eligible entities in their respective regions. **(40 U.S.C. 15101 *et seq.*)** Authorizes annual appropriations of $30 million to each of the commissions. Not more than 10% of appropriated funds to any commission can be used for administrative expenses. **(40 U.S.C. 15751(b))**	
Definition of rural area for purposes of the Housing Act of 1949. *Rural area* is defined as any area so defined between 1990 and 2010 to remain so classified until receipt of the 2020 decennial census. The provision also caps the eligible rural population threshold at 35,000 residents or less for rural areas in excess of 10,000 and with a serious lack of mortgage credit for lower and moderate-income families. **(42 U.S.C. 1490)**	Amends the definition by defining *rural area* as any area so defined between 1990 and 2020 to remain so classified until receipt of the 2030 decennial census. The provision keeps the 35,000 population threshold for areas rural in character and with a serious lack of mortgage credit for lower and moderate-income families. **(§6504)**
Program Repeals	
Elimination of unfunded programs. The following programs of the ConAct, as amended, no longer receive funding: • Multijurisdictional regional planning organizations (Section • 306(a)(23) of ConAct); • Grants to broadcasting systems (Section 310B(f) of ConAct); • Rural telework organizations (Section 379 of ConAct); • Historical barn preservation (Section 379A of ConAct); • Grants to train farm workers in new technologies and to train farm workers in specialized skills necessary for higher value crops (Section 379C of ConAct); • Grants to Delta Region Agricultural Economic Development • Program (Section 379D of ConAct); • Grants for expansion of employment opportunities for individuals with disabilities in rural areas (Section 379F of ConAct);	Repeals unfunded programs. **(§6601)**

Current Law/Policy	House Passed Bill (H.R.2)
• Regional rural collaborative investment program (Subtitle I of ConAct). **(7 U.S.C. 1926 *et seq.*)**	
Rural Telephone Bank. Establishes a corporate body called the Rural Telephone Bank whose general purpose is securing funds and making loans to support a telephone bank in rural areas. **(7 U.S.C. 941-950b)**	Repeals the Rural Telephone Bank. **(§6602)**
Launching Our Communities' Access to Local Television Act of 2000. Facilitates access to signals of local television stations for households located in nonserved areas and underserved areas by providing loans and loan guarantees. Authorizes such sums as necessary. **(P.L. 106-553)**	Amends the act by striking Sections 1001-1007 and 1009-1012 and inserting Title X—Satellite Carrier Retransmission Eligibility. **(§6603)**
Technical Corrections	
No comparable provision.	Provides technical corrections related to various provisions of the Consolidated Farm and Rural Development Act, as amended. **(§6701)**
No comparable provision. **(7 U.S.C. 901 *et seq.*)**	Provides technical corrections related to various provisions of the Rural Electrification Act, as amended. **(§6702)**

Table 9. Title VII: Research, Extension, and Related Matters

Current Law/Policy	House Passed Bill (H.R. 2)
Subtitle A—National Agricultural Research, Extension, and Teaching Policy Act of 1977(NARETP)	
Agricultural research, extension, and education. Provides support to enhance the competitiveness of the agricultural research, extension, and education capabilities of the United States. **(7 U.S.C. 3101)**	Adds the objective of supporting international scientific collaboration that leverages resources and advances the food and agricultural interests of the United States. **(§7101)**
Non-land-grant colleges of agriculture (7 U.S.C. 3103(14)(A))	Establishes a process of review within 90 days of enactment of each Non-Land Grant College of Agriculture (NLGCA) to ensure compliance in the colleges with appropriate study of food and agricultural sciences and to propose revocation of the designated NLGCA for non-compliance. Permits NLGCAs and Hispanic-serving agricultural colleges until FY2023 to no longer be designated as such institutions. **(§7102)**

Table 9. (Continued)

Current Law/Policy	House Passed Bill (H.R. 2)
National advisory board. Establishes the National Agricultural Research, Extension, Education, and Economics Advisory Board. **(7 U.S.C. 3123)**	Amends the membership composition of the Advisory Board. Directs the Advisory Board to make recommendations and to address long- and short-term national priorities consistent with various priorities of the Agriculture and Food Research Initiative and the NARETP Act. **(§7103)**
Citrus disease subcommittee. Establishes a citrus disease subcommittee within the specialty crops committee to advise USDA on citrus research and establish priorities for grants and regularly consult and collaborate with USDA and other groups and institutions. **(7 U.S.C. 3123a(a)(2))**	Extends the citrus disease subcommittee through FY2023 and changes the composition of the subcommittee. **(§7104)**
Renewable energy committee. Establishes a renewable energy committee, directs the Advisory Board to appoint committee members, and establishes the committee's duties. **(7 U.S.C. 3121(b))**	Discontinues the renewable energy committee. **(§7105)**
Duties of the Secretary of Agriculture. Sets out the duties of the Secretary of Agriculture as concerns extension and agricultural research at 1890 land-grant colleges, including Tuskegee University. **(7 U.S.C. 3221, 3222)**	Directs the Secretary to transmit to Congress annually a report on the allocations made to, and matching funds received by, 1890 land-grant institutions. **(§7106)**
Grants and fellowships for food and agriculture sciences education. Authorizes the Secretary to make grants and conduct fellowships to strengthen higher education in food and agricultural sciences. **(7 U.S.C. 3152(m)(2))**	Reauthorizes appropriations for grants and fellowships for FY2019-FY2023. **(§7107)**
Agriculture and food policy research centers. Authorizes competitive grants to, or to enter into cooperative agreements with, policy research centers to conduct research and education programs that are objective, operationally independent, and external to the federal government and that concern the effect of public policies and trade agreements on agriculture. **(7 (U.S.C. 3155(e))**	Reauthorizes appropriations for FY2019-FY2023. **(§7108)**
Education grants to Alaska Native–serving institutions and Native Hawaiian–serving institutions. Authorizes competitive grants to Alaska Native–serving institutions for the purpose of promoting and strengthening the ability of Alaska Native–serving institutions to carry out	Reauthorizes appropriations for FY2019-FY2023. **(§7109)**

Current Law/Policy	House Passed Bill (H.R. 2)
education, applied research, and related community development programs. **(7 U.S.C. 3156)**	
Nutrition Education Program. Authorizes establishment of a National Education Program to disseminate results of food and human nutrition research funded by USDA. **(7 U.S.C. 3175)**	Repeals the Nutrition Education Program. **(§7110)**
Continuing animal health and disease research programs. Directs deans of accredited colleges and the state agricultural experiment station to develop a comprehensive animal health and disease research program for the state based on the animal health research capacity of each eligible institution in the state, which shall be submitted to the Secretary for approval and shall be used for the allocation of funds available to the state under this section. **(7 U.S.C. 3195(c)(1))**	Reauthorizes appropriations for FY2019-FY2023. **(§7111)**
Extension at 1890 land-grant colleges, including Tuskegee University. Limits carryover of federal funding to no more than 20% of the funds received for conducting extension activities. **(7 U.S.C. 3221(a))**	Amends by striking paragraph 4 that prohibits 1890 colleges from carrying forward to the succeeding fiscal year more than 20% of the funds they receive in a given fiscal year. **(§7112)**
Agricultural extension at 1890 land-grant universities. Authorizes such sums as Congress may determine necessary to support continuing agricultural and forestry extension at 1890 land-grant universities. **(7 U.S.C. 3222)**	Amends by establishing a scholarship grant program at 1890 institutions for accepted students who intend to pursue a career in agribusiness, energy and renewable fuels, or financial management. **(§7113)**
Grants to upgrade agricultural and food sciences facilities at 1890 land-grant colleges, including Tuskegee University. (7 U.S.C. 3222b(b))	Reauthorizes appropriations for FY2019-FY2023. **(§7114)**
Grants to upgrade agricultural and food sciences facilities and equipment at insular area land-grant institutions. Authorizes appropriations of $25 million for each of FY2002-FY2018 for the acquisition and improvement of agricultural and food sciences facilities and equipment, including libraries, so that the eligible institutions may participate fully in the production of human capital. **(7 U.S.C. 3222b-2(d))**	Reauthorizes appropriations for FY2019-FY2023. **(§7115)**
Education grants program at Hispanic-serving institutions. Authorizes competitive grants to promote and strengthen Hispanic-serving institutions to carry out education, applied	Reauthorizes appropriations for FY2019-FY2023. **(§7116)**

Table 9. (Continued)

Current Law/Policy	House Passed Bill (H.R. 2)
research, and related community development programs. **(7 U.S.C. 3241(c))**	
No comparable provision.	**Land-grant designation.** Prohibits any additional entity from being designated as eligible to receive funds for agricultural research, extension, and related programs under Hatch Act, Smith-Lever Act, and McIntire-Stennis Act. **(§7117)**
Competitive grants for international agricultural science and education programs. Authorizes grants to colleges and universities that will enhance international content of curricula, promote extension of U.S. scientists' research to international peers, and enhance collaborative research with other countries. **(7 U.S.C. 3292b(c)(2))**	Reauthorizes appropriations for FY2019-FY2023. **(§7118)**
Limitation on indirect costs for agricultural research, education, and extension programs. Sets limits on indirect cost recovery on grants awarded to support research, education, and extension activities to 22% of total federal funding. **(7 U.S.C. 3310)**	Amends the provision to allow indirect cost recovery charged against any agricultural research, education, or extension grant awarded to increase from 22% of total federal funds received to 30% of funding. **(§7119)**
No comparable provision.	**Research equipment grants**. Adds new section to Section 1462 of NARETP Act establishing a competitive grants program for research equipment. Grant amounts may not exceed $500,000 to an eligible institution. Authorizes $5 million for each of FY2019-FY2023. **(§7120)**
Authorization of appropriations for research. Authorizes formula funds for agricultural research at land- grant universities. **(7 U.S.C. 3311)**	Reauthorizes Hatch Act funding to state agricultural experiment stations at the current level for FY2019-FY2023. **(§7121)**
Authorization of appropriations for extension education. Authorizes formula funds for agricultural extension at land-grant universities. **(7 U.S.C. 33312)**	Reauthorizes such sums as necessary to carry out extension programs of USDA for FY2019-FY2023. **(§7122)**
Supplemental and alternative crops. Requires USDA to develop and implement a program to develop supplemental and alternative crops. Authorizes $1 million in appropriations for each of FY2014-FY2018. **(7 U.S.C. 3319d)**.	Extends program and funding levels through FY2023. Amends the program to include canola and alternative crops "for agronomic rotational purposes and for use as a habitat for honey bees and other pollinators," among other changes. **(§7123)**

Current Law/Policy	**House Passed Bill (H.R. 2)**
Capacity-building grants for NLGCA institutions. Authorizes competitive grants program for NLGCAs. **(7 U.S.C. 3319i(b))**	Reauthorizes appropriations for FY2019-FY2023. **(§7124)**
Aquaculture assistance programs. Provides competitive grants to support aquaculture research and assistance. **(7 U.S.C. 3324(a)(2))**	Reauthorizes appropriations for FY2019-FY2023. **(§7125)**
Rangeland research programs. Provides competitive grants to support rangeland research and assistance. **(7 U.S.C. 3336(a)(2))**	Reauthorizes appropriations for FY2019-FY2023. **(§7126)**
Special authorization for biosecurity planning and response. Authorizes $20 million annually for research, education, and extension activities for biosecurity planning and response. **(7 U.S.C. 3351)**	Authorizes appropriations of $30 million for each of FY2019-FY2023. Adds that the Secretary shall, in addition to other stated activities, use the funds to coordinate tactical science activities of USDA's mission areas to protect the agricultural system of the U.S. against biosecurity threats from pests, diseases, contaminants, and disasters. **(§7127)**
Distance education and resident instruction grants program for insular area institutions of higher education. Authorizes distance education grants and resident instruction grants for insular area institutions. **(7 U.S.C. 3362(f)(2), 3363(c)(2))**	Reauthorizes appropriations for FY2019-FY2023. **(§7128)**
Matching funds requirement. Requires the recipient of a competitive grant that is awarded by the Secretary under a covered law to provide funds, in-kind contributions, or a combination of both from sources other than funds provided through such grant in an amount that is at least equal to the amount of such grant. **(7 U.S.C. 3371(d))**	Strikes paragraph 5, which excludes competitive, special, and facilities research grants from the matching requirement. **(§7129)**
Subtitle B—Food, Agriculture, Conservation, and Trade Act of 1990	
Best utilization of biological applications. Authorizes appropriations under the Sustainable Agriculture Research and Education Program of $40 million annually for FY2013-FY2018. **(7 U.S.C. 5814)**	Reauthorizes appropriations for FY2019-FY2023. **(§7201)**
Integrated management systems. Authorizes a research and education program concerning integrated resource management and integrated crop management to enhance research related to farming operations, practices, and systems that optimize crop and livestock production potential and are environmentally sound. Authorizes $20 million annually for FY2013-FY2018. **(7 U.S.C. 5821(d))**	Reauthorizes appropriations for FY2019-FY2023. **(§7202)**

Table 9. (Continued)

Current Law/Policy	House Passed Bill (H.R. 2)
Technical guides and handbooks. (7 U.S.C. 5831(f)(2))	Reauthorizes appropriations for FY2019-FY2023. **(§7203)**
National Training Program. Authorizes a National Training Program in Sustainable Agriculture to provide education and training for Cooperative Extension Service agents and other professionals involved in the education and transfer of technical	Reauthorizes appropriations for FY2019-FY2023. **(§7204)**
information concerning sustainable agriculture. Authorizes $20 million annually for FY2013-FY2018. **(7 U.S.C. 5832(1))**	
National Genetics Resources Program. Authorizes a National Genetics Resources Program with an appropriation of $1million annually for FY2013-FY2018. **(7 U.S.C. 5844(b)(2)).**	Reauthorizes appropriations for FY2019-FY2023. **(§7205)**
National Agricultural Weather Program. Authorizes a National Agricultural Weather Program with an authorized appropriation of $1 million annually for FY2014-FY2018. **(7 U.S.C. 5855(c))**	Reauthorizes appropriations for FY2019-FY2023. **(§7206)**
Agricultural genome initiative. Establishes an Agricultural Genome Program to expand the knowledge of public and private sector entities and persons concerning genomes for species of importance to the food and agriculture sectors in order to maximize the return on the investment in genomics of agriculturally important species. **(7 U.S.C. 5924)**	Adds the phrase *to Phenome* after *Genome*. Outlines goals of research to expand knowledge concerning genomes and phenomes of crops important to the United States. Authorizes appropriation of $30 million each fiscal year for FY2019-FY2023. **(§7207)**
High-priority research and extension. Provides for "high- priority research and extension" areas and initiatives and other programs. **(7 U.S.C. 5925)**	Retains, amends, and/or adds research areas as a "high-priority." Added initiatives that cover macadamia tree health, national turfgrass research, fertilizer management, cattle fever ticks, and laying hen and turkey research. **(§7208)**
Organic Agriculture Research and Extension Initiative. Establishes the Organic Agriculture Research and Extension Initiative. Provides grants to facilitate the development of organic agriculture production and processing. Provides mandatory CCC funds of $20 million annually for FY2014-FY2018. **(7 U.S.C. 5925b)**	Reauthorizes program and increases annual CCC funding levels to $30 million for FY2019-FY2023. **(§7209)**
Farm business management. Authorizes competitive research and extension grants for	Amends to permit the Secretary to make competitive research and extension grants

Current Law/Policy	House Passed Bill (H.R. 2)
improving the farm management knowledge and skills of agricultural producers and for establishing and maintaining a national, publicly available farm financial management database to support improved farm management. **(7 U.S.C. 5925f)**	for the purpose of improving farm management knowledge and skills of agricultural producers by maintaining a national, publicly available farm financial management database to support improved farm management. **(§7210)**
Assistive Technology Program for Farmers with Disabilities. Authorizes demonstration grants to support cooperative programs between State Cooperative Extension Service agencies and private nonprofit disability organizations to provide on-the-farm agricultural education and assistance directed at accommodating disability in farm operations for individuals with disabilities who are engaged in farming and farm-related occupations and their families. **(7 U.S.C. 5933)**	Clarifies language to make the provision apply to veterans engaged in farming or pursuing new farming opportunities. **(§7211)**
National Rural Information Center Clearinghouse. Establishes within the National Agricultural Library, in coordination with the National Institute of Food and Agriculture, a National Rural Information Center Clearinghouse to provide and distribute information and data to any industry, organization, or federal, state, or local government entity, on request, about programs and services provided by federal, state, and local agencies and private nonprofit organizations and institutions under which individuals residing in, or organizations and state and local government entities operating in, a rural area may be eligible for any kind of assistance, including job training, education, health care, and economic development assistance and emotional and financial counseling. **(7 U.S.C. 3125b(e))**	Reauthorizes appropriations for FY2019-FY2023. **(§7212)**
Subtitle C—Agriculture, Research, Extension, and Education Reform Act of 1998	
Ending limitation on funding. Limits grant funding to no more than three years and prohibits further funding after an eligible entity has received three years of funding. **(7 U.S.C. 7625(e)(3))**	Removes limitation on funding that restricts USDA from providing additional grant funding once an entity has received three years of grant funding. **(§7300)**
National food safety training. Authorizes appropriations of such sums as necessary for competitive grants to support training, education, extension, outreach, and technical assistance projects to increase the adoption of established food safety standards, guidance, and protocols. **(7 U.S.C. 7625(j))**	Reauthorizes appropriations through FY2023. **(§7301)**

Table 9. (Continued)

Current Law/Policy	House Passed Bill (H.R. 2)
Integrated research, extension, and education competitive grant program. (7 U.S.C. 7626(e))	Reauthorizes appropriations for FY2019-FY2023. **(§7302)**
Support for research regarding diseases of wheat, triticale, and barley caused by Fusarium graminearum or by Tilletia indica. Authorizes grants to consortia of land- grant colleges and universities to enhance the ability of the consortia to carry out multi-state research projects aimed at understanding and combating diseases of wheat, triticale, and barley caused by Fusarium gramin-earum and related fungi. **(7 U.S.C. 7628(e)(2))**	Reauthorizes appropriations for FY2019-FY2023. **(§7303)**
Grants for youth organizations. Authorizes grants through the director of NIFA, which shall make grants to the Girl Scouts of the United States of America, the Boy Scouts of America, the National 4–H Council, and the National Future Farmers of America Organization to establish pilot projects to expand the programs carried out by the organ-izations in rural areas and small towns. **(7 U.S.C. 7630(d)(2))**	Reauthorizes appropriations for FY2019-FY2023. **(§7304)**
Specialty Crop Research Initiative. Provides mandatory CCC funds of $80 million for FY2014 and each fiscal year thereafter and authorizes appropriations of $100 million annually for FY2014-FY2018. **(7 U.S.C. 7632(b))** Reserves at least $25 million in funding for the emergency citrus disease research and extension program and includes an additional $25 million in authorized appropriations annually for FY2014- FY2018. **(7 U.S.C. 7632(j))**	Extends and funding levels through FY2023, including funding for the emergency citrus disease research and extension program. Expands program eligibility to include “size-controlling rootstock systems for perennial crops” and “emerging and invasive species,” among other production practices and technologies. **(§7305)**
Food Animal Residue Avoidance Database Program. Establishes a database to provide livestock producers, extension specialists, scientists, and veterinarians with information to prevent drug, pesticide, and environmental contaminant residues in food animal products. **(7 U.S.C. 7642(e))**	Reauthorizes appropriations for FY2019-FY2023. **(§7306)**
Office of Pest Management Policy. Establishes the Office of Pest Management Policy to coordinate USDA’s policies and activities related to pesticides and pest management tools. Authorizes appropriations of such sums as necessary through FY2018. **(7 U.S.C. 7653)**	Reauthorizes appropriations for FY2019-FY2023. **(§7307)**

Current Law/Policy	House Passed Bill (H.R. 2)
Forestry products advanced utilization research. Establishes forestry and forestry products research and extension initiative to develop and disseminate science-based tools that address the needs of the forestry sector and their respective regions; forest and timberland owners and managers; and forestry products engineering, manufacturing, and related interests. **(7 U.S.C. 7655b(f)(1))**	Reauthorizes appropriations for FY2019-FY2023. No change to current law. **(§7308)**
Subtitle D—Food, Conservation, and Energy Act of 2008 (FCE)	
Agricultural Biosecurity Communication Center. Establishes a communication center within USDA to collect and disseminate information and prepare for an agricultural disease emergency, agroterrorist act, or other threat to agricultural biosecurity and to coordinate activities among agencies and offices within the USDA. Authorizes $2 million annually for FY2013-FY2018. **(7 U.S.C. 8912(c)(2))**	Reauthorizes appropriations for FY2019-FY2023. **(§7401)**
Assistance to build local capacity in agricultural biosecurity planning, preparation, and response. Authorizes a competitive grant program to support the development and expansion of advanced training programs in agricultural biosecurity planning and response for food science profess-ionals and veterinarians. Authorizes $15 million annually for FY2013-FY2018. **(7 U.S.C. 8913)**	Reauthorizes appropriations for FY2019-FY2023. **(§7402)**
Research and development of agricultural countermeasures. Authorizes a competitive grant program to encourage basic and applied research and the development of qualified agricultural countermeasures. Authorizes $15 million annually for FY2013-FY2018. **(7 U.S.C. 8921(b)(2))**	Reauthorizes appropriations for FY2019-FY2023. **(§7403)**
Agricultural Biosecurity Grant Program. Authorizes a competitive grant program to promote the development of teaching programs in agriculture, veterinary medicine, and disciplines closely allied to the food and agriculture system to increase the number of trained individuals with an expertise in agricultural biosecurity. **(7 U.S.C. 8922(e)(2))**	Reauthorizes appropriations for FY2019-FY2023. **(§7404)**
Grazinglands Research Laboratory. Establishes a research laboratory for grazingland research. **(§7502, P.L. 110-246)**	Amends provision to state that the Grazinglands Research Laboratory shall not be declared excess or surplus federal property for the 15-year period beginning on the date of enactment of the FCE Act.

Table 9. (Continued)

Current Law/Policy	House Passed Bill (H.R. 2)
	The amendment increases the time period from 10 years to 15 years. **(§7405)**
Natural products research program. Authorizes a natural products research program to improve human health and agricultural productivity through the discovery, development, and commercialization of products and agrichemicals from bioactive natural products, including products from plant, marine, and microbial sources. Authorizes $7 million annually for FY2014-2018. **(7 U.S.C. 5937(e))**	Reauthorizes appropriations for FY2019-FY2023. **(§7406)**
Sun grant program. Establishes six sun grant centers and authorizes competitive grants to enhance national energy security through the development, distribution, and implementation of biobased energy technologies. Authorizes $75 million annually through FY2018. **(7 U.S.C. 8114(g))**	Reauthorizes appropriations for FY2019-FY2023. **(§7407)**
Subtitle E—Amendments to Other Laws	
Critical Agricultural Materials Act. Authorizes a research program into the use of agricultural materials that are of strategic and industrial importance to the United States. Authorizes $2 million annually for FY2014-FY2018. **(7 U.S.C. 178n(a)(2)**.	Reauthorizes appropriations for FY2019-FY2023. **(§7501)**
Equity in Educational Land-Grant Status Act of 1994. Establishes land-grant aid to colleges. **(7 U.S.C. 301 note)**	Amends provision to define 36 tribal colleges as "1994 land-grant institutions." Reauthorizes endowment funding, capacity-building grants, and research grants for the 36 tribal colleges for FY2019-FY2023. **(§7502)**
Research Facilities Act. Defines and authorizes funding for agricultural research facilities. **(7 U.S.C. 390 *et seq.*)**	Amends the Research Facilities Act (7 U.S.C. 390(1)) by striking *a college, university, or nonprofit institution* and inserting *an entity eligible to receive funds under a capacity and infrastructure program as defined in Section 251(f)(1)(C) of the 1994 Agriculture Reorganization Act.* Adds a new section authorizing competitive grants appropriation and limiting those funds made available to no more than 25% for any one project. Limits an eligible entity to

Current Law/Policy	House Passed Bill (H.R. 2)
	receiving funds for only one project at a time. **(§7503)**
Competitive, Special, and Facilities Research Grant Act. Authorizes a competitive grants program at USDA to address various areas of importance to the agricultural production, food, and nutrition sectors. **(7 U.S.C. 3157(b))**	Amends the act by making technical corrections and adding clauses that accelerate research in the use of automation or mechanization for labor- intensive tasks in crop production and distribution and remove barriers to entry for young, beginning, socially disadvantaged, veteran, and immigrant farmers and ranchers. **(§7504)**
Renewable Resources Extension Act of 1978. Authorizes $30 million annually for FY2002-FY2018 for forestry-related extension activities. **(16 U.S.C. 1675, 1671)**	Reauthorizes appropriations for FY2019-FY2023. **(§7505)**
National Aquaculture Act of 1980. Authorizes appropriations of $1 million annually for FY1991-FY2018 to the Departments of Agriculture, Commerce, and the Interior to support research on aquaculture. **(16 U.S.C. 2809)**	Reauthorizes appropriations for FY2019-FY2023. **(§7506)**
Beginning Farmer and Rancher Development Program. Authorizes a beginning farmer and rancher development program to provide training, education, outreach, and technical assistance initiatives for beginning farmers or ranchers. Authorizes $20 million in mandatory funding annually for FY2014-FY2018 and $30 million annually for FY2014-FY2018 in discretionary spending. **(7 U.S.C. 3319f)**	Reauthorizes mandatory and discretionary appropriations for FY2019-FY2023. Amends to require that grant recipients provide a match in the form of cash or in-kind contributions equal to 25% of the grant funds provided. The Secretary is authorized to waive the matching requirement to effectively reach an underserved area or population. Amendment adds new subsection outlining the purposes of the competitive grants. Requires that not less than 5% of the funds be made available to socially disadvantaged farmers and ranchers, limited resource farmers and ranchers, and farm workers who desire to become farmers and ranchers. Also requires not less than 5% of the funds be made available to support programs and services that address the needs of veteran farmers. **(§7507)**
Federal agricultural research facilities. Provides funding for federal agricultural research facilities. **(Title XIV, Public Law 99-198)**	Reauthorizes appropriations for FY2019-FY2023. No change to current law. **(7508)**

Table 9. (Continued)

Current Law/Policy	House Passed Bill (H.R. 2)
Biomass research and development. Establishes a research initiative between USDA and the Department of Energy to coordinate research and development programs and activities relating to biofuels and biobased products that are carried out by their respective departments. Authorizes $20 million in discretionary funding annually for FY2014-2018. **(7 U.S.C. 8108(h))**	Reauthorizes appropriations of $20 million for each fiscal year for FY2019-FY2023. **(§7509)**
Subtitle F—Other Matters	
Enhanced Use Lease Authority Program. Concerns the National Agricultural Library's authority under a pilot program to lease non-excess property. **(7 U.S.C. 3125a note)**	Transitions the lease authority program from a pilot program to a permanent program and changes the dates of report submission requirements. **(§7601)**
Functions and duties of the Under Secretary for Research, Education, and Economics. (7 U.S.C. 6971(d)(2))	Declares that certain duties of the Secretary with respect to coordination of research across disciplines and to address the priority research areas of the Agriculture and Food Research Initiative. **(§7602)**
Reinstatement of District of Columbia matching requirement for certain land-grant university assistance. (P.L. 93-471, §38-1202.09(e), D.C. Official Code)	Amends Section 209 of the District of Columbia Postsecondary Education Reorganization Act to pay no more than one-half of the total cost of providing certain extension work. **(§7603)**
No comparable provision.	**Farmland tenure, transition, and entry data initiative.** Directs the Secretary to collect and report annually data and analysis on farmland ownership, tenure, transition, and entry of beginning farmers. Authorizes $2 million each fiscal year for FY2019-FY2023. **(§7604)**
No comparable provision.	**Transfer of administrative jurisdiction, portion of Henry A. Wallace Beltsville Agricultural Research Center, Beltsville, Maryland.** Authorizes the Secretary to transfer a parcel of real property at the Henry A. Wallace Beltsville Agricultural Research Center to the administrative jurisdiction of the Secretary of the Treasury and specifies the conditions of the transfer. **(§7605)**

Current Law/Policy	House Passed Bill (H.R. 2)
Smith-Lever Act of 1916, Sections 3 and 4; Hatch Act of 1887, Section 3; National Agricultural Research, Extension, and Teaching Policy Act, Sections 1444 and 1445. (7 U.S.C. 343(h)(2)); (7 U.S.C 344); (7 U.S.C 366(c)); (7 U.S.C 361g); (7 U.S.C> 3221(d)); (7 U.S.C. 3222(e))	Amends provisions requiring submission of plans of work by land-grant institutions with respect to the use of formula funds and state matching funds provided under the Hatch Act, Smith-Lever Act, and similar formula funds provided to the 1890 land-grant universities. Provides that the procedures of such plans of work are not subject to audits to determine their sufficiency. **(§7606)**
Department of Agriculture Reorganization Act of 1994, Section 251. (7 U.S.C. 6971(f)(1)(C))	Exempts entities receiving certain funds from time and effort reporting requirements under Part 200 of Title 2 of the *Code of Federal Regulations* with respect to the use of such funds. **(§7607)**
No comparable provision	Provides that USDA, in consultation with the Food and Drug Administration (FDA), shall develop and carry out a national science-based education campaign to increase public awareness regarding the use of biotechnology in food and agriculture production. **(§7608)**

Table 10. Title VIII: Forestry

Current Law/Policy	House Passed Bill (H.R. 2)
Subtitle A—Reauthorization and Modification of Certain Forestry Programs	
Funding. Authorizes up to $10 million in annual appropriations between FY2008 and FY2018 to implement the requirements for statewide forest resource assessments and strategies. **(16 U.S.C. 2101a)**	Reauthorizes funding at the current authorized level of up to $10 million annually through FY2023. **(§8101)**
Permanently authorizes such sums as necessary to be appropriated to carry out the **Forest Legacy Program**, which was created to protect forests from conversion to non-forest uses and received average annual appropriations of approximately $59 million from FY2014 through FY2018. **(16 U.S.C. 2103c)**	Eliminates permanent authority to receive annual appropriations of such sums as necessary and instead authorizes the program to receive $35 million annually through FY2023, subject to appropriations. **(§8102)**
Permanently authorizes such sums as necessary to be appropriated to carry out the **Community Forest and Open Space Conservation** program. The program provides financial assistance to local governments, federally	Eliminates permanent authority to receive annual appropriations of such sums as necessary and instead authorizes the program to receive $5 million annually through FY2023, subject to appropriations. **(§8103)**

Table 10. (Continued)

Current Law/Policy	House Passed Bill (H.R. 2)
recognized Indian tribes, and nonprofit organizations to establish community forests by acquiring and protecting private forests threatened by conversion to non- forest uses. It received an average of $2.4 million annually in appropriations between FY2014 and FY2018. **(16 U.S.C. 2103d)**	
Permanently authorizes up to 5% of the funds made available for all CFAA programs to be appropriated to carry out a program to support innovative regional or national forest restoration projects that address priority landscapes. The **Landscape Scale Restoration** program received average annual appropriations of $14 million from FY2014 through FY2018. **(16 U.S.C. 2109a)**	Eliminates the existing program and establishes a State and Private Forest Landscape-Scale Restoration program to provide technical and financial assistance for landscape-scale restoration projects on state, tribal, or private forest land. Authorizes the program to receive $10 million annually through FY2023, subject to appropriations. **(§8104)**
Authorizes up to $5 million annually through FY2018 for the **Rural Revitalization Technologies** program. **(7 U.S.C. 6601(d)(2))**	Reauthorizes the program at the current authorized level of up to $5 million annually through FY2023. **(§8105)**
Authorizes financial assistance for communities to plan and install wood energy systems in public buildings and authorizes appropriations of $5 million annually through FY2018. The program has never received appropriations. **(7 U.S.C. 8113)**	Expands the program to provide financial assistance for the installation of public or private wood energy systems or the construction of manufacturing or processing plants that use or produce innovative wood products. Changes the name to the **Community Wood Energy and Wood Innovation Program**. Authorizes the program to receive $25 million annually through FY2023, subject to appropriations. **(§8106)**
Establishes the **Healthy Forests Reserve Program** (HFRP) to assist private and tribal landowners in restoring and enhancing forest ecosystems using 10-year agreements, 30-year contracts, 30-year easements, and permanent easements for the purposes of species recovery, improving biodiversity, and enhancing carbon sequestration as outlined in restoration plans. Authorizes appropriations for HFRP of $12 million annually through FY2018. **(16 U.S.C. 6571-6578)** Authorizes the use of procedures intended to expedite the environmental analysis, administrative review, and judicial review for	Expands the purposes, eligibility requirements, and enrollment priorities of the program to include species recovery and habitat conservation considerations. Authorizes federally recognized Indian tribes to sell permanent easements on lands they own in fee simple. Specifies that restoration plans may include a variety of land management practices if necessary to achieve habitat restoration objectives. Reauthorizes HFRP at the current authorized level of $12 million annually through FY2023, subject to appropriations. Permanently authorizes the procedures for priority projects within designated treatment

Current Law/Policy	**House Passed Bill (H.R. 2)**
specified priority forest health projects within NFS areas designated as insect and disease treatment areas under the Healthy Forests Restoration Act (HFRA) through FY2018. Section 603(c) categorically excludes priority projects from the requirements to produce an environmental assessment or environmental impact statement under NEPA (P.L. 91-109) if the project was developed through a collaborative process, is located within or in proximity to designated landscapes and specified Fire Regime Condition Classes, and involves less than 3,000 acres. **(16 U.S.C. 6591a-b)**	areas, adds hazardous fuels reduction projects as a priority project category subject to the expedited procedures, and expands the availability of the NEPA categorical exclusion (CE) to projects up to 6,000 acres. **(§8107)**
Authorizes the Secretary of Agriculture to provide matching funds to the **National Forest Foundation** (NFF) for administrative expenses through FY2018. Section 410(b) authorizes $3 million in annual appropriations through FY2018 to provide matching funds for the NFF. **(16 U.S.C. 583j)**	Reauthorizes the Secretary's authority to provide matching funds for NFF administrative expenses and appropriations at the current authorized level of $3 million through FY2023. **(§8108)**
Subtitle B—Secure Rural Schools and Community Self-Determination Act of 2000 Amendments	
The **Secure Rural Schools and Community Self- Determination Act of 2000** (SRS, P.L. 106 393), as amended, requires that 50% of the funds authorized by Title II of SRS are used on (1) road maintenance, decommissioning, or obliteration or (2) stream or watershed restoration projects. **(16 U.S.C. 7124(f))**	Changes the requirements to provide that 50% of the funds are to be used on timber or forest product sales, fire risk reduction, water supply, or forest stewardship projects. **(§8201)**
Establishes local **Resource Advisory Committees** (RACs) to coordinate, review, and recommend Title II projects to the Secretary to implement on NFS lands through FY2018 and specifies that RACs shall consist of 15 members, with five members representing a balance of specified community interests. Members must reside within the state in which the RAC has jurisdiction. **(16 U.S.C. 7125)**	Extends the authorization for RACs through FY2023 and reduces the membership requirement to nine members, with three members representing the specified community interests. Restricts membership to the county or adjacent counties within the RAC jurisdiction. Authorizes the Secretary to designate an appointee to perform certain functions. **(§8202)**
No comparable provision.	Adds a new Section 209 to SRS, establishing a program for 10 select RACs to retain and use the revenues generated by projects they propose, through FY2023. **(§8203)**
Subtitle C—Availability of Categorical Exclusions to Expedite Forest Management Activities	

Table 10. (Continued)

Current Law/Policy	House Passed Bill (H.R. 2)
No comparable provision.	Defines relevant terms and specifies that the Secretary concerned refers to the Secretary of Agriculture for NFS lands or the Secretary of the Interior for the public lands. **(§8301)**
No comparable provision.	Excludes from the authorities established in the subtitle NFS or public lands that are designated wilderness areas, inventoried roadless areas except under specific conditions, or lands on which timber harvesting is prohibited by law. **(§8302)**
The Endangered Species Act (ESA, P.L. 93-205) requires consultation with the Secretary of the Interior to determine if a federal action may adversely impact a species—or its habitat—listed as endangered or threatened. **(16 U.S.C. 1536)**	Provides for an expedited ESA consultation for forest management activities carried out under this subtitle on NFS or public lands or, if the Secretary concerned determines that the activity is not likely to adversely affect a listed species or designated critical habitat, removes the requirement for consultation. **(§8303)**
No comparable provision.	Authorizes the Secretary to choose which CE to use if a forest management activity on NFS or public lands qualifies for multiple CEs under this subtitle. (§8304)
No comparable provision.	Establishes a CE for projects up to 6,000 acres and for any combination of addressing an insect or disease infestation; reducing hazardous fuel loads; protecting a municipal water source; maintaining, enhancing, or modifying critical habitat to protect it from catastrophic disturbances; or increasing water yield on NFS or public lands. **(§8311)**
No comparable provision.	Establishes a CE for projects to prevent wildfire as a result of a catastrophic event or to use and generate revenue from the sale of forest products impacted by a catastrophic event on NFS or public lands, subject to a maximum project size of 6,000 acres and a requirement to prepare a reforestation plan. **(§8312)**
No comparable provision.	Establishes a CE for projects up to 6,000 acres to improve, enhance, or create early successional forests for wildlife habitat improvement and other purposes on NFS or public lands. Projects should maximize production and regeneration of priority species. **(§8313)**

Current Law/Policy	**House Passed Bill (H.R. 2)**
No comparable provision.	Establishes a CE for projects to remove hazardous trees to protect public health or safety, water supply, or public infrastructure on NFS or public lands. **(§8314)**
No comparable provision.	Establishes a CE for forest restoration or improvement projects up to 6,000 acres to reduce the risk of wildfire on NFS or public lands, including the removal of specified vegetation, including conifer trees, through livestock grazing, prescribed burns, and mechanical treatments; performance of hazardous fuels management; creation of fuel and fire breaks; modification of fences for livestock grazing; installation of erosion control devices; construction and maintenance of livestock grazing infrastructure; various specified soil treatments; and use of herbicides in accordance with applicable land and resource management plan and agency procedures. **(§8315)**
No comparable provision.	Establishes a CE for projects up to 6,000 acres to improve forest resiliency, reduce hazardous fuels, or improve wildlife and aquatic habitat on NFS or public lands, including timber, salvage, and regeneration harvests; prescribed burning; stream restoration and erosion control; and road and trail decommissioning activities. Projects may include permanent roads up to three miles or temporary roads for up to three years. **(§8316)**
No comparable provision.	Establishes a CE for projects on NFS lands to construct, reconstruct, or decommission NFS roads up to three miles; reclassify or add NFS roads; reconstruct, rehabilitate, or decommission bridges; remove dams; or maintain facilities through the use of pesticides according to federal and state requirements. **(§8317)**
No comparable provision.	Establishes a CE for projects to operate, maintain, modify, reconstruct, or decommission existing developed recreation sites on NFS lands, including activities related to facility and site maintenance and road and trail construction, reconstruction, maintenance or decommissioning, subject to a maximum of

Table 10. (Continued)

Current Law/Policy	House Passed Bill (H.R. 2)
	three miles for permanent roads or three years for temporary roads. **(§8318)**
No comparable provision.	Establishes a CE for projects on NFS lands to construct, reconstruct, maintain, decommission, relocate, or dispose of an administrative site. Projects may include road and trail construction, reconstruction, or maintenance activities, subject to a maximum of three miles for permanent roads or three years for temporary roads. **(§8319)**
No comparable provision.	Establishes a CE for projects on NFS lands to issue new special use authorizations or renew or modify existing or expired special use authorizations for the use or occupancy of NFS lands under certain specified conditions. Specifies that the Secretary of Agriculture is not required to prepare a project file for such actions. **(§8320)**
Establishes a CE for certain projects located within or in proximity to the wildland-urban interface or in areas classified as Condition Class 2 or 3 in Fire Regime groups I, II, or III. **(16 U.S.C. 6591b(c))**	Expands the availability of the CE to include projects located in areas classified as Condition Class 2 or 3 in Fire Regimes IV and V. **(§8321)**
Permanently authorizes the Forest Service and BLM to enter into **Good Neighbor Agreements** with states to perform authorized forest restoration activities on NFS or public lands. **(16 U.S.C. 2113a)**	Expands the availability of Good Neighbor Agreements to include federally recognized Indian tribes. **(§8331)**
Authorizes the prioritization of hazardous fuel reduction projects on NFS lands. **(16 U.S.C. 6513)**	Encourages the Secretary to use any funds appropriated for hazardous fuels management in excess of $300 million annually for projects on federal and nonfederal land, including the use of up to 20% or $20 million of any excess funds annually to provide financial assistance to states for cross-boundary hazardous fuels reduction projects. **(§8332)**
Export prohibition. Prohibits the foreign export of unprocessed logs from the contiguous federal lands west of the 100th Meridian unless the Secretary concerned determines through a rulemaking process that certain grades or species of lumber are surplus to domestic needs. **(16 U.S.C. 620a)**	Directs the Secretary to undertake a rulemaking to issue a determination exempting unprocessed dead and dying trees on NFS lands in California from the export prohibition for 10 years. **(§8333)**

Current Law/Policy	House Passed Bill (H.R. 2)
	three miles for permanent roads or three years for temporary roads. **(§8318)**
Subtitle D—Tribal Forestry Participation and Protection	
Authorizes the Secretary concerned to enter into an agreement with federally recognized Indian tribes to implement forest or rangeland projects on tribal lands or on federal lands adjacent to tribal lands. **(25 U.S.C. 3115a(b))**	Requires the Secretary concerned to respond to a tribal request within 120 days and, if the project is accepted, requires the project analysis to be completed within two years. **(§8401)**
No comparable provision.	Authorizes the Secretary concerned and federally recognized Indian tribes, on a demonstration basis, to enter into contracts to allow tribes to perform administrative, management, and other functions of the Tribal Forest Protection Act. **(§8402)**
Subtitle E—Other Matters	
No comparable provision.	Establishes a research, development, education, and technical assistance program to facilitate the use of wood products in construction projects. **(§8501)**
No comparable provision.	Establishes a pilot program through December 21, 2027, for owners or operators of rights-of-way on NFS land to develop and implement vegetation management plans and perform projects on NFS lands within and up to 75 feet from the right-of-way. **(§8502)**
No comparable provision.	Prohibits the Forest Service from considering certain criteria when considering if **extraordinary circumstances** exist that would potentially require further review and documentation under NEPA than would normally be required under a CE, such as wilderness designations, sensitive species, cumulative impacts, threatened or endangered species, or critical habitat. Eliminates the requirements to prepare an environmental impact statement for activities that would substantially alter a potential wilderness area. Directs the Forest Service to initiate rulemaking to implement these procedures within 60 days of enactment and issue final regulations within 120 days of enactment. **(§8503)**
No comparable provision.	States that nothing in this title or any amendments made to the title would impact the availability of funds or other resources for wildfire suppression. **(§8504)**

Table 10. (Continued)

Current Law/Policy	House Passed Bill (H.R. 2)
The Wildfire Suppression Funding and Forest Management Activities Act, enacted as Title I of Division O of the FY2018 Consolidated Appropriations Act (P.L. 115-141), establishes a new mechanism for funding federal wildfire suppression activities.	Makes technical amendments. **(§8505)**
Subtitle A—Reauthorization and Modification of Certain Forestry Programs	
Funding. Authorizes up to $10 million in annual appropriations between FY2008 and FY2018 to implement the requirements for statewide forest resource assessments and strategies. **(16 U.S.C. 2101a)**	Reauthorizes funding at the current authorized level of up to $10 million annually through FY2023. **(§8101)**
Permanently authorizes such sums as necessary to be appropriated to carry out the **Forest Legacy Program**, which was created to protect forests from conversion to non-forest uses and received average annual appropriations of approximately $59 million from FY2014 through FY2018. **(16 U.S.C. 2103c)**	Eliminates permanent authority to receive annual appropriations of such sums as necessary and instead authorizes the program to receive $35 million annually through FY2023, subject to appropriations. **(§8102)**
Permanently authorizes such sums as necessary to be appropriated to carry out the **Community Forest and Open Space Conservation** program. The program provides financial assistance to local governments, federally recognized Indian tribes, and nonprofit organizations to establish community forests by acquiring and protecting private forests threatened by conversion to non- forest uses. It received an average of $2.4 million annually in appropriations between FY2014 and FY2018. **(16 U.S.C. 2103d)**	Eliminates permanent authority to receive annual appropriations of such sums as necessary and instead authorizes the program to receive $5 million annually through FY2023, subject to appropriations. **(§8103)**
Permanently authorizes up to 5% of the funds made available for all CFAA programs to be appropriated to carry out a program to support innovative regional or national forest restoration projects that address priority landscapes. The **Landscape Scale Restoration** program received average annual appropriations of $14 million from FY2014 through FY2018. **(16 U.S.C. 2109a)**	Eliminates the existing program and establishes a State and Private Forest Landscape-Scale Restoration program to provide technical and financial assistance for landscape-scale restoration projects on state, tribal, or private forest land. Authorizes the program to receive $10 million annually through FY2023, subject to appropriations. **(§8104)**
Authorizes up to $5 million annually through FY2018 for the **Rural Revitalization Technologies** program. **(7 U.S.C. 6601(d)(2))**	Reauthorizes the program at the current authorized level of up to $5 million annually through FY2023. **(§8105)**

Current Law/Policy	House Passed Bill (H.R. 2)
Authorizes financial assistance for communities to plan and install wood energy systems in public buildings and authorizes appropriations of $5 million annually through FY2018. The program has never received appropriations. **(7 U.S.C. 8113)**	Expands the program to provide financial assistance for the installation of public or private wood energy systems or the construction of manufacturing or processing plants that use or produce innovative wood products. Changes the name to the **Community Wood Energy and Wood Innovation Program**. Authorizes the program to receive $25 million annually through FY2023, subject to appropriations. **(§8106)**
Establishes the **Healthy Forests Reserve Program** (HFRP) to assist private and tribal landowners in restoring and enhancing forest ecosystems using 10-year agreements, 30-year contracts, 30-year easements, and permanent easements for the purposes of species recovery, improving biodiversity, and enhancing carbon sequestration as outlined in restoration plans. Authorizes appropriations for HFRP of $12 million annually through FY2018. **(16 U.S.C. 6571-6578)** Authorizes the use of procedures intended to expedite the environmental analysis, administrative review, and judicial review for specified priority forest health projects within designated insect and disease treatment areas, within the NFS through FY2018. Section 603(c) categorically excludes priority projects from the requirements to produce an environmental assessment or environmental impact statement under NEPA (P.L. 91-109) if the project was developed through a collaborative process, is located within or in proximity to designated landscapes and specified Fire Regime Condition Classes, and involves less than 3,000 acres. **(16 U.S.C. 6591a-b)**	Expands the purposes, eligibility requirements, and enrollment priorities of the program to include species recovery and habitat conservation considerations. Authorizes federally recognized Indian tribes to sell permanent easements on lands they own in fee simple. Specifies that restoration plans may include a variety of land management practices if necessary to achieve habitat restoration objectives. Reauthorizes HFRP at the current authorized level of $12 million annually through FY2023, subject to appropriations. Permanently authorizes the procedures for priority projects within designated treatment areas, adds hazardous fuels reduction projects as a priority project category subject to the expedited procedures, and expands the availability of the NEPA categorical exclusion (CE) to projects up to 6,000 acres. **(§8107)**
Authorizes the Secretary of Agriculture to provide matching funds to the **National Forest Foundation** (NFF) for administrative expenses through FY2018. Section 410(b) authorizes $3 million in annual appropriations through FY2018 to provide matching funds for the NFF. **(16 U.S.C. 583j)**	Reauthorizes the Secretary's authority to provide matching funds for NFF administrative expenses and appropriations at the current authorized level of $3 million through FY2023. **(§8108)**
Subtitle B—Secure Rural Schools and Community Self-Determination Act of 2000 Amendments	

Table 10. (Continued)

Current Law/Policy	House Passed Bill (H.R. 2)
The **Secure Rural Schools and Community Self- Determination Act of 2000** (SRS, P.L. 106-393), as amended, requires that 50% of the funds authorized by Title II of SRS are used on (1) road maintenance, decommissioning, or obliteration or (2) stream or watershed restoration projects. **(16 U.S.C. 7124(f))**	Changes the requirements to provide that 50% of the funds are to be used on timber or forest product sales, fire risk reduction, water supply, or forest stewardship projects. **(§8201)**
Establishes local **Resource Advisory Committees** (RACs) to coordinate, review, and recommend Title II projects to the Secretary to implement on NFS lands through FY2018 and specifies that RACs shall consist of 15 members, with five members representing a balance of specified community interests. Members must reside within the state in which the RAC has jurisdiction. **(16 U.S.C. 7125)**	Extends the authorization for RACs through FY2023 and reduces the membership requirement to nine members, with three members representing the specified community interests. Restricts membership to the county or adjacent counties within the RAC jurisdiction. Authorizes the Secretary to designate an appointee to perform certain functions. **(§8202)**
No comparable provision.	Adds a new Section 209 to SRS, establishing a program for 10 select RACs to retain and use the revenues generated by projects they propose, through FY2023. **(§8203)**
Subtitle C—Availability of Categorical Exclusions to Expedite Forest Management Activities	
No comparable provision.	Defines relevant terms and specifies that the Secretary concerned refers to the Secretary of Agriculture for NFS lands or the Secretary of the Interior for the public lands. **(§8301)**
No comparable provision.	Excludes from the authorities established in the subtitle NFS or public lands that are designated wilderness areas, inventoried roadless areas except under specific conditions, or lands on which timber harvesting is prohibited by law. **(§8302)**
The Endangered Species Act (ESA, P.L. 93-205) requires consultation with the Secretary of the Interior to determine if a federal action may adversely impact a species—or its habitat—listed as endangered or threatened. **(16 U.S.C. 1536)**	Provides for an expedited ESA consultation for forest management activities carried out under this subtitle on NFS or public lands or, if the Secretary concerned determines that the activity is not likely to adversely affect a listed species or designated critical habitat, removes the requirement for consultation. **(§8303)**
No comparable provision.	Authorizes the Secretary to choose which CE to use if a forest management activity on NFS or public lands qualifies for multiple CEs under this subtitle. **(§8304)**

Current Law/Policy	**House Passed Bill (H.R. 2)**
No comparable provision.	Establishes a CE for projects up to 6,000 acres and for any combination of addressing an insect or disease infestation; reducing hazardous fuel loads; protecting a municipal water source; maintaining, enhancing, or modifying critical habitat to protect it from catastrophic disturbances; or increasing water yield on NFS or public lands. **(§8311)**
No comparable provision.	Establishes a CE for projects to prevent wildfire as a result of a catastrophic event or to use and generate revenue from the sale of forest products impacted by a catastrophic event on NFS or public lands, subject to a maximum project size of 6,000 acres and a requirement to prepare a reforestation plan. **(§8312)**
No comparable provision.	Establishes a CE for projects up to 6,000 acres to improve, enhance, or create early successional forests for wildlife habitat improvement and other purposes on NFS or public lands. Projects should maximize production and regeneration of priority species. **(§8313)**
No comparable provision.	Establishes a CE for projects to remove hazardous trees to protect public health or safety, water supply, or public infrastructure on NFS or public lands. **(§8314)**
No comparable provision.	Establishes a CE for forest restoration or improvement projects up to 6,000 acres to reduce the risk of wildfire on NFS or public lands, including the removal of specified vegetation, including conifer trees, through livestock grazing, prescribed burns, and mechanical treatments; performance of hazardous fuels management; creation of fuel and fire breaks; modification of fences for livestock grazing; installation of erosion control devices; construction and maintenance of livestock grazing infrastructure; various specified soil treatments; and use of herbicides in accordance with applicable land and resource management plan and agency procedures. **(§8315)**
No comparable provision.	Establishes a CE for projects up to 6,000 acres to improve forest resiliency, reduce hazardous fuels, or improve wildlife and aquatic habitat on

Table 10. (Continued)

Current Law/Policy	House Passed Bill (H.R. 2)
	NFS or public lands, including timber, salvage, and regeneration harvests; prescribed burning; stream restoration and erosion control; and road and trail decommissioning activities. Projects may include permanent roads up to three miles or temporary roads for up to three years. **(§8316)**
No comparable provision.	Establishes a CE for projects on NFS lands to construct, reconstruct, or decommission NFS roads up to three miles; reclassify or add NFS roads; reconstruct, rehabilitate, or decommission bridges; remove dams; or maintain facilities through the use of pesticides according to federal and state requirements. **(§8317)**
No comparable provision.	Establishes a CE for projects to operate, maintain, modify, reconstruct, or decommission existing developed recreation sites on NFS lands, including activities related to facility and site maintenance and road and trail construction, reconstruction, maintenance or decommissioning, subject to a maximum of three miles for permanent roads or three years for temporary roads. **(§8318)**
No comparable provision.	Establishes a CE for projects on NFS lands to construct, reconstruct, maintain, decommission, relocate, or dispose of an administrative site. Projects may include road and trail construction, reconstruction, or maintenance activities, subject to a maximum of three miles for permanent roads or three years for temporary roads. **(§8319)**
No comparable provision.	Establishes a CE for projects on NFS lands to issue new special use authorizations or renew or modify existing or expired special use authorizations for the use or occupancy of NFS lands under certain specified conditions. Specifies that the Secretary of Agriculture is not required to prepare a project file for such actions. **(§8320)**
Establishes a CE for certain projects located within or in proximity to the wildland-urban interface or in areas classified as Condition	Expands the availability of the CE to include projects located in areas classified as Condition Class 2 or 3 in Fire Regimes IV and V. **(§8321)**

Current Law/Policy	**House Passed Bill (H.R. 2)**
Class 2 or 3 in Fire Regime groups I, II, or III. **(16 U.S.C. 6591b(c))**	
Permanently authorizes the Forest Service and BLM to enter in to **Good Neighbor Agreements** with states to perform authorized forest restoration activities on NFS or public lands. **(16 U.S.C. 2113a)**	Expands the availability of Good Neighbor Agreements to include federally recognized Indian tribes. **(§8331)**
Authorizes the prioritization of hazardous fuel reduction projects on NFS lands. **(16 U.S.C. 6513)**	Encourages the Secretary to use any funds appropriated for hazardous fuels management in excess of $300 million annually for projects on federal and nonfederal land, including the use of up to 20% or $20 million of any excess funds annually to provide financial assistance to states for cross-boundary hazardous fuels reduction projects. **(§8332)**
Export prohibition. Prohibits the foreign export of unprocessed logs from the contiguous federal lands west of the 100th Meridian unless the Secretary concerned determines through a rulemaking process that certain grades or species of lumber are surplus to domestic needs. **(16 U.S.C. 620a)**	Directs the Secretary to undertake a rulemaking to issue a determination exempting unprocessed dead and dying trees on NFS lands in California from the export prohibition for 10 years. **(§8333)**
Subtitle D—Tribal Forestry Participation and Protection	
Authorizes the Secretary concerned to enter into an agreement with federally recognized Indian tribes to implement forest or rangeland projects on tribal lands or on federal lands adjacent to tribal lands. **(25 U.S.C. 3115a(b))**	Requires the Secretary concerned to respond to a tribal request within 120 days and, if the project is accepted, requires the project analysis to be completed within two years. **(§8401)**
No comparable provision.	Authorizes the Secretary concerned and federally recognized Indian tribes, on a demonstration basis, to enter into contracts to allow tribes to perform administrative, management, and other functions of the Tribal Forest Protection Act. **(§8402)**
Subtitle E—Other Matters	
No comparable provision.	Establishes a research, development, education, and technical assistance program to facilitate the use of wood products in construction projects. **(§8501)**
No comparable provision.	Establishes a pilot program through December 21, 2027, for owners or operators of rights-of-way on NFS land to develop and implement vegetation management plans and perform projects on NFS lands within and up to 75 feet from the right-of-way. **(§8502)**

Table 10. (Continued)

Current Law/Policy	House Passed Bill (H.R. 2)
No comparable provision.	Prohibits the Forest Service from considering certain criteria when considering if **extraordinary circumstances** exist that would potentially require further review and documentation under NEPA than would normally be required under a CE, such as wilderness designations, sensitive species, cumulative impacts, threatened or endangered species, or critical habitat. Eliminates the requirements to prepare an environmental impact statement for activities that would substantially alter a potential wilderness area. Directs the Forest Service to initiate rulemaking to implement these procedures within 60 days of enactment and issue final regulations within 120 days of enactment. **(§8503)**
No comparable provision.	States that nothing in this title or any amendments made to the title would impact the availability of funds or other resources for wildfire suppression. **(§8504)**
The Wildfire Suppression Funding and Forest Management Activities Act, enacted as Title I of Division O of the FY2018 Consolidated Appropriations Act (P.L. 115-141), establishes a new mechanism for funding federal wildfire suppression activities.	Makes technical amendments. **(§8505)**

Table 11. Title IX: Horticulture

Current Law/Policy	House Passed Bill (H.R. 2)
Specialty Crop, Organic Agriculture, and Local Foods Programs	
Specialty crop market news. Authorizes support for the collection and dissemination of market news for specialty crops. Authorized appropriations of $9 million annually through FY2018 to remain available until expended. **(7 U.S.C. 1622b(b))**	Reauthorizes program and funding levels through FY2023. **(§9001)**
Farmers' Market and Local Food Promotion Program. Authorizes the promotion of (1) farmers' markets, community- supported agriculture programs, and other direct producer-	Amends 7 U.S.C. 3005(g)(3) only, which authorizes discretionary appropriations for these programs. Reorganizes the paragraph and authorizes appropriations of $30 million

Current Law/Policy	**House Passed Bill (H.R. 2)**
to- consumer market opportunities and (2) local and regional food business enterprises. Authorizes CCC funding of $30 million annually (FY2014 through FY2018) and authorized appropriations of $10 million each year (FY2014-FY2018). **(7 U.S.C. 3005)**	annually for FY2019-FY2023. Does not make changes to the mandatory funding Section in (g)(1) and does not add any mandatory funding beyond FY2018. **(§9002)**
Food safety education initiatives. Amends the Agricultural Research, Extension, and Education Reform Act of 1998 (P.L. 105-185) to implement a program to educate fresh produce industry personnel and consumers on ways to reduce pathogens in fresh produce. Authorizes appropriations of $1 million annually to remain available until expended. **(7 U.S.C. 7655a(c))**	Reauthorizes program and funding levels through FY2023. **(§9003)**
Block grants to states. The Specialty Crops Competitiveness Act of 2004 (P.L. 108-465), as amended, authorizes block grants to states to support projects in marketing, research, pest management, and food safety, among other purposes. Authorizes CCC funding of $72.5 million annually (FY2014-FY2017) and $85 million for FY2018 and each fiscal year thereafter. Funding for multi-state project grants shall remain available until expended, rising from $1 million (FY2014) to $5 million (FY2018). **(7 U.S.C. 1621 note)**	Reauthorizes program and funding levels through FY2023. Requires USDA enter into a cooperative agreement to conduct program evaluation with state government and industry stakeholders **(§9004)**
Plant Variety Protection Act. Provides legal intellectual property rights protection to breeders of new varieties of plants that are sexually reproduced (by seed) or tuber-propagated. USDA issues Certificates of Protection that protect varieties for 20 years (25 years for vines and trees). **(7 U.S.C. 2401(a), 2402(a), 2541(a)(3), and 2568(a))**	Amends the Plant Variety Protection Act to include certain protections for sexually reproduced varieties. **(§9005)**
National Organic Program (NOP). The Organic Foods Production Act of 1990 authorizes NOP to develop and enforce national standards for organically produced agricultural products. Authorizes the creation of NOSB and the creation of the "National List of Approved and Prohibited Substances for Organic Farming and Handling Operations." Authorized appropriations were $15 million annually	Amends NOP to include provisions in H.R. 3871 (Organic Farmer and Consumer Protection Act of 2017), including the following: limits the types of operations excluded from NOP certification; requires electronic import documentation; establishes mechanisms for collaborative investigations and enforcement; requires increased documentation; increases accreditation

Table 11. (Continued)

Current Law/Policy	House Passed Bill (H.R. 2)
(FY2014-FY2018). **(7 U.S.C. 6522)** Provides $5 million in CCC funding for technology upgrades. **(7 U.S.C. 6519)** Section 7407(d) of the 2002 farm bill, as amended, requires USDA to collect data under the Organic Production and Market Data Initiatives (ODI), providing $5 million in mandatory CCC funds in FY204 (to remain available until expended). **(7 U.S.C. 5925c)** Section 10606 establishes the National Organic Certification Cost Share Program (NOCCSP) to help producers and handlers of organic products obtain certification. Provides $11.5 million in FY2014, to remain available until expended. **(7 U.S.C. 6523)**	authority of NOP over certifying agents; requires audits of satellite offices; ensures coordination and access to data; and requires additional reporting. **(§9006(a),(e)-(f))** Reauthorizes NOP appropriations, increasing from $16.5 million (FY2019) to $24 million (FY2023), and provides $5 million for technology upgrades to improve tracking and verification of organic imports. **(§9006(g)-(h))** Reauthorizes ODI funds at current levels. **(§9006(i))** Funding for NOCCSP is not reauthorized. Requires USDA to establish procedures for expedited petitions for postharvest handling substances related to food safety pertaining to the NOP's "National List of Approved and Prohibited Substances." **(§9006 (b))** Amends the eligibility and consultation requirements of the NOSB. **(§9006(c)-(d))**
Pecan marketing orders. Section 8e of the Agricultural Marketing Agreement Act of 1937 requires U.S. import of fruit, vegetable, and specialty crops to meet the same or comparable grade, size, quality, and maturity standards as domestic products covered by federal marketing orders. **(7 U.S.C. 608e–1(a))**	Adds pecans to the list of products with import prohibitions regulating the grade, size, quality, or maturity of certain crops. **(§9202)**
Food labeling. The Nutrition Labeling and Education Act of 1990 (P.L. 101-535) amended the Federal Food, Drug, and Cosmetic Act and provides the FDA with the authority to require nutrition labeling on most packaged foods. **(21 U.S.C. 343(q))**	Requires USDA to submit a report to the House and Senate Agriculture Committees examining the effect of a final FDA regulation, ''Food Labeling: Revision of the Nutrition and Supplement Facts Labels'' (81 *Federal Register* 33742) and whether the nutrition facts panel on the labeling of packaged food regarding ''added sugar'' should apply for foods with added honey and maple syrup. **(§9203)**
Regulation of Pesticides and Other Agricultural Chemicals	
Role of states in regulation of pesticides. The Federal Insecticide, Fungicide, and Rodenticide Act (FIFRA) governs the sale, distribution, and use of pesticides through registration (i.e., licensing), which includes the approval of a label specifying its proper use. FIFRA requires EPA to cooperate with federal and state	Amends FIFRA to define *State lead agency* and requires EPA to cooperate with federal agencies and state agencies regarding FIFRA regulations. Authorizes EPA to award cooperative agreements to states and tribes to ensure uniformity of FIFRA regulations.

Current Law/Policy	House Passed Bill (H.R. 2)
agencies in administering the act and its regulations and authorizes EPA to award cooperative agreements to enforce the act. FIFRA provides that states may regulate the sale or use of any federally registered pesticide in their respective jurisdictions but only if and to the extent the regulation does not permit any sale or use prohibited under the act. **(7 U.S.C. 136, 136t, 136u, 136v, 136w)**	Expressly preempts political subdivisions of a state, but not a state, from regulating the sale and use of pesticides within their respective jurisdictions. **(§9101)**
Pesticide registrations; experimental use permits. FIFRA Section 3 specifies criteria for the registration of a pesticide by EPA, establishes a process for the periodic review of existing pesticide registrations, and authorizes EPA to conditionally grant the registration of a pesticide if it meets certain criteria. FIFRA Section 5 governs the issuance of experimental use permits for pesticides. **(7 U.S.C. 136a, 136c, 136d)** ESA authorizes federal agencies, such as EPA, to consult with the Interior Department's Fish and Wildlife Service (FWS) and the Commerce Department's National Marine Fisheries Service (NMFS) when federal agency actions may likely jeopardize the continued existence of any endangered or threatened species or adversely modify their critical habitat. **(16 U.S.C. 1536)**	Amends FIFRA to require EPA to determine that certain agency actions are not likely to jeopardize the survival of a federally listed threatened or endangered species or alter critical habitat in a way that affects the survival and recovery of such species and expressly states that EPA is not required to consult with FWS and NMFS under ESA unless requested by an applicant for a pesticide registration. Requires EPA to consider certain information when making such a determination and engage in collaboration with other federal agencies. **(§9111, 9112)**
Administrative review; suspension. FIFRA Section 6 governs the cancellation, change in classification, or suspension of a pesticide registration. **(7 U.S.C. 136d)**	Authorizes EPA to initiate proceedings to cancel a pesticide registration or change a pesticide's classification if the agency determines that the proper use of the registered pesticide jeopardizes the survival of a federally listed species or alters critical habitat in a way that affects the survival and recovery of such species. **(§9113)**
Unlawful acts. FIFRA Section 12 specifies unlawful acts that are subject to civil or criminal penalties. **(7 U.S.C. 136j)**	Clarifies that any taking of federally listed species incidental to the lawful use of a pesticide that EPA has determined not to jeopardize the survival of such species or alter their critical habitat shall not be considered unlawful under ESA. **(§9114)**

Table 11. (Continued)

Current Law/Policy	House Passed Bill (H.R. 2)
Authority of states. FIFRA Section 24 authorizes a state to register EPA-registered pesticides for additional uses to meet special local needs within the state if EPA had not previously disapproved such uses. **(7 U.S.C. 136v)**	Amends requirements regarding state pesticide registrations and federally listed species considerations. Repeals EPA authority to suspend the authority of a state to register pesticides for not exercising adequate controls. **(§9115)**
No comparable provision.	Directs EPA to publish, and revise as appropriate, a work plan and processes for completing determinations on whether the registration of a pesticide would jeopardize the survival of federally listed threatened or endangered species or would alter their critical habitat. **(§9116)**
Use and discharges of authorized pesticides. FIFRA Section 3 directs EPA to register pesticides that have a pesticidal effect and, when used in conformance with labeling directions, do not present unreasonable adverse effects on human health or the environment. Pesticide registrations govern the sale, distribution, and use of a pesticide. **(7 U.S.C. 136a)** The Clean Water Act (CWA) makes it unlawful to discharge any pollutant into navigable waters unless specifically authorized by a permit, such as a permit for the discharge of a pollutant or group of pollutants from a point source into navigable waters under Section 402. Any person who unlawfully discharges a pollutant is subject to civil/criminal penalties. **(33 U.S.C. 1342)** Pesticide general permits cover most discharges of biological and chemical pesticides into navigable waters.	Amends FIFRA to prohibit EPA or a state from requiring a permit for point source discharges of a pesticide registered under FIFRA into navigable waters except in specific circumstances provided under new CWA Section 402(s). **(§9117)** Amends the CWA to prohibit EPA or a state from requiring a permit for point source discharges of a pesticide registered under FIFRA into navigable waters. Defines circumstances where a permit would be required (e.g., pesticide applications in violation of FIFRA, stormwater discharges, industrial or treatment works effluents, and certain vessel discharges). **(§9118)**
Pesticide registration fees reauthorization. FIFRA authorizes EPA to collect fees from pesticide manufacturers for the maintenance of existing pesticide registrations and evaluation of applications to register new pesticides, amend existing registrations, or related activities. **(7 U.S.C. 136 *et seq.*)**	Enacts into law H.R. 1029 of the 115th Congress, entitled the Pesticide Registration Improvement Enhancement Act of 2017. As passed by the House on March 20, 2017, H.R. 1029 would amend FIFRA to extend the authority to collect pesticide fees and for other purposes. **(§9119)**
Methyl bromide. Section 419 of the Plant Protection Act provides that USDA—in consultation with state, local and tribal	Requires USDA to establish a process to determine authorized methyl bromide uses in response to an emergency event. Amends the

Current Law/Policy	**House Passed Bill (H.R. 2)**
authorities— shall establish a program to identify alternatives to methyl bromide for treatment and control of plant pests and weeds. For uses where no registered, effective, economically feasible alternatives available can currently be identified, USDA shall initiate research programs to develop alternative methods of control and treatment. **(7 U.S.C. 7719)**	definition of an emergency event. Sets limitations on use per emergency event to allow for up to 20 metric tons of methyl bromide to be used per event at a specific location. **(§9121)**
Definition of *retail facilities*. Occupational Safety and Health Act of 1970 (OSHA) regulations exempt retail facilities from its standards for Process Safety Management (PSM) of Highly Hazardous Chemicals. While current regulations do not define the term *retail facility*, OSHA, in accordance with a ruling of the U.S. Court of Appeals, considers a facility to be a retail facility if more than half of the facility's income is obtained from direct sales to end users. **(29 U.S.C. 655)**	Requires OSHA to revise the PSM standard to formally define *retail facility* in accordance with its current, income-based definition. **(§9131)**
Report on regulation of plant biostimulants. *Plant biostimulant* is not defined in current law or regulation. Plant biostimulants that meet the definition of a "plant regulator" under FIFRA (7 U.S.C. §136 *et seq.*) are subject to requirements under the act.	Requires USDA—in consultation with EPA, states, and stakeholders—to submit a report to the President and Congress that identifies potential regulatory and legislative reforms to ensure the expeditious and appropriate review, approval, uniform national labeling, and availability of plant biostimulant products to agricultural producers. Defines *plant biostimulant* for purposes of the section. **(§9201)**

Table 12. Title X: Crop Insurance

Current Law/Policy—Crop Insurance	**House Passed Bill (H.R.2)**
Treatment of Forage and Grazing	
Catastrophic risk protection. Requires FCIC to offer catastrophic risk protection (high-deductible coverage) for all crops except for "crops and grasses used for grazing." **(7 U.S.C. 1508(b)(1))**	Strikes the exception that provides that catastrophic risk protection plans shall not be available for crops and grasses used for grazing. **(§10001(a))**
Ineligible producers. Makes producers ineligible to receive both catastrophic risk protection benefits and other assistance for the	Provides an exception to the limitation on multiple benefits for the same loss for coverage described in the new Section 508D of the

Table 12. (Continued)

Current Law/Policy—Crop Insurance	House Passed Bill (H.R.2)
same loss under any program administered by the Secretary of Agriculture, with the exception of certain emergency loans. **(7 U.S.C. 1508(n)(1),(2))**	Federal Crop Insurance Act. **(§10001(b))**
No comparable provision.	**Expanded coverage for forage and grazing.** Adds a new Section 508D, which permits separate crop insurance policies, including a catastrophic risk protection plan, to be purchased for crops that can be both grazed and mechanically harvested on the same acres during the same growing season. Such separate policies can be independently indemnified for each intended use. **(§10001(c))**
Administrative Basic Fee	
CAT fees. Sets the administrative fee for catastrophic risk protection (commonly referred to as CAT fees) at $300 per crop per county. **(7 U.S.C. 1508(b)(5)(A))**	Increases the administrative basic fee from $300 to $500 per crop per county. **(§10002)**
Prevention of Duplicative Coverage	
Additional coverage. Requires FCIC to offer plans of insurance that provide additional coverage, including additional coverage based on an individual yield and loss basis, an area yield and loss basis, an individual yield and loss basis supplemented with coverage based on an area yield and loss basis, or a margin basis. **(7 U.S.C. 1508(c)(1))**	Provides that crops for which the producer has elected agriculture risk coverage or that are enrolled in the stacked income protection plan are ineligible for coverage based on an area yield and loss basis or coverage based on the supplemental coverage option. **(§10003(a))** Adds conforming amendments. **(§10003(b))**
Repeal of Authority for Performance-Based Premium Discounts	
Performance-based premium discounts. Authorizes FCIC to provide performance-based premium discounts to producers with "good insurance or production experience relative to other producers" of the same crop in the same area. **(7 U.S.C. 1508(d))**	Repeal the authority for performance-based discounts for producers. **(§10004(a))** Adds conforming amendments. **(§10004(b))**
Addition of Producer Option to Limit APH Decreases	
Calculation of APH yields. Details how FCIC determines yields and provides exceptions to the calculation of actual production history (APH) yields, such as transitional yields and yield exclusion options. **(7 U.S.C. 1508(g))**	Requires FCIC to establish underwriting rules that would give producers the choice to limit their APH decreases to 10% of the previous year's APH. Requires actuarially sound premiums to cover the additional risk. **(§10005)**

Current Law/Policy—Crop Insurance	House Passed Bill (H.R.2)
Program Administration—Reviews, Compliance, and Integrity	
Funding for reviews, compliance, and program integrity. Provides up to $9,000,000 per fiscal year from the insurance fund for expenses, including operating and reviewing plans of insurance (including actuarial and related information) and for maintaining the actuarial soundness and financial integrity of the program. Allows the Secretary to merge some or all of the funds into the accounts of the Risk Management Agency (RMA) and to obligate the funds. **(7 U.S.C. 1516(b)(2)(C)(i) and (ii))**	Reduces the funds available for review, compliance, and program integrity from $9 million to $7 million per fiscal year. **(§10006)**
Reimbursement of Private Submissions	
Research, development, and maintenance costs. Authorizes FCIC to contract with private submitters to research and develop new crop insurance policies. FCIC may approve up to 75% of the projected total research and development costs to be paid in advance to an applicant. Provides for reimbursement of "reasonable research and development costs." **(7 U.S.C. 1522(b))**	Allows for reimbursement of "reasonable and actual research and development costs" related to policies that have been approved by the FCIC board. Defines *reasonable and actual costs* as costs based on (1) wage rates equal to two times Bureau of Labor Statistics hourly wage rates plus benefits or (2) actual documented costs incurred by the applicant. Prohibits disapproval of a user fee based on (1) it being compared to a maintenance fee or (2) the potential for the fee to result in a financial gain/loss to the applicant. Limits discretion of the FCIC board in approval of user fees. **(§10007(a))**
No comparable provision.	**Resubmission of reimbursement requests.** Provides that this section applies to reimbursement requests made on or after October 1, 2016, and that requests for reimbursement previously denied between October 1, 2016, and the date of enactment of this act may be resubmitted. **(§10007(b))**
Research and Development	
Priorities. Authorizes FCIC to conduct activities or contract for research and development efforts to maintain or improve existing policies or develop new policies. Directs FCIC to conduct or contract for specific types of coverage for specific crops or livestock. **(7 U.S.C. 1522(c))**	Strikes 16 completed studies and research and development contracts. **(§10008(a))** Defines *beginning farmer or rancher* for the purposes of research and development of whole farm insurance plans as having actively operated and managed a farm or ranch for less than 10 years. **(§10008(b))**

Table 12. (Continued)

Current Law/Policy—Crop Insurance	House Passed Bill (H.R.2)
	Requires FCIC to contract with one or more qualified entities to conduct research and development on (1) a policy to insure certain crops due to losses due to tropical storms or hurricanes; (2) create a separate practice for subsurface irrigation; (3) the difference in rates, average yields, and coverage levels of grain sorghum policies as compared to other feed grains within a county (with a reporting requirement of sorghum study results within a year of enactment) and; (4) establish an alternative (and optional) method of adjusting for quality losses that does not impact the APH of producers. **(§10008(c))**
Funding. Under Sections 522 and 523 of the Federal Crop Insurance Act, FCIC may enter into contracts to carry out research and development for new crop insurance policies but may not conduct research itself. **(7 U.S.C. 1522)**	Amends the act to discontinue partnerships for risk management development and implementation and to reduce CCC funding for research and development contracting from $12.5 million to no more than $8 million for FY2019 and each subsequent fiscal year. **(§10009)**
Education and Risk Management Assistance	
Underserved states. Authorizes FCIC to establish a program for crop insurance education and information to producers in states where federal crop insurance participation and availability are low and producers are underserved by the federal crop insurance program. **(7 U.S.C. 1524(a)(2))** **Partnerships for risk management education.** Authorizes the Secretary, through NIFA, to establish a program of competitive grants for public and private entities to educate agricultural producers about the full range of risk management activities, including futures, options, agricultural trade options, and crop insurance, among others. **(7 U.S.C. 1524(a)(3))** **Agricultural Management Assistance (AMA) Program.** Authorizes the AMA program, which provides financial and technical to producers in 16 specified states for conservation practices, risk mitigation, and market diversification.	Eliminates the crop insurance education and information program for targeted states carried out by RMA and AMA and reauthorizes the risk management education and assistance carried out through NIFA. Directs the FCIC insurance fund to transfer $5 million for FY2018 and each fiscal year thereafter to fund partnerships for risk management education. **(§10010)**

Current Law/Policy—Crop Insurance	House Passed Bill (H.R.2)
Provides $15 million in annual mandatory funding in FY2008-FY2014 and $10 million each fiscal year thereafter. Requires 50% to NRCS, 40% to RMA, and 10% to AMS. **(7 U.S.C. 1524(a)(2) and 1524(b))**	

Table 13. Title XI: Miscellaneous

Current Law/Policy	House Passed Bill (H.R. 2)
Subtitle A—Livestock	
Animal Health Protection Act (AHPA). AHPA contains provisions to prevent, detect, control, and eradicate diseases and pests to protect animal health. **(7 U.S.C. 8301 *et seq.*)** The 2014 farm bill (P.L. 113-79) establishes a National Animal Health Laboratory Network to develop and enhance national veterinary diagnostic capabilities, with an emphasis on surveillance planning, vulnerability analysis, and technology development and validation. Authorizes appropriations of $15 million per year for FY2014-FY2018. **(7 U.S.C. 8308a)**	Requires USDA to establish the **National Animal Disease Preparedness and Response Program** to address the risk of the introduction and spread of animal pests and diseases that affect the U.S. livestock and related industries, including export expansion. Directs USDA to sign cooperative agreements or other legal agreements with state departments of agriculture, offices of the chief animal health state official, land-grant colleges or universities or non-land-grant colleges of agriculture, colleges of veterinary medicine, state or national livestock producer organizations, state emergency agencies, veterinarian organizations recognized by the American Veterinary Medical Association, Indian tribes, federal agencies, or a combination of entities. To the extent practicable, activities include enhancing animal pest and disease analysis and surveillance; expanding outreach and education; targeting domestic inspection at vulnerable points; strengthening threat identification; improving biosecurity; enhancing emergency response capabilities; conducting technology development (veterinary biologics, diagnostics, animal drugs, and animal medical devices); enhancing electronic sharing of health data and risk analysis; and other activities as determined by USDA.

Table 13. (Continued)

Current Law/Policy	House Passed Bill (H.R. 2)
	USDA will notify entities of information required to enter into cooperative agreements, requirements for the use of funds, and criteria to evaluate the activities. USDA may consider entities' ability to contribute nonfederal funds but may not require entities to contribute funds. Requires recipients to use funds according to cooperative agreements. Recipients may enter sub-agreements with state entities responsible for animal disease prevention, surveillance, and response. Requires recipients to submit to USDA reports describing the purposes and results of activities no later than 90 days after completion of activities. Requires USDA to establish a **National Animal Health Vaccine Bank** to protect U.S. agriculture and food systems against terrorist attack, major disaster, and other emergencies. Requires the Vaccine Bank to maintain sufficient quantities of animal vaccine, antiviral, therapeutic, or diagnostic products for rapid response to animal disease outbreak that would have a damaging effect on human health or the economy. Directs it to leverage existing mechanisms and infrastructure of the National Veterinary Stockpile of APHIS. Also requires USDA to prioritize the acquisition of sufficient quantities of foot- and-mouth disease vaccine and consider contracting with one or more entities capable of producing foot-and-mouth disease vaccines and having surge production capacity. For FY2019, requires mandatory funding of $250 million from the CCC, of which $30 million is for **the National Animal Health Laboratory Network**, $70 million for the **National Animal Disease Preparedness and Response Program**, and $150 million for the **National Animal Health Vaccine Bank**. In FY2020-FY2023, $50 million per year in mandatory CCC funds is available for the three programs, of which not less than $30 million per year is for the National

Current Law/Policy	House Passed Bill (H.R. 2)
	Animal Disease Preparedness and Response Program. In addition, authorizes appropriations of $15 million per year for FY2019-FY2023 for the National Animal Health Laboratory Network. Funds made available may be used until expended. **(§11101)**
National Aquatic Animal Health Plan. Authorizes USDA to enter into cooperative agreements for the purpose of detecting, controlling, or eradicating diseases of aquaculture species and promoting species-specific best management practices on a cost-share basis. The Secretary may use authorities from AHPA **(7 U.S.C. 8301 *et seq.*)** to carry out the plan. Authorizes such sums as necessary to be appropriated in each of FY2008-FY2018. **(7 U.S.C. 8322)**	Authorizes appropriations of such sums as necessary to administer the program through FY2023. **(§11102)**
Veterinary training. Allows USDA to develop a program to maintain a sufficient number of federal and state veterinarians who are trained in the recognition and diagnosis of exotic and endemic animal diseases. **(7 U.S.C. 8318)**	Amends the section to include "veterinary teams, including those based at colleges of veterinary medicine" and inserts *and who are capable of providing effective services before, during, and after emergencies* at the end of the section. **(§11103)**
No comparable provision.	**Report on Food Safety Inspection Service (FSIS) guidance and outreach to small meat processors.** Requires the USDA inspector general to provide the Secretary of Agriculture a report on the effectiveness of existing FSIS guidance materials and tools for small and very small establishments. The report is to include (1) an evaluation of the outreach conducted by FSIS, (2) an evaluation of guidance materials and tools used by FSIS, (3) an evaluation of FSIS responsiveness to inquiries and issues, and (4) recommendations FSIS should take to improve regulatory clarity and consistency. **(§11104)**
Subtitle B—Beginning, Socially Disadvantaged, and Veteran Producers	
Outreach and assistance for socially disadvantaged farmers and ranchers and veteran farmers and ranchers. Provides for an outreach and technical assistance program to assist socially disadvantaged farmers and ranchers and veteran farmers and ranchers in	Reauthorizes $10 million in mandatory spending each year for FY2019-FY2023. Prioritizes grants under the program for agricultural education for youth under the age of 18, for agricultural employment and volunteer opportunities for youth under the age of 18, and

Table 13. (Continued)

Current Law/Policy	House Passed Bill (H.R. 2)
owning and operating farms and ranches and in participating equitably in the full range of agricultural programs offered by USDA. **(7 U.S.C. 2279(a)(4))**	for projects that demonstrate experience in providing such education and opportunities to socially disadvantaged youth. Reauthorizes appropriations of $20 million each for FY2019-FY2023. **(§11201)**
Office of Advocacy and Outreach. Leads USDA in implementing outreach and assistance to socially disadvantaged farmers and ranchers and veteran farmers and ranchers. Also carries out the functions and duties of the Office of Outreach and Diversity under the Assistant Secretary for Civil Rights, oversees the Office of Small Farms Coordination, and coordinates with NIFA on the administration of the beginning farmer and rancher development program. **(7 U.S.C. 6934)**	Renames the Office of Advocacy and Outreach as the **Office of Partnerships and Public Engagement**. Amends the section to improve access to USDA programs to limited resource producers, veteran farmers and ranchers, and tribal farmers and ranchers. Also adds **"promoting youth outreach"** as an objective of the newly named office. Reauthorizes appropriations funding of $2 million each fiscal year for FY2019- FY2023. **(§11202)**
No comparable provision.	**Commission on farm transition needs for 2050.** Establishes a commission to conduct a study on issues affecting the transition of agricultural operations from established farmers and ranchers to the next generation of farmers and ranchers. Outlines the composition and operation of the commission. Not later than one year from enactment, the commission is required to submit to the House Committee on Agriculture and the Senate Committee on Agriculture, Nutrition, and Forestry a report on the study results and recommendations the commission considers appropriate. **(§11203)**
The **Department of Agriculture Reorganization Act of 1994** authorizes the Secretary to streamline, reorganize, and manage USDA programs and activities**. (7 U.S.C. 6901** ***et seq.*****)**	**Agricultural youth organization coordinator.** Establishes the position of Agricultural Youth Coordinator to promote the role of youth-serving organizations and school-based agricultural education. Outlines contracts and cooperative agreements the coordinator may engage in with land- grant universities, research centers of the Agricultural Research Service, and nonprofit organizations. **(§11204)**
Subtitle C—Textiles	
Pima Agriculture Cotton Trust Fund. Establishes a trust fund in the Treasury of the United States for the purpose of reducing the injury to domestic manufacturers resulting	Repeals the Pima Cotton Trust Fund. **(§11301)**

Current Law/Policy	House Passed Bill (H.R. 2)
from tariffs on cotton fabric that are higher than tariffs on certain apparel articles made of cotton fabric. The Secretary may make payments to nationally recognized associations that promote pima cotton use, yarn spinners who produce ring spun cotton yarns, and manufacturers that cut and sew cotton shirts in the United States and that certify that they used imported cotton fabric in 2013. Payments to spinners and manufacturers are based on a production ratio and must be certified through affidavit. The Secretary shall transfer $16 million for each of the calendar years 2014-2018 from the CCC to the trust fund, which are to remain available until expended. **(7 U.S.C. 2101 note)**	
Agriculture Wool Apparel Manufacturers Trust Fund. Establishes a trust fund in the Treasury of the United States for the purpose of reducing the injury to domestic manufacturers resulting from tariffs on wool fabric that are higher than tariffs on certain apparel articles made of wool fabric. Annual payments based on one of four funding mechanisms are to be made to eligible domestic manufacturers of wool fabric and processors of wool material. The Secretary shall transfer up to $30 million in CCC funds for each of the calendar years 2014-2019 to the Agriculture Wool Trust. The funds remain available until expended. **(7 U.S.C. 7101 note)**	Repeals the Wool Apparel Manufacturers Trust Fund. **(§11302)**
Wool Research, Development, and Promotion Trust Fund. Establishes a trust fund for the purpose of assisting U.S. wool producers to improve the competitiveness of the American wool market. The trust fund sunsets effective January 1, 2015. Section 12316 of the 2014 farm bill provided $2.25 million of CCC funds for grants as defined in the trust fund for each of the calendar years 2015-2019. The funds remain available until expended. **(7 U.S.C. 7101 note)**	Repeals Wool Research and Promotion Grants Funding. **(§11303)**

Table 13. (Continued)

Current Law/Policy	House Passed Bill (H.R. 2)
No comparable provision.	Establishes the **Textile Trust Fund** for the purpose of reducing injury for domestic manufacturers resulting from tariffs on pima fabric and wool products that are higher than tariffs on certain apparel items made of pima cotton fabric and wool. The Secretary may make payments to nationally recognized associations who promote pima cotton use, yarn spinners who produce ring spun cotton yarns in the United States and certify through affidavit that they used pima cotton during the year in which the affidavit is filed and the previous calendar year, and manufacturers that cut and sew cotton shirts in the United States and that certify through affidavit that they used imported cotton fabric during the previous calendar year. In addition, the Textile Trust Fund is established for the purpose of reducing economic injury to domestic manufacturers resulting from tariffs on wool fabric that are higher than tariffs on certain apparel articles made of wool fabric. Payments to eligible wool manufacturers and processors must be certified through affidavit. For each of the calendar years 2019-2023, the Secretary shall transfer $8 million of CCC funds to the Textile Trust Fund for eligible manufacturers of pima cotton, $15 million to eligible wool manufacturers, and $2.25 million in grants for wool research and promotion. Funds are to remain available until expended. **(§11304)**
Sheep Production and Marketing Grant Program. Establishes a competitive grant program through USDA's Agricultural Marketing Service to improve the sheep industry, including infrastructure, business, resource development, or innovative approaches for long-term needs. Provided $1.5 million in CCC mandatory funds for FY2014 to remain available until expended. **(7 U.S.C. 1627a)**	Authorizes $2 million of CCC funds for FY2019 for the purposes of strengthening and enhancing the production of sheep and sheep products in the United States, with funds remaining available until expended. **(§11304)**

Current Law/Policy	**House Passed Bill (H.R. 2)**
Subtitle D—United States Grains Standards Act	
United States Grain Standards Act (USGSA). Establishes official marketing standards for grains and oilseeds and sets procedures for grain inspection and weighing services. Authorizes user fees for services. **(7 U.S.C. 71 *et seq.*)**	Restores exceptions created in the 2003 regulation **(7 C.F.R. 800.117)** that were revoked on or after September 30, 2015, upon the reauthorization of the USGSA
Exceptions to geographic areas for official agencies under the USGSA. Revises USGSA regulations to establish criteria to allow more than one designated official agency to inspect or weigh grain within a single geographic area. Criteria to consider for exceptions are (1) timely service, (2) nonuse of service, and (3) barge probe service. The rule enhances the orderly marketing of grain by providing segments of the grain industry with more cost-effective and responsive official grain inspection and weighing services without undermining the integrity of the official system. **(68 *Federal Register* 19137 (April 18, 2003))**	(Title III of P.L. 114-54). Grain handling facilities must request the restoration of exceptions within 180 days of enactment. **(§11401)**
Subtitle E—Nonisnsured Crop Disaster Assistance Program	
National Crop Assistance Program. Authorized to receive such sums as necessary in mandatory funding to make insurance available to growers of crops that are not insurable under the federal crop insurance program. Provides a payment to an eligible producer whose actual production is less than 50% of the established (historical) yield for the crop. Producers pay a fee of $250 per crop per county or $750 per producer per county, not to exceed $1,875 per producer. **(7 U.S.C. 7333)**	Amends the definition of *eligible crop* to include those crops that may be insurable under the crop insurance program but only for whole farm plans or policies that provide coverage for specific intervals based on weather indexes. **(§11501)** Increases the service fees to $350 per crop per county or $1,050 per producer per county, not to exceed $2,100 per producer. **(§11502)** Reauthorizes buy-up coverage through FY2023 and amends the premium for additional coverage to be proportional to a producer's share of the crop. **(§11503)**
Subtitle F—Other Matters	
In May 2017, USDA announced an agency reorganization that created an Under Secretary for Trade and Foreign Agricultural Affairs, an Under Secretary for Farm Production and Conservation, and an Assistant to the Secretary for Rural Development.	References to the former Under Secretary of Agriculture for Farm and Foreign Agricultural Services in various laws are changed to either the Under Secretary of Agriculture for Production and Conservation or the Under

Table 13. (Continued)

Current Law/Policy	House Passed Bill (H.R. 2)
The duties of the new Under Secretaries were previously assigned to the Under Secretary of Farm and Foreign Agricultural Affairs and the Under Secretary for Natural Resources and Environment. The duties of the Assistant to the Secretary were formerly assigned to the Under Secretary for Rural Development **(7 U.S.C. 6901 *et seq.*)** and the Reorganization Plan No. 2 of 1953 **(7 U.S.C. 2201 note)**	Secretary for Trade and Foreign Agricultural Affairs. References to the Under Secretary for Rural Development in various laws are amended by inserting *or other official designated by the Secretary*. **(§11601)**
Food for Peace Act. **(7 U.S.C. 1725(b))**	Removes Under Secretary of Agriculture for Farm and Foreign Agricultural Services and inserts Under Secretary for Trade and Foreign Agricultural Affairs in the Food Aid Consultative Group.
Department of Agriculture Reorganization Act of 1994. **(7 U.S.C. 6933(d)(1))**	Removes Under Secretary of Agriculture for Farm and Foreign Agricultural Services and inserts Under Secretary of Agriculture for Production and Conservation in the Office of Risk Management.
Department of Agriculture Reorganization Act of 1994. **(7 U.S.C. 6952(b)(3))**	Removes Under Secretary of Agriculture for Farm and Foreign Agricultural Services and inserts Under Secretary for Trade and Foreign Agricultural Affairs in the Multiagency Task Force.
Higher Education Act of 1965. **(20 U.S.C. 1131c(c)(1)(A))**	Removes Under Secretary of Agriculture for Farm and Foreign Agricultural Services and inserts Under Secretary of Agriculture for Trade and Foreign Agricultural Affairs in the Interagency Committee on Minority Careers in International Affairs.
Agricultural Act of 1961 and Consolidated Farm and Rural Development Act. **(7 U.S.C. 1991(a)(13)(D))**	In the definitions, inserts *or other official designated by the Secretary of Agriculture* after *Under Secretary for Rural Development* where it appears and inserts *or designated official* after *Under Secretary* where it appears.
Agricultural Marketing Act of 1946. **(7 U.S.C. 1627b(f)(3)(B)(i))**	Inserts *or other official designated by the Secretary* after *Under Secretary of Agriculture for Rural Development* in the National Sheep Industry Improvement Center.
Native American Business Development, Trade Promotion, and Tourism Act of 2000. **(25 U.S.C. 4305(a)(2)(A))**	Inserts *or other official designated by the Secretary of Agriculture* after *Under Secretary of Agriculture for Rural Development* in the Intertribal Tourism Demonstration Projects.

Current Law/Policy	**House Passed Bill (H.R. 2)**
Rehabilitation Act of 1973. **(29 U.S.C. 721(a)(11)(C))**	Inserts *or other official designated by the Secretary of Agriculture* after *Under Secretary for Rural Development of the Department of Agriculture* in the State Plans for Vocational Rehabilitation Services.
Department of Agriculture Reorganization Act of 1994. Ends the Secretary of Agriculture's authority to reorganize USDA two years after the enactment of the act and lists functions that are not affected by the two-year termination date. **(7 U.S.C. 7014(b)(8))**	Amends the code to insert *section 772 of the Agriculture, Rural Development, Food and Drug Administration, and Related Agencies Appropriations Act, 2018, or the Agriculture and Nutrition Act of 2018.* **(§11602)** Section 772 establishes the position of Under Secretary of Farm Production and Conservation, which replaces the Under Secretary of Agriculture for Farm and Foreign Agricultural Services. Section 772 also amends 5 U.S.C. 5314, which lists Level III positions of the Executive Schedule, by striking *Under Secretary for Farm and Foreign Agricultural Services* and inserting *Under Secretary of Farm Production and Conservation* and *Under Secretary of Agriculture for Trade and Foreign Agricultural Affairs*.
USDA conference transparency. Requires USDA to provide annual reports to the House Committee on Agriculture and the Senate Committee on Agriculture, Nutrition, and Forestry on conferences sponsored or held by USDA or attended by USDA employees. Conferences that cost the federal government less than $10,000 are excluded from reporting requirements. **(7 U.S.C. 2255b(a)(3)(A))**	Amends the subsection by raising the exclusion to $75,000. **(§11603)**
No comparable provision.	**National Agriculture Imagery Program.** Requires USDA, through the Farm Service Agency, to carry out a national agriculture imagery program to annually acquire aerial imagery during the agricultural growing season. Requires the data to (1) include high resolution processed digital imagery; (2) be available in a format that can be provided to federal, state, and private sector entities; (3) be technologically compatible with geospatial information technology; and (4) be consistent with the standards of the Federal Geographic Data

Table 13. (Continued)

Current Law/Policy	House Passed Bill (H.R. 2)
	Committee. Authorizes an appropriation of $23 million for FY2019 and each fiscal year thereafter. **(§11604)**
Commodity Promotion, Research, and Information Act of 1996. Authorizes the establishment of commodity promotion and research programs (i.e., checkoff programs). **(7 U.S.C. 7401 *et seq.*)**	**Report on inclusion of natural stone products in Commodity Promotion, Research, and Information Act of 1996.** Requires that not later than 180 days after enactment, USDA is required to submit a report to the House Committee on Agriculture that examines the effects of establishing a promotion and research program for natural stone. The report is to cover the effects a program would have on (1) research and promotion of natural stone, (2) development and expansion of domestic markets, (3) economic activity of the natural stone industry subject to a promotion board, (4) economic development in rural areas, and (5) benefits to U.S. consumers of natural stone. **(§11605)**
Peanuts Standards Board. Establishes a board consisting of producers and industry representatives from peanut-producing states. Board members are appointed from three regions: Southeast (Alabama, Georgia, and Florida); Southwest (Texas, Oklahoma, and New Mexico); and Virginia/Carolina (Virginia and North Carolina). Members of the board are to advise the Secretary on quality and handling standards for domestic and import peanuts. **(7 U.S.C. 7958(c))**	**South Carolina inclusion in Virginia/Carolina peanut-producing region.** Amends the designated Virginia/Carolina region by adding South Carolina as a state represented on the Peanut Standards Board. **(§11606)**
USDA reorganization. Provides the Secretary with the authority to streamline, reorganize, and manage USDA programs and activities. **(7 U.S.C. 6901 *et seq.*)**	Authorizes USDA to establish, within the Office of the Secretary, a **Food Loss and Waste Reduction Liaison** to coordinate federal programs to measure and reduce the incidence of food loss and waste, provide information and resources, and raise awareness of the liability protections for donated foods. **(§11607)**
Cotton classification services. Authorizes USDA to make cotton classification and classification fee collection services available to cotton producers. **(7 U.S.C. 473a)**	Amends the cotton classification section by allowing employees who are hired to classify cotton to work up to 240 days in a service year and be rehired non-competitively every year for the same position, or a successor position, if they meet performance standards. **(§11608)**

Current Law/Policy	**House Passed Bill (H.R. 2)**
No comparable provision.	**Century Farms Program.** Establishes a program under which the Secretary of Agriculture recognizes any farm or ranch, as defined in Cooperative Services Grant Programs, which has been in continuous operation for at least 100 years, and has been owned by the same family for at least 100 consecutive years, as verified through appropriate documentation. **(§11609)**
No comparable provision.	**Report on agricultural innovation.** Requires USDA, in consultation with EPA and FDA, to prepare and submit a report to the House Committee on Agriculture and the Senate Committee on Agriculture, Nutrition, and Forestry on plans for improving federal government policies and procedures with respect to gene editing and other precision plant breeding methods. **(§11610)**
No comparable provision.	**Report on dog importation.** USDA, in consultation with the Secretaries of Commerce, Health and Human Services, and Homeland Security, is to submit a report to the House Committee on Agriculture and the Senate Committee on Agriculture, Nutrition, and Forestry on the importation of dogs. The report is to include (1) an estimate of the number of dogs imported annually, (2) the number of dogs imported for resale, (3) the number imported for resale but denied importation due to failure of Animal Welfare Act (7 U.S.C. 2148) requirements, and (4) Secretary recommendations of federal statutory changes needed for importation for resale. **(§11611)**
No comparable provision.	**Prohibition on slaughter of dogs and cats for human consumption.** Amends the Animal Welfare Act (7 U.S.C. 2131 *et seq.*) to prohibit knowingly slaughtering dogs or cats for human consumption. Also prohibits the transporting, possessing, buying, selling, or donation of a dog or cat for such purposes and imposes penalties for violations. The provision does not limit any state or local law to protect animal welfare. **(§11612)**

Table 13. (Continued)

Current Law/Policy	House Passed Bill (H.R. 2)
Subtitle G—Protecting Interstate Commerce	
No comparable provision.	**Prohibition against interference by state and local governments with production of agricultural products from other states.** Prohibits any state or local government from setting standards or conditions on the production or manufacture of agricultural products from other states if the products are produced or manufactured according to federal law or the laws of the state or locality. **(§11701)** **Federal cause of action to challenge state regulation of interstate commerce.** Empowers producers, consumers, trade organizations, governments, and others affected by a state standard or condition for products sold in interstate commerce to bring action in the appropriate court to invalidate the state standard or condition and to seek damages for economic losses, subject to a 10-year statute of limitations. Requires courts to issue a preliminary injunction on the state standard or condition unless the state provides convincing evidence it would prevail in the case or the injunction would cause irreparable harm. **(§11702)**

APPENDIX

Table A-1. Summary of House-Adopted Amendments to H.R. 2 Amendments Adopted as of May 18, 2018

Title/Amendment	Summary Description
Title I, Commodities	
H.Amdt. 606	Exempts APHIS as one of the agencies (along with Natural Resources Conservation Service and the Farm Service Agency) to which exempted producers would not be required to make annual reports on their agricultural enterprises. Exempted producers are producers or landowners eligible to participate in any conservation or commodity program administered by the Secretary.

Title/Amendment	Summary Description
H.Amdt. 608	Amends the Title I ARC and PLC programs under current law by streamlining their sign-up process. USDA is directed to change the regulatory requirements from an annual sign up to a `one and done' process through crop year 2023 for ARC and PLC only.
Title II, Conservation	
H.Amdt. 586	Amends a new provision under EQIP allowing USDA to contract with irrigation districts, irrigation associations, and acequias to also include drainage districts. Expands payments for water conservation activities under EQIP to also include the use of existing drainage systems or to upgrade drainage systems to provide irrigation or water efficiency.
H.Amdt. 587	Adds a sense of Congress statement encouraging partnerships at the watershed level between nonpoint sources and regulated point sources to advance the goals of the Federal Water Pollution Control Act (Clean Water Act).
H.Amdt. 610	Amends the Soil and Water Resources Conservation Act of 1977 (P.L. 95-192) to require USDA to conduct two comprehensive appraisals of soil, water, and related natural resources (completed by year-end 2022). Adds a new requirement for assessing and monitoring USDA programs and initiatives and their progress in reaching natural resource and environmental objectives. Requires a report in the third fiscal year after enactment and periodically thereafter. Authorizes appropriations equal to 1% of all mandatory conservation program funding (excluding CRP).
Title III, Trade	
H.Amdt. 612	Amends the Farmer-to-Farmer (F2F) program (7 U.S.C. 1737) to add specificity to the types of technical assistance provided by American volunteers under this program. Also establishes both a geographically defined crop yield metrics system for evaluating the degree of F2F program success and a grant program to facilitate new partnerships and innovative activities under the F2F program.
Title IV, Nutrition	
H.Amdt. 588	Amends the current law definition of *food* to allow the purchase of multivitamin- mineral dietary supplements (as defined by the amendment) with SNAP benefits.
H.Amdt. 606 (Nutrition)	Amends Nutrition title of reported H.R. 2 provisions as follows: • Amends changes to categorical eligibility (§4006 in reported bill) to make them effective October 1, 2020. • Expands exceptions to standard utility allowances changes (§4010 in reported bill), holding harmless households with elderly *or disabled* members.
	• Amends changes to work-related rules (§4015 in reported bill): • Volunteer work only meets work requirements if no more than 6 months in a 12-month period.

Table A-1. (Continued)

Title/Amendment	Summary Description
	• Amends definition of work program to include a program of employment and training for veterans operated by the Department of Labor or Department of Veterans Affairs and approved by the Secretary. • Amends FY2019-FY2020 transition period to require proposal's unemployment-based waiver policies to apply during transition period. • Makes one of the grounds for unemployment-based waivers more permissive, by, among other criteria, requiring areas applying for waivers to have 24-month average unemployment rates below 7%, increased from 6% in the reported bill. • Amends states' limits on individual exemptions to create different rules based on year. For FY2021-FY2025, 15% of covered individuals, as defined by bill, in FY2019. For FY2026 and thereafter, 12% of covered individuals in FY2019. • Restores a state's authority to offer workfare. Amends workfare to exempt those under 18 years of age, instead of 16 years of age. Eliminates state option to exempt an individual complying with TANF work requirements from workfare requirements. • Amends student ineligibility rules to make eligible those responsible for the care of an incapacitated person, also expands certain parent eligibility rules to apply to other household members responsible for children. • Strikes authority to reallocate Employment & Training funds, instead requiring states' unspent allocated funding to be returned to the Treasury. • Allows a state to request earned income data from the Internal Revenue Service for purposes of ensuring equitable treatment among all households (including those containing a married couple). • Amends mobile technologies provision (§ 4017 in reported bill) to: require non- exempt retail food stores to bear the costs of equipment and supplies for the redemption of benefits, including fees; requires that states make the demonstration projects voluntary for all retail food stores and allow recipients to redeem benefits at non-participating retail food stores. • Amends the nutrition education provision (§4033 in reported bill) to: allow some specified nutrition education administrative costs to be eligible for federal matching funds authorized by Section 16(a) of the Food and Nutrition Act; make nutrition education funds available for obligation for two fiscal years.

Title/Amendment	Summary Description
	• Adds to the Nutrition title two sections that were not in H.R. 2 as reported: • Requires a minimum certification period of not less than one year for the Commodity Supplemental Food Program (CSFP) and allows the Secretary to approve state request for longer certification periods if certain requirements are met. • Requires the Secretary to review the 2012 and 2016 regulations which updated the school meal nutrition standards and created nutrition standards for foods served outside of the meal program, including any requirements for milk. Revised final regulations are to be based on research focused on school-age children, not add costs to the operation of the program, and maintain healthy meals for students.
H.Amdt. 613	Adds language seeking to ensure that if an individual becomes ineligible to participate in SNAP as a household member due to failure to meet the work requirements, the remaining household members (including children), shall not become ineligible to apply to participate in the supplemental nutrition assistance program due to such individual's ineligibility.
H.Amdt. 614	Amends SNAP law to disqualify individuals convicted of specified federal crimes (including murder, rape, and certain crimes against children) and state offenses determined by the Attorney General to be substantially similar from receiving SNAP, regardless of whether they are fleeing felons or compliant with the terms of their sentence.
H.Amdt. 615	Requires the Secretary of Agriculture to conduct a feasibility study on developing a Thrifty Food Plan to calculate the funding for the Nutritional Assistance Program for Puerto Rico.
H.Amdt. 616	Amends SNAP law to provide states the authority to contract out certification or any other SNAP administrative function. Contractor must have no direct or indirect financial interest in an approved retail food store.
H.Amdt. 617	Amends a 2014 farm bill provision on service of Indian and Alaska Native traditional foods in public facilities, expanding the list of specified public programs and facilities included and protected from liability.
H.Amdt. 618	Amends a provision of the 2008 farm bill to require the Secretary to again carry out a study of the feasibility and effects of including Puerto Rico in SNAP as opposed to the Nutrition Assistance for Puerto Rico block grant. Provides $1 million in mandatory funding and an authorization for additional discretionary funding.
Title VI, Rural Infrastructure and Economic Development	
H.Amdt. 590	Amends the Consolidated Farm and Rural Development Act to permit funding for the Community Facilities program to include refinancing a debt obligation of a rural hospital as an eligible loan or loan guarantee if the assistance would help preserve access to health service in a rural community and improve the financial position of the hospital.

Table A-1. (Continued)

Title/Amendment	Summary Description
H.Amdt. 591	Amends the Consolidated Farm and Rural Development Act and the Rural Electrification Act of 1936 to exclude the first 1,500 individuals residing in housing located on a military base from being included in determining whether an area is "rural" or a "rural area." Also amends the Rural Electrification Act of 1936 for purposes of the Distance Learning and Telemedicine program to define *rural area* as any area other than a city or town that has a population of greater than 50,000 inhabitants, any urbanized area contiguous and adjacent to a city or town of 50,000 inhabitants, or any city or town with a population greater than 20,000.
H.Amdt. 592	Adds a new section to the Rural Development Title to establish a task force under the Federal Communications Commission (FCC) to review the connectivity and technological needs of precision agriculture. The task force will consult with the Secretary and collaborate with public and private stakeholders to develop policy recommendations, recommend new rules or amendments to the FCC to achieve the goals of the task force, and recommend specific steps that the FCC should consider to ensure that available farm data are reflected in existing or future programs of the FCC supporting broadband deployment, and to direct available funding to unserved agricultural lands where needed. Directs the Secretary to submit to the task force a list of all federal programs available for the expansion of broadband access on unserved agricultural land. Defines composition of the task force and directs it to submit a report to the chairman of the FCC detailing steps being taken to measure the availability of broadband access service on agricultural land.
Title VII, Research	
H.Amdt. 593	Amends the Food, Agriculture, Conservation and Trade Act of 1990 to add chronic wasting disease as an eligible activity for research and extension grants under the High- Priority Research and Development Initiative.
H.Amdt. 621	Amends the National Agricultural Research, Extension, and Teaching Policy Act to deem any "recently designated"1890 institutions as having been designated an "eligible institution" on or after September 1978. A "recently designated" 1890 institution is one designated as an 1890 institution after September 1999. An "eligible institution" is eligible to receive research and extension formula funding.
Title VIII, Forestry	
H.Amdt. 594	Establishes that receipts from Stewardship Contracting projects shall be considered monies received from the NFS, making those receipts subject to revenue-sharing laws.
H.Amdt. 595	Replaces Section 8331 and expands the availability of Good Neighbor Agreements to include federally recognized Indian tribes and county governments.

Title/Amendment	Summary Description
H.Amdt. 596	Requires the Secretary of Agriculture or the Secretary of the Interior to complete the environmental assessment for a salvage operation or reforestation activity within 60 days after the conclusion of a catastrophic event with specified time frames for public scoping, comments, and objections. Prohibits federal courts from issuing restraining orders or injunctions for any salvage operation or reforestation activity in response to a large-scale catastrophic event.
H.Amdt. 597	Requires the Secretary of Agriculture or the Secretary of the Interior to consider only the proposed action and no-action alternative while preparing an environmental assessment pursuant to NEPA for a forest management activity within areas designated as insect and disease treatment areas under HFRA (16 U.S.C. 6591a).
H.Amdt. 598	Exempts all National Forest System land in Alaska from the Forest Service Roadless Area Conservation Rule as published in 66 *Federal Register* 9, January 12, 2001.
H.Amdt. 599	Authorizes the Secretary to convey 1,520 acres of NFS land to the village of Santa Clara, NM.
H.Amdt. 600	Directs the Secretary of Agriculture to promulgate regulations revising the process to issue special use authorizations for communications sites or rights-of-ways on NFS lands.
H.Amdt. 601	Directs the Secretary of Agriculture and Secretary of the Interior to submit annual reports to Congress on specified wildfire and forest management metrics.
H.Amdt. 602	Reauthorizes the Collaborative Forest Landscape Restoration Program (16 U.S.C. 7303) through FY2023 and authorizes the Secretary to extend projects beyond 10 years.
H.Amdt. 603	Authorizes the Secretary to convey 3.61 acres of NFS land to Dolores County, CO, for specified purposes, subject to a reversionary clause.
H.Amdt. 622	Adds invasive vegetation to the definition of a forest that is experiencing declining forest health for purposes of designating insect and disease treatment areas within the NFS under HFRA (16 U.S.C. 6591a).
H.Amdt. 623	Directs the Secretary to make vacant grazing allotments available to holders of existing grazing permits under certain conditions.
H.Amdt. 624	Creates a pilot research program on the Lincoln, Cibola, and Gila National Forests to study the effectiveness of silvicultural management technique to address natural resource concerns. Projects in the pilot program are subject to the refusal of the county government in which the project is located. Establishes an arbitration program as an alternative dispute resolution process for challenges to projects in the pilot program.
H.Amdt. 625	Creates a new competitive forestry research program.
Title XI, Horticulture	
H.Amdt. 626	Amends the Plant Protection Act (7 U.S.C 770 *et seq.*) to apply import restrictions to prevent the arrival of forest pests. Directs the Forest Service and Animal Plant Health Inspection Service to cooperate in responding to forest plant pests. Instructs the Secretary to produce a report on

Table A-1. (Continued)

Title/Amendment	Summary Description
	"Interception of Forest Pests" to Congress by March 1, 2021. Directs the use of available funds for all activities necessary for pest eradication, including pest identification, development of pest-specific management plan, and implementation of that plan.
Title XI, Miscellaneous	
H.Amdt. 604	Requires USDA to establish not more than three regional Cattle and Carcass Grading Correlation and Training Centers to provide education and training for cattle and carcass beef graders of the Agricultural Marketing Service, cattle producers, and other professionals involved in the reporting, delivery, and grading of feeder cattle, live cattle, and carcasses. The centers are to be located near cattle feeding or slaughtering areas and are to coordinate the existing resources of USDA, state agricultural extension and research centers, relevant contract markets, and producers. Funding for the centers may not be used for new construction or remodeling of facilities but may be used for rental space. The centers may accept in-kind donations to cover such spaces.
H.Amdt. 629	Amends Section 309 of the Federal Crop Insurance Reform and Department of Agriculture Reorganization Act of 1994 (7 U.S.C. 6921) to require the Secretary of Agriculture to (1) establish an Office of Tribal Relations within the Office of Partnerships and Public Engagement to advise the Secretary on policies related to Indian tribes and (2) establish the "New Beginnings Initiative," under which the Secretary shall provide funds to a land-grant college or university in the amount equal to the amount such land-grant college or university expends for providing educational programs and services for, or tuition paid with respect to, Indians at a land-grant college or university.
H.Amdt. 630	Amends Section 26 of the Animal Welfare Act (7 U.S.C. 2156) to extend to the territories the existing prohibition on animal fighting to which the 50 states are currently subject. Makes it unlawful to sell, buy, or transport in interstate or foreign commerce any knife or sharp object to be used on the leg of a bird as a weapon in animal fighting.
H.Amdt. 632	Allows the Secretary of the Interior, in conjunction with the director of the U.S. Fish and Wildlife Service, to authorize the issuance of depredation permits to livestock farmers for black vultures, otherwise prohibited by federal law, to prevent black vultures from taking livestock during the calving season. Allows permits to be issued only in states or regions where producers are affected by black vultures. Requires producers to report takings to the proper enforcement agencies.

Source: Congress.gov.

Notes: The amendments to H.R. 2 in this table do not have assigned section numbers within the bill. As such, the listing of these amendments by title is an effort to categorize them based on CRS's understanding of their substantive content. It is not meant to indicate to which title they may ultimately be assigned.

In: The Farm Bill
Editor: Billie Grant
ISBN: 978-1-53615-294-4

Chapter 2

THE PRESIDENT'S FY2018 BUDGET REQUEST FOR AGRICULTURE APPROPRIATIONS AND THE FARM BILL*

Congressional Research Service

BACKGROUND

The Trump Administration released its first full budget request on May 23, 2017. It proposes specific amounts for the FY2018 Agriculture appropriation as well as legislative changes to various mandatory spending programs, including those in the farm bill.

The Administration's budget outline, released on March 16, 2017, proposed an overall 21% reduction for the U.S. Department of Agriculture, and it mentioned seven specific discretionary programs for elimination or reduction. It did not address any mandatory spending proposals.

---

* This is an edited, reformatted and augmented version of Congressional Research Service Publication No. IN10710, dated June 2, 2017.

This chapter separates the President's budget request into proposed changes for agriculture based on congressional jurisdiction. The proposals are likely to be treated differently in Congress because of separate appropriations and authorizing committee jurisdictions. The Appropriations committees will determine funding levels for FY2018 through the budget and appropriations process and may incorporate elements of the request. The Agriculture committees may respond to the mandatory spending proposals, which would need separate legislative action to be enacted, and the committees may wait until 2018, when the current farm bill is due for reauthorization.

Agriculture Appropriations Request

The President's budget request for FY2018 proposes an estimated $5.1 billion reduction (-24%) in discretionary spending for accounts that are in the Agriculture and Related Agencies Appropriations bill (*Figure 1, Table 1*). This CRS estimate is preliminary and subject to rescoring by the Congressional Budget Office (CBO). The estimate is based on Agriculture appropriations jurisdiction, which does not cover all of USDA. It excludes the Forest Service, includes the Food and Drug Administration and, in the House, includes the Commodity Futures Trading Commission. It is also relative to the enacted FY2017 appropriation (P.L. 115-31) rather than the FY2017 continuing resolution that existed when the budget request was assembled.

The $5.1 billion reduction to Agriculture appropriations is comprised largely of the following proposals:

- $1.7 billion reduction in foreign food aid (-90%, by eliminating Food for Peace and McGovern-Dole Food for Education),
- $912 million reduction to rural development (-30%, including eliminating rural water and waste disposal grants, and the Rural Business Cooperative Service),
- $382 million reduction to agricultural research agencies (-13%),

- $260 million reduction to conservation programs (-25%),
- $250 million reduction to discretionary domestic nutrition assistance programs, primarily the Supplemental Nutrition Program for Women, Infants and Children (WIC, -3%),
- $234 million reduction to the Food and Drug Administration (-8.5%),
- $136 million reduction to animal and plant health inspection (-14%),
- $115 million reduction to Farm Service Agency operations (-7%), including a 13% reduction in the amount of ownership and operating loans that can be made to farmers,
- $1.1 billion of rescissions and limitations beyond the FY2017 level of $1.8 billion (including a $212 million rescission of prior-year funds for research facilities, and $410 million of limitations to mandatory programs beyond the FY2017 level of $744 million).

The request also proposes reducing USDA staffing by over 5,000 employees (-5%), including an 8% reduction at the Farm Service Agency (headquarters and county offices), 19% at Rural Development, and 10% at the Agricultural Research Service.

Farm Bill and Other Legislative Requests

The President's budget request proposes nearly $240 billion of reductions over 10 years to mandatory spending programs that are in the jurisdiction of the House and Senate Agriculture Committees. The reduction includes $229 billion affecting farm bill programs, nearly $2 billion in rural development programs, and $9 billion of proposed user fees (*Table 2*). This Office of Management and Budget estimate is subject to rescoring by CBO.

This request may be an indicator of the Administration's priorities for the next farm bill, which is expected to receive legislative attention by 2018, when the current farm bill expires. The request proposes reducing the Supplemental Nutrition Assistance Program (SNAP), capping crop insurance premiums, eliminating a crop insurance option, tightening income eligibility requirements for farm subsidies, reducing conservation programs, and eliminating various smaller farm bill programs such as trade promotion and specialty crop support.

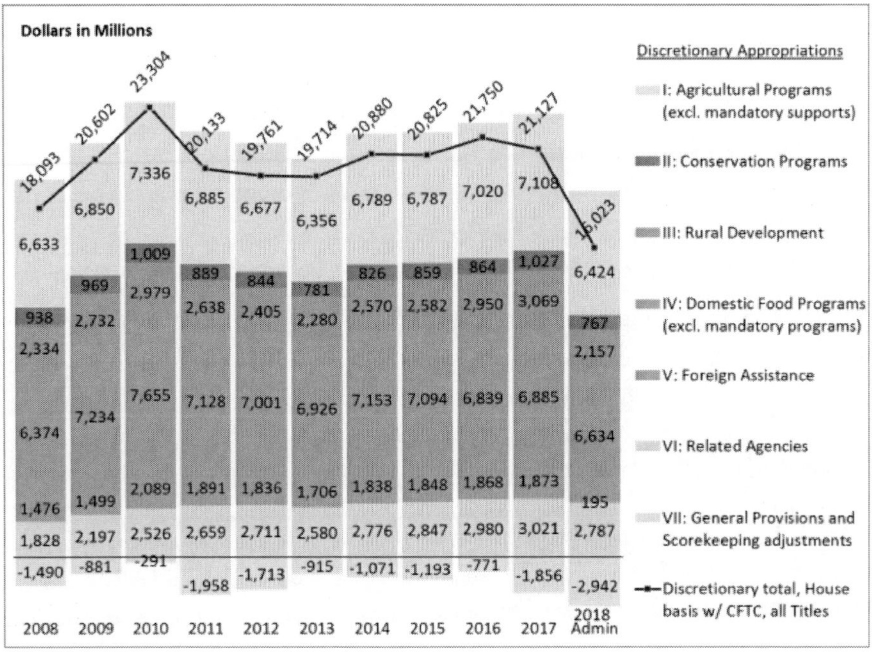

Source: CRS.

Notes: FY0218 data are a preliminary compilation by CRS of congressional appropriations jurisdiction based on the President's budget. Includes CFTC in Related Agencies in all years for comparability, regardless of jurisdiction.

Figure 1. Discretionary Agriculture Appropriations, by Title, Since FY2008.

These reductions are relative to a farm bill baseline of about $870 billion for the same period based on the January 2017 CBO baseline projection. If enacted, the $229 billion subtotal of farm bill reductions would imply a 26% reduction to the farm bill baseline over FY2018-FY2027. The SNAP proposals would be a 28% reduction to its $672 billion 10-year baseline, and the crop insurance proposals would be a 35% reduction to its $79 billion baseline.

Table 1. President's FY2018 Request for Agriculture and Related Agencies Appropriations (discretionary budget authority in millions of dollars)

	FY2017	**FY2018**	**Change from FY2017 to FY2018 Request**	
Agency or Major Program	P.L. 115-31	Admin. Request		
Title I. Agricultural Programs				
Departmental Administration	410.1	383.0	-27.1	-6.6%
Agricultural Research Service	1,269.8	993.1	-276.7	-21.8%
National Institute of Food and Agriculture	1,362.9	1,252.8	-110.1	-8.1%
National Agricultural Statistics Service	171.2	185.7	+14.4	+8.4%
Economic Research Service	86.8	76.7	-10.1	-11.6%
Animal and Plant Health Inspection Service	949.4	812.9	-136.5	-14.4%
Agricultural Marketing Service	86.2	78.6	-7.6	-8.8%
Grain Inspection, Packers and Stockyards Administration	43.5	43.0	-0.5	-1.2%
Food Safety and Inspection Service	1,032.1	1,038.1	+6.0	+0.6%
Farm Service Agency	1,623.5	1,508.3	-115.2	-7.1%
Risk Management Agency	74.8	55.0	-19.8	-26.5%
Subtotal	7,110.3	6,427.1	-683.2	-9.6%
FSA Farm Loan Authority	8,002.6	6,953.9	-1,048.7	-13.1%
Title II. Conservation Programs				
Conservation Operations	864.5	766.0	-98.5	-11.4%
Watershed and Flood Prevention	150.0	0.0	-150.0	-100.0%
Watershed Rehabilitation Program	12.0	0.0	-12.0	-100.0%
Subtotal	1,026.5	766.0	-260.5	-25.4%
Title III. Rural Development				
Salaries and Expenses (including transfers)	675.8	624.0	-51.8	-7.7%
Rural Economic Infrastructure Grants	—	161.9	+161.9	—
Rural Housing Service	1,654.9	1,365.3	-289.6	-17.5%
Rural Business-Cooperative Service	97.7	0.0	-97.7	-100.0%
Rural Utilities Service	639.9	5.4	-634.5	-99.2%
Subtotal	3,068.3	2,156.6	-911.7	-29.7%
Rural Development Loan Authority	37,288.9	33,477.0	-3,811.9	-10.2%
Title IV. Domestic Food Programs				
Women, Infants, and Children (WIC) Program	6,350.0	6,150.0	-200.0	-3.1%

Table 1. (Continued)

	FY2017	FY2018	Change from FY2017 to FY2018 Request	
Agency or Major Program	P.L. 115-31	Admin. Request		
Commodity Assistance Programs	315.1	293.6	-21.5	-6.8%
Nutrition Programs Administration	170.7	148.5	-22.2	-13.0%
Discretionary amounts in child nutrition, SNAP	48.0	40.9	-7.1	-14.7%
Subtotal	6,883.9	6,633.1	-250.8	-3.6%
Title V. Foreign Assistance				
Foreign Agricultural Service and other admin.	205.3	195.1	-10.2	-5.0%
Food for Peace Title II	1,466.0	0.0	-1,466.0	-100.0%
McGovern-Dole Food for Education	201.6	0.0	-201.6	-100.0%
Subtotal	1,872.9	195.1	-1,677.8	-89.6%
Title VI. Related Agencies				
Food and Drug Administration	2,771.2	2,536.7	-234.4	-8.5%
Commodity Futures Trading Commission	[250.0]	250.0[a]	+0.0	+0.0%
Subtotal	[3,021.2]	2,786.7	-234.4	-7.8%
Title VII. General Provisions				
Changes in Mandatory Program Spending	-744.0	-1,154.2	-410.2	+55.1%
Rescissions	-854.0	-1,424.7	-570.7	+66.8%
Other appropriations	266.0	0.0	-266.0	-100.0%
Scorekeeping adjustments	-524.0	-363.0	+161.0	-30.7%
Subtotal	-1,855.9	-2,941.9	-1,086.0	+58.5%
Totals				
Discretionary: Senate basis w/o CFTC	20,877.0	15,772.5	-5,104.5	-24.5%
Discretionary: House basis w/ CFTC	[21,127.0]	16,022.5	-5,104.5	-24.2%

Source: CRS, using P.L. 115-31, and Office of Management and Budget, President's Budget for FY2018: Appendix, May 2017.

Notes: FY0218 data are a preliminary compilation by CRS of congressional appropriations jurisdiction, based on the President's budget. Bracketed amounts are not in the official totals due to differing House-Senate appropriations jurisdiction for the Commodity Futures Trading Commission.

[a] As an independent agency, CFTC submits its budget concurrently to Congress and the Administration. CFTC is requesting a different amount in its budget justification: $281.5 million, an increase of $31.5 million (+12.6%). See CRS Insight IN10715, When an Agency's Budget Request Does Not Match the President's Request: The FY2018 CFTC Request and "Budget Bypass", by [author name scrubbed], [author name scrubbed], and [author name scrubbed].

Table 2. President's Request for Mandatory Programs in Agriculture and the Farm Bill

	10-year reduction FY2018-FY2027 ($ billion)
Farm Bill Savings	
SNAP reform (including categorical eligibility, able-bodied waivers, state matching)	-190.9
Crop Insurance Premium Subsidy Limit (create new $40,000 limit)	-16.2
Eliminate Harvest Price Option (reduce crop insurance)	-11.9
AGI Eligibility Limit (tighten the limit from $900,000 to $500,000)	-1.1
Conservation programs (including reductions to Agricultural Management Assistance, Regional Conservation Partnership Program, Conservation Stewardship Program)	-5.8
Eliminate other programs (including Specialty Crop Block Grants, Farmers Markets Promotion, Market Access Program, Foreign Market Development, Pima Cotton and Wool trust funds)	-3.1
Subtotal of farm bill programs	-229.0
Other reductions	
Eliminate Interest Payments to Rural Utilities (cushion of credit account)	-1.4
Eliminate Rural Economic Development Program (cushion of credit account)	-0.5
Create user fees	
Food Safety and Inspection Service (fee for inspections)	-5.9
SNAP Retailer Application Fee (fee to become a retailer)	-2.4
Grain Inspection, Packers, and Stockyards Admin. (licensing and standards development)	-0.3
Agricultural Marketing Service (to pay for marketing orders)	-0.2
Animal and Plant Health Inspection Service (animal welfare, biotechnology, veterinary biologics)	-0.2
Total	-239.8

Source: CRS, compiled from Office of Management and Budget, President's Budget for FY2018: Major Savings and Reforms, and Appendix, May 2017. Other parts of the budget may propose changes to programs that were not included in the Major Savings list.

In: The Farm Bill
Editor: Billie Grant
ISBN: 978-1-53615-294-4

Chapter 3

BUDGET ISSUES SHAPING THE 2018 FARM BILL*

Jim Monke

ABSTRACT

The farm bill is an omnibus, multi-year law that governs an array of agricultural and food programs. It provides an opportunity for policymakers to periodically address a broad range of agricultural and food issues. The farm bill has typically undergone reauthorization about every five years. The 115th Congress has considered a new farm bill but has not enacted one to date. Both the House and the Senate passed versions of a 2018 farm bill (H.R. 2) in June 2018. Conference proceedings officially began in September 2018 but have not reached agreement.

The farm bill provides an opportunity for Congress to choose how much support, if any, to provide for various agriculture and nutrition programs and how to allocate it among competing constituencies. Under congressional budgeting rules, many programs are assumed to continue beyond the end of a farm bill. From a budgetary perspective, this provides

* This is an edited, reformatted and augmented version of Congressional Research Service Publication No. R45425, Updated December 6, 2018.

funding to reauthorize programs, reallocate funding to other programs, or be taken for deficit reduction.

Budget for a 2018 Farm Bill

(dollars in millions, FY2019-FY2028)

Farm bill titles	CBO baseline	CBO score House-passed	CBO score Senate-passed
Commodities	61,151	+284	-408
Conservation	59,754	-795	+0
Trade	3,624	+470	+515
Nutrition	663,828	-1,426	+94
Credit	-4,558	+0	+0
Rural Development	168	+0	-2,340
Research	604	+250	+685
Forestry	10	+0	+5
Energy	612	-517	+375
Horticulture	1,547	+10	+626
Crop Insurance	78,037	-161	-2
Miscellaneous	2,423	+566	+517
Subtotal	**867,200**	**-1,320**	**+68**
Increase in Revenue	-	+465	+68
Total	**867,200**	**-1,785**	**0**

Source: CRS, compiled using the CBO Baseline by Title (unpublished; April 2018), based on the CBO baseline (April 2018), and the CBO cost estimates for H.R. 2 as passed by the House and as passed by the Senate (July 24, 2018).

The farm bill authorizes programs in two spending categories: mandatory spending and discretionary spending. The Congressional Budget Office (CBO) baseline is a projection at a particular point in time of future federal spending on mandatory programs under current law. When a new bill is proposed that would affect mandatory spending, the cost impact (*score*) is measured in relation to the baseline. Changes that increase spending relative to the baseline have a positive score; those that decrease spending relative to the baseline have a negative score. Federal budget rules such as "PayGo" may require budgetary offsets to balance new spending so that there is no increase in the federal deficit. Discretionary spending may be authorized in a farm bill but is not actually provided until budget decisions are made in a future annual appropriations act.

Since 2000, farm bill budgets have varied: The 2002 farm bill increased overall spending, the 2008 farm bill was essentially budget neutral, the 2014 farm bill reduced spending, and the 2018 farm bill is projected to be essentially budget neutral.

The April 2018 CBO baseline for farm bill programs, used as the official benchmark in 2018, contains $867 billion over FY2019-FY2028—77% of which stems from the nutrition title ($664 billion) and its largest program, the Supplemental Nutrition Assistance Program. The remaining $203 billion baseline is for agricultural programs, mostly in crop insurance, farm commodity programs, and conservation. Other titles of the farm bill contribute about 1% of the baseline, some of which are funded primarily with discretionary spending.

The budgetary impact of the 2018 farm bill proposals are measured relative to the CBO baseline—that is, what the 2014 farm bill (current law) would have spent had it continued. Relative to the baseline, the House-passed bill would reduce federal outlays by $1.8 billion over 10 years (-0.2%), and the Senate-passed bill would remain budget neutral (+0%) over the same 10-year period. These overall relatively small scores are the net result of sometimes relatively larger increases and reductions across individual titles. Some of the overall scores within a single title of the farm bill are the net result of sometimes large changes in individual programs that may reflect changes in the direction of policy.

- The House bill would achieve its overall 10-year net reduction primarily by reducing net outlays in four titles (Nutrition, Conservation, Energy, and Crop Insurance). It would increase spending by less than the total of these reductions across five other titles (Miscellaneous, Trade, Commodities, Research, and Horticulture). The Nutrition title has provisions that sum to a $22 billion reduction over 10 years (including those for work requirements) and provisions that would add to $20.6 billion in increased spending. Similarly, the Conservation title has provisions that sum to a $12.6 billion reduction (including repealing the Conservation Stewardship Program), as well as provisions that add spending totaling $11.8 billion.
- The Senate bill would achieve a budget-neutral outcome by reducing net spending primarily in the Rural Development title but also in the Commodities and Crop Insurance titles. It would increase spending across seven titles (Research, Horticulture, Miscellaneous, Trade, Energy, Nutrition, and Forestry).

For some of the programs without baseline, both the House-passed and the Senate-passed bills would provide continuing funding and, in some cases, permanent baseline.

INTRODUCTION

The farm bill is an omnibus, multi-year law that governs an array of agricultural and food programs. It provides an opportunity for policymakers to periodically address a broad range of agricultural and food issues. The farm bill has typically undergone reauthorization about every five years.[1]

From its beginning in the 1930s, farm bills have focused primarily on farm commodity programs to support a handful of staple commodities—corn, soybeans, wheat, cotton, rice, dairy, and sugar. In recent decades, farm bills have expanded in scope to include a Nutrition title since 1973 and since then Conservation, Horticulture, Bioenergy, Credit, Research, and Rural Development titles, among others.

Recent farm bills have been subject to various procedural hurdles, such as insufficient votes to pass the House floor, presidential vetoes, or—as in the case of 2008 and 2014 farm bills—shortterm extensions.[2] The current farm bill (the Agricultural Act of 2014, P.L. 113-79) has many provisions that expire in 2018.[3]

FARM BILL STATUS

The 115th Congress has begun but not finished a new farm bill. An initial House vote on H.R. 2 (the Agriculture and Nutrition Act of 2018) in May 2018 failed by vote of 198-213, but floor procedures allowed that vote to be reconsidered, and it passed in June by a second vote of 213- 211. The Senate passed its bill as an amendment to H.R. 2 (the Agriculture Improvement Act

[1] CRS In Focus IF10187, *Farm Bill Primer: What Is the Farm Bill?*
[2] CRS Report R45210, *Farm Bills: Major Legislative Actions, 1965-2018.*
[3] CRS Report R45341, *Expiration of the 2014 Farm Bill.*

of 2018) in June 2018 by a vote of 86-11. Conference proceedings officially began on September 5, 2018, but have not reached agreement.[4]

FARM BILLS FROM A BUDGET PERSPECTIVE

The farm bill provides an opportunity for Congress to choose how much support to provide for agriculture and nutrition and how to allocate it among competing constituencies. Generally, farm bills authorize spending in two categories: mandatory and discretionary. From a budgetary perspective, many programs are assumed to continue beyond the end of a farm bill, even though their authorizations may expire. That projection—for certain mandatory programs as explained below—provides funding to reauthorize programs, reallocate funding to other programs, or take offsets for deficit reduction. For new programs, those without baseline, or discretionary programs, funding must come from other means.

Types of Spending Authorized in the Farm Bill

Mandatory spending. A farm bill authorizes outlays and pays for them with multiyear budget estimates when the law is enacted. Budget enforcement is through "baseline" projections under current law, "scores" of the effect of proposed bills, and "PayGo" budget rules that may prevent deficit increases.

Discretionary authorizations. A farm bill establishes parameters for discretionary programs and authorizes them to receive funding in subsequent appropriations acts but does not provide or assure actual funding. Budget enforcement is through future appropriations and budget resolutions.

Recent farm bills have faced various budget situations, including spending more under a budget surplus, cutting spending for deficit reduction, and remaining basically budget neutral—with or without offsets. For example

[4] CRS Report R45275, *The House and Senate 2018 Farm Bills (H.R. 2): A Side-by-Side Comparison with Current Law.*

- The 2002 farm bill (the Farm Security and Rural Investment Act of 2002, P.L. 107-171) was enacted under a budget surplus that allowed it to make changes that were projected to increase spending by $73 billion over a 10-year budget window, more than half of which was for the farm commodity programs.[5]
- The 2008 farm bill (the Food, Conservation, and Energy Act of 2008, P.L. 110 246) was officially budget neutral, though it included $10 billion of offsets over 10 years from tax-related and other provisions that allowed it to increase spending on the Nutrition, Conservation, and Disaster titles.[6]
- The 2014 farm bill (the Agricultural Act of 2014, P.L. 113-79) was enacted under deficit reduction and budget sequestration that influenced its legislative development. It made changes that projected a net reduction of $16 billion over 10 years ($23 billion including sequestration).[7]
- The 2018 farm bill—the current bill under consideration (H.R. 2)—is being held to a budget-neutral position, though budget amounts may be reallocated across programs within issue areas and across titles of the farm bill (*Table 1*).

Mandatory spending is authorized throughout the farm bill, but four titles presently account for about 99% of the mandatory farm bill spending: Commodity, Nutrition, Crop Insurance, and Conservation.[8] The Supplemental Nutrition Assistance Program (SNAP) and crop insurance have their own mandatory spending sources, but the farm commodity programs, conservation, and most other mandatory outlays are paid through the U.S. Department of Agriculture's (USDA) Commodity Credit Corporation (CCC).[9]

---

[5] CRS Report RL31704, *A New Farm Bill: Comparing the 2002 Law with Previous Law and House and Senate Bills* (available from the author).

[6] CRS Report RL34696, *The 2008 Farm Bill: Major Provisions and Legislative Action*.

[7] CRS Report R42484, *Budget Issues That Shaped the 2014 Farm Bill*. For more about continuing sequestration issues for the farm bill, see the Appendix in CRS Report R45230, *Agriculture and Related Agencies: FY2019 Appropriations*.

[8] CRS Report RS22131, *What Is the Farm Bill?*

[9] CRS Report R44606, *The Commodity Credit Corporation: In Brief*.

Discretionary spending is authorized throughout the farm bill, including most rural development, credit, and research programs, among others. Some smaller research, bioenergy, and rural development programs are authorized to receive both mandatory and discretionary funding. Most agency operations (salaries and expenses) are financed with discretionary funds. Discretionary appropriations are made through the annual Agriculture appropriations act.[10]

While both types of programs are significant, mandatory programs often dominate the farm bill debate. Therefore, the majority of this chapter focuses on mandatory spending.

IMPORTANCE OF BASELINE TO THE FARM BILL

The Congressional Budget Office (CBO) *baseline* is a projection at a particular point in time of future federal spending on mandatory programs under current law. The baseline is the *benchmark* against which proposed changes in law are measured. The CBO develops the budget baseline under various laws and follows the supervision of the House and Senate Budget Committees.

When a new bill is proposed that would affect mandatory spending, the cost impact (*score*) is measured in relation to the baseline. Changes that increase spending relative to the baseline have a *positive* score; those that decrease spending relative to the baseline have a *negative* score.[11]

Having a baseline essentially gives programs built-in future funding if policymakers decide that the programs should continue—that is, straightforward reauthorization would not have a scoring effect (budget neutral). However, some programs do not have a continuing baseline beyond the expiration of a farm bill and do not have assured future funding. Their reauthorization would have a positive score that increases the bill's cost.

---

[10] For example, see CRS Report R45230, *Agriculture and Related Agencies: FY2019 Appropriations*.

[11] See CRS Report 98-560, *Baselines and Scorekeeping in the Federal Budget Process*.

Development of the Baseline

CBO projects future government spending via its budget baselines and evaluates proposed bills via scoring estimates. The baseline incorporates domestic and international market conditions at the time the baseline is projected, government policies, and expectations for future economic conditions. Generally, a program with estimated mandatory spending in the last year of its authorization may be assumed to continue in the baseline as if there were no change in policy and it did not expire. This is the situation for most of the major, long-standing farm bill provisions such as the farm commodity programs or supplemental nutrition assistance.[12] However, some programs may not be assumed to continue in the budget baseline beyond the end of a farm bill because they are either[13]

- programs with estimated mandatory spending less than a minimum $50 million scoring threshold in the last year of the farm bill, or
- new programs established after 1997 for which the Budget Committees have determined that the mandatory spending shall not extend beyond expiration. This decision may have been made in consultation with the Agriculture Committees for a number of reasons, such as to reduce the program's 10-year cost when a farm bill is written or to prevent the program from having a continuing baseline.

April 2018 CBO Baseline

The baseline for scoring the 2018 farm bill currently under consideration is the CBO baseline that was released in April 2018. This baseline is to be used until a new annual scoring baseline is released in the spring of 2019.

---

[12] For example, the CBO baselines for the primary farm commodity and nutrition programs remain positive through FY2027, even though their current authority under the 2014 farm bill generally expires after FY2018.

[13] See Section 257 of the Balanced Budget and Emergency Deficit Control Act of 1985 (2 U.S.C. 907), as explained by CBO, *The Budget and Economic Outlook: Fiscal Years 2018 to 2028*, April 2018, pp. 47 and 54, https://www.cbo.gov/ publication/53651.

Table 1. Budget for a 2018 Farm Bill: Baseline and Scores, by Title (projected outlays in millions of dollars, 5- and 10-year totals)

Farm Bill Titles	5 years (FY2019-FY2023)			10 years (FY2019-FY2028)		
	CBO Baseline	CBO Score		CBO Baseline	CBO Score	
		House-Passed	Senate-Passed		House-Passed	Senate-Passed
Commodities	31,340	+198	-23	61,151	+284	-408
Conservation	28,715	+656	+290	59,754	-795	+0
Trade	1,809	+235	+258	3,624	+470	+515
Nutrition	325,922	+862	+224	663,828	-1,426	+94
Credit	-2,205	+0	+0	-4,558	+0	+0
Rural Development[a]	98	+0	-832	168	+0	-2,340
Research	329	+168	+426	604	+250	+685
Forestry	5	+0	+5	10	+0	+5
Energy[a]	362	-267	+311	612	-517	+375
Horticulture	772	+10	+323	1,547	+10	+626
Crop Insurance	38,057	-70	-1	78,037	-161	-2
Miscellaneous	1,259	+553	+594	2,423	+566	+517
Subtotal	426,462	+2,344	+1,573	867,200	-1,320	+68
Increase in Revenue	-	+115	+33	-	+465	+68
Total	426,462	+2,229	+1,540	867,200	-1,785	0

Source: CRS. Compiled from the CBO Baseline by Title (unpublished; April 2018), based on the CBO baseline, https://www.cbo.gov/about/products/baseline-projections-selected-programs, April 2018, and the CBO cost estimates for H.R. 2 as passed by the House of Representatives and the Senate Amendment to H.R. 2 as passed by the Senate, https://www.cbo.gov/publication/54284, July 24, 2018.

Note:

[a] The House bill combined rural development and energy provisions into a Rural Infrastructure and Economic Development title. This table retains the separate titles, based on provisions, to maintain consistency with the 2014 farm bill, the CBO baseline, and the Senate bill.

The April 2018 mandatory spending baseline for farm bill programs contains $867 billion over FY2019-FY2028, 77% of which is in the Nutrition

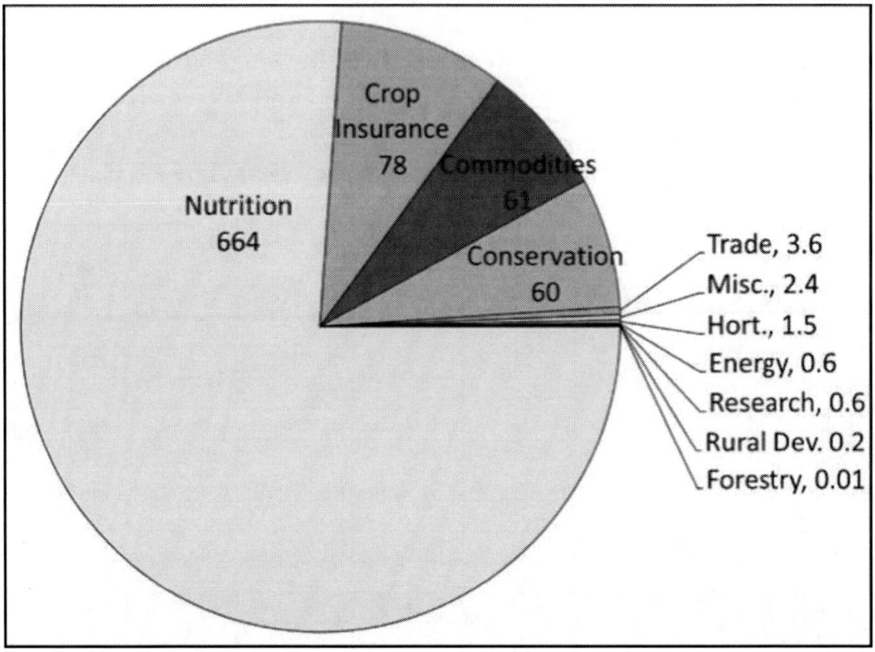

Source: CRS, using CBO Baseline by Title (unpublished; April 2018), based on the CBO baseline, https://www.cbo.gov/about/products/baseline-projections-selected-programs, April 2018.

Figure 1. CBO Baseline for Farm Bill Titles. (10-year projected outlays under current law, FY2019-FY2028, billions of dollars)

title for SNAP ($664 billion). The remaining $203 billion baseline is for agricultural programs, mostly in the Crop Insurance, Farm Commodity Programs, and Conservation titles.[14] Other titles contribute about 1% of the baseline because they are funded mostly with discretionary spending.

---

[14] CBO, "Baseline Projections," https://www.cbo.gov/about/products/baseline-projections-selected-programs, April 2018; and the CBO Baseline by Title (unpublished; April 2018); and in the table notes in CBO, "Cost Estimates for H.R. 2 as Passed by the House of Representatives and as Passed by the Senate," https://www.cbo.gov/publication/ 54284, July 24, 2018. See also the analysis in CRS In Focus IF10783, *Farm Bill Primer: Budget Issues*.

The April 2018 CBO baseline is the benchmark of available funding from which the House and Senate wrote bills for a new farm bill in 2018. The 5-year and 10-year columns in *Table 1* show the CBO baseline for the titles of the 2014 farm bill over the next 10 years. (The score columns will be discussed later in "Scores of the 2018 Farm Bill Proposals".) *Figure 1* illustrates the 10- year baseline by title. *Table 2* adds details at the program level and with the annual projections, for the Farm Commodity Programs, Conservation, Trade, and Miscellaneous titles. *Figure 2* illustrates the 10-year, program-level baseline for agriculture (non-nutrition) programs.[15]

Programs Without Baseline

As explained above, most of the major farm bill provisions are assumed to continue in the baseline. However, some programs may not be assumed to continue, because they had estimated mandatory spending below the minimum scoring threshold of $50 million or the Budget and/or Agriculture Committees determined that mandatory spending should not continue.

The 2014 farm bill contains 39 programs that received mandatory funding that do not have baseline beyond FY2018 (*Figure 3*). These programs had estimated mandatory spending totaling $2.824 billion over the five-year farm bill.[16]

Among this group are certain conservation programs; most of the Bioenergy, Rural Development, and Research title programs; various Nutrition title pilot programs and studies; organic agriculture and farmers' market programs; trade promotion; and outreach to farmers.[17]

[15] Although the farm bill is generally considered a five-year authorization, budget rules assess federal spending over a 10-year budget window.

[16] CRS Report R44758, Farm Bill Programs Without a Budget Baseline Beyond FY2018.

[17] CRS In Focus IF10780, Farm Bill Primer: Programs Without Baseline Beyond FY2018.

Table 2. CBO Baseline for the 2018 Farm Bill, by Title and Program (projected outlays in millions of dollars, April 2018 baseline)

	Fiscal year										**5 years**	**10 years**
	2019	2020	2021	2022	2023	2024	2025	2026	2027	2028	FY2019-23	FY2019-28
Title I: Farm Commodity Programs												
Agricultural Risk Coverage	*2,627*	*2,155*	*464*	*430*	*479*	*431*	*463*	*482*	*505*	*492*	*6,155*	*8,529*
Price Loss Coverage	*2,727*	*2,653*	*5,742*	*5,006*	*4,574*	*4,639*	*4,603*	*4,854*	*4,558*	*4,566*	*20,702*	*43,921*
Marketing Loan Program	*58*	*51*	*51*	*48*	*45*	*44*	*43*	*47*	*48*	*50*	*254*	*486*
Dairy	*186*	*161*	*160*	*177*	*173*	*177*	*191*	*128*	*134*	*137*	*857*	*1,624*
Disaster assistance programs	*364*	*361*	*391*	*390*	*388*	*386*	*389*	*388*	*387*	*425*	*1,893*	*3,868*
Other	*524*	*241*	*228*	*235*	*251*	*252*	*244*	*253*	*255*	*240*	*1,479*	*2,723*
Subtotal, Title I	6,487	5,621	7,035	6,286	5,910	5,930	5,934	6,151	5,886	5,910	31,340	61,151
Title II: Conservation												
Conservation Reserve Program	*1,819*	*1,999*	*2,042*	*2,083*	*2,126*	*2,169*	*2,209*	*2,223*	*2,213*	*2,214*	*10,069*	*21,097*
Emergency Forestry Conservation Reserve	*1*	*1*	*1*	*1*	*1*	*1*	*1*	*1*	*1*	*1*	*5*	*10*
CRP Technical Assistance	*100*	*37*	*77*	*72*	*147*	*106*	*169*	*91*	*94*	*85*	*433*	*978*
Conservation Security/Stewardship Program	*1,607*	*1,822*	*1,743*	*1,772*	*1,820*	*1,771*	*1,768*	*1,810*	*1,808*	*1,808*	*8,764*	*17,729*
Environmental Quality Incentives Program	*1,509*	*1,545*	*1,600*	*1,640*	*1,674*	*1,729*	*1,750*	*1,750*	*1,750*	*1,750*	*7,968*	*16,697*
Agricultural Conservation Easement Program	*310*	*271*	*266*	*250*	*250*	*250*	*250*	*250*	*250*	*250*	*1,347*	*2,597*

	Fiscal year										5 years	10 years
	2019	2020	2021	2022	2023	2024	2025	2026	2027	2028	FY2019-23	FY2019-28
Regional Conservation Partnership Program	*127*	*125*	*121*	*107*	*98*	*100*	*100*	*100*	*100*	*100*	*578*	*1,078*
Agricultural Management Assistance	*9*	*9*	*9*	*10*	*10*	*10*	*10*	*10*	*10*	*10*	*47*	*97*
Programs repealed in 2014 and user fees	*-4*	*-4*	*-4*	*-4*	*-4*	*-4*	*-4*	*-4*	*-4*	*-4*	*-20*	*-40*
Other, incl. announced FY2019 sequestration	*-233*	*-75*	*-75*	*-51*	*-42*	*-27*	*15*	*-1*	*0*	*0*	*-476*	*-489*
Subtotal, Title II	5,245	5,730	5,780	5,880	6,080	6,105	6,268	6,230	6,222	6,214	28,715	59,754
Title III: Trade												
Market Access Program	200	200	200	200	200	200	200	200	200	200	1,000	2,000
Food for Progress	153	154	154	154	154	155	155	155	155	155	769	1,544
Emerging Markets Program	8	8	8	8	8	8	8	8	8	8	40	80
Subtotal, Title III	361	362	362	362	362	363	363	363	363	363	1,809	3,624
Title IV: Nutrition	65,817	65,268	65,033	64,857	64,947	65,477	66,247	67,151	68,720	70,311	325,922	663,828
Title V: Credit	-435	-437	-440	-444	-449	-455	-462	-471	-478	-487	-2,205	-4,558
Title VI: Rural Development	35	21	14	14	14	14	14	14	14	14	98	168
Title VII: Research	82	78	59	55	55	55	55	55	55	55	329	604
Title VIII: Forestry	1	1	1	1	1	1	1	1	1	1	5	10
Title IX: Energy	102	89	70	51	50	50	50	50	50	50	362	612
Title X: Horticulture	153	154	155	155	155	155	155	155	155	155	772	1,547
Title XI: Crop Insurance	7,230	7,471	7,684	7,811	7,860	7,903	7,942	8,006	8,047	8,082	38,057	78,037
Title XII: Miscellaneous												
Noninsured Crop Disaster Assistance Program	223	223	223	223	223	223	223	223	223	223	1,114	2,229
Other	71	37	12	12	12	10	10	10	10	10	145	195
Subtotal, Title XII	294	259	235	235	235	233	233	233	233	233	1,259	2,423

Table 2. (Continued)

	Fiscal year										**5 years**	**10 years**
	2019	2020	2021	2022	2023	2024	2025	2026	2027	2028	FY2019-23	FY2019-28
Total	85,372	84,617	85,989	85,263	85,221	85,831	86,800	87,938	89,268	90,901	426,462	867,200
Nutrition (Title IV)	65,817	65,268	65,033	64,857	64,947	65,477	66,247	67,151	68,720	70,311	325,922	663,828
Non-nutrition (other titles)	19,555	19,350	20,955	20,406	20,274	20,354	20,553	20,787	20,548	20,590	100,540	203,372

Source: CRS, compiled using the CBO Baseline by Title (unpublished; April 2018; in bold), and based on additional details for programs from the CBO baseline, https:// www.cbo.gov/about/products/baseline-projections-selected-programs, April 2018 (in italics).

Note: Near-term amounts may include outlays for programs that expired before FY2019. Among titles without program detail, Nutrition includes SNAP, Credit includes receipts to FCS Insurance Fund. Research includes SCRI. Energy includes REAP, Horticulture includes SCBG, PPDM, and promotion orders, as noted in Figure 2.

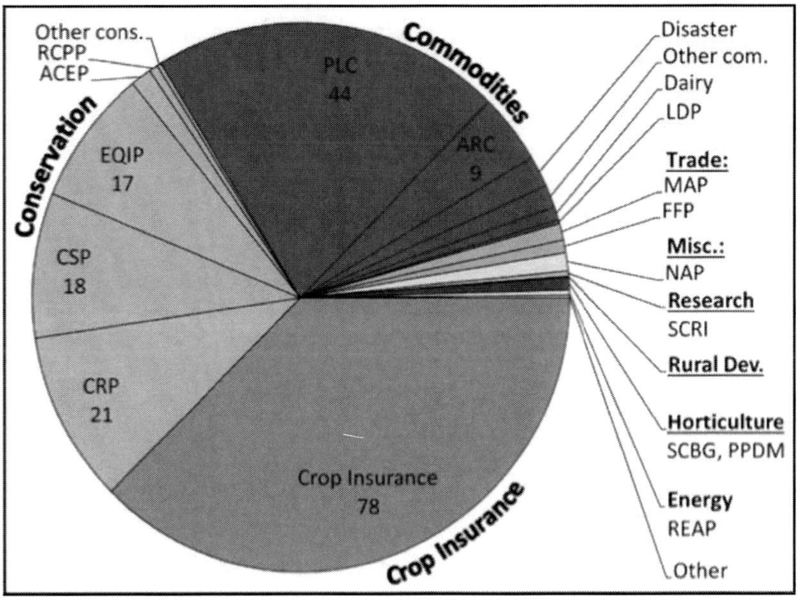

Source: CRS, using CBO Baseline by Title (unpublished; April 2018), and CBO Baseline for USDA Mandatory Farm Programs, https://www.cbo.gov/about/products/baseline-projections-selected-programs#25, April 2018.

Notes: CRP = Conservation Reserve Program, CSP = Conservation Stewardship Program, EQIP = Environmental Quality Incentives Program, ACEP = Agricultural Conservation Easement Program, RCPP = Regional Conservation Partnership Program, PLC = Price Loss Coverage, ARC = Agricultural Risk Coverage, LDP = Loan Deficiency Payments, MAP = Market Assistance Program, FFP = Food for Progress, NAP = Noninsured Crop Disaster Assistance Program, SCRI = Specialty Crop Research Initiative, SCBG = Specialty Crop Block Grants, PPDM = Plant Pest and Disease Management, REAP = Rural Energy for America Program.

Figure 2. CBO Baseline for USDA Agriculture Programs. (10-year projected outlays under current law, FY2019-FY2028, billions of dollars)

SCORES OF THE 2018 FARM BILL PROPOSALS

The budgetary impact of the 2018 farm bill proposals (House-passed H.R. 2 and the Senate-passed amendment to H.R. 2) are measured relative to the CBO baseline—that is, what the 2014 farm bill (current law) would

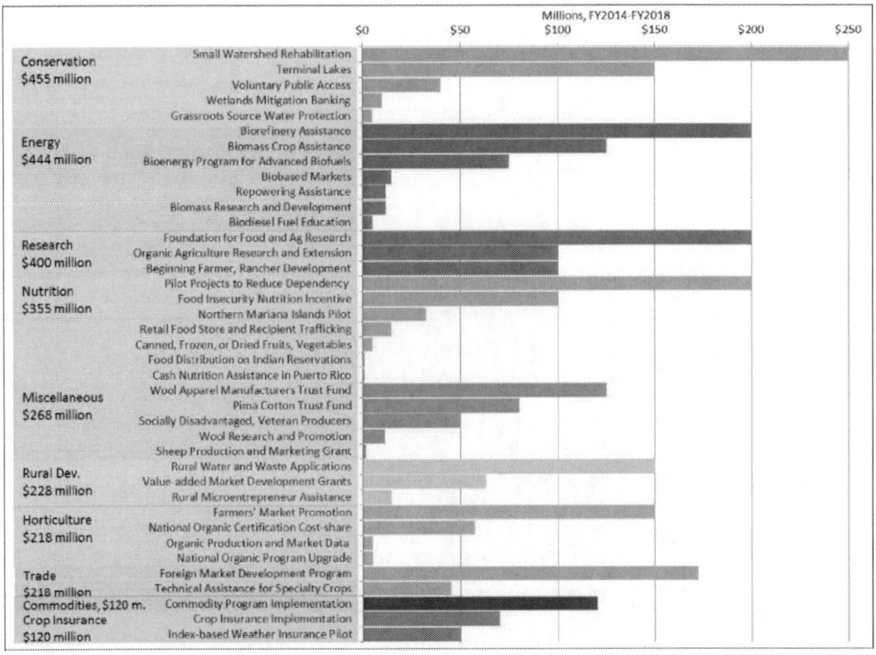

Sources: Compiled by CRS using the text of the 2014 farm bill (P.L. 113-79); the CBO score of the Agricultural Act of 2014, Table 4, "Detailed Effects on Direct Spending," January 28, 2014, https://www.cbo.gov/publication/ 45049; and the CBO Baseline Projection for USDA Mandatory Farm Programs, April 2018.

Figure 3. 2014 Farm Bill Programs Without a Budget Baseline After FY2018.

have spent had it continued. Budget enforcement uses the April 2018 baseline and these scores to follow an array of federal budget rules, such as "PayGo," that require budgetary offsets to balance new spending to avoid increasing the federal deficit.[48]

Although the farm bill is generally considered a 5-year authorization—the potential 2018 farm bill would cover FY2019-FY2023—budget rules require it to be scored over a 10-year budget window. Thus, when the legislation is discussed during its development, the farm bill may be presented more in terms of its effect over the 10-year budget window than the score of the bill over the intended 5-year duration of the law. Separately,

[48] CRS Report RL31943, *Budget Enforcement Procedures: The Senate Pay-As-You-Go (PAYGO) Rule.*

other statements about the total cost of the farm bill may be in terms of its five-year baseline (i.e., projected spending over the five-year life of the farm bill). Both are appropriate measures depending on one's perspective, but the two can be very different in magnitude, so it is important to differentiate between them.

CBO has released several scores of the 2018 farm bill in the various stages of its development. The most recent is an update that was released jointly for both bills on July 24, 2018, for the versions of H.R. 2 as passed by the House and the Senate and is the basis for the analysis here.[49]

Prior to the July 24 scores, CBO released its analyses of the original House-introduced bill,[50] the House-reported bill after it passed the full committee and was initially considered on the floor,[51] and the Senate-reported bill.[52] The July 24 scores incorporate floor amendments from both chambers' bills that caused the House bill to reduce spending compared with the House-reported bill—particularly in the Nutrition title—and the Senate bill to spend slightly more than the Senate-reported bill in the Nutrition, Farm Commodities, and Miscellaneous titles. Subsequent to the July 24 scores, CBO released a more detailed assessment of payment limit provisions in the House-passed bill that did not change the score but explained it in more detail.[53]

Summaries of the House- and Senate-Passed Bill Scores

Relative to the 10-year $867 billion baseline (*Table 1, Figure 1*), the House-passed bill would reduce outlays by $1.8 billion over 10 years

---

[49] CBO, "Cost Estimates for H.R. 2 as Passed by the House of Representatives and as Passed by the Senate."

[50] CBO, "H.R. 2, Agriculture and Nutrition Act of 2018, as Introduced in the House," https://www.cbo.gov/publication/ 53760, April 13, 2018.

[51] CBO, "H.R. 2, Agriculture and Nutrition Act of 2018, as Reported by the House Agriculture Committee," https:// www.cbo.gov/publication/53819, May 2, 2018.

[52] CBO, "S. 3042, Agriculture Improvement Act of 2018, as Reported by the Senate Agriculture Committee," https:// www.cbo.gov/publication/54092, June 21, 2018.

[53] CBO, "Payment Limitations in H.R. 2, the Agriculture and Nutrition Act of 2018," https://www.cbo.gov/publication/ 54450, September 6, 2018.

(-0.2%), and the Senate-passed bill would remain budget neutral (+0%) over the same 10-year period (as indicated by the diamonds in *Figure 4*).

The overall relatively small scores are the net result of sometimes relatively larger increases and reductions across titles (indicated by bar segments in *Figure 4, Table 1*).

- The House-passed bill would achieve its overall net reduction by reducing net outlays in four titles (Nutrition, Conservation, Energy, and Crop insurance) and by raising revenue from fees paid by contractors in the SNAP program. It would increase spending by less than the total of these reductions across five other titles (Miscellaneous, Trade, Commodities, Research, and Horticulture).
- The Senate-passed bill would achieve its budget-neutral outcome by reducing net spending in three titles (Rural Development, Commodities, and Crop insurance) and raising revenue for an oilheat program. It would increase spending across seven titles (Research, Horticulture, Miscellaneous, Trade, Energy, Nutrition, and Forestry).

Net Increases in Five-Year Outlays Are Followed by Net Decreases

For the House-passed bill, the net reduction of $1.8 billion over 10 years may be disaggregated into 2 time periods. On a shorter-time-period basis, the five-year score for the authorized life of the bill (FY2019-FY2023) shows a net increase of $2.2 billion over the comparable baseline of $426 billion (*Table 1*). This projected increase is more than offset by planned reductions that would not be realized until the second five years of the budget window (*Figure 5*).

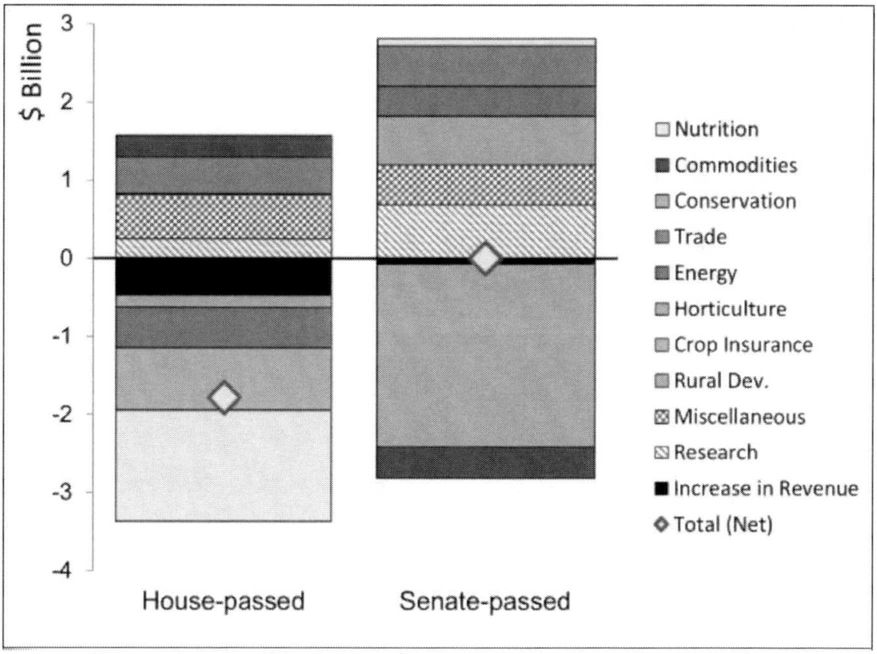

Source: CRS, using the CBO cost estimates for H.R. 2 as passed by the House of Representatives and the Senate Amendment to H.R. 2 as passed by the Senate, https://www.cbo.gov/publication/54284, July 24, 2018.

Note: Does not show amounts less than $50 million that are presented in Table 1.

Figure 4. CBO Scores of the House-Passed and Senate-Passed Farm Bills, by Title. (projected change in 10-year outlays relative to baseline, FY2019-FY2028)

For the Senate-passed bill, when the budget-neutral 10-year score is disaggregated, the effect is similar. The five-year FY2019-FY2023 score of the Senate bill shows a net increase of $1.6 billion that is offset by net reductions that would occur during the second five years (*Figure 6*).

In both bills, some of the titles that have increases in the first five years have decreases in the second five years (e.g., the Nutrition and Conservation titles in both the House- and Senate-passed bills). This may occur because of the time needed to implement changes and may make provisions more appealing in the early years despite having less baseline for a future farm bill.

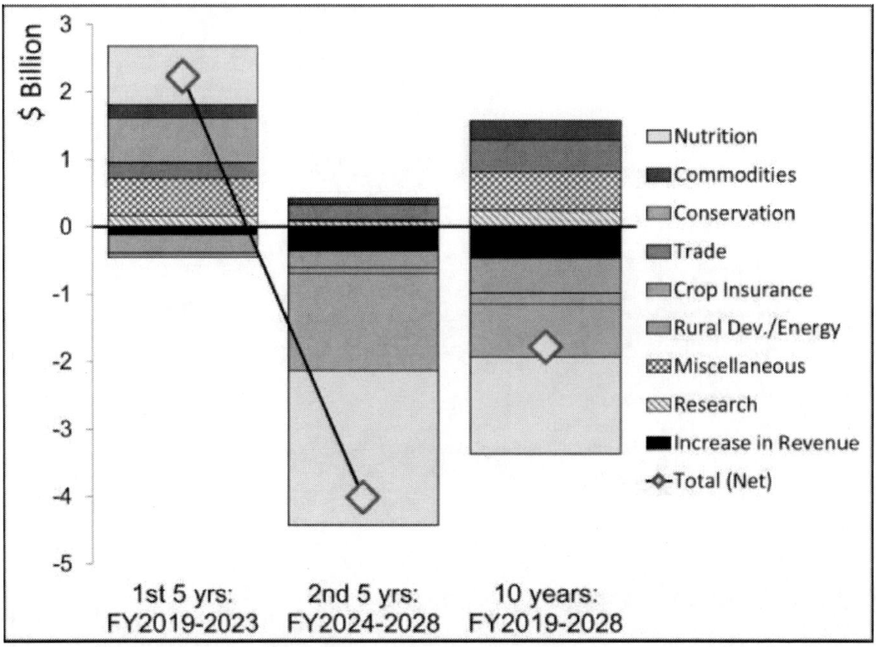

Source: CRS, using the CBO cost estimates for H.R. 2 as passed by the House, https://www.cbo.gov/ publication/54284, July 24, 2018.

Note: Does not show amounts less than $50 million that are indicated in Table 1.

Figure 5. CBO Score of House-Passed H.R. 2, by Period and Title. (projected change in 5- and 10-year outlays relative to baseline, FY2019-FY2028)

Section-by-Section Scores for Some Titles Exceed Net Scores

Some of the overall scores within a single title are the net result of increases in some sections (provisions) that are offset by reductions in other sections. Sometimes, these increases or decreases are relatively large compared to the net title-level effect. These budget effects may reflect the policy preferences of particular constituencies that may be less apparent in the net title-level scores. For example

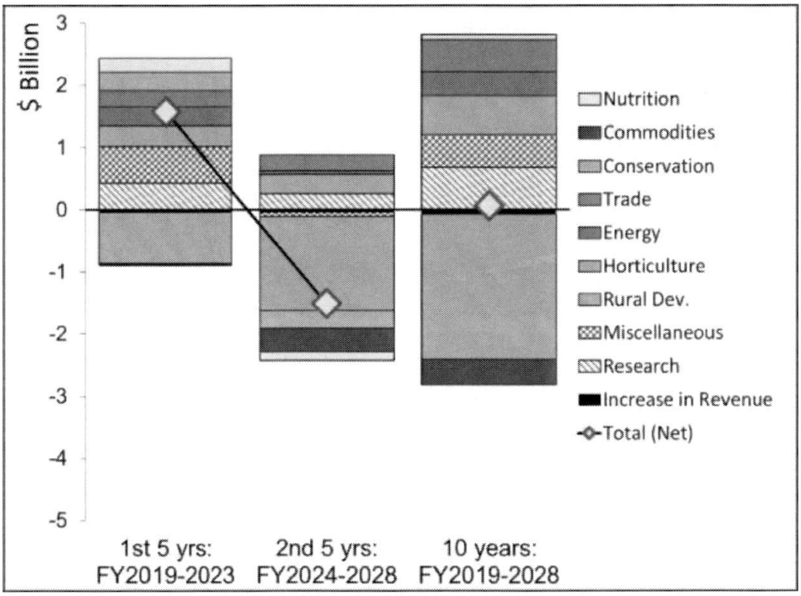

Source: CRS, using the CBO cost estimates for the Senate Amendment to H.R. 2 as passed by the Senate, https://www.cbo.gov/publication/54284, July 24, 2018.

Note: Does not show amounts less than $50 million that are indicated in Table 1.

Figure 6. CBO Score of the Senate-Passed Amendment to H.R. 2, by Period and Title. (projected change in 5- and 10-year outlays relative to baseline, FY2019-FY2028)

- In the House-passed bill, the Nutrition title has six sections that sum to a $22.0 billion reduction over 10 years (including those for work requirements) and 18 sections that add to $20.6 billion in increased spending—for a relatively small $1.4 billion net decrease in the title-level score. Similarly, the Conservation title has two sections that sum to a $12.6 billion reduction over 10 years (including repealing the Conservation Stewardship Program) and eight sections that add to $11.8 billion in increased spending—for the relatively small net $0.8 billion decrease (Figure 7, Table 3).
- In the Senate-passed bill, none of the titles' section-by-section scores are as large as for the Nutrition and Conservation titles in the House-passed bill. Nonetheless, the section-by-section scores of the Senate-passed bill show both increases and decreases within some

titles, such as Conservation, Nutrition, and Commodities (Figure 8, Table 4).

Programs without Baseline

For some of the programs without baseline, both the House-passed and Senate-passed bills would provide continuing funding and, in some cases, permanent baseline. Permanent baseline for a program may be indicated by the continuation of funding in the FY2024-FY2028 period that is similar to FY2019-FY2023 (*Table 3* and *Table 4*).

- In the House bill, programs that receive permanent baseline include Trade title programs that are combined into a new program ($470 million), and a food insecurity program in the Nutrition title ($472 million). Other affected programs that receive mandatory funding, but not permanent baseline, include organic research and beginning farmer programs in the Research title ($250 million), two organic programs in the Horticulture title ($10 million), and outreach for socially disadvantaged farmers and the wool and cotton trust funds in the Miscellaneous title ($150 million). In the Conservation title, small watershed rehabilitation, wetlands mitigation, voluntary public access, and grassroots source water protection programs receive over $500 million of mandatory funding.
- In the Senate bill, more programs receive permanent baseline than in the House bill, including Trade title programs ($515 million), organic research ($450 million), the beginning farmer program that would be combined with other outreach programs ($466 million),

Table 3. CBO Score of House-Passed H.R. 2, by Section (projected change in outlays relative to April 2018 baseline, millions of dollars)

	Fiscal year										5 years	10 years
	2019	2020	2021	2022	2023	2024	2025	2026	2027	2028	2019-23	2019-28
Title I—Commodity Programs												
Agriculture Risk Coverage—Individual[a]	+0	+0	-16	-17	-18	-18	-17	-19	-18	-20	-51	-143
Agriculture Risk Coverage—County[a]	+0	+0	+23	-34	-26	-17	-6	-15	-25	-11	-37	-111
Dairy Program	-45	-2	+4	+3	-1	-3	-6	-4	+18	+17	-41	-20
Nonrecourse Marketing Assistance Loansa	+0	+0	+0	+0	+0	+0	+0	+0	+0	+0	+0	+0
Economic Adjustment Assistance Textile Mills	+2	+2	+2	+2	+2	+2	+2	+2	+2	+2	+11	+23
Implementation	+24	+1	+0	+0	+0	+0	+0	+0	+0	+0	+25	+25
Payment Limitations[b]	+4	+4	+4	+4	+4	+4	+4	+4	+4	+4	+20	+40
Supplemental Agriculture Disaster Assistance	+13	+6	+5	+5	+5	+5	+5	+5	+5	+6	+35	+62
Price Loss Coverage[a]	+0	+0	+137	+55	+43	+50	+134	-59	-16	+64	+235	+408
Subtotal, Title I	-3	+12	+160	+18	+10	+23	+115	-85	-30	+62	+198	+284
Title II—Conservation												
Repeal Conservation Stewardship Program	-28	-405	-725	-1,072	-1,422	-1,771	-1,768	-1,810	-1,808	-1,808	-3,653	-12,618
Conservation Reserve Program	-21	+70	+98	+96	+83	+73	-43	-76	-137	-166	+326	-23
Grassroots Source Water Protection[c]	+2	+2	+1	+0	+0	+0	+0	+0	+0	+0	+5	+5
Wetlands Mitigation Banking[c]	+2	+2	+2	+2	+2	+0	+0	+0	+0	+0	+10	+10
Voluntary Public Access and Habitat Protection[c]	+10	+10	+10	+10	+10	+0	+0	+0	+0	+0	+50	+50

Table 3. (Continued)

	Fiscal year										5 years	10 years
	2019	2020	2021	2022	2023	2024	2025	2026	2027	2028	2019-23	2019-28
Feral Swine Eradication and Control Pilot	+20	+30	+25	+15	+10	+0	+0	+0	+0	+0	+100	+100
Small Watershed Rehabilitation Program[c]	+3	+16	+38	+58	+74	+81	+73	+52	+32	+32	+189	+459
Regional Conservation Partnership Program	+60	+106	+118	+131	+143	+150	+150	+150	+150	+150	+558	+1,308
Agricultural Conservation Easement Program	+90	+187	+221	+234	+247	+247	+248	+248	+249	+250	+979	+2,221
Environmental Quality Incentives Program	+55	+227	+424	+608	+777	+921	+1,056	+1,164	+1,217	+1,243	+2,092	+7,693
Subtotal, Title II	+193	+244	+212	+82	-76	-299	-284	-272	-297	-299	+656	-795
Title III—Trade												
International Development Program[d]	+47	+47	+47	+47	+47	+47	+47	+47	+47	+47	+235	+470
Subtotal, Title III	+47	+47	+47	+47	+47	+47	+47	+47	+47	+47	+235	+470
Title IV—Nutrition												
Workforce Solutions: Benefits	+0	-300	-1,330	-1,350	-1,340	-1,370	-1,560	-1,920	-2,280	-2,650	-4,320	-14,100
Update to Categorical Eligibility	+0	+0	-200	-525	-520	-530	-530	-540	-555	-565	-1,245	-3,965
Standard Utility Allowances Based on Receipt	-130	-310	-310	-310	-300	-300	-310	-310	-320	-330	-1,360	-2,930
Duplicative Enrollment Database	+0	-8	-25	-45	-60	-80	-90	-90	-95	-95	-138	-588
State Performance Indicators	+0	-48	-48	-48	-48	-48	-48	-48	-48	-48	-192	-432
Disqualification of Certain Convicted Felons	*	*	*	-1	-2	-2	-3	-4	-5	-6	-3	-23
Benefit Recovery	*	*	*	*	*	*	*	*	*	*	*	*

	Fiscal year										5 years	10 years
	2019	2020	2021	2022	2023	2024	2025	2026	2027	2028	2019-23	2019-28
Tolerance Level for Payment Errors	*	*	*	*	*	*	*	*	*	*	*	*
Administrative Flexibility for States	*	*	*	*	*	*	*	*	*	*	*	*
Multivitamin-Mineral Dietary Supplements	*	+0	+0	+0	+0	+0	+0	+0	+0	+0	*	*
Review of SNAP Operations	*	*	*	+0	+0	+0	+0	+0	+0	+0	*	*
Mobile Technologies	+0	+1	+1	+1	+1	+1	+1	+2	+2	+2	+4	+12
SNAP Benefit Transfer Data Report	+4	+3	+2	+3	+3	+3	+3	+3	+3	+3	+15	+30
Interactions	-2	-3	*	+2	-4	-3	-2	+12	+10	+25	-7	+35
Simplified Homeless Housing Costs	+4	+8	+8	+8	+8	+8	+8	+8	+8	+8	+36	+76
Percent Recovered Funds Retained by States	+10	+10	+10	+10	+10	+10	+10	+10	+11	+11	+50	+102
Basic Allowance for Housing	+8	+11	+11	+11	+11	+12	+12	+13	+13	+14	+52	+116
Implementation Funds	+128	+17	+3	+3	+0	+0	+0	+0	+0	+0	+150	+150
Prohibited Fees	+0	+3	+7	+13	+20	+20	+20	+20	+25	+25	+43	+153
Asset Limits; Vehicle Allowance; Savings	+1	-15	+5	+30	+30	+30	+30	+30	+30	+30	+51	+201
Food Insecurity Nutrition Incentive Program[d]	+7	+17	+30	+46	+55	+59	+63	+65	+65	+65	+155	+472
Emergency Food Assistance	+45	+46	+47	+48	+49	+50	+52	+53	+54	+55	+235	+499
National Gateway	+8	+10	+10	+68	+70	+78	+81	+90	+95	+95	+165	+601
Nutrition Education	+57	+53	+59	+61	+62	+64	+65	+67	+69	+70	+297	+632
Transitional Benefits	+75	+90	+90	+90	+90	+90	+90	+90	+95	+95	+435	+895
Retailer-Funded Incentives Pilot	+2	+132	+180	+120	+120	+120	+120	+120	+120	+120	+604	+1,204
Cooperation with Child Support Agencies	+140	+304	+321	+335	+345	+355	+375	+396	+446	+476	+1,446	+3,494

Table 3. (Continued)

	Fiscal year										5 years	10 years
	2019	2020	2021	2022	2023	2024	2025	2026	2027	2028	2019-23	2019-28
Earned Income Deduction	+350	+470	+470	+470	+470	+470	+470	+480	+490	+500	+2,230	+4,640
Workforce Solutions: Administration	+0	+140	+600	+680	+740	+810	+920	+1,020	+1,140	+1,250	+2,160	+7,300
Subtotal, Title IV	+707	+685	-59	-280	-190	-153	-223	-434	-628	-850	+862	-1,426
Title V—Credit	+0	+0	+0	+0	+0	+0	+0	+0	+0	+0	+0	+0
Title VI—Rural Infrastructure and Economic Development[e]												
Rural Energy for America Programe	-10	-30	-45	-50	-50	-50	-50	-50	-50	-50	-185	-435
Biorefinery Assistance[e]	-35	-31	-16	+0	+0	+0	+0	+0	+0	+0	-82	-82
Subtotal, Title VI[e]	-45	-61	-61	-50	-50	-50	-50	-50	-50	-50	-267	-517
Title VII—Research and Extension												
Beginning Farmer and Rancher Development[c]	+3	+10	+15	+19	+20	+17	+10	+5	+1	+0	+67	+100
Organic Agricultural Research and Extension[c]	+5	+15	+23	+29	+30	+26	+15	+8	+2	+0	+101	+150
Subtotal, Title VII	+8	+25	+38	+48	+50	+43	+25	+13	+3	+0	+168	+250
Title VIII—Forestry	+0	+0	+0	+0	+0	+0	+0	+0	+0	+0	+0	+0
Title IX—Horticulture												
National Organic Program Technology Update[c]	+1	+1	+1	+1	+1	+0	+0	+0	+0	+0	+5	+5
Organic Production and Market Data Initiative[c]	+1	+1	+1	+1	+1	+0	+0	+0	+0	+0	+5	+5
Subtotal, Title IX	+2	+2	+2	+2	+2	+0	+0	+0	+0	+0	+10	+10
Title X—Crop Insurance												
Education and Risk Management Assistance	-1	-11	-17	-13	-14	-14	-15	-15	-15	-15	-52	-125

	Fiscal year										5 years	10 years
	2019	2020	2021	2022	2023	2024	2025	2026	2027	2028	2019-23	2019-28
Increase Catastrophic Administration Fee	-1	-7	-8	-8	-8	-8	-8	-8	-8	-8	-32	-72
Research and Development Priorities	-5	-5	-5	-5	-5	-5	-5	-5	-5	-5	-23	-45
Program Administration	+0	-2	-2	-2	-2	-2	-2	-2	-2	-2	-8	-18
Whole Farm Application to Beginning Farmers	+0	+1	+1	+1	+1	+1	+1	+1	+1	+1	+4	+9
Treatment of Forage and Grazing	+1	+9	+10	+10	+10	+10	+10	+10	+10	+10	+40	+90
Subtotal, Title X	-6	-14	-16	-17	-17	-18	-18	-18	-18	-18	-70	-161
Title XI—Miscellaneous												
Noninsured Crop Disaster Assistance	-4	-4	-4	-4	-4	-4	-4	-4	-4	-4	-19	-37
Outreach to Socially Disadvantaged Producers[c]	+5	+8	+10	+10	+10	+5	+2	+0	+0	+0	+43	+50
Textile Trust Fund[c]	+1	+26	+25	+25	+25	+0	+0	+0	+0	+0	+103	+103
Animal Disease Preparedness and Response	+150	+125	+50	+50	+50	+25	+0	+0	+0	+0	+425	+450
Subtotal, Title XI	+152	+156	+82	+82	+82	+26	-2	-4	-4	-4	+553	+566
Total Changes in Direct Spending	+1,055	+1,096	+406	-68	-142	-381	-390	-803	-977	-1,112	+2,344	-1,320
Increases in Revenue: Title IV—Nutrition	+0	+0	–0	+55	+60	+60	+65	+70	+75	+80	+115	+465
Net Effect on the Deficit	+1,055	+1,095	–405	-124	-203	-441	-455	-874	-1,052	-1,192	+2,229	-1,785

Source: CRS, sorted within titles using the CBO cost estimates for H.R. 2 as passed by the House, https://www.cbo.gov/publication/54284, July 24, 2018.

Notes: * denotes score between -$500,000 and +$500,000. + denotes additional spending or, in the case of revenue, additional revenue. – denotes reduced spending.

[a] Details by commodity within these programs is available in Table 3 of the original CBO score of the House bill, at https://www.cbo.gov/publication/53760 (April 13, 2018). The total across commodities matches the score of these provisions (ARC, PLC, and marketing loan gains) in both the original CBO estimate and the July 24 score used in this table.

[b] Details about CBO's score of the payment limits provision are explained in "Payment Limitations in H.R. 2, the Agriculture and Nutrition Act of 2018," https://www.cbo.gov/publication/54450, September 6, 2018.

[c] Denotes a "program without baseline" after FY2018 from the 2014 farm bill (Figure 3) that received new funding in FY2019-2023 but not permanent baseline.

[d] Denotes a "program without baseline" after FY2018 from the 2014 farm bill (Figure 3) that received new funding in FY2019-2028 and permanent baseline.

[e] The House bill combined rural development and energy provisions (e.g., Titles VI and IX in the 2014 farm bill, respectively) into a single title, Title VI—Rural Infrastructure and Economic Development. Elsewhere in this chapter, such as in Table 1 and the figures, the two House provisions that scored in Title VI are assigned to an Energy title for comparison to the Senate bill and the CBO baseline.

Table 4. CBO Score of the Senate-Passed Amendment to H.R. 2, by Section (projected change in outlays relative to April 2018 baseline, millions of dollars)

	Fiscal year										5 years	10 years
	2019	2020	2021	2022	2023	2024	2025	2026	2027	2028	2019-23	2019-28
Title I—Commodities Economic Adjustment to Users of Upland												
Cotton	+0	+0	+0	-46	-46	-47	-47	-47	-47	-47	-92	-328
AGI Limitation of $700,000	-2	-3	-38	-33	-31	-31	-31	-32	-31	-31	-107	-263
Actively Engaged in Farming Requirement	+0	-2	-31	-27	-25	-25	-25	-26	-25	-25	-85	-211
Dairy Product Donation Program	-5	-5	-6	-6	-5	-5	-6	-5	-5	-5	-27	-53
Producer Election (ARC Default Choice)	+0	+0	-2	-1	-1	-1	-1	-1	-1	-1	-4	-9
Catastrophic Coverage $5.00 with 40% Cap	+6	-3	+3	+3	+3	+5	-3	-5	-1	-12	+13	-3
Supplemental Agriculture Disaster Assistance	+1	+1	+1	+1	+1	+1	+1	+1	+1	+1	+6	+11
Loss of Peach, Blueberry Crops Due to Cold	+18	+0	+0	+0	+0	+0	+0	+0	+0	+0	+18	+18

	Fiscal year										5 years	10 years
	2019	2020	2021	2022	2023	2024	2025	2026	2027	2028	2019-23	2019-28
Additional Assistance for Volcanic Activity	+27	+3	+0	+0	+0	+0	+0	+0	+0	+0	+30	+30
Milk Donation Program	+8	+5	+5	+5	+5	+5	+5	+5	+5	+5	+28	+53
Repayment Dairy Risk Coverage Premiums	+78	+0	+0	+0	+0	+0	+0	+0	+0	+0	+78	+78
Dairy Risk Coverage	+24	+14	+9	+6	+6	+7	+0	-1	+16	+16	+59	+97
Agriculture Risk Coverage (ARC)	+0	+0	+23	+17	+20	+21	+21	+23	+22	+23	+61	+172
Subtotal, Title I	+155	+10	-35	-81	-73	-70	-85	-88	-66	-76	-23	-408
Title II—Conservation												
Environmental Quality Incentives Program	-61	-120	-138	-149	-158	-171	-187	-176	-163	-158	-626	-1,481
Conservation Stewardship Program	-3	-25	-46	-67	-88	-112	-133	-155	-175	-196	-229	-1,000
Conservation Reserve Program	-11	+42	+47	+49	+15	+11	-22	-30	-50	-51	+142	+0
Regional Conservation Partnership Program	+41	+71	+79	+87	+96	+100	+100	+100	+100	+100	+374	+874
Agricultural Conservation Easement Program	+56	+115	+134	+149	+175	+188	+194	+197	+199	+200	+629	+1,607
Subtotal, Title II	+22	+83	+76	+69	+40	+16	-48	-64	-89	-105	+290	+0
Title III—Trade												
Trade Promotion, Development and Assistance[a]	+52	+52	+52	+52	+52	+52	+52	+52	+52	+52	+258	+515
Subtotal, Title III	+52	+52	+52	+52	+52	+52	+52	+52	+52	+52	+258	+515
Title IV—Nutrition												
Interstate Data Matching/Multiple Issuance	+0	-8	-25	-45	-60	-80	-90	-90	-95	-95	-138	-588

Table 4. (Continued)

	Fiscal year										5 years	10 years
	2019	2020	2021	2022	2023	2024	2025	2026	2027	2028	2019-23	2019-28
Quality Control	-42	-42	-42	-42	-42	-42	-42	-42	-42	-42	-210	-420
Assistance for Community Food Projects	-4	-4	-4	-4	-4	-4	-4	-4	-4	-4	-20	-40
Interactions	*	*	*	*	*	*	*	*	*	*	*	*
Income Verification	*	+2	+4	+3	+1	+0	+0	+0	+0	+0	+10	+10
Harvesting Health Pilot Projects	+4	+4	+4	+4	+4	+0	+0	+0	+0	+0	+20	+20
Improvements to EBT System	+0	+2	+5	+9	+8	+4	+0	+0	+0	+0	+24	+28
Food Distribution on Indian Reservations	+3	+3	+3	+4	+4	+4	+4	+4	+4	+4	+17	+37
Definition of Certification Period	*	*	+5	+20	+30	+30	+30	+30	+30	+30	+55	+205
Emergency Food Assistance Programs	+12	+24	+23	+23	+23	+19	+20	+20	+21	+21	+105	+206
Work Requirements for SNAP	+5	+40	+55	+55	+55	+5	+5	+5	+5	+5	+210	+235
Food Insecurity Nutrition Incentive[a]	+8	+18	+30	+45	+50	+50	+50	+50	+50	+50	+151	+401
Subtotal, Title IV	-14	+39	+58	+72	+69	-14	-27	-27	-31	-31	+224	+94
Title V—Credit	+0	+0	+0	+0	+0	+0	+0	+0	+0	+0	+0	+0
Title VI—Rural Development												
Cushion of Credit: No New, Reduce Rate	-140	-140	-150	-190	-220	-260	-280	-300	-320	-350	-840	-2,350
Rural Electric Development Loan and Grants	+0	+0	+0	+4	+4	+2	+0	+0	+0	+0	+8	+10
Subtotal, Title VI	-140	-140	-150	-186	-216	-258	-280	-300	-320	-350	-832	-2,340

	Fiscal year										5 years	10 years
	2019	2020	2021	2022	2023	2024	2025	2026	2027	2028	2019-23	2019-28
Title VII—Research and Extension												
Biomass Research and Development	+0	+1	+2	+3	+3	+3	+2	+1	+0	+0	+8	+15
Emerging Agricultural Production Research and Extension	+2	+3	+4	+4	+4	+2	+1	+0	+0	+0	+17	+20
Foundation for Food and Agricultural Research[b]	+200	0	0	0	0	0	0	0	0	0	+200	+200
Organic Agricultural Research and Extension Initiative[a]	+24	+36	+43	+48	+50	+50	+50	+50	+50	+50	+200	+450
Subtotal, Title VII	+226	+40	+48	+54	+57	+55	+53	+51	+50	+50	+426	+685
Title VIII—Forestry	+1	+1	+1	+1	+1	+0	+0	+0	+0	+0	+5	+5
Title IX—Energy												
Carbon Utilization Education Program	+2	+2	+2	+2	+2	0	0	0	0	0	+10	+10
Bio-based Market Program[b]	+3	+3	+3	+3	+3	+0	+0	+0	+0	+0	+15	+15
Bioenergy Program for Advanced Biofuels[b]	+3	+9	+13	+14	+15	+12	+6	+2	+1	+0	+54	+75
Biomass Crop Assistance Program[b]	+9	+16	+20	+22	+25	+16	+8	+5	+4	+0	+92	+125
Bio-refinery Assistance[b]	+0	+20	+40	+45	+35	+10	+0	+0	+0	+0	+140	+150
Subtotal, Title IX	+17	+50	+78	+86	+80	+38	+14	+7	+5	+0	+311	+375
Title X—Horticulture												
Organic Production and Market Data[b]	+1	+1	+1	+1	+1	+0	+0	+0	+0	+0	+5	+5
Organic Certification/Trade Tracking/Data Collection	+1	+1	+1	+1	+1	+0	+0	+0	+0	+0	+5	+5
National Organic Certification Cost Share[b]	+9	+12	+12	+12	+12	+3	0	0	0	0	+55	+58
Local Agriculture Market Program[a]	+33	+45	−60	+60	+60	+60	+60	+60	+60	+60	+258	+558
Subtotal, Title X	+44	+59	−74	+74	+74	+63	+60	+60	+60	+60	+323	+626
Title XI—Crop Insurance												

Table 4. (Continued)

	Fiscal year										5 years	10 years
	2019	2020	2021	2022	2023	2024	2025	2026	2027	2028	2019-23	2019-28
Enterprise Units Across County Lines	+0	-3	-3	-3	-3	-3	-3	-3	-3	-3	-12	-27
Crop Production on Native Sod	+0	-1	-1	-1	-1	-1	-1	-1	-1	-1	-3	-7
Funding for Information Technology	+0	+1	+1	+0	+0	+0	+0	+0	+0	+0	+2	+2
Submission of Policies and Materials to Board	+0	+0	+1	+1	+1	+1	+1	+1	+1	+1	+3	+8
Whole Farm Revenue Agent Incentives	+0	+1	+1	+1	+1	+1	+1	+1	+1	+2	+3	+10
Pasture, Range, Forage Policy Indian Tribes	+0	+1	+1	+1	+1	+1	+1	+1	+1	+1	+5	+12
Subtotal, Title XI	+0	+0	+0	-1	-1	+0	+0	+0	+0	+0	-1	-2
Title XII—Miscellaneous												
Extension of Merchandise Processing Fee	+0	+0	+0	+0	+0	+0	+0	+0	-371	+0	+0	-371
Direct Operation Microloans	+1	+1	+1	+1	+1	+0	+0	+0	+0	+0	+5	+5
Cattle Tick Inspection Emergency Livestock	+1	+1	+1	+1	+1	+1	+1	+1	+1	+1	+4	+7
Administrative Units	+0	+0	+1	+1	+1	+1	+1	+1	+1	+1	+3	+7
Wool Research and Promotion	+0	+2	+2	+2	+2	+0	+0	+0	+0	+0	+9	+10
National Oilheat Research Alliance	+5	+7	+7	+7	+7	+7	+7	+7	+7	+7	+33	+68
Pima Agriculture Cotton Trust Fund[b]	+16	+16	+16	+16	+16	+0	+0	+0	+0	+0	+80	+80
Agriculture Wool Apparel Manufacturing Trust Fund[b]	+0	+30	+30	+30	+30	+0	+0	+0	+0	+0	+120	+121
Emergency Citrus Trust Fund[b]	+25	+25	+25	+25	+25	+0	+0	+0	+0	+0	+125	+125
Farming Opportunities Training and Outreach[a]	+26	+40	+50	+50	+50	+50	+50	+50	+50	+50	+216	+466

	Fiscal year										**5 years**	**10 years**
	2019	2020	2021	2022	2023	2024	2025	2026	2027	2028	2019-23	2019-28
Subtotal, Title XII	+73	+122	+133	+133	+133	+59	+59	+59	-312	+59	+594	+517
Total Changes in Direct Spending	+436	+314	+334	+273	+215	-61	-203	-250	-651	-341	+1,573	+68
Increases in Revenue: Title XII—Oilheat	+5	+7	+7	+7	+7	+7	+7	+7	+7	+7	+33	+68
Net Effect on the Deficit	+431	+307	+327	+266	+208	-68	-210	-257	-658	-348	+1,540	+0

Source: CRS, sorted within titles using the CBO cost estimates for the Senate-passed amendment to H.R. 2, https://www.cbo.gov/ publication/54284, July 24, 2018.

Notes: * denotes score between -$500,000 and +$500,000. + denotes additional spending or, in the case of revenue, additional revenue. - denotes reduced spending.

[a] Denotes a "program without baseline" after FY2018 from the 2014 farm bill (Figure 3) that received new funding in FY2019-2028 and permanent baseline.

[b] Denotes a "program without baseline" after FY2018 from the 2014 farm bill (Figure 3) that received new funding in FY2019-2023 but not permanent baseline.

farmers market and value-added promotion programs that are combined ($558 million), and a food insecurity program in the Nutrition title ($401 million). Other affected programs that receive mandatory funding, but not permanent baseline, include an agricultural research foundation ($200 million); various bioenergy programs ($375 million); two other horticulture programs ($63 million); and the Pima cotton, wool, and citrus programs in the Miscellaneous title ($326 million).

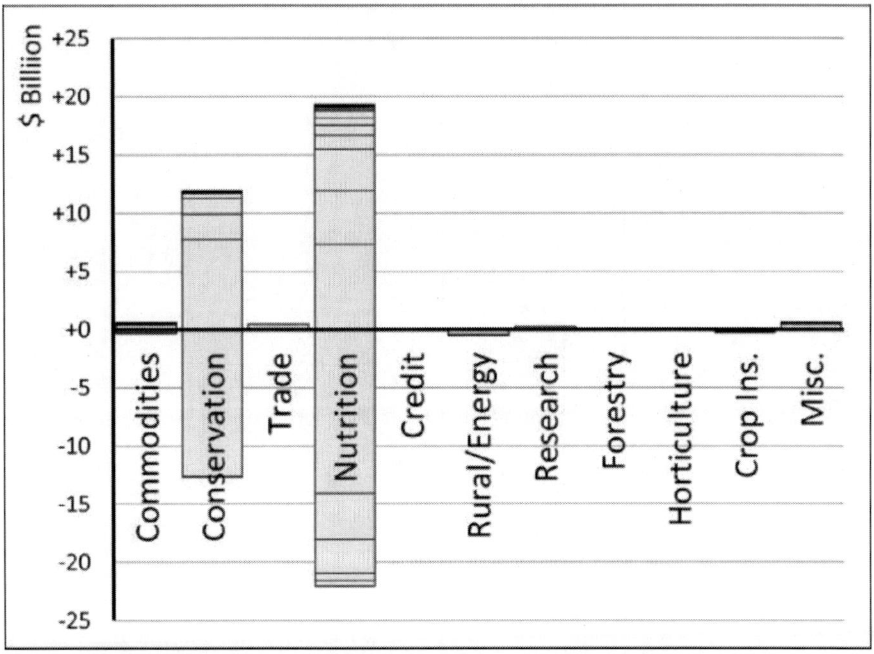

Source: CRS, sorted within titles using the CBO cost estimate for H.R. 2 as passed by the House, July 24, 2018.

Note: Figure indicates magnitude of changes within titles. Details about individual sections are in Table 3.

Figure 7. CBO Score of House-Passed H.R. 2, by Section and Title. (projected change in 10-year outlays relative to baseline, FY2019-FY2028)

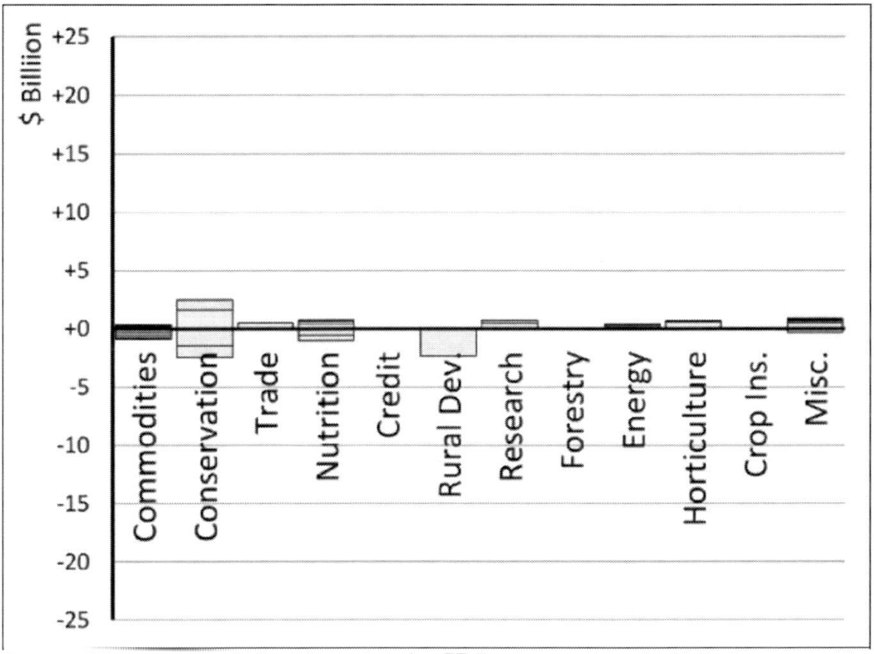

Source: CRS, sorted within titles using the CBO cost estimate for H.R. 2 as passed by the Senate, July 24, 2018.

Note: Figure indicates magnitude of changes within titles. Details about individual sections are in Table 4.

Figure 8. CBO Score of Senate-Passed Amendment to H.R. 2, by Section and Title. (projected change in 10-year outlays relative to baseline, FY2019-FY2028)

AUTHORIZATIONS FOR DISCRETIONARY APPROPRIATION

In addition to the mandatory spending figures above, the farm bill authorizes appropriations for a variety of existing and new USDA programs. The CBO scores include an estimate of the discretionary spending that would be needed to implement provisions that have authorizations of appropriations. As discussed before, these authorizations are not actual costs to the score of the farm bill (in terms of mandatory spending baseline and score) because such discretionary spending is ultimately determined in future annual appropriations acts.

For the House-passed farm bill, CBO estimated that implementing the provisions of H.R. 2 that specify authorizations of appropriations would cost $24.5 billion over the five-year period FY2019-FY2023, assuming appropriation of the specified amounts. For the Senate-passed version, the amount would be slightly smaller at $23.7 billion.[54]

For both of these estimates of chamber-passed authorized appropriations, the projection is for the total of the bill and is not disaggregated across titles or programs. However, the earlier committee-reported scores of the respective farm bills do estimate amounts by title, as shown in *Table 5*.[55] The committee-reported totals are nearly the same as the chamber-passed totals, thus making the earlier title-level estimates relatively reliable indicators of the distribution across titles for the authorizations of appropriation that are made in each chamber-passed bill.

The title-level CBO estimate of discretionary spending that is authorized in the farm bill is similar between the House and Senate bills. Three titles account for about 85% of the discretionary authorizations: Trade, Research, and Rural Development.

The bill-level estimates that sum to between $2 billion and $6 billion per year do not reflect total annual appropriations for agencies or programs in the roughly $20 billion Agriculture appropriations act.[56] Not all of the authorizations of appropriations that are funded in the Agriculture appropriations act are made in the farm bill. For example, the annual Agriculture appropriations act includes funding for (1) agencies or programs that are not in the jurisdiction of the farm bill authorizing committees (e.g., the roughly $6 billion Special Supplemental Nutrition Assistance Program for Women, Infants, and Children is not in the jurisdiction of the House Agriculture Committee or the farm bill) and (2) appropriations for salaries

---

[54] CBO, "Cost Estimates for H.R. 2 as Passed by the House of Representatives and as Passed by the Senate."

[55] CBO, "H.R. 2, Agriculture and Nutrition Act of 2018, as Reported by the House Agriculture Committee"; and CBO, "S. 3042, Agriculture Improvement Act of 2018, as Reported by the Senate Agriculture Committee."

[56] For example, see CRS Report R45230, *Agriculture and Related Agencies: FY2019 Appropriations.*

Table 5. Farm Bill Authorizations That Are Subject to Appropriation (dollars in millions)

	Fiscal year					Five years
	2019	2020	2021	2022	2023	FY2019-23
House						
Commodities	na	na	na	na	na	na
Conservation	106	144	157	165	165	737
Trade	874	2,130	2,417	2,533	2,578	10,532
Nutrition	74	79	80	80	80	393
Credit	248	257	257	257	257	1,274
Rural Infrastructure and Economic Development	179	490	826	1,159	1,292	3,945
Research	756	1,183	1,479	1,479	1,479	6,374
Forestry	56	81	94	102	105	437
Horticulture	51	62	65	67	69	313
Crop Insurance	na	na	na	na	na	na
Miscellaneous	34	54	60	60	60	268
Subtotal (committee-reported score)	2,378	4,479	5,433	5,900	6,084	24,273
Changes added after floor passage	37	40	41	41	41	200
Total (House-passed score)	2,415	4,519	5,474	5,941	6,125	24,473
Senate						
Commodities	na	na	na	na	na	na
Conservation	178	259	293	315	315	1,359
Trade	878	2,139	2,427	2,544	2,589	10,577
Nutrition	7	14	11	10	5	47
Credit	172	173	173	173	173	862
Rural Development	132	333	520	690	764	2,440
Research	864	1,278	1,566	1,559	1,559	6,826
Forestry	-24	-14	9	23	31	26
Energy	31	78	126	159	176	570
Horticulture	37	51	54	56	58	255
Crop Insurance	na	na	na	na	na	na
Miscellaneous	95	149	157	157	157	713
Subtotal (committee-reported score)	2,370	4,461	5,334	5,685	5,825	23,675
Changes added after floor passage	1	4	4	1	0	10
Total (Senate-passed score)	2,371	4,465	5,338	5,686	5,825	23,685

Source: CRS, compiled from (1) title-level amounts in CBO, "H.R. 2, as Reported by the House Agriculture Committee," May 2, 2018; and CBO, S. 3042 as Reported by the Senate Agriculture Committee," June 21, 2018; and (2) the updated total in CBO, "Cost Estimates for H.R. 2 as Passed by the House and as Passed by the Senate," July 24, 2018.

Note: "na" indicates that CBO did not estimate a specific authorization amount.

and expenses that may be permanently authorized or not necessarily reauthorized in the farm bill. CBO did not estimate the cost of implementing provisions that do not have a specific authorization amount.

In: The Farm Bill
Editor: Billie Grant
ISBN: 978-1-53615-294-4

Chapter 4

FARM BILLS: MAJOR LEGISLATIVE ACTIONS, 1965-2018 (UPDATED)*

Jim Monke

ABSTRACT

The farm bill provides an opportunity for Congress to address agricultural and food issues comprehensively about every five years. Over time, farm bills have tended to become more complicated and politically sensitive. As a result, the timeline for reauthorization has become less certain. With the exception of the 2018 farm bill, recent farm bills have taken longer to enact than in previous decades. Beginning in 2008, farm bills have been subject to various developments that have delayed enactment, such as insufficient votes to pass the House floor, presidential vetoes, or short-term extensions.

The Agriculture Improvement Act of 2018 (P.L. 115-334), often called the "2018 farm bill," was enacted on December 20, 2018. In the House, the Agriculture Committee reported the bill on April 18, 2018. An initial floor vote on May 18 failed in the House 198-213, but floor procedures allowed that vote to be reconsidered (H.Res. 905). The House

* This is an edited, reformatted and augmented version of Congressional Research Service, Publication No. R45210, dated December 21, 2018.

passed H.R. 2 in a second vote of 213-211 on June 21. In the Senate, the Agriculture Committee reported its bill (S. 3042) on June 13, 2018, by a vote of 20-1. The Senate passed its bill as an amendment to H.R. 2 by a vote of 86-11 on June 28. Conference proceedings officially began on September 5, 2018, and concluded in December with a Senate vote of 87-13 and a House vote of 369-47 (H.Rept. 115-1072).

The 2018 farm bill took 8 months from introduction to passage. By comparison, the 2014 farm bill took more than 21 months from introduction to enactment, and spanned the 112th and 113th Congresses. The 2008 farm bill took more than a year to enact and was complicated by revenue provisions from another committee of jurisdiction, temporary extensions, and vetoes.

Most farm bills have been introduced in the first session of a two-year Congress (the odd-numbered year). Three of the farm bills that were introduced in the second session—the 1970, 1990, and 2018 farm bills—were enacted during a lame duck Congress of the same year. The 2014 farm bill was the first farm bill to start in one Congress (2012), remain unfinished, and require reintroduction in a subsequent Congress.

This chapter examines the major legislative milestones for the last 12 farm bills covering 54 years.

INTRODUCTION

The farm bill provides an opportunity for Congress to address agricultural and food issues comprehensively about every five years.[1] Over time, farm bills have tended to become more complicated and politically sensitive. This has made the timeline for reauthorization less certain. Recent farm bills have been subject to developments that have delayed enactment, such as insufficient votes to pass the House floor, presidential vetoes, and short-term extensions.

The Agriculture Improvement Act of 2018 (P.L. 115-334), often called the "2018 farm bill," was enacted on December 20, 2018. In the House, the Agriculture Committee reported the bill on April 18, 2018. An initial floor vote on May 18 failed by 198-213, but procedures allowed that vote to be reconsidered (H.Res. 905). The House passed H.R. 2 in a second vote of 213-211 on June 21. In the Senate, the Agriculture Committee reported its

[1] See CRS In Focus IF10187, *Farm Bill Primer: What Is the Farm Bill?*

bill (S. 3042) on June 13, 2018, by a vote of 20-1. The Senate passed its bill as an amendment to H.R. 2 by a vote of 86-11 on June 28. Conference proceedings officially began September 5 and concluded on December 10.

The 1973 farm bill was enacted less than 3 months after being introduced. In contrast, the 2014 farm bill took more than 21 months from introduction to enactment, spanning two Congresses.[2] The House rejected a bill in 2013 and then passed separate farm and nutrition assistance components—the first time a chamber-passed farm bill did not include a nutrition title since 1973. The House later procedurally recombined them for conference with the Senate.

Both the 2002 and 2008 farm bills had expired for about three months (from October through December in 2007 and 2012) before extensions were enacted. In each case, the fiscal year began under a continuing resolution for appropriations. The extensions of the 2002 farm bill were for relatively short periods totaling about five months during final House-Senate negotiations. However, the extension of the 2008 farm bill in 2013 was for a full year.

This chapter examines the major legislative milestones for the last 12 farm bills over 54 years, a period representing modern farm bills with growing complexity. Table 1 contains a history of major legislative action on farm bills since 1965. Figure 1 shows the major dates on a timeline.

TIMELINES FOR ENACTMENT, EXTENSION, AND VETOES

Different parts of a farm bill are authorized for different periods of time. Fiscal years, calendar years, and crop years can be important to different programs. Programs authorized by the 2018 farm bill (the Agriculture Improvement Act of 2018) would generally expire either at the end of

[2] These dates span only the official introduction of a bill marked up by committee until the President signed the bill. They do not include background hearings before committee markup, which would extend the timeline.

FY2023 (September 30, 2023) or after the 2023 crop year, which varies among crops.

Timeline Relative to Fiscal Years

Enacting farm bills after the end of the final fiscal year for which programs have been authorized has been a common occurrence. In the past 42 years covering the nine farm bills since 1976— when the federal government began using a fiscal year that began on October 1[3]—only the 1977 and 2002 farm bills were enacted before the September 30 expiration date for programs that would have been affected by the fiscal year.[4]

The 1981, 1985, 1990, and 2018 farm bills were enacted within three months after the final fiscal year for which programs were authorized ended. The 1996 farm bill was enacted in April 1996 following the September 30, 1995, expiration of some of the authorizations in the 1990 farm bill.[5] The 2008 and 2014 farm bills were enacted well after their original September 30 expirations and following the enactment of extensions.

Expiration at the end of a fiscal year (September 30) matters for programs with fiscal year authorizations. These programs include certain nutrition, conservation, and trade programs; various agricultural programs, excluding the Title I commodity programs; and many authorizations for discretionary appropriations. The consequences of expiration of a farm bill are discussed in Chapter 6.

---

[3] The federal fiscal year changed in 1976. A "transition quarter" was added to move the beginning of the fiscal year from July 1 to October 1. See Office of Management and Budget, *Historical Tables: Budget of the U.S. Government.*

[4] Before the 1973 farm bill, which was the first to incorporate reauthorization of the food stamp program that had a fiscal year expiration, the focus of the farm bill was the farm commodity programs that operated by crop years.

[5] While the 1996 farm bill was not pressured by the expiration of farm commodity programs in the 1990 farm bill— since budget reconciliation in 1993 had extended them through the 1996 and 1997 crop years (see footnote 7)—some of the original FY1995 expiration dates for food stamps, certain conservation programs, and various authorizations of appropriations continued unchanged and had not been extended by the reconciliation act.

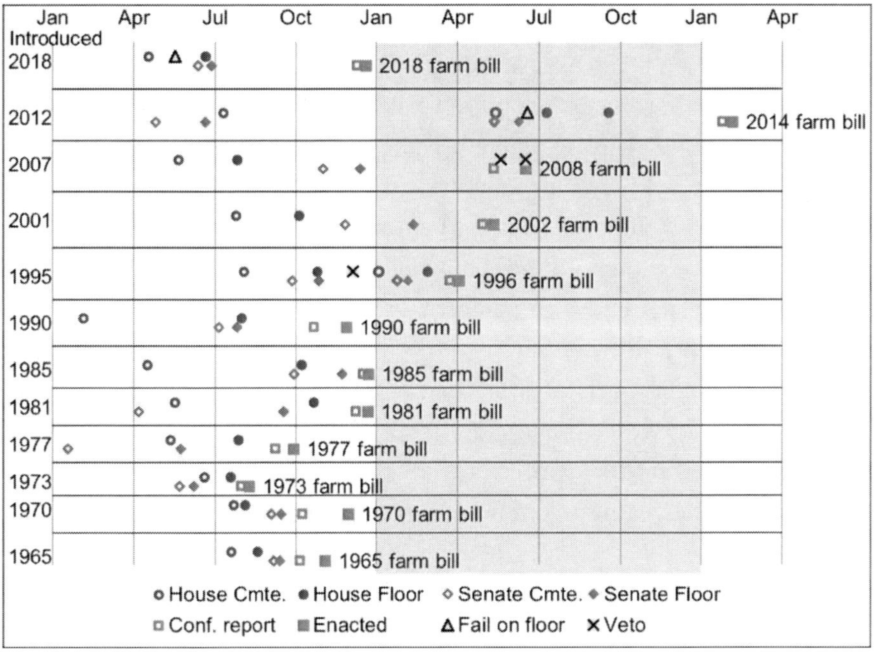

Source: CRS, using http://www.congress.gov.

Figure 1. Major Legislative Actions on Farm Bills, 2018-1965.

Timeline Relative to Calendar Years

All farm bills since 1965—except the 2008 and 2014 farm bills—have been enacted before December 31 in the year of their expirations.[6] Therefore, only the 2008 and 2014 farm bills have required extensions (see "Short-Term Extensions" below).

[6] The 1965 farm bill was extended for one year, but that extension occurred more than a year before expiration and before the reauthorization process had begun in 1970. The 1996 and 2002 farm bills may appear to have been delayed by being reintroduced (1996) or going through the new year into May (2002), but their predecessors did not require extensions. The 1990 farm bill's original expiration date of the end of the 1995 crop year had less of an effect on the 1996 farm bill's timeline because budget reconciliation in 1993 had extended the farm commodity programs through at least 1996 and, in some cases, the 1997 crops. The 2002 farm bill was enacted before the 1996 farm bill expired on September 30, 2002, and before the 2002 crop year ended. In fact, the 2002 farm bill superseded the last year of the 1996 farm bill by beginning with the 2002 crop year.

From another perspective, the 1990 farm bill was the last farm bill prior to the 2018 farm bill that was enacted by December 31—within three months from the start of fiscal-year expiration but before the spring-planted crops covered by the new law were planted. The 1996, 2002, 2008, and 2014 farm bills were enacted in a calendar year after their introduction—in April (1996), May (2002), June (2008), and February (2014)—but still prior to the first crop covered by the farm bill being harvested.

Expiration at the end of a calendar year matters mostly for the dairy program, one of the farm commodity programs in Title I of recent farm bills. The farm commodity programs are tied to crop years—that is, the year in which a crop is harvested—and dairy is the first commodity that would be affected by reverting to "permanent law," since its crop year begins on January 1 after the year of expiration.[7]

Timeline Relative to the Two-Year Congressional Term

Since 1965, 8 out of 12 enacted farm bills were introduced in the first session of a two-year Congress (the odd-numbered year). The other four (1970, 1990, 2014, and 2018) were introduced in the second session of a two-year Congress (the even-numbered year).[8] The 2018 farm bill was the first time since before 1965 that both chambers completed floor action before the end of June.

---

[7] *Permanent law* refers to non-expiring farm commodity programs that are generally from the 1938 and 1949 farm bills. The temporary suspension of permanent law is included as a section in all recent farm bills. If the suspension of permanent law were to expire at the end of a crop year, the permanent law provisions would take effect unless a new farm bill, or an extension of the most recent bill, continues the suspension. For more details about permanent law and its consequences, see the heading on permanent law in CRS Report R45341, *Expiration of the 2014 Farm Bill.*

[8] Technically, the bill that became the 2014 farm bill (H.R. 2642) was introduced in 2013 (the first session of the 113th Congress), but many consider it a reintroduction of the bills started in 2012 (the second session of the 112th Congress).

Of the four bills introduced in a second session, the 1970, 1990, and 2018 farm bills were enacted during a lame duck Congress (after an election) in November and December of the same year. The 2014 farm bill, which was introduced in 2012, was the first farm bill to start in one Congress, remain unfinished, and require reintroduction in a subsequent Congress.

House or Senate Action First

The House and Senate have taken turns in initiating action on a farm bill. Since 1965, the Senate was first to mark up farm bills in 1973, 1977, 1981, 2012, and 2013. The House was first to mark up bills in 1965, 1970, 1985, 1990, 1995 (and 1996), 2001, 2007, and 2018.

Short-Term Extensions

Extensions of a prior farm bill while its successor is being written have been atypical. Only the 2002 and 2008 farm bills have required extensions in 2007-2008 and 2013, respectively, as their successors were being written.[9]

When the 2002 farm bill expired, portions of it were extended six times for less than a year total beginning in December 2007.[10] When the 2008 farm bill expired, the entire farm bill was extended in January 2013 for all of FY2013 and the 2013 crop year.[11] While the 2014 farm bill was expired from October 1 until the 2018 farm bill was enacted, the continuing resolution for appropriations continued many operations, though some new program activity ceased.[12]

---

[9] See also footnote 7 and the section "Timeline Relative to Calendar Years."

[10] CRS Report RL34154, *Possible Expiration (or Extension) of the 2002 Farm Bill*.

[11] CRS Report R42442, *Expiration and Extension of the 2008 Farm Bill*.

[12] CRS Report R45341, *Expiration of the 2014 Farm Bill*.

Presidential Vetoes

Presidential vetoes of farm bills are not common. Since 1965, only the 2008 farm bill has been vetoed as stand-alone measure; it was vetoed twice. A 1995 farm bill was vetoed as part of a larger budget reconciliation package.

President George W. Bush vetoed the 2008 farm bill (H.R. 2419). When Congress overrode the veto to enact P.L. 110-234, it accidentally enrolled the law without Title III (the trade title). Congress immediately reintroduced the same bill with the trade title (H.R. 6124). President Bush vetoed this version as well, and Congress again overrode the veto to enact P.L. 110-246, a complete 2008 farm bill that included the trade title. The overrides in 2008 were the only time that a farm bill was enacted as a result of a veto override.

President Clinton vetoed a 1995 budget reconciliation package that included the first version of what became the 1996 farm bill, but the veto was not due to the farm bill itself but rather the controversial nature of the reconciliation bill in which the farm bill was embedded.

Prior to 1965, the first veto of a farm bill was in 1956, when President Eisenhower vetoed H.R. 12 (84th Congress), the first version of the Agricultural Act of 1956.

Implications for Congress

As farm bill reauthorization has tended to become more complex and engender greater political sensitivity, the process of enacting a new farm bill prior to the expiration of the existing law has become more difficult.

As stakeholders in the farm bill have become more diverse, more people are affected by the legislative uncertainty around this process. This lack of certainty may translate into questions about the availability of future program benefits, some of which may affect agricultural production decisions or market uncertainty for agricultural commodities.

Table 1. Major Legislative Actions on Farm Bills, 2018-1965

	House		Senate		Conference Report Approval			
	Cmte.	Passage	Cmte.	Passage	Conf. Report	House Passage	Senate Passage	Public Law
2018 farm bill Agriculture Improvement Act of 2018 Covers 2019-2023 crops or until 9/30/2023	4/18/2018 H.R. 2 Vote of 26-20 5/3/2018 H.Rept. 115-661	5/18/2018 H.R. 2 Initial vote failed by 198-213 Reconsidered under H.Res. 905 6/21/2018 Passed by vote of 213-211	6/13/2018 S. 3042 Vote of 20-1	6/28/2018 H.R. 2 Vote of 86-11	12/10/2018 H.Rept. 115-1072	12/12/2018 H.R. 2 Vote of 369-47	12/11/2018 H.R. 2 Vote of 87-13	12/20/2018 P.L. 115-334
2014 farm bill Agricultural Act of 2014 *(113th Congress)* Covers 2014-2018 crops or until 9/30/2018	5/15/2013 H.R. 1947 Vote of 36-10 5/29/2013 H.Rept. 113-92	6/20/2013 H.R. 1947 Failed by vote 195-234 7/11/2013 H.R. 2642 Farm portion vote of 216-208 9/19/2013 H.R. 3102 Nutrition part vote of 217-210 9/28/2013 H.Res. 361 combined House bills	5/14/2013 S. 954 Vote of 15-5 9/4/2013 S.Rept. 113-88	6/10/2013 S. 954 Vote of 66-27	1/27/2014 H.Rept. 113-333	1/29/2014 H.R. 2642 Vote of 251-166	2/4/2014 H.R. 2642 Vote of 68-32	2/7/2014 P.L. 113-79

Table 1. (Continued)

	House		Senate		Conference Report Approval			
	Cmte.	Passage	Cmte.	Passage	Conf. Report	House Passage	Senate Passage	Public Law
Agriculture Reform, Food, and Jobs Act *(112th Congress)*	7/11/2012 H.R. 6083 Vote of 35-11 9/13/2012 H.Rept. 112-669	—	4/26/2012 S. 3240 Vote of 16-5 8/28/2012 S.Rept. 112-203	6/21/2012 S. 3240 Vote of 64-35	—	—	—	—
Early extension:	Extended five conservation programs of the 2008 farm bill through FY2014 (AMA, CSP, EQIP, FPP, and WHIP).							11/18/2011 P.L. 112-55
Extension:	One-year extension of the 2008 farm bill until 9/30/2013 and for the 2013 crop year (dairy price support extended until 12/31/2013, and MILC extended until 9/30/2013). Did not provide funding for programs without mandatory baseline.							1/2/2013 P.L. 112-240 Title VII
2008 farm bill Food, Conservation, and Energy Act of 2008 Covers 2008-2012 crops or until 9/30/2012	5/22/2007 H.R. 2419 Introduced 7/23/2007 H.Rept. 110-256	7/27/2007 H.R. 2419 Vote of 231-191	11/2/2007 S. 2302 S.Rept. 110-220	12/14/2007 Amdt. to H.R. 2419 Vote of 79-14	5/13/2008 H.Rept. 110-627 Re-passed as new bill w/Title III	5/14/2008 H.R. 2419 Vote of 318-106 5/21/2008 Passed over veto 316-108	5/15/2008 H.R. 2419 Vote of 81-15 5/22/2008 Passed over veto 82-13	5/21/2008 Enrolling error omits Title III Vetoed 5/22/2008 P.L. 110-234

	House		Senate		Conference Report Approval			
	Cmte.	Passage	Cmte.	Passage	Conf. Report	House Passage	Senate Passage	Public Law
						5/22/2008 H.R. 6124 Vote of 306-110 6/18/2008 Passed over veto 317-109	6/5/2008 H.R. 6124 Vote of 77-15 6/18/2008 Passed over veto 80-14	6/18/2008 Vetoed 6/18/2008 P.L. 110-246
Early extensions:	Extended the early-expiring MILC program of the 2002 farm bill for two years from 9/2005 through 8/2007 and two conservation programs (EQIP and Conservation Security Program) until FY2010.							2/8/2006 P.L. 109-171
Extensions:	Extended parts of the 2002 farm bill until 3/15/2008 but did not extend the direct and counter cyclical farm commodity programs. See Division A, §751. Continued extension until 4/18/2008 and added extension of suspension of permanent law. Continued extension until 4/25/2008. Continued extension until 5/2/2008. Continued extension until 5/16/2008. Continued extension until 5/23/2008.							12/26/2007 P.L. 110-161 3/14/2008 P.L. 110-196 4/18/2008 P.L. 110-200 4/25/2008 P.L. 110-205 5/2/2008 P.L. 110-208 5/18/2008 P.L. 110-231

Table 1. (Continued)

	House		Senate		Conference Report Approval			
	Cmte.	Passage	Cmte.	Passage	Conf. Report	House Passage	Senate Passage	Public Law
2002 farm bill Farm Security and Rural Investment Act Covers 2002-2007 crops or until 9/30/2007	7/26/2001 H.R. 2646 8/2/2001 H.Rept. 107-191	10/5/2001 H.R. 2646 Vote of 291-120	11/27/2001 S. 1731 12/7/2001 S.Rept. 107-117	2/13/2002 Amdt. to H.R. 2646 Vote of 58-40	5/1/2002 H.Rept. 107-424	5/2/2002 H.R. 2646 Vote of 280-141	5/8/2002 H.R. 2646 Vote of 64-35	5/13/2002 P.L. 107-171
1996farm bill Federal Agriculture Improvement and Reform Act of 1996 Covers 1996-2002 crops or until 9/30/2002	1/5/1996 H.R. 2854 introduced Vote of 29-17 2/9/1996 H.Rept. 104-462	2/29/1996 H.R. 2854 Vote of 270-155	1/26/1996 S. 1541 introduced	2/7/1996 S. 1541 Vote of 64-32 3/12/1996 Amdt. To H.R. 2854 Voice vote	3/25/1996 H.Rept. 104-494	3/29/1996 H.R. 2854 Vote of 318-89	3/28/1996 H.R. 2854 Vote of 74-26	4/4/1996 P.L. 104-127
Balanced Budget Act of 1995	10/26/1995 H.R. 2491 includes H.R. 2195	10/26/1995 H.R. 2491 Vote of 227-203	10/28/1995 S. 1357 includes Senate bill	10/28/1995 Amdt. to H.R. 2491 Vote of 52-47	11/16/ 1995 H.Rept. 104-347	11/20/1995 H.R. 2491 Vote of 235-192	11/17/1995 H.R. 2491 Vote of 52-47	12/6/1995 Vetoed
Freedom to Farm Act	8/4/1995 H.R. 2195 introduced 9/20/1995 fails cmte.	—	9/28/1995 unnumbered bill	—	—	—	—	—

	House		Senate		Conference Report Approval			
	Cmte.	Passage	Cmte.	Passage	Conf. Report	House Passage	Senate Passage	Public Law
Extension:	More than a year before expiration, extended the dairy program of the 1990 farm bill until 1996 and extended programs for wheat, feed grains, cotton, rice, peanuts, wool, and mohair until 1997 and honey until 1998.							8/10/1993 P.L. 103-66
1990 farm bill Food, Agriculture, Conservation, and Trade Act of 1990 Covers 1991-1995 crops or until 9/30/1995	2/5/1990 H.R. 3950 introduced 7/3/1990 H.Rept. 101-569	8/1/1990 H.R. 3950 Vote of 327-91	7/6/1990 S. 2830 S.Rept. 101-357	7/27/1990 S. 2830 Vote of 70-21	10/22/ 1990 H.Rept. 101-916	10/23/1990 S. 2830 Vote of 318-102	10/25/1990 S. 2830 Vote of 60-36	11/28/1990 P.L. 101-624
1985 farm bill Food Security Act of 1985 Covers 1986-1990 crops or until 9/30/1990	4/17/1985 H.R. 2100 introduced 9/13/1985 H.Rept. 99-271	10/8/1985 H.R. 2100 Vote of 282-141	9/30/1985 S. 1714 S.Rept. 99-145	11/23/1985 H.R. 2100 Vote of 61-28	12/17/ 1985 H.Rept. 99-447	12/18/1985 H.R. 2100 Vote of 325-96	12/18/1985 H.R. 2100 Vote of 55-38	12/23/1985 P.L. 99-198
1981 farm bill Agriculture and Food Act of 1981 Covers 1982-1985 crops or until 9/30/1985	5/18/1981 H.R. 3603 introduced 5/19/1981 H.Rept. 97-106	10/22/1981 S. 884 Vote of 192-160	4/7/1981 S. 884 introduced 5/27/1981 S.Rept. 97-126	9/18/1981 S. 884 Vote of 49-32	12/9/1981 H.Rept. 97-377 12/10/ 1981 S.Rept. 97-290	12/16/1981 S. 884 Vote of 205-203	12/10/1981 S. 884 Vote of 67-32	12/22/1981 P.L. 97-98

Table 1. (Continued)

	House		Senate		Conference Report Approval			
	Cmte.	Passage	Cmte.	Passage	Conf. Report	House Passage	Senate Passage	Public Law
1977 farm bill Food and Agriculture Act of 1977 Covers 1978-1981 crops or until 9/30/1981	5/13/1977 H.R. 7171 introduced 5/16/1977 H.Rept. 95-348	7/28/1977 Amdt. to S. 275 Vote of 294-114	1/18/1977 S. 275 introduced 5/16/1977 S.Rept. 95-180	5/24/1977 S. 275 Vote of 69-18	9/9/1977 S.Rept. 95-418	9/16/1977 S. 275 Vote of 283-107	9/9/1977 S. 275 Vote of 63-8	9/29/1977 P.L. 95-113
1973 farm bill Agriculture and Consumer Protection Act Covers 1974-1977 crops or until 6/30/1977	6/20/1973 H.R. 8860 introduced 6/27/1973 H.Rept. 93-337	7/19/1973 Amdt. to S. 1888 Vote of 226-182	5/23/1973 S. 1888 introduced S.Rept. 93-173	6/8/1973 S. 1888 Vote of 78-9	7/31/1973 H.Rept. 93-427	8/3/1973 S. 1888 Vote of 252-151	7/31/1973 S. 1888 Vote of 85-7	8/10/1973 P.L. 93-86
1970 farm bill Agricultural Act of 1970 Covers 1971-1973 crops	7/23/1970 H.R. 18546 H.Rept. 91-1329	8/5/1970 H.R. 18546 Vote of 212-171	9/4/1970 Amdt. to H.R. 18546 S.Rept. 91-1154	9/15/1970 Amdt. to H.R. 18546 Vote of 65-7	10/9/1970 H.Rept. 91-1594	10/13/1970 H.R. 18546 Vote of 191-145	11/19/1970 H.R. 18546 Vote of 48-35	11/30/1970 P.L. 91-524
Extension:	More than a year before expiration, extended the 1965 farm bill for one-year until 12/31/1970.							10/11/1968 P.L. 90-559

	House		**Senate**		**Conference Report Approval**			
	Cmte.	Passage	Cmte.	Passage	Conf. Report	House Passage	Senate Passage	Public Law
1965 farm bill Food and Agricultural Act Covers 1966-1969 crops	7/20/1965 H.R. 9811 H.Rept. 89-631	8/19/1965 H.R. 9811 Vote of 221-172	9/7/1965 Amdt. to H.R. 9811 S.Rept. 89-687	9/14/1965 Amdt. to H.R. 9811 Vote of 72-22	10/6/1965 H.Rept. 89-1123	10/8/1965 H.R. 9811 Vote of 219-150	10/12/1965 H.R. 9811 Voice vote	11/4/1965 P.L. 89-321

Source: CRS, using http://www.congress.gov. Includes only major legislative actions. Excludes subsequent revisions, such as in budget reconciliation, except for extensions as noted.

In: The Farm Bill
Editor: Billie Grant

ISBN: 978-1-53615-294-4

Chapter 5

ENERGY PROVISIONS IN THE 2014 FARM BILL (P.L. 113-79): STATUS AND FUNDING*

Kelsi Bracmort

ABSTRACT

Title IX, the energy title of the 2014 farm bill (Agricultural Act of 2014; P.L. 113-79), contains authority for the energy programs administered by the U.S. Department of Agriculture (USDA). USDA energy programs have incentivized research, development, and adoption of renewable energy projects, including solar, wind, and anaerobic digesters. However, the primary focus of USDA energy programs has been to promote U.S. biofuels production and use—including corn starch-based ethanol (the predominant biofuel produced and consumed in the United States), cellulosic ethanol, and soybean-based biodiesel. The USDA energy programs via the farm bill are separate from the Renewable Fuel Standard (RFS) and tax incentives contained in separate energy and tax legislation.

Three farm bills have contained an energy title: the 2002 farm bill, the 2008 farm bill, and the 2014 farm bill. For all three farm bills, the major

* This is an edited, reformatted and augmented version of Congressional Research Service, Publication No. R43416, dated July 12, 2018.

energy programs expire and lack baseline funding. The enacted 2014 farm bill extended most of the energy provisions of the 2008 farm bill with new funding authority, with the exception of the Rural Energy Self-Sufficiency Initiative, the Forest Biomass for Energy Program, the Biofuels Infrastructure Study, and the Renewable Fertilizer Study, which were either omitted or repealed. At issue for Congress is what oversight, programs, and initiatives, if any, an energy title under the forthcoming farm bill might support. The 2014 farm bill energy title provisions may be of interest during the upcoming farm bill debate, as Congress may decide to modify or reauthorize many of the programs.

The 2014 farm bill continued the attempt to refocus U.S. biofuels policy initiatives to favor non-corn feedstocks (e.g., cellulosic feedstocks). The most critical programs to this end are the Bioenergy Program for Advanced Biofuels, which pays producers for production of eligible advanced biofuels; the Biorefinery, Renewable Chemical, and Biobased Product Manufacturing Assistance Program (formerly Biorefinery Assistance Program), which assists in the development of new and emerging technologies for advanced biofuels; the Biomass Crop Assistance Program (BCAP), which assists farmers in developing nontraditional crops for use as feedstocks for the eventual production of cellulosic biofuels; and the Renewable Energy for America Program (REAP), which has funded a variety of biofuels-related projects. In addition, the 2014 farm bill included a new provision that precludes the use of REAP funding for any mechanism for dispensing energy at the retail level (e.g., blender pumps). Also, despite several amendments to the contrary, and its explicit exclusion from all financial support in the House-passed version of the 2014 farm bill (H.R. 2642), BCAP funding for the collection, harvest, storage, and transportation (CHST) component was retained in the 2014 farm bill. Finally, the 2014 farm bill added a new reporting requirement on energy use and efficiency at USDA facilities.

Over the five-year reauthorization period (FY2014-FY2018), the 2014 farm bill contained a total of $694 million in new mandatory funding and authorizes discretionary funding (i.e., subject to annual appropriations) of $765 million for the various farm bill renewable energy programs. This is a significant reduction from the 2008 farm bill, which had authorized slightly over $1 billion in mandatory funding over the five-year period of FY2008-FY2012, along with $1.7 billion in discretionary appropriations to Title IX energy programs. The mandatory funding has been the primary support for these programs, as appropriators have not provided funding for most of the discretionary authorizations.

OVERVIEW AND HISTORY

Agriculture-based renewable energy can take several forms, including biofuels such as corn-based ethanol or soy-based biodiesel, wind-driven turbines located on farmland or in rural areas, anaerobic digesters that convert animal waste into methane and electric power, or biomass harvested for burning as a processing fuel or to generate heat as part of an industrial activity.

Since the late 1970s, U.S. policymakers at both the federal and state levels have adopted a variety of incentives, regulations, and programs to encourage the production and use of agriculture-based renewable energy (mostly biofuels).[1] Over the years, the two most widely used biofuels—ethanol produced primarily from corn starch and biodiesel produced primarily from soybean oil—have received significant federal support in the form of tax incentives, loans and grants, and regulatory programs.[2] Many of these support programs originate in legislation outside of the farm bill. For instance, the Energy Tax Act of 1978 (P.L. 95-618) provided an exemption for ethanol from the excise tax on motor fuels. Congress subsequently provided a tax credit for blending ethanol with gasoline, which expired after 2011. By executive order[3] the Bioenergy Program was established in 1999 and in FY2001 began making payments from the U.S. Department of Agriculture's (USDA's) Commodity Credit Corporation (CCC)[4] to eligible producers of ethanol and biodiesel based on year-to-year production increases in these fuels. The Biomass Research and Development Act of 2000 (P.L. 106-224) directed USDA and the U.S. Department of Energy (DOE) to cooperate and coordinate research and development activities for

---

[1] For a list of federal incentives in support of biofuels production, see CRS Report R42566, *Alternative Fuel and Advanced Vehicle Technology Incentives: A Summary of Federal Programs*.

[2] See CRS Report R41282, *Agriculture-Based Biofuels: Overview and Emerging Issues*.

[3] The Bioenergy Program was initiated on August 12, 1999, by President Clinton's Executive Order 13134.

[4] The CCC is a U.S. government-owned and -operated corporation, created in 1933 with broad powers to support farm income and prices and to assist in the export of U.S. agricultural products. Toward this end, the CCC finances USDA's domestic farm commodity price and income support programs and certain export programs using its permanent authority to borrow up to $30 billion at any one time from the U.S. Treasury.

biobased industrial products, including biofuels. The 2002 farm bill (P.L. 107-171) authorized several new biofuel programs and added an energy title, Title IX. The 2008 farm bill (P.L. 110-246) subsequently extended and expanded the programs promoting biofuels renewable energy, emphasizing particularly those utilizing biomass feedstock. Motivations cited for these legislative initiatives included energy security concerns, reduction of greenhouse gas emissions from traditional fossil fuels, and raising domestic demand for U.S.-produced farm products.

By FY2011, federal biofuels subsidies peaked at approximately $7.7 billion,[5] of which an estimated $5.7 billion was attributable to the Volumetric Ethanol Excise Tax Credit (VEETC) of $0.45/gallon. However, the VEETC expired at the end of FY2011, and federal subsidies fell to an estimated $1.3 billion in FY2012—consisting primarily of tax credits of approximately $1 billion for biodiesel producers. The remaining biofuels tax credits—for biodiesel and second generation (formerly cellulosic) biofuel, and including a tax credit for small producers are temporary incentives, currently scheduled to expire at the end of 2017. In recent years, these credits have since been extended several times, most recently in the Bipartisan Budget Act of 2018 (BBA; P.L. 115-123).[6] In addition to these types of tax incentives and the Renewable Fuel Standard (RFS) that mandates a minimum level of renewable fuel usage, the provisions of Title IX of the 2014 farm bill, the Agricultural Act of 2014 (P.L. 113-79), represents a significant source of federal support for biofuels production and use in the United States.

Title IX of the 2014 farm bill continued long-standing congressional support for the production of renewable energy from agriculturally sourced materials. This chapter focuses on those policies contained in the 2014 farm bill that support agriculture-based renewable energy, especially biofuels.

---

[5] CRS estimates based on ethanol production data, tax incentives, and congressional appropriations. These estimates do not account for the implicit subsidy inherent in biofuels import tariffs.

[6] For more information, see CRS Report R44990, *Energy Tax Provisions That Expired in 2017 ("Tax Extenders")*, by Molly F. Sherlock, Donald J. Marples, and Margot L. Crandall-Hollick, and CRS Report R44677, *Tax Provisions that Expired in 2016 ("Tax Extenders")*, by Molly F. Sherlock.

The introductory sections of this chapter briefly describe how USDA bioenergy policies evolved and how they fit into the larger context of U.S. biofuels policy. Then, each of the bioenergy provisions of the 2014 farm bill are defined in terms of their function, goals, administration, funding, and implementation status.

In an appendix at the end of this chapter, Table A-1 presents data on 2014 farm bill budgetary authority for energy provisions, while Table A-2 presents the original budget authority for Title IX programs under the previous 2008 farm bill. A third table (Table A-3) provides a side-by-side comparison of Title IX energy-related provisions for current versus previous law.

Renewable energy production plays a key role not just in agricultural policy, but also in energy, tax, and environmental policy. As a result, many of the federal programs that support renewable energy production in general, and agriculture-based energy production in particular, are outside the purview of USDA and have origins outside of omnibus farm bill legislation. For example, the three principal federal biofuels policies of the past decade were all established outside of farm bills

- The Renewable Fuel Standard (RFS) mandates an increasing volume of biofuels use and has its origins in the Energy Policy Act of 2005 (P.L. 109-58). The RFS was expanded in the Energy Independence and Security Act of 2007 (EISA; P.L. 110-140) and divided into four distinct, but nested categories—total, advanced, cellulosic, and biodiesel—each with its own mandated volume.[7]
- The volumetric ethanol excise tax credit (VEETC), originally established in the American Jobs Creation Act of 2004 (P.L. 108-357), provided a tax credit that varied in value over the years, which amounted to $0.45 per gallon of pure ethanol blended with gasoline when it expired on December 31, 2011.[8]

---

[7] See CRS Report R43325, *The Renewable Fuel Standard (RFS): An Overview*, by Kelsi Bracmort.

[8] For more information, see CRS Report R41282, *Agriculture-Based Biofuels: Overview and Emerging Issues*.

- The ethanol import tariff (a most-favored-nation duty of $0.54 per gallon) was intended to offset the blending tax credit and was originally established by the Omnibus Reconciliation Act of 1980 (P.L. 96-499). The ethanol import tariff also expired on December 31, 2011.

In addition to the RFS, VEETC, and ethanol import tariff, several other tax credits that originated outside of farm bills were available for biodiesel production as well as for small producers (less than 60 million gallons per year per plant) of ethanol and biodiesel. A substantial number of federal programs also support renewable energy sources other than biofuels.[9] In addition to federal programs, many states offer additional support to biofuels producers, blenders, and consumers.[10]

An awareness of the non-USDA federal programs is important for appreciating the role envisioned for the energy title of the 2014 farm bill, which was designed to provide incentives for the research and development of new agriculture-based renewable fuels, especially second-generation biofuels (those based on non-food crop biomass such as cellulose and algae), and to expand their distribution and use. A summary of the evolution of these programs follows.

2002 Farm Bill—First Energy Title

The 2002 farm bill (Farm Security and Rural Investment Act of 2002; P.L. 107-171) was the first omnibus farm bill to explicitly include an energy title (Title IX). The energy title authorized grants, loans, and loan guarantees to foster research on agriculture-based renewable energy, to share development risk and to promote the adoption of renewable energy

---

[9] For a complete listing of federal programs that support all types of renewable energy, see CRS Report R40913, *Renewable Energy and Energy Efficiency Incentives: A Summary of Federal Programs*, by Lynn J. Cunningham.

[10] For information on state programs, see "Database of State Incentives for Renewables & Efficiency (DSIRE)," at http://www.dsireusa.org/.

systems.[11] Since enactment of the 2002 farm bill, interest in renewable energy has grown rapidly, due in large part to periods of steep increases in domestic and international petroleum prices and a dramatic acceleration in domestic biofuels production (primarily corn-based ethanol).

2008 Farm Bill—Refocus on Non-Corn-Based Biofuels

Annual U.S. ethanol production expanded rapidly between 2002 and 2007, rising from approximately 2 billion gallons to over 6.5 billion gallons during that period.[12] Similarly, corn use for ethanol grew from an 11% share of the U.S. corn crop in 2002 to an estimated 23% share of the 2007 corn crop.[13] During the 2008 farm bill debate, projections had ethanol's corn-use share rising rapidly, sparking concerns about unintended consequences of the policy-driven expansion of U.S. corn ethanol production. Dedicating an increasing share of the U.S. corn harvest to ethanol production evoked fears of higher prices for all grains and oilseeds that compete for the same land, which could lead to higher livestock feed costs, higher food prices, and lower U.S. agricultural exports. In addition, several environmental concerns emerged regarding the expansion of corn production onto nontraditional lands, including native grass and prairie land. In response, policymakers sought to refocus biofuels policy initiatives in the 2008 farm bill (the Food, Conservation, and Energy Act of 2008; P.L. 110-246) in favor of non-corn starch feedstock, especially cellulosic-based feedstock, by introducing a number of programs aimed at facilitating the production and use of bioenergy from nonfood feedstock, mainly biomass.

Renewable energy policy in the 2008 farm bill became law six months after the enactment of the EISA. A key component of EISA was a significant

---

[11] For an overview of the 2002 farm bill's energy title, see CRS Report RL33037, *Previewing a 2007 Farm Bill*.

[12] U.S. Energy Information Administration, *Short-Term Energy Outlook*, 2017. For a discussion of the rapid growth of the U.S. biofuels sector, see CRS Report R41282, *Agriculture-Based Biofuels: Overview and Emerging Issues*.

[13] U.S. Department of Energy, *Maps and Data - U.S. Total Corn Production and Corn Used for Fuel Ethanol Production*, September 2016.

expansion of the RFS, which in part mandates the increasing use of "advanced biofuels" (i.e., non-corn starch biofuels), whose minimum use was scheduled to increase from zero gallons in 2008 to 21 billion gallons by 2022.[14] The energy provisions of the 2008 farm– bill were intended to reinforce EISA's program goals via a further refocusing of federal incentives toward non-corn sources of renewable energy.

2014 Farm Bill—Extends Most Programs with New Funding

All of the major energy programs from the 2008 farm bill expired at the end of FY2013 and lacked baseline funding going forward. The enacted 2014 farm bill (P.L. 113-79) extended most of the renewable energy provisions of the 2008 farm bill and provided new mandatory funding, with some notable exceptions. Again, most of these 2014 farm bill energy programs lack a mandatory funding baseline going forward beyond FY2018.[15] Key energy-related provisions in the 2014 farm bill include

- Section 9002, which extended the Biobased Markets Program that promotes biobased products through a federal purchasing requirement and a labeling initiative;
- Section 9003, which extended the Biorefinery Assistance Program with new funding and renamed as the Biorefinery, Renewable Chemical, and Biobased Product Manufacturing Assistance Program;
- Section 9004, which extended the Repowering Assistance Program with new funding;
- Section 9005, which extended the Bioenergy Program for Advanced Biofuels with new funding;
- Section 9006, which extended the Biodiesel Fuel Education Program with new funding;

---

[14] 42 U.S.C. §7545(o).

[15] For more information, see CRS Report R44758, *Farm Bill Programs Without a Budget Baseline Beyond FY2018*, by Jim Monke.

- Section 9007, which extended the Renewable Energy for America Program (REAP)—which provides support for rural energy efficiency and self-sufficiency and biofuels marketing infrastructure—with new funding, but included a new provision which precludes the use of REAP funding for any mechanism for dispensing energy at the retail level (for example, blender pumps);
- Section 9008, which extended the Biomass Research and Development Initiative (BRDI) with new funding for biofuels research programs within USDA and DOE;
- Section 9009, which extended the sugar-to-ethanol Feedstock Flexibility Program;
- Section 9010, which extended the Biomass Crop Assistance Program (BCAP), including the collection, harvesting, storage, and transportation (CHST) component designed to incentivize the production of cellulosic ethanol feedstock;
- Section 9011, which repealed the Forest Biomass for Energy Program;
- Section 9012, which extended the Community Wood Energy Program with new funding;
- Section 9013, which repealed the Biofuels Infrastructure Study;
- Section 9014, which repealed the Renewable Fertilizer Study;
- Section 9015, which added a new reporting requirement on energy use and efficiency at USDA facilities;
- Section 7212, which repealed the Agricultural Bioenergy Feedstock and Energy Efficiency Research and Extension Initiative; and
- Section 7526, which reauthorized, with new funding, the Sun Grant Initiative programs that provide funding for competitive grants and coordinate research on advanced biofuels at land-grant universities and federally funded laboratories.

The 2014 farm bill excluded the Rural Energy Self-Sufficiency Initiative of the 2008 farm bill. Each of the above-cited programs is described in more detail in the section below entitled "Major Energy Provisions in the 2014 Farm Bill."

FUNDING FOR AGRICULTURE-BASED ENERGY PROGRAMS

In general, two types of funding are authorized by Congress in a farm bill—mandatory and discretionary. Some farm bill programs identified as receiving mandatory funds (including most of the bioenergy programs) are automatically funded at levels "authorized" in the farm bill unless Congress limits funding to a lower amount through the appropriations or legislative process.[16] For many of these programs, mandatory funding is provided through the borrowing authority of USDA's Commodity Credit Corporation (CCC).[17] The farm bill may also specify some discretionary funding as "authorized to be appropriated"—such discretionary funding is actually determined each year through the annual appropriations process and may or may not reflect the funding level suggested in the authorizing legislation.

Funding under the 2008 Farm Bill

The 2008 farm bill authorized slightly over $1 billion in mandatory funding and $1.1 billion in discretionary appropriations to Title IX energy programs for FY2008-FY2012 (Table A-2). Mandatory authorizations included $320 million to the Biorefinery Assistance Program, $300 million to the Bioenergy Program for Advanced Biofuels, and $255 million to the

---

[16] Mandatory funding remains subject to sequestration under the Budget Control Act of 2011 (P.L. 112-25). Mandatory funding may also be reduced by appropriation acts via Changes in Mandatory Program Spending (CHIMPS).

[17] The CCC is the funding mechanism for the mandatory payments that are administered by various agencies of USDA, including all of the farm commodity price and income support programs and selected conservation programs. For more information on the CCC, see CRS Report R44606, *The Commodity Credit Corporation: In Brief*, by Megan Stubbs. For more information on mandatory versus discretionary authorizations, CHIMPS, and sequestration, see CRS Report R44588, *Agriculture and Related Agencies: FY2017 Appropriations*, coordinated by Jim Monke.

Rural Energy for America Program (REAP). The Biomass Crop Assistance Program (BCAP) was authorized to receive such sums as necessary (i.e., funding is open-ended and depends on program participation); however, limits were later set on BCAP outlays under the annual appropriations process beginning in FY2010.[18]

The $1.1 billion of discretionary funding authorization included $600 million for the Biorefinery Assistance Program. Authorized discretionary appropriations included $100 million for both the Bioenergy Program for Advanced Biofuels and REAP. However, actual discretionary appropriations of $106 million through FY2012 to all Title IX energy programs were substantially below authorized levels.

As regards mandatory funding, all of the bioenergy provisions of Title IX—with the exception of Section 9010, the Feedstock Flexibility Program for Bioenergy Producers, which is authorized indefinitely—had mandatory funding only for the life of the 2008 farm bill, FY2008 through FY2012. As a result, all of the bioenergy provisions in Title IX of the 2008 farm bill, with the exception of the Feedstock Flexibility Program for Bioenergy Producers (§9010), expired on September 30, 2012.[19]

Funding under Continuing Resolutions for FY2013

The 112th Congress did not complete action on any of the regular FY2013 appropriations bills during 2012. Instead, a continuing resolution (CR) for the first half of FY2013 (P.L. 112-175) was signed into law on September 28, 2012.[20] This was followed by a second CR to provide appropriations for the second half of FY2013 (P.L. 113-6).[21] The Rural Energy for America Program was the sole Title IX bioenergy program that received an appropriation of discretionary funds ($3.4 million) in FY2013.

[18] See CRS Report R41296, *Biomass Crop Assistance Program (BCAP): Status and Issues*, by Mark A. McMinimy.

[19] For more information, see CRS Report R42442, *Expiration and Extension of the 2008 Farm Bill.*

[20] See out-of-print CRS Report R42782, *FY2013 Continuing Resolutions: Analysis of Components and Congressional Action*, available upon request for congressional staff from the author.

[21] Consolidated and Further Continuing Appropriations Act, 2013, P.L. 113-6, March 26, 2013.

Funding under ATRA—The 2008 Farm Bill Extension

Many of the 2008 farm bill programs were extended through September 30, 2013, by Section 701 of the American Taxpayer Relief Act of 2012 (ATRA; P.L. 112-240) signed into law by President Obama on January 2, 2013. Under ATRA, discretionary funding was authorized to be appropriated at the rate that programs were funded under the 2008 farm bill.

Funding under the 2014 Farm Bill

The five-year reauthorization period (FY2014-FY2018) of the 2014 farm bill (P.L. 113-79) contained a total of $694 million in new mandatory funding and authorized $765 million to be appropriated for the various farm bill renewable energy programs (Table A-1). Details of the actual funding levels provided in FY2014-FY2016 appropriations bills are provided in the discussion of individual provisions below and are summarized in the appendix tables. Under the 2014 farm bill, Congress has acted through annual appropriations bills to lower the amount of mandatory funding available to four of these programs (§9003, §9004, §9005, and §9010) and has not appropriated discretionary funding for most of these programs.

Major Energy Provisions in the 2014 Farm Bill

What follows is a summary of the bioenergy-related authorities found in the 2014 farm bill, including (where applicable) a brief description of each program, funding levels, and the status of program implementation, including any noteworthy changes made by the 2014 farm bill.

Like the two preceding farm bills, the 2014 farm bill (P.L. 113-79) contained a distinct energy title (Title IX) that extends many of the previous bioenergy programs.[22] Four previous provisions are omitted or repealed, and

[22] For a side-by-side comparison of previous law with the energy provisions of the 2014 farm bill, see Table A-3 at the end of this chapter.

a new provision, Section 9015, was added to require USDA to submit a report to the House and Senate Agriculture Committees on energy use and energy efficiency projects at USDA facilities. Two bioenergy-related provisions in the Research Title (Title VII)—one extended, one repealed—are also included in the following discussion.

TITLE IX—ENERGY PROVISIONS

Section 9001: Definitions

The 2014 farm bill made four substantive modifications to bioenergy related definitions as follows (7 U.S.C. §8101):

1) "biobased product"—similar to prior law except for the explicit inclusion of forestry materials that meet biobased content requirements, notwithstanding the market share the product holds, the age of the product, or whether the market for the product is new or emerging;
2) "forest product"—defined as a product made from materials derived from the practice of forestry or the management of growing timber, including pulp, paper, paperboard, pellets, lumber, and wood products, and any recycled products derived from forest materials;
3) "renewable chemical"—defined as a monomer, polymer, plastic, formulated product, or chemical substance produced from renewable biomass; and
4) "renewable energy system"—defined as a system that produces energy from a renewable source, including distribution components necessary to move energy produced by such a system to the initial point of sale, but not any mechanism for dispensing energy at retail (e.g., a blender pump).

The first three modifications were designed to expand access to federal support for renewable energy to forestry products and renewable chemicals.

The new definition for renewable energy systems was intended to prohibit REAP funds from being used for blender pumps.

Section 9002: Biobased Markets Program

Administered by

Assistant Secretary for Administration, USDA.[23]

Program Overview

The Biobased Markets Program was originally established under the 2002 farm bill as a federal procurement preference program that required federal agencies to purchase biobased products under certain conditions (7 U.S.C. §8102). The 2008 farm bill renamed the federal biobased procurements preference program as the Biobased Markets Program. USDA refers to the program as the BioPreferred® Program.[24] The BioPreferred® Program promotes biobased products—those derived from marine and forestry materials—through two initiatives: (1) a mandatory purchasing requirement for federal agencies and their contractors and (2) a voluntary labeling initiative for biobased products. Products that meet the minimum biobased content criteria may display the USDA Certified Biobased Product label.[25]

Under the Biobased Markets Program, federal agencies and their contractors are generally required to purchase biobased products from 97 categories of goods—among which are cleaners, carpets, lubricants, office supplies, and paints—when an agency procures $10,000 or more worth of an item within these categories during the course of a fiscal year, or where

---

[23] The official USDA biobased markets program website is at http://www.biopreferred.gov/.

[24] OEPNU, OCE, USDA, *Metrics to Support Informed Decision Making for Consumers of Biobased Products*, by Marvin Duncan, Barbara C. Lippiatt, Zia Haq, Michael Wang, and Roger Conway, AIB No. 803, October 2008.

[25] For policies and laws, see http://www.biopreferred.gov/BioPreferred/faces/pages/PoliciesAndLaws.xhtml.

the quantity of such items or of functionally equivalent items purchased during the preceding fiscal year was $10,000 or more.[26]

Changes in 2014 Farm Bill

The 2014 farm bill (P.L. 113-79) extended the Biobased Markets Program through FY2018 while adding several new implementation requirements, including reporting of quantities and types of biobased purchases by federal agencies with a focus on biobased content requirements (explicitly including forest products); mandating (within one year of enactment) designation of intermediate ingredients or feedstocks and assembled and finished biobased products according to guidelines; adding auditing and compliance activities to ensure proper use of biobased labeling; mandating a study and report by USDA to assess the economic impact of the biobased product industry (due 180 days after enactment); and encouraging expedited coordination, review, and approval (with appropriate technical assistance) of forest-related biobased products. USDA issued two final rules implementing these changes on June 15, 2015: 7 C.F.R. 3201 on designating biobased products for federal procurement and 7 C.F.R. 3202 on voluntary labeling for biobased products.

Funding

The 2014 farm bill authorized mandatory CCC funding of $3 million for each of FY2014-FY2018 for biobased products testing and labeling. Discretionary funding of $2 million was authorized to be appropriated for each of FY2014-FY2018. However, through FY2018 no discretionary funding has ever been appropriated for the Biobased Markets Program. This compares with mandatory funding authorized by the 2008 farm bill of $9 million—including $1 million for FY2008 and $2 million for each of FY2009-FY2012—for biobased products testing and labeling. In the 2008 farm bill, discretionary funding of $2 million was authorized to be appropriated for each of FY2009-FY2012. The program went unfunded in

[26] For more detail and exceptions to this requirement, see http://www.ecfr.gov/cgi-bin/text-idx?SID=f511776b8ee3c0092343d0e8736f5224&mc=true&node=se7.15.3201_13&rgn=div8.

FY2013, as ATRA provided no mandatory funding for it. Discretionary funds of $2 million were authorized to be appropriated, but no appropriations were provided under either of the CRs for FY2013 (P.L. 112-175 or P.L. 113-6).

Section 9003: Biorefinery, Renewable Chemical, and Biobased Product Manufacturing Assistance Program

Administered by

Rural Business and Cooperative Service, Rural Development Agency (RD), USDA in consultation with DOE.

Program Overview

Originally called the Biorefinery Assistance Program (BAP) as authorized in the 2008 farm bill, this program assists in the development of new and emerging technologies for advanced biofuels.[27] Competitive grants and loan guarantees are available for construction and/or retrofitting of demonstration-scale biorefineries to demonstrate the commercial viability of one or more processes for converting renewable biomass to advanced biofuels. Biorefinery grants can provide for up to 30% of total project costs. Each loan guarantee is limited to $250 million or 80% of project cost (7 U.S.C. §8103). Mandatory funds are used for the loan guarantee portion of BAP, whereas discretionary appropriations are to be used to fund grants.[28] However, since Congress never appropriated any discretionary funds for BAP during the life of the 2008 farm bill, USDA has only moved forward with the loan guarantee portion of BAP. Rural Development administers the program under 7 C.F.R. 4279, Subpart C, and 7 C.F.R. 4287, Part D.

---

[27] For more program information, see Biorefinery, Renewable Chemical, and Biobased Product Manufacturing Assistance Program, Business and Cooperative Programs (BCP), Rural Development (RD), USDA, at https://www.rd.usda.gov/programs-services/biorefinery-renewable-chemical-and-biobased-product-manufacturing-assistance.

[28] Based on information received by CRS from Kelly Oehler, Branch Chief, Energy Division, RD, USDA.

For loan guarantees, project lenders (not prospective borrowers) must submit the application.[29] Each loan guarantee application undergoes at least three rounds of review within USDA, including review by the Rural Development Agency, USDA; the National Renewable Energy Laboratory (NREL), DOE; and the Office of the Chief Economist (OCE), USDA.

Changes in 2014 Farm Bill

Renamed the Biorefinery Assistance Program as the Biorefinery, Renewable Chemical, and Biobased Product Manufacturing Assistance Program. Funding for grants is eliminated. The program assists in the development of new and emerging technologies for advanced biofuels, renewable chemicals, and biobased products. The lender or borrower may submit a letter of intent to apply for the loan guarantee. Also, P.L. 113-79 directs USDA to ensure diversity in the types of projects approved and caps the funds used for loan guarantees to promote biobased product manufacturing at 15% of the total available mandatory funds.

Funding

Under the 2014 farm bill, mandatory CCC funding of $100 million in FY2014 and $50 million each for FY2015 and FY2016 (to remain available until expended) was authorized to support making loan guarantees. Thus, there is no new baseline funding after FY2016 except for any carryover. The FY2014 appropriations act (P.L. 113-76) rescinded $40.7 million of funds available, while the FY2015, FY2016, and FY2017 appropriations acts (P.L. 113-235, P.L. 114-113, and P.L. 115-31) limited funding to $30 million, $27 million, and $151 million, respectively.[30] Discretionary funding of $75 million annually is authorized for FY2014-FY2018, but no discretionary funds have been appropriated through FY2018. Under the 2008 farm bill, mandatory CCC funding amounted to $75 million for FY2009, $245 million for FY2010 (to remain available until expended), and $0 for FY2011 and

[29] More information on the BAP loan guarantee applications is available at https://www.ecfr.gov/cgi-bin/text-idx?SID=053b4252b720dd2ab341a62759c8032c&pitd=20150624&node=20150624y1.19.

[30] §9003 was subject to changes in mandatory spending (CHIMPS) of $20 million for FY2017.

FY2012, with any mandatory funding unspent from the FY2010 allocation of $245 million to remain available through FY2013. Discretionary funding of $150 million annually was authorized for FY2009-FY2013 for grants under the 2008 farm bill and the ATRA extension. However, no discretionary funding was appropriated for BAP through FY2013.

Section 9004: Repowering Assistance Program (RAP)

Administered by Rural Business and Cooperative Service, RD, USDA.

Program Overview

The Repowering Assistance Program (RAP) was originally established under the 2002 farm bill as a grant program to help finance the cost of developing and constructing bio-refineries and biofuels production plants to carry out projects to demonstrate the commercial viability of converting biomass to fuels or chemicals. The 2008 farm bill altered RAP's orientation to focus on converting fossil fuel-burning plants to biomass or some other renewable fuel source for processing energy.

RAP makes payments to eligible biorefineries (i.e., those in existence on the date of enactment of the 2008 farm bill, June 18, 2008) to encourage the use of renewable biomass as a replacement for fossil fuels used to provide heat for processing or power in the operation of these eligible biorefineries.[31] Not more than 5% of the funds shall be made available to eligible producers with a refining capacity exceeding 150 million gallons of advanced biofuel per year.[32] Individual project awards are limited to $5 million or 50% of total eligible project costs, whichever is less (7 C.F.R., Part 4288, Subpart A).

[31] For more program information, see "Section 9004: Repowering Assistance Program," BCP, RD, USDA, at https://www.rd.usda.gov/programs-services/repowering-assistance-program.

[32] 7 C.F.R. §4288.131.

Changes in 2014 Farm Bill

RAP was extended without changes to program implementation other than new funding levels.

Funding

The 2014 farm bill authorized mandatory CCC funding of $12 million for FY2014 to remain available until expended (i.e., no new baseline funding after FY2014). The FY2015 appropriations act reduced available funds by $8 million. Discretionary funding of $10 million annually for FY2014-FY2018 was authorized to be appropriated, but through FY2018 no discretionary funding had been appropriated. The 2008 farm bill authorized mandatory CCC funding of $35 million for FY2009 to remain available until expended. Discretionary funding of $15 million annually for FY2009-FY2013 was authorized to be appropriated under the 2008 farm bill and the ATRA extension; however, during this period the only appropriation was $15 million in FY2010. No new mandatory funding was included for RAP under the ATRA farm bill extension; however, any mandatory funding unspent from the FY2009 allocation of $35 million remained available through FY2013.

Section 9005: Bioenergy Program for Advanced Biofuels

Administered by Rural Business and Cooperative Service, RD, USDA.

Program Overview

Originally created by a 1999 executive order during the Clinton Administration, the bioenergy program provided mandatory CCC incentive payments to biofuels producers based on year-to-year increases in the quantity of biofuel produced. The 2002 farm bill provided mandatory funding for the program of $150 million annually for FY2002 through FY2006, but the program lapsed without funding in FY2007. The 2008 farm bill established a new Bioenergy Program for Advanced Biofuels to support and expand production of advanced biofuels—that is, fuel derived from renewable biomass other than corn kernel starch—under which USDA would enter into contracts with advanced biofuel producers to pay them for production of eligible advanced biofuels.[33] The policy goal is to create long-term, sustained increases in advanced biofuels production (7 U.S.C. §8105). Payments are of two types: one based on actual production, and a second based on incremental production increases. Not more than 5% of the funds in any year can go to facilities with total refining capacity exceeding 150 million gallons per year (7 C.F.R. Part 4288, Subpart B).

Changes in 2014 Farm Bill

Extended the Bioenergy Program for Advanced Biofuels through FY2018 without changes to program implementation other than new funding levels.

Funding

The 2014 farm bill authorized mandatory CCC funding of $15 million for each of FY2014-FY2018 to remain available until expended. The FY2014 appropriations act reduced funds available by $8 million in that year. Discretionary funding of $20 million annually for FY2014-FY2018 was authorized to be appropriated under the 2014 farm bill. However, no discretionary funding has been appropriated for the Bioenergy Program for Advanced Biofuels program through FY2018. The 2008 farm bill authorized mandatory CCC funding of $55 million for 2009, $55 million for FY2010, $85 million for FY2011, and $105 million for FY2012 to remain available until expended. Subsequently, the final FY2012 agriculture appropriations act (P.L. 112-55) limited mandatory spending to $65 million. Discretionary funding of $25 million annually for FY2009-FY2013 was authorized to be appropriated under the 2008 farm bill and the ATRA extension.

---

[33] For more program information, see the "Advanced Biofuel Payment Program," RD, USDA at https://www.rd.usda.gov/programs-services/advanced-biofuel-payment-program.

Section 9006: Biodiesel Fuel Education Program

Administered by National Institute of Food and Agriculture (NIFA) and Office of Energy Policy and New Uses (OEPNU), OCE, USDA.

Program Overview

Originally established under the 2002 farm bill, the Biodiesel Fuel Education Program was extended by both the 2008 and 2014 farm bills (7 U.S.C. §8106). The Biodiesel Fuel Education Program awards competitive grants to nonprofit organizations that educate governmental and private entities that operate vehicle fleets, and educates the public about the benefits of biodiesel fuel use. The program is implemented by USDA through continuation grants.[34] The final rule for the program was published on September 30, 2003 (68 *Federal Register* 56137).

Changes in 2014 Farm Bill

Extended the Biodiesel Fuel Education Program from FY2014 through FY2018 without changes to program implementation other than new funding levels.

Funding

Under the 2014 farm bill, mandatory CCC funds of $1 million were provided annually for FY2014-FY2018. Discretionary funds of $1 million each for FY2014-FY2018 were authorized to be appropriated, but through FY2018 no discretionary funding has been provided. Under the 2008 farm bill, mandatory CCC funds of $1 million were provided annually for FY2008-FY2012.

---

[34] USDA reports that a new continuation grant is an award for a successful project application that has not been previously submitted, and by which the Department agrees to support a specified level of effort for a predetermined project period with a statement of intention to provide additional support at a future date, contingent upon the availability of appropriated funds and the satisfactory progress of this project, and the determination that continued support would be in the best interest of the federal government and the public. U.S. Department of Agriculture, *Biodiesel Fuel Education Program, Fiscal Year 2014 Request for Applications*, June 27, 2014.

Section 9007: Rural Energy for America Program (REAP)

Administered by REAP is administered by the Rural Business and Cooperative Service, Rural Development, USDA.

Program Overview

The 2008 farm bill combined elements of two existing programs from the 2002 farm bill—the Energy Audit and Renewable Energy Development Program and the RES and EEI Program—into a single program renamed the Rural Energy for America Program (REAP), (7 U.S.C. §8107).

REAP provides various types of financial assistance under a cost-share arrangement for the following purposes:

- grants, guaranteed loans, and combined grants and guaranteed loans for the development and construction of renewable energy systems (RES) and for energy efficiency improvement (EEI) projects (eligible entities include rural small businesses and agricultural producers);
- grants for conducting energy audits and for conducting renewable energy development assistance (eligible entities include state, tribe, or local governments; land-grant colleges and universities; rural electric cooperatives; and public power entities); and
- grants for conducting renewable energy systems (RES) feasibility studies (eligible entities include rural small businesses and agricultural producers).

The cost share feature of REAP limits the government's contribution to no more than 75% of eligible project costs for RES systems and energy efficiency improvement funding for guaranteed loan-only requests and for combination guaranteed loan and grant requests, while government's share of the grant portion may not exceed 25% of the total project costs whether the grant is grant-only or part of a combination request. Under energy audit and renewable energy development assistance grants, a grantee must pay a minimum of 25% of the cost of the energy audit. RES systems include those that generate energy from bioenergy (but excluding any mechanism for dispensing energy at retail—e.g., a blender pump), anaerobic digesters, geothermal, hydrogen, solar, wind, and hydropower. Energy-efficiency improvement (EEI) projects typically involve installing or upgrading equipment to significantly reduce energy use. REAP operates under regulations published under 7 C.F.R. Part 4280, subpart B.

Changes in 2014 Farm Bill

Extended REAP through FY2018, plus added new funding and a three-tiered application process with separate application processes for grants and loan guarantees for RES and EEI projects based on the project cost: tier-1 for projects < $80,000; tier-2 for projects > $80,000 but < $200,000; and tier-3 for projects > $200,000. In addition, a renewable energy system (RES) was redefined to exclude any mechanism for dispensing energy at retail—most notably blender pumps.

Funding

Under the 2014 farm bill, mandatory CCC funds of $50 million were authorized for FY2014 and each fiscal year thereafter (thus, unlike other farm bill renewable energy programs, REAP's mandatory funding authority does not expire with the 2014 farm bill). Mandatory funds are to remain available until expended. Discretionary funding of $20 million annually was authorized to be appropriated for FY2014-FY2018; of this amount, $3.5 million was appropriated for FY2014, $1.35 million in FY2015, $0.5 million for FY2016, $352,000 in FY2017, and $293,000 in FY2018 under annual appropriations acts. Under the 2008 farm bill, mandatory CCC funds of $55 million in FY2009, $60 million in FY2010, $70 million in FY2011, and $70 million in FY2012 were authorized, to remain available until expended. Discretionary funding of $25 million annually was authorized to be appropriated for FY2009-FY2012. Actual discretionary appropriations were $5 million in FY2009, $39.3 million in FY2010, $5 million in FY2011, and $3.4 million in FY2012 and in FY2013. The FY2011 appropriations act (Department of Defense and Full-Year Continuing Appropriations Act, 2011; P.L. 112-10) reduced REAP discretionary funds from $25 million to

$5 million, but left REAP's mandatory funding of $70 million intact. The FY2012 Agriculture Appropriations Act (P.L. 112-55) limited REAP mandatory spending to $22 million, while $3.4 million in discretionary funds was appropriated, to be divided evenly between grants and loan guarantees. Under ATRA, no new mandatory funding was included for REAP; however, discretionary funding of $25 million was authorized to be appropriated for FY2013.

Section 9008: Biomass Research and Development Initiative (BRDI)

Administered by National Institute of Food and Agriculture (NIFA), USDA, and DOE, jointly.

Program Overview

BRDI—created originally under the Biomass Research and Development Act of 2000 (BRDA; P.L. 106-224)—seeks to foster significant commercial production of biofuels, biobased energy innovations, development of biobased feedstocks, and biobased products and processes, including cost-competitive cellulosic ethanol. To this end, the program provides competitive funding in the form of grants, contracts, and financial assistance for research, development, and demonstration of technologies and processes. Eligibility is limited to institutions of higher learning, national laboratories, federal or state research agencies, private-sector entities, and nonprofit organizations.

BRDI provides for coordination of biomass research and development, including life-cycle analysis of biofuels, between USDA and DOE by creating the Biomass Research and Development Board to coordinate government activities in biomass research, and the Biomass Research and Development Technical Advisory Committee to advise on proposal direction and evaluation.[35] The 2008 farm bill moved BRDA in statute to

[35] For more information on the Biomass Research and Development Board, the Technical Advisory Committee, and project selection, https://biomassboard.gov/.

Title IX of the 2008 farm bill and expanded the BRDI technical advisory committee (7 U.S.C. §8108).

Since 2002 USDA and DOE jointly have announced annual solicitations and awards of funding allocations under BRDI.[36] Pursuant to the 2008 farm bill, applicants seeking BRDI funding must propose projects that integrate science and engineering research in the following three technical areas that are critical to the broader success of alternative biofuels production: feedstock development, biofuels and biobased products development, and biofuels development analysis. A minimum of 15% of funding must go to each area.[37] The minimum cost-share requirement for demonstration projects was increased to 50%, and for research projects to 20%.

Changes in 2014 Farm Bill

Extended BRDI through FY2018 without changes to program implementation other than new funding levels.

Funding

The 2014 farm bill authorized mandatory funding (to remain available until expended) of $3 million for four fiscal years—FY2014-FY2017—with baseline funding authority expiring after FY2017. Discretionary funding of $20 million was authorized to be appropriated annually for FY2014-FY2018. However, no discretionary funding from USDA has been appropriated for BRDI through FY2018. A DOE funding match of up to $3 million annually of discretionary funding is subject to annual appropriations.[38] DOE reports it contributed up to $3 million for FY2017, and that it will not contribute funding for FY2018.[39] The 2008 farm bill authorized mandatory funding (to remain available until expended) of $20

[36] For BRDI current and historical (FY2003-FY2015) solicitations and awards, visit https://nifa.usda.gov/funding-opportunity/biomass-research-and-development-initiative-brdi and https://biomassboard.gov/initiative/ past_solicitations.html.

[37] For details on BRDI technical areas, see https://biomassboard.gov/initiative/initiative.html.

[38] U.S. Department of Energy in Partnership with U.S. Department of Agriculture, *Financial Assistance Funding Opportunity Announcement Fiscal Year 2017 Biomass Research and Development Request for Applications,* DE-FOA-0001637, June 5, 2017.

[39] Emails from DOE on September 5, 2017, and April 17, 2018. DOE reports it provides funding for this program every other year.

million for FY2009, $28 million for FY2010, $30 million for FY2011, and $40 million for FY2012. Discretionary funding of $35 million was authorized to be appropriated annually for FY2009-FY2012. Under ATRA, no new mandatory funding was included for BRDI; however, discretionary funding of $35 million was authorized to be appropriated for FY2013.

Section 9009: Feedstock Flexibility Program (FFP) for Bioenergy Producers

Administered by Farm Service Agency (FSA), USDA.

Program Overview

Under the 2008 farm bill, the Feedstock Flexibility Program required that USDA establish and administer a sugar-for-ethanol program using sugar intended for food use but deemed to be in surplus. USDA would subsidize the use of sugar for ethanol production through federal purchases of surplus sugar for resale to ethanol producers. USDA would implement the program only in those years where purchases are determined to be necessary to ensure that the sugar program operates at no cost to the federal government (7 U.S.C. §8110).

The intent of the FFP is to provide the CCC a tool for avoiding sugar forfeitures. Under the sugar program, domestic sugar beet or sugarcane processors may borrow from the CCC, pledging their sugar production as collateral for any such loan, and then satisfy their loans either by repaying the loan on or before loan maturity, or by transferring the title for the collateral to the CCC immediately following loan maturity, also known as "forfeiture" of collateral (as specified in 7 C.F.R. 1435). The CCC is required to operate the sugar program, to the maximum extent practicable at no cost to the federal government, by avoiding forfeitures to CCC. If domestic sugar market conditions are such that market rates are less than forfeiture level (i.e., forfeitures appear likely), current law requires CCC to use FFP to purchase sugar and sell such sugar to bioenergy producers to avoid forfeitures.

The FFP became effective upon publication of the final rule by USDA in the *Federal Register* on July 29, 2013.[40] By late July 2013, U.S. sugar prices were below effective federal support levels, compelling USDA to activate FFP on August 15, 2013, and use an estimated $148 million of CCC funds to avoid possible sugar forfeitures.[41]

Changes in 2014 Farm Bill

Extended the Feedstock Flexibility Program through FY2018 with no changes to program implementation.

Funding

Under the 2014 farm bill, mandatory funding authority of such sums as necessary was extended through FY2018 by the 2014 farm bill. Under the 2008 farm bill, mandatory CCC funds of such sums as necessary also were made available. Funding authority was extended through FY2013 by ATRA.

Section 9010: Biomass Crop Assistance Program (BCAP)

Administered by Farm Service Agency (FSA), USDA.

Program Overview

The Biomass Crop Assistance Program (BCAP) provides financial assistance to owners and operators of agricultural land and nonindustrial private forest land who wish to establish, produce, and deliver biomass feedstocks to eligible processing plants.[42] BCAP provides two categories of assistance[43]

---

[40] Sugar Program: Feedstock Flexibility Program for Bioenergy Producers," *Federal Register*, Vol. 78, No. 145, July 29, 2013.

[41] For more information see USDA, Economic Research Service (ERS), *Sugar and Sweeteners Outlook*, SSS-M-305, January 16, 2014.

[42] For more information, see CRS Report R41296, *Biomass Crop Assistance Program (BCAP): Status and Issues*, by Mark A. McMinimy, and U.S. Department of Agriculture, "Biomass Crop Assistance Program," 80 *Federal Register*, February 27, 2015.

[43] Farm Service Agency, USDA, "Biomass Crop Assistance Program for Fiscal Year 2017, Fact Sheet," at https://www.fsa.usda.gov/Assets/USDA-FSA-Public/usdafiles/FactSheets/2016/bcap_fact_sheet_nov2016.pdf.

1) establishment and annual payments, including a one-time payment of up to 50% of the cost of establishment for perennial crops, and annual payments (i.e., rental rates based on a set of criteria) of up to five years for nonwoody and 15 years for woody perennial biomass crops; and
2) matching payments, at a rate of $1 for each $1 per ton provided, up to $20 per ton, for a period of two years, which may be available to help eligible material owners with collection, harvest, storage, and transportation (CHST) of eligible material for use in a qualified biomass conversion facility.

Establishment and annual payments are available to certain producers who enter into contracts with USDA to produce eligible biomass crops on contract acres within designated BCAP project areas.[44] Eligible land for BCAP project area contracts includes agricultural land and nonindustrial private forestland, but does not include federal or state-owned land, land that is native sod. Lands enrolled in existing land retirement programs for conservation purposes—the Conservation Reserve Program (CRP) or the Agricultural Conservation Easement Program (ACEP)—also become eligible during the fiscal year that their land retirement contract expires. Generally, crops that receive payments under Title I (the commodity title) of the farm bill (e.g., corn, wheat, rice, and soybeans) and noxious weeds or invasive species are not eligible for annual payments.

Matching payments are available to eligible material owners who deliver eligible material to qualified biomass conversion facilities. Eligible material must be harvested directly from the land and separate from a higher-value product (e.g., Title I crops). Invasive and noxious species are considered eligible material, and land ownership (private, state, federal, etc.) is not a limiting factor to receive matching payments (7 U.S.C. §8111).

---

[44] See FSA, USDA, "BCAP Project Area Information," at https://www.fsa.usda.gov/programs-and-services/energy-programs/BCAP/bcap-project-area/index.

Changes in 2014 Farm Bill

Extended BCAP through FY2018. Changes enrolled land eligibility by including land under expiring CRP or ACEP easement contracts; included residue from crops receiving Title I payments as eligible material, but extended exclusion to any whole grain from a Title I crop, as well as bagasse and algae. One-time establishment payments are limited to no more than 50% of cost of establishment from 75% previously, not to exceed $500 per acre ($750 per acre for socially disadvantaged farmers or ranchers). CHST matching payments may not exceed $20 per dry ton (down from $45 per dry ton) and are available for a two-year period. CHST funding shall be available for technical assistance. Not less than 10% or more than 50% of funding may be used for CHST. Not later than four years after enactment of the 2014 farm bill, USDA shall submit to the House and Senate Agriculture Committees a report on best practices from participants receiving assistance under BCAP.

Funding

Under the 2014 farm bill, mandatory funding of $25 million was authorized for each of FY2014-FY2018. No discretionary funding was authorized. The FY2015, FY2016, and FY2017 appropriations acts (P.L. 113-235, P.L. 114-113, and P.L. 115-31, respectively) limited mandatory funds to $23 million in FY2015, $3 million in FY2016, and $3 million in FY2017.[45] The FY2018 appropriations act provides no mandatory funding for BCAP. Under the 2008 farm bill, BCAP was meant to facilitate a broadening of the feedstock supply base for biofuel production beyond food crops by helping to establish a reliable supply of biomass for cellulosic biofuel production. Thus, under the 2008 farm bill, mandatory CCC funds of such sums as necessary were made available for each of FY2008-FY2012, with outlays to be determined by the number of BCAP participants. Actual outlays during FY2008-FY2012 were $290 million. Congress began to place limitations on the scope of BCAP funding with the 2010 Supplemental Appropriations Act (P.L. 111-212), which limited BCAP funding to $552

---

[45] §9010 was subject to changes in mandatory spending (CHIMPS) of $20 million for FY2017.

million in FY2010 and $432 million in FY2011. The Department of Defense and Full-Year Continuing Appropriations Act, 2011 (P.L. 112-10), further reduced BCAP funding for FY2011 to $112 million. The FY2012 Agriculture Appropriations Act (P.L. 112-55) limited BCAP mandatory spending to $17 million. Under ATRA, no new mandatory funding was included for BCAP for FY2013; however, discretionary funding of $20 million was authorized to be appropriated. Actual outlays for FY2013 were $9 million.

Section 9011: Forest Biomass for Energy (Repealed)

Administered by Forest Service, USDA.

Program Overview

The 2008 farm bill authorized the Forest Biomass for Energy program to function as a research and development program to encourage use of forest biomass for energy. The Forest Service, other federal agencies, state and local governments, Indian tribes, land-grant colleges and universities, and private entities were to be eligible to compete for program funds. Priority was to be given to projects that use low-value forest byproduct biomass for the production of energy; develop processes to integrate bioenergy from forest biomass into existing manufacturing streams; develop new transportation fuels; and improve the growth and yield of trees for renewable energy (7 U.S.C. §8112). In the end, the Forest Service never announced any regulations for this program.

Changes in 2014 Farm Bill

The Forest Biomass for Energy program was repealed.

Funding

Under the 2008 farm bill, discretionary funding of $15 million annually was authorized to be appropriated for FY2009-FY2012. Under ATRA, discretionary funding of $15 million was authorized to be appropriated for

FY2013; however, no funding was appropriated through FY2013, and funding authority for the program expired after FY2013.

Section 9012: Community Wood Energy Program

Administered by Forest Service, USDA.

Program Overview

The 2008 farm bill authorized the Community Wood Energy Program to provide matching grants—up to $50,000 and subject to a match of at least 50%—to state and local governments to acquire community wood energy systems for public buildings. Participants must also implement a community wood energy plan to meet energy needs with reduced carbon intensity through conservation, reduced costs, utilizing low-value wood sources, and increased awareness of energy consumption (7 U.S.C. §8113).

Changes in 2014 Farm Bill

Extended the Community Wood Energy Program through FY2018; defined a Biomass Consumer Cooperative and authorizes grants of up to $50,000 to be made to establish or expand biomass consumer cooperatives that will provide consumers with services or discounts relating to the purchase of biomass heating systems or products (including their delivery and storage); and required that any biomass consumer cooperative that receives a grant must match at least the equivalent of 50% of the funds toward the establishment or expansion of a biomass consumer cooperative.

Funding

Under the 2014 farm bill, no mandatory funding was provided. Discretionary funding of $5 million annually was authorized to be appropriated for FY2014-FY2018, but no funds have been appropriated through FY2018. Under the 2008 farm bill, discretionary funding of $5 million annually was authorized to be appropriated for FY2009-FY2012.

ATRA subsequently extended authority for the program through FY2013, but no funds were appropriated through FY2013.

Section 9013: Biofuels Infrastructure Study (Repealed)

Program Overview

Section 9002 of the 2008 farm bill requested that USDA, DOE, EPA, and the Department of Transportation (DOT) jointly report on the infrastructure needs, requirements, and development approaches for expanding the domestic production, transportation, and distribution of biofuels given current and likely future market trends. A report including the study results was to be submitted to various related committees in Congress. No deadline was specified, and the report was never undertaken.

Changes in 2014 Farm Bill

The Biofuels Infrastructure Study requirement was repealed.

Funding

Program funding authority expired after FY2013. Under the 2008 farm bill, no specific funding was announced for this study, and no funding was ever authorized. In addition, no new funding authority was included in ATRA.

Section 9014: Renewable Fertilizer Study (Repealed)

Program Overview

Section 9003 of the 2008 farm bill required that a report be submitted to the House and Senate Agriculture Committees within one year of receipt of the appropriations to carry out the study on the production of fertilizer from renewable energy sources in rural areas. The report was to be based on a study of the challenges to commercialization of rural fertilizer production from renewable sources, potential processes and technologies, and the potential impacts of renewable fertilizer on fossil fuel use and the environment. The study was never undertaken.

Changes in 2014 Farm Bill

The Renewable Fertilizer Study requirement was repealed.

Funding

Program funding authority expired after FY2013. Under the 2008 farm bill, discretionary funding of $1 million was authorized to be appropriated for FY2009; however, no discretionary funding was ever authorized, and no new funding authority was included in ATRA.

Section 9015: Energy Efficiency Report for USDA Facilities

Program Overview

Under the 2014 farm bill, USDA was directed to submit a report to the House and Senate Agriculture Committees on energy use and energy efficiency projects at USDA facilities. USDA transmitted the report to the House and Senate Agriculture Committees on October 8, 2014.

Funding

No specific funding was authorized for this study.

No Provision: Rural Energy Self-Sufficiency Initiative

Administered by Rural Business and Cooperative Service, RD, USDA.

Program Overview

The 2008 farm bill authorized the Rural Energy Self-Sufficiency Initiative to assist rural communities with community-wide energy systems that reduce conventional energy use and increase the use of energy from renewable sources. Grants were to be made available to assess energy use in a rural community, evaluate ideas for reducing energy use, and develop and install integrated renewable energy systems. Grants were not to exceed 50% of the total cost of the activity (7 U.S.C. §8109). No funding was ever appropriated, and regulations were never announced for this program.

Changes in 2014 Farm Bill

No provision was included in the 2014 farm bill for the Rural Energy Self-Sufficiency Initiative, with the result that program funding authority expired after FY2013.

Funding

Program funding authority expired after FY2013. Under the 2008 farm bill and the ATRA extension, discretionary funding of $5 million annually was authorized to be appropriated for FY2009-FY2013; however, no funding was ever appropriated.

TITLE VII—ENERGY-RELATED AGRICULTURAL RESEARCH AND EXTENSION PROVISIONS

Three provisions from the Research title (Title VII) of the 2014 farm bill relate directly to renewable energy initiatives, which are described below.

Section 7210: Nutrient Management Research and Extension Program (Repealed)

Administered by USDA.

Program Overview

This program provided research and extension grants for the purpose of finding innovative methods and technologies to allow agricultural operators to make use of animal waste, such as fertilizer, methane digestion, composting, and other useful by-products (7 U.S.C. §5925a).

Changes in 2014 Farm Bill

The 2014 farm bill repealed the Nutrient Management Research and Extension Program.

Section 7212: Agricultural Bioenergy Feedstock and Energy Efficiency Research and Extension Initiative (Repealed)

Function

Established for the purpose of using competitive grants to support research and extension activities that enhance the production of biomass energy crops and the energy efficiency of agricultural operations (7 U.S.C. §5925e).

Administered by USDA.

Changes in 2014 Farm Bill

The 2014 farm bill repealed the Agricultural Bioenergy Feedstock and Energy Efficiency Research and Extension Initiative.

Section 7516: Sun Grant Program

Administered by NIFA, USDA. Each regional Sun Grant center manages the programs and activities within its region, although a process based on peer and merit review is used to administer grants.

Program Overview

Under the 2008 farm bill, the Sun Grant Initiative (SGI) is a national network of land-grant universities and federally funded laboratories—coordinated through regional Sun Grant centers—working together to further establish a biobased economy.[46] Competitive grants are available to

[46] See "Sun Grant Initiative," at http://www.sungrant.org/.

land-grant schools within each region to be used toward integrated, multistate research, extension, and education programs on technology development and implementation. Sun Grant centers are also charged with reviving America's farming communities by placing an emphasis on rural economic development through the production of biobased renewable energy feedstocks.

A provision creating the Sun Grant Program was added subsequent to the 2002 farm bill under the Sun Grant Research Initiative Act of 2003 (§778, Consolidated Appropriations Act, 2004; P.L. 108-199). The initiative was originally established with five national Sun Grant research centers based at land-grant universities, each covering a different national region, to enhance coordination and collaboration among USDA, DOE, and land-grant universities in the development, distribution, and implementation of biobased energy technologies. The 2008 farm bill established the Sun Grant Program and added a sixth regional center (7 U.S.C. §8114). NIFA administers the program under 7 C.F.R. part 3430.

Changes in 2014 Farm Bill

The 2014 farm bill extended the Sun Grant Program with its discretionary funding authority (i.e., subject to appropriations) of $75 million annually through FY2018. It also consolidates and amends the Sun Grant Program to expand input from other appropriate federal agencies and replace authority for gasification research with bioproducts research and makes the program competitive by removing designation of certain universities as regional centers.

Funding

Under the 2014 farm bill, discretionary funding of $75 million annually was authorized to be appropriated for FY2014-FY2018. Of this amount, $2.5 million was appropriated for FY2014-FY2016, and $3 million for FY2017 and FY2018.[47] Under the 2008 farm bill, discretionary funding of $75 million annually was authorized to be appropriated for FY2008-FY2012, but

[47] Funding amounts provided in USDA budget explanatory notes and the bill explanatory statement.

actual appropriations amounted to $2.25 million for FY2010 and $2.2 million for FY2012. ATRA contained no new funding authority for FY2013.

APPENDIX. SUPPLEMENTARY TABLES

Table A-1. Authorized Funding for 2014 Farm Bill Title IX Energy Provisions, FY2014-FY2018 (budget authority in $ millions)

Section	Provision Name	Type[a]	FY 2014	FY 2015	FY 2016	FY 2017	FY 2018	Total FY 2014-FY 2018
Section 9002	Federal Biobased Markets Program	M	3	3	3	3	3	15
		D[b]	2	2	2	2	2	10
Section 9003	Biorefinery, Renewable Chemical, and Biobased Product	M[c]	100[d]	50[e]	50[f]	0[g]	0	200
	Manufacturing Assistance Program (formerly BAP)	D[b]	75	75	75	75	75	375
Section 9004	Repowering Assistance Program	M[c]	12	0[h]	0	0	0	12
		D[b]	10	10	10	10	10	50
Section 9004	Repowering Assistance Program	M[c]	12	0[h]	0	0	0	12
		D[b]	10	10	10	10	10	50
Section 9005	Bioenergy Program for Adv. Biofuels	M[c]	15[i]	15	15	15	15	75
		D[b]	20	20	20	20	20	100
Section 9006	Biodiesel Fuel Education Program	M	1	1	1	1	1	5
		D[b]	1	1	1	1	1	5
Section 9007	Rural Energy for America Program (REAP)	M[c]	50	50	50	50	50	250
		D[b]	20	20	20	20	20	100
Section 9008	Biomass Research and Dev. Act (BRDA)	M[c]	3	3	3	3	0	12
		D[b]	20	20	20	20	20	100
Section 9009	Feedstock Flexibility Program for Bioenergy Production[j]	M	SSAN[k]	SSAN	SSAN	SSAN	SSAN	SSAN
Section 9010	Biomass Crop Assistance Program (BCAP)	M	25	25[l]	25[m]	25[n]	25	125
		D	0	0	0	0	0	0
Section 9012	Community Wood Energy Program	D[b]	5	5	5	5	5	25

Table A-1. (Continued)

Section	Provision Name	Type[a]	FY 2014	FY 2015	FY 2016	FY 2017	FY 2018	Total FY 2014-FY 2018
Section 9015	Energy Efficiency Report for USDA facilities	Unfunded						
Total Mandatory Funding Authorized			209	147	147	97	94	694
Total Discretionary Funding Authorized			153	153	153	153	153	765

Source: P.L. 113-79 (Agricultural Act of 2014).

Notes: The following Title IX sections are unfunded repeals of programs from the 2008 farm bill: Section 9011, Forest Biomass for Energy; Section 9013, Biofuels Infrastructure Study; Section 9014, Renewable Fertilizer Study. The previous Rural Energy Self-Sufficiency Initiative was repealed by omission. In addition, three energy-related provisions from Title VII (Research, Extension, and Related Matters) were dealt with as follows: the Nutrient Management Research and Extension program was repealed by Section 7210, the Biofeedstock and Energy Efficiency Research and Extension Program was repealed by Section 7212, and the Sun Grant Program was extended (§7516) with authorization for discretionary funding of $75 million for each of FY2014-FY2018.

[a] M = mandatory funding; D = discretionary funding.

[b] In the past, many of the discretionary programs have never received any funding or received lesser amounts in the annual appropriations process than originally authorized in the farm bill.

[c] Mandatory funding is to remain available until expended for Title IX programs under the following provisions: Section 9003, Section 9004, Section 9005, Section 9007, and Section 9008.

[d] The FY2014 appropriations act (P.L. 113-76) rescinded $40.7 million of funds available.

[e] The FY2015 appropriations act (P.L. 113-235) limited funding to $30 million.

[f] The FY2016 appropriations act (P.L. 114-113) limited funding to $27 million.

[g] The FY2017 appropriations act (P.L. 115-31) limited funding to $151 million in carryover funding.

[h] The FY2015 appropriations act reduced available funds for FY2015 by $8 million.

[i] The FY2014 appropriations act reduced funds available by $8 million.

[j] This program is triggered when a sugar surplus exists.

[k] SSAN = Such sums as necessary.

[l] The FY2015 appropriations act limited funding to $23 million.

[m] The FY2016 appropriations act limited funding to $3 million.

[n] The FY2017 appropriations act limited funding to $3 million.

Table A-2. Authorized Funding for 2008 Farm Bill Title IX Energy Provisions, FY2008-FY2012 (budget authority in $ millions)

Section[a]	Provision Name	Type	FY2008	FY2009	FY2010	FY2011	FY2012	Total
Section 9002[a]	Federal Biobased Markets Program	Mand.	1	2	2	2	2	9
		Discr.[b]	0	2	2	2	2	8
		Mand.	0	75	245	0	0	320

Section[a]	Provision Name	Type	FY2008	FY2009	FY2010	FY2011	FY2012	Total
Section 9003[a]	Biorefinery Assistance Program (BAP)	Discr.[b]	0	150	150	150	150	600
Section 9004[a]	Repowering Assistance Program	Mand.	0	35	0	0	0	35
		Discr.[b]	0	15	15	15	15	60
Section 9005[a]	Bioenergy Program for Adv. Biofuels	Mand.	0	55	55	85	105c	300
		Discr.[b]	0	25	25	25	25	100
Section 9006[a]	Biodiesel Fuel Education Program	Mand.	1	1	1	1	1	5
Section 9007[a]	Rural Energy for America Prog. (REAP)	Mand.	0	55	60	70	70d	255
		Discr.[b]	0	25	25	25	25	100
Section 9008[a]	Biomass Research and Dev. Act (BRDA)	Mand.	0	20	28	30	40	118
		Discr.[b]	0	35	35	35	35	140
Section 9009[a]	Rural Energy Self-Sufficiency Initiative	Discr.[b]	0	5	5	5	5	20
Section 9010[a]	Feedstock Flex. Prog. for Bioenergy Prod.	Mand.	SSAN	SSAN	SSAN	SSAN	SSAN	SSAN
Section 9011[a]	Biomass Crop Assistance Prog. (BCAP)	Mand.	SSAN	SSAN	SSAN[e]	SSAN[e]	SSAN[e]	SSAN
Section 9012[a]	Forest Biomass for Energy	Discr.[b]	0	15	15	15	15	60
Section 9013a	Community Wood Energy Program	Discr.[b]	0	5	5	5	5	20
Section 9002	Biofuels Infrastructure Study	None	0	0	0	0	0	0
Section 9003	Renewable Fertilizer Study	Discr.[b]	0	1	0	0	0	1
Total Discretionary Funding Authorized[b]			0	278	277	277	277	1,109
Total Mandatory Funding Authorized			2	243	391	188	218	1,042

Source: P.L. 110-246 (Food, Conservation, and Energy Act of 2008) and P.L. 113-6 (Consolidated and Further Continuing Appropriations Act, 2013).

Notes: All mandatory funding authority expired at the end of FY2012, with the exception of the Feedstock Flexibility Program. Authority for discretionary funding was extended under the Continuing Resolution (P.L. 112-175), for the first half of FY2013 effective October 1, 2012, through March 27, 2013; the American Taxpayer Relief Act of 2012 (ATRA; P.L. 112-240, §701), and P.L. 113-6 (Consolidated and Further Continuing Appropriations Act, 2013) which appropriated funds for the second half of FY2013.

Abbreviations: "SSAN" = such sums as necessary.

[a] Section 9001 of the 2008 farm bill (P.L. 110-246) amends Title IX of the 2002 farm bill (P.L. 107-171). Sections 9001 through 9013 of the table are the amended section numbers.

[b] Many of the discretionary programs never received any funding or received lesser amounts through the annual appropriations process than originally authorized in the farm bill.

[c] The FY2012 Agriculture Appropriations Act (P.L. 112-55) limited funding to $65 million.

[d] The FY2012 Agriculture Appropriations Act limited funding to $22 million.

[e] The authority for funding under BCAP was reduced to $552 million in FY2010 and $432 million in FY2011 under the Supplemental Appropriations Act of 2010 (P.L. 111-212). BCAP funding for FY2011 was reduced a second time to $112 million under the Department of Defense and Full-Year Continuing Appropriations Act, 2011 (P.L. 112-10). Finally, the FY2012 Agriculture Appropriations Act reduced BCAP funding to $17 million for FY2012.

Table A-3. Title IX- Energy: Comparison of 2014 Farm Bill with Prior Law

Prior Law/Policy—Energy	Enacted 2014 Farm Bill (P.L. 113-79)
Definitions	
Advanced Biofuel. Fuel derived from renewable biomass other than corn kernel starch. Includes biofuel derived from sugar and starch other than corn kernel starch, renewable biodiesel, biogas produced from organic matter, as well as other fuels (e.g., home heating fuels, and aviation and jet fuels) from cellulosic biomass (including organic waste material).*[7U.S.C.8101(3)]*	Same as prior law. *[§9001]*
Biobased Product. A commercial or industrial product—i.e., intermediate, feedstock, or end product (other than food or feed)—composed in whole or in part of biological products including renewable agricultural and forestry materials.*[7U.S.C. 8101(4)]*	Same as prior law. *[§9001]*
Biofuel. A fuel derived from renewable biomass.*[7U.S.C. 8101(5)]*	Same as prior law. *[§9001]*
Biomass Conversion Facility. A facility that converts renewable biomass into heat, power, biobased products, or advanced biofuels.*[7U.S.C.8101(6)]*	Same as prior law. *[§9001]*
Biorefinery. A facility (including equipment and processes) that converts renewable biomass into biofuels and biobased products, and may produce electricity.*[7U.S.C. 8101(7)]*	Same as prior law. *[§9001]*
No comparable provision.	**Forest Product.** A product made from materials derived from the practice of forestry or the management of growing timber including pulp, paper, paperboard, pellets, lumber, and wood products, and any recycled

Prior Law/Policy—Energy	**Enacted 2014 Farm Bill (P.L. 113-79)**
	products derived from forest materials. *[§9001]*
Renewable Biomass. Includes (1) materials, precommercial thinnings, or invasive species from National Forest System land and public lands that are: byproducts of designated preventive treatments (removed to reduce hazardous fuels, to reduce or to contain disease or insect infestation, or to restore ecosystem health), not used for higher value products, and harvested in accordance with applicable law and land management plans and requirements for old-growth maintenance, restoration, and management and large-tree retention, or (2) any organic matter available on a recurring basis from nonfederal or Indian land including: renewable plant material (including agricultural commodities, plants and trees, and algae) and waste material (including crop residue, vegetative waste, wood waste and residues, animal waste and byproducts, and food and yard waste).*[7U.S.C.8101(12)]*	Same as prior law. *[§9001]*
No comparable definition.	**Renewable Chemical.** A monomer, polymer, plastic, formulated product, or chemical substance produced from renewable biomass. *[§9001]*
Renewable Energy. Energy derived from a wind, solar, renewable biomass, ocean (including tidal, wave, current, and thermal), geothermal, or hydroelectric source. *[7U.S.C. 8101(13)]*	Same as prior law. *[§9001]*
No comparable definition.	**Renewable Energy System.** A system that produces energy from a renewable source including distribution components necessary to move energy produced by such a system to
	the initial point of sale, but not any mechanism for dispensing energy at retail (e.g., a blender pump). *[§9001]*
Authorized Programs	
Biobased Markets Program. Requires federal agencies to purchase products with maximum biobased content subject to availability and flexibility and performance standards. Minimum biobased content standards applied to federal contracts on case-by-case basis.	Extends the Biobased Markets Program through FY2018including, in addition to preference for biobased products, establish a targeted biobased-only procurement requirement for federal agencies. Limits reporting on the availability, relative price,

Table A-3. (Continued)

Prior Law/Policy—Energy	Enacted 2014 Farm Bill (P.L. 113-79)
Continued voluntary labeling. Authorized mandatory funding of $1 million for FY2008 and $2 million annually for FY2009-FY2012; no mandatory funding was authorized for FY2013. Authorized to be appropriated $2 million annually for FY2009-FY2013for testing and labeling. *[7U.S.C. 8102]*	performance and environmental and public health benefits of biobased materials subject to the availability of data. Adds reporting requirements of quantities and types of biobased products purchased by procuring federal agencies and a focus on biobased content requirements (explicitly including forest products). Mandates (within one year of enactment) designation of intermediate ingredients or feedstocks and assembled and finished biobased products according to guidelines. Adds auditing and compliance activities to ensure proper use of biobased labeling. Mandates study (and report) by USDA to assess economic impact of biobased product industry, due within one year of enactment. Encourages expedited coordination, review and approval (with appropriate technical assistance) of forest-related biobased products. Authorizes mandatory funding of $3million annually for FY2014-FY2018. Authorizes to be appropriated $2 million annually for FY2014-FY2018. *[§9002]*
Biorefinery Assistance Program. Assists in development of new and emerging technologies for advanced biofuels by providing competitive grants (up to 30% of total project costs) and loan guarantees (limited to $250 million or 80% of project cost) for construction and/or retrofitting of demonstration-scale biorefineries to demonstrate the commercial viability of one or more processes for converting renewable biomass to advanced biofuels. Provided mandatory funding of $75 million in FY2009 and $245 million in FY2010, available until expended, for loan guarantees. Authorized to be appropriated $150 million annually for FY2009-13for grants. *[7U.S.C. 8103]*	Renamed as the Biorefinery, Renewable Chemical, and Biobased Product Manufacturing Assistance Program. Extends and expands the program to include renewable chemical (as defined above in §9001) and biobased product manufacturing (defined as development, construction, and retrofitting of technologically new commercial-scale processing and manufacturing equipment and required facilities used to convert renewable chemicals and other biobased outputs into commercial-scale end products). Extends loan guarantee availability to the development and construction of renewable chemical and biobased product manufacturing facilities, directs USDA to ensure diversity in types of projects approved, and caps the funds used for loan

Prior Law/Policy—Energy	Enacted 2014 Farm Bill (P.L. 113-79)
	guarantees to promote biobased product manufacturing at 15% of the total available mandatory funds. Eliminates grant funding. Authorizes mandatory funding of $100 million for FY2014and $50million each for FY2015-FY2016 to remain available until expended, plus it authorizes to be appropriated $75 million for each of FY2014-FY2018. *[§9003]*
Repowering Assistance Program. Provides funds to reduce or eliminate the use of fossil fuels for processing or power in biorefineries in existence at enactment. Not more than 5% of funds are available to eligible producers with a refining capacity exceeding 150 million gallons of advanced biofuel per year. Provided mandatory CCC funding of $35 million for FY2009, available until expended. Authorized to be appropriated $15 million annually for FY2009-FY2013. *[7U.S.C. 8104]*	Extends prior law through FY2018. Authorizes mandatory funding of $12million for FY2014, available until expended. Authorizes to be appropriated $10million annually for FY2014-FY2018. *[§9004]*
Bioenergy Program for Advanced Biofuels. Provides payments to producers to support and expand production of advanced biofuels by entering into contracts to pay producers for production of eligible advanced biofuels. Provided mandatory funding of $55 million (FY2009), $55 million (FY2010), $85 million (FY2011), and $105 million (FY2012), available until expended. Authorized to be appropriated $25 million annually (FY2009-13)*[7U.S.C. 8105]*	Extends the Bioenergy Program for Advanced Biofuels Program through FY2018. Authorizes mandatory funding of $15million for each of FY2014-FY2018, available until expended. Authorizes to be appropriated $20 million annually for FY2014-FY2018. *[§9005]*
Biodiesel Fuel Education Program. Awards competitive grants to nonprofit organizations that educate fleet operators and the public on biodiesel benefits. Provided mandatory CCC funding of $1 million annually (FY2008-FY2012). Authorized to be appropriated $1million for FY2013.*[7U.S.C. 8106]*	Extends the Biodiesel Fuel Education Program through FY2018. Authorizes mandatory funding of $1 million annually for FY2014-FY2018. Authorizes to be appropriated $1million annually forFY2014-FY2018. *[§9006]*
Rural Energy for America Program (REAP). Provides financial assistance of grants, guaranteed loans, and combined grants and guaranteed loans for the development and construction of renewable energy systems (RES) and for energy efficiency improvement (EEI) projects (eligible entities include rural small businesses and agricultural producers); grants for conducting energy audits and	Extends REAP through FY2018.Adds a council (as defined in Section 1528 of the Agriculture and Food Act of 1981) as an eligible entity. Adds a 3-tiered application process with separate application processes for grants and loan guarantees for RES and EEI projects based on the project cost: tier-1 for projects <$80,000; tier-2 for $80,000 <

Table A-3. (Continued)

Prior Law/Policy—Energy	Enacted 2014 Farm Bill (P.L. 113-79)
for conducting renewable energy development assistance (eligible entities include state, tribe, or local governments, land-grant colleges and universities, rural electric cooperatives, and public power entities); and grants for conducting RES feasibility studies (eligible entities include rural small businesses and agricultural producers). Grants are limited to $500,000 for RES and $250,000 for EEI activities up to 25% of the cost of the RES or EEI activity. Loan guarantees are limited to a max of $25 million and a min of $5,000 up to 75% of the cost of a funded activity. Provides mandatory funds: $55 million (FY2009), $60 million (FY2010), $70 million (FY2011), and $70 million (FY2012), available until expended. Authorizes $25 million annually, subject to appropriations (FY2009-FY2013). *[7U.S.C.8107]*	projects < $200,000; andtier-3 for projects > $200,000. Mandatory funding of $50million is authorized for FY2014 and each fiscal year thereafter, to remain available until expended. Authorizes to be appropriated $20 million annually for FY2014-FY2018. *[§9007]*
Biomass Research & Development Initiative (BRDI). Provides competitive funding as grants, contracts, and financial assistance for research, development, and demonstration of technologies and processes leading to commercial production of biofuels and biobased products. Provides for coordination between USDA and DOE work related to biofuels and biobased products research and development programs through the Biomass Research and Development Board. Provides mandatory funding: $20 million (FY2009), $28 million (FY2010), $30 million (FY1022), and $40 million (FY2012). Authorizes to be appropriated $35 million annually (FY2009-FY2013). *[7U.S.C. 8108]*	Extends BRDI through FY2018. Authorizes mandatory funding of $3million annually for four fiscal years, FY2014-FY2017, to remain available until expended. Authorizes to be appropriated $20million annually for FY2014-FY2018. *[§9008]*
Rural Energy Self-Sufficiency Initiative. Provides cost-share grants (up to 50%) for rural communities to assess energy systems and make improvements. Authorizes to be appropriated $5 million annually (FY2009-FY2013); however, no funds were ever appropriated and no rules were ever promulgated. *[7U.S.C.8109]*	No provision. Hence, program funding authority expired after FY2013.

Prior Law/Policy—Energy	**Enacted 2014 Farm Bill (P.L. 113-79)**
Feedstock Flexibility Program. Authorizes use of CCC funds (such sums as necessary) to purchase sugar (intended for food use but deemed to be in surplus) for resale as a biomass feedstock to produce bioenergy. USDA would implement the program only in those years where purchases are determined to be necessary to ensure that the sugar program operates at no cost to the federal government. *[7 U.S.C. 8110]*	Extends the Feedstock Flexibility Program through FY2018. *[§9009]*
Biomass Crop Assistance Program (BCAP). Provides financial assistance to owners and operators of agricultural land and nonindustrial private forest land who wish to establish, produce, and deliver biomass feedstocks under two categories of assistance: (1) establishment and annual payments provided under contract between USDA and participating producers, including a one-time payment of up to 75% of cost of establishment for perennial crops, and annual payments (rental rates based on a set of criteria)of up to 5 years for non-woody and 15 years for woody perennial biomass crops, and (2) matching payments at a rate of $1 for each $1 per ton provided, up to $45 per ton, for a period of 2 years to help eligible material owners with collection, harvest, storage, and transportation (CHST) of eligible material for use in a qualified biomass conversion facility. Eligible material excludes Title I crops, animal waste and byproducts, food and yard waste, and algae. Provides mandatory CCC funding of such sums as necessary annually for FY2008-FY2012. Authorized to be appropriated $20million for FY2013. *[7U.S.C. 8111]*	Extends BCAP through FY2018. Changes enrolled land eligibility; includes residue from crops receiving Title I payments as eligible material, but extends exclusion to any whole grain from a Title I crop, as well as bagasse and algae. One-time establishment payments are limited to no more than 50% of cost of establishment, not to exceed $500 per acre ($750per acre for socially disadvantaged farmers or ranchers). CHST matching payments may not exceed $20 per dry ton but are available for a 2-year period. Not later than 4 years after enactment, USDA shall submit a report on best practice data and information gathered from participants. Also, it provides that funding under the subsection shall be available for technical assistance. Mandatory funding of $25million is authorized for each of FY2014-FY2018. Not less than 10%or more than 50%of funding may be used for CHST. *[§9010]*
Forest Biomass for Energy Program. Requires the Forest Service to conduct a competitive research and development program to encourage use of forest biomass for energy. Authorized to be appropriated $15 million annually (FY2009-FY2013). *[7 U.S.C. 8112]*	Repeals the Forest Biomass for Energy Program. *[§9011]*

Table A-3. (Continued)

Prior Law/Policy—Energy	Enacted 2014 Farm Bill (P.L. 113-79)
Community Wood Energy Program. Provides grants of up to $50,000 for up to 50% of the cost for communities to plan and install wood energy systems in public buildings. The energy system acquired with grant funds shall not exceed an output of 50,000,000 Btu per hour for heating and 2 megawatts for electric power production. Authorized to be appropriated $5 million annually (FY2009-FY13). *[7 U.S.C. 8113]*	Extends the Community Wood Energy Program through FY2018. Defines Biomass Consumer Cooperative. Authorizes grants of up to $50,000 to be made to establish or expand biomass consumer cooperatives that will provide consumers with services or discounts relating to the purchase of biomass heating systems or products (including their delivery and storage). Any biomass consumer cooperative that receives a grant must match at least the equivalent of 50% of the funds toward the establishment of expansion of a biomass consumer cooperative. Authorizes to be appropriated $5million annually for FY2014-FY2018. *[§9012]*
Biofuels Infrastructure Study. Required USDA to conduct a study (and report) to assess the infrastructure needs for expanding the domestic production, transport, and distribution of biofuels given current and likely future market trends with recommendations for such infrastructure through 2025 based on needs, costs, and other factors. No specific time frame or funding was provided. *[§9002 of* P.L. 110-246*]*	Repeals the requirement to conduct the study (and report). *[§9013]*
Renewable Fertilizer Study. Required USDA to conduct a study to assess the current state of knowledge on the potential for the production of fertilizer from renewable energy sources in rural areas. Study was to be completed within one year of receiving an appropriation. Authorized to be appropriated $1 million for FY2009. *[§9003 of* P.L. 110-246*]*	Requirement to conduct the study is repealed. [§9014]
No comparable provision.	**Energy Efficiency Report for USDA Facilities.** Within 180 days after enactment, USDA is required to submit a report to the House and Senate Agriculture Committees on energy use and energy efficiency projects at USDA facilities. *[§9015]*

Source: Title IX- Energy, Agricultural Act of 2014; P.L. 113-79.

Notes: For a comparison of prior and enacted law with the provisions in the House and Senate versions of the 2014 farm bill (i.e., the Senate-passed S. 954 and the House-passed H.R. 2642), see CRS Report R43076, *The 2014 Farm Bill (P.L. 113-79): Summary and Side-by-Side*.

In: The Farm Bill
Editor: Billie Grant

ISBN: 978-1-53615-294-4

Chapter 6

EXPIRATION OF THE 2014 FARM BILL*

Jim Monke, Randy Alison Aussenberg and Megan Stubbs

ABSTRACT

The farm bill is an omnibus, multi-year law that governs an array of agricultural and food programs. It provides an opportunity for policymakers to periodically address a broad range of agricultural and food issues. The farm bill is typically reauthorized about every five years.

Recent farm bills have been subject to various developments, such as insufficient votes to pass the House floor, presidential vetoes, or—as in the case of 2008 and 2014 farm bills—short-term extensions.

The current farm bill (the Agricultural Act of 2014, P.L. 113-79) has many provisions that expire in 2018. The 115th Congress has begun but not finished a new farm bill. An initial House vote on H.R. 2 failed by vote of 198-213, but floor procedures allowed that vote to be reconsidered, and it passed by a second vote of 213-211. The Senate passed its bill as an amendment to H.R. 2 by a vote of 86-11. Conference proceedings officially began on September 5, 2018, but have not yet reached agreement. The timing and consequences of expiration vary by program across the breadth of the farm bill. There are two principal expiration dates: September 30 and

* This is an edited, reformatted and augmented version of Congressional Research Service Publication No. R45341, Updated October 11, 2018.

December 31. The 2014 farm bill generally expires either at the end of FY2018 (September 30, 2018), or with the 2018 crop year. Crop years vary by commodity, but the first to be affected by a new crop year is dairy, whose 2018 crop year ends on December 31, 2018. The possible consequences of expiration include minimal disruption (if the program is able to be continued via appropriations), ceasing new activity (if its authorization to use mandatory funding expires), or reverting to permanent laws enacted decades ago (for the farm commodity programs). For example

- An appropriations act or a continuing resolution can continue some farm bill programs even though an authority has expired. Programs using discretionary funding—and programs using appropriated mandatory funding like those in the SNAP account—can continue to operate via appropriations action.
- Most farm bill programs with mandatory funding (except the Supplemental Nutrition Assistance Program (SNAP), the farm commodity programs, and crop insurance) generally cease new operations when they expire (e.g., the Conservation Reserve Program (CRP), and Market Assistance Program (MAP)).
- The mandatory farm commodity programs would begin reverting to permanent law beginning with the 2019 crop year, for which dairy is the first to be affected, beginning on January 1, 2019.
- Crop insurance is an example of a program with mandatory funding that is permanently authorized outside of the farm bill and does not expire.

"Permanent law" refers to nonexpiring farm commodity programs that are generally from the 1938 and 1949 farm bills. A temporary suspension of permanent law has been included in all recent farm bills, but reverting to permanent law would occur if the suspension expires. The commodity support provisions of permanent law are commonly viewed as being fundamentally different from current policy—and inconsistent with today's farming practices, marketing system, and international trade agreements—as well as potentially costly to the federal government. Among the mandatory-funded programs that are usually the focus of the farm bill, there are two subcategories that may affect congressional action—some have baseline beyond FY2018 and some do not have baseline after FY2018. In an expiration, both categories of mandatory programs can face similar disruption when their authorizations expire. But the difference in having or not having a baseline is important if Congress considers an extension to deal with an expiration. Providing funding for those programs without baseline could make extension more difficult if budget offsets are needed to keep an extension budget-neutral.

FARM BILL EXPIRATION: TIMING AND EFFECTS VARY[1]

The farm bill is an omnibus, multi-year law that governs an array of agricultural and food programs. It provides an opportunity for policymakers to periodically address a broad range of agricultural and food issues. The farm bill has typically undergone reauthorization about every five years.

In the past, farm bills have focused primarily on farm commodity program support for a handful of staple commodities—corn, soybeans, wheat, cotton, rice, dairy, and sugar. Farm bills have become increasingly expansive in their topical scope since 1973, when a nutrition title was included. Other prominent additions include conservation, horticulture, and bioenergy programs.[2]

Recent farm bills have been subject to various developments, such as insufficient votes to pass the House floor, presidential vetoes, or—as in the case of 2008 and 2014 farm bills—short-term extensions. The 2002 farm bill was the most recent to be enacted before the fiscal year expiration date for some programs.[3]

The current farm bill (the Agricultural Act of 2014, P.L. 113-79) has many provisions that expire in 2018. The 115th Congress has begun but not finished a new farm bill. An initial House vote on H.R. 2 failed by vote of 198-213, but floor procedures allowed that vote to be reconsidered, and it passed by a second vote of 213-211. The Senate passed its bill as an amendment to H.R. 2 by a vote of 86-11. Conference proceedings officially began on September 5, 2018, but have not reached agreement.[4]

---

[1] See also CRS In Focus IF10989, *Expiration of the 2014 Farm Bill: Some Potential Implications*, by Jim Monke.

[2] CRS In Focus IF10187, *Farm Bill Primer: What Is the Farm Bill?*, by Renée Johnson and Jim Monke.

[3] CRS Report R45210, *Farm Bills: Major Legislative Actions, 1965-2018*, by Jim Monke.

[4] CRS Report R45275, *The House and Senate 2018 Farm Bills (H.R. 2): A Side-by-Side Comparison with Current Law*, coordinated by Mark A. McMinimy.

Timing of Expiration

The timing and consequences of expiration vary by program across the breadth of the farm bill. There are two principal expiration dates: September 30 and December 31. The 2014 farm bill generally expires either at the end of FY2018 (September 30, 2018), or at the end of the 2018 crop year.[5] Crop years vary by commodity, but the first to be affected by a new crop year is dairy, which has a 2018 crop year that ends on December 31, 2018.

Expiration by Fiscal Year

Expiration of a farm bill on September 30 matters for programs with fiscal year authorizations. These programs include certain nutrition, conservation, trade, and agricultural support programs (excluding the Title I commodity programs), along with many authorizations for discretionary appropriations. Although the Supplemental Nutrition Assistance Program (SNAP) has an authorization of appropriations ending on September 30, it (and other related programs in the SNAP account) can continue to operate with an appropriation.

Expiration by Crop Year

Farm commodity programs expire on a crop year. A crop year is the year in which crops are harvested and may extend into a new calendar year. In the case of dairy, the crop year is the calendar year. Following the expiration of the current farm law without replacement legislation or an extension, the first farm commodity program to be affected would be dairy, whose new crop year begins on January 1, 2019.

Consequences of Expiration

The possible consequences of expiration include minimal disruption (if the program is able to be continued via appropriations), ceasing new activity

---

[5] A crop year refers to the year in which a commodity is harvested. A marketing year follows the crop year and is the 12 months following harvest during which that crop is typically sold, perhaps participating in a government program.

(if its authorization to use mandatory funding expires), or reverting to permanent laws enacted decades ago (for the farm commodity programs).[6] For example

- An appropriations act or a continuing resolution can continue some farm bill programs even though an authority has expired. Programs using discretionary funding—and programs using appropriated mandatory funding such as those in the SNAP account—can continue to operate via appropriations action.[7]
- Most farm bill programs with mandatory funding generally cease new operations when they expire (e.g., the Conservation Reserve Program (CRP), and Market Assistance Program (MAP)).[8] However, existing contracts under prior-year authority could generally continue to be paid. Exceptions include SNAP and programs in the SNAP account (as discussed above), the farm commodity programs, and crop insurance (as discussed below).
- The mandatory farm commodity programs would begin reverting to permanent law beginning with the 2019 crop year, for which dairy is the first to be affected, beginning on January 1, 2019. However, payments for the 2018 crop year would continue to be authorized from the 2014 farm bill, including final payments for corn and soybeans that would be made as late as October 2019 after the 2018 crop's marketing year.

---

[6] "Permanent law" refers to nonexpiring farm commodity programs that are generally from the 1938 and 1949 farm bills. The temporary suspension of permanent law is included as a section in all recent farm bills. If the suspension of permanent law were to expire at the end of a crop year, the permanent law provisions would take effect unless a new farm bill, or an extension of the most recent bill, continues the suspension.

[7] CRS Report RS20129, *Entitlements and Appropriated Entitlements in the Federal Budget Process*, by Bill Heniff Jr.

[8] One mandatory conservation program—the Environmental Quality Incentives Program—was extended through FY2019 prior to expiration, and therefore did not expire like other programs.

- Crop insurance is an example of a program with mandatory funding that is permanently authorized outside of the farm bill and does not expire.[9]

Funding Sources Affect Consequences of Expiration

The funding source that is authorized matters, since some programs use discretionary appropriations and some are mandatory spending. These differences affect how the farm bill is constructed under normal circumstances. They also affect what happens when the farm bill expires or if there is an extension. Farm bill programs are generally funded in two ways:[10]

1. *Discretionary authorizations.* A farm bill sets the parameters for programs and authorizes them to receive funding in subsequent appropriations, but does not provide or assure actual funding. Budget enforcement is through future appropriations acts and budget resolutions.
2. *Mandatory spending.* A farm bill authorizes outlays and pays for them with multiyear budget estimates when the farm bill is enacted. Budget enforcement is through "PayGo" budget rules, baseline projections, and scores of the effect of proposed bills. The baseline is a projection of future federal spending on mandatory programs under current law. It is a benchmark against which proposed changes in law are measured (i.e., the score of a bill).

Discretionary Funding

Discretionary spending is authorized throughout the farm bill. Discretionary programs include most rural development, credit, and research

---

[9] Federal crop insurance is permanently authorized by the Federal Crop Insurance Act (7 U.S.C. §1501 et seq.) and would continue to operate without enactment of a new farm bill. Past farm bills, however, have amended the crop insurance program's underlying authority.

[10] CRS In Focus IF10783, *Farm Bill Primer: Budget Issues*, by Jim Monke.

programs, and some conservation and nutrition programs. Some smaller research, bioenergy, and rural development programs are authorized to receive both mandatory and discretionary funding. Most agency operations are financed with discretionary funds. SNAP—a mandatory program—also requires an appropriation and can be continued in expiration situation via appropriations action.[11]

Without a new farm bill or extension, many programs may not appear to have statutory authority to receive appropriations (an "authorization of appropriations").[12] However, appropriations law allows the continued operation of a program where only appropriations action has occurred.

The Government Accountability Office (GAO) says there is no constitutional or statutory requirement for an appropriation to have a prior authorization.[13] Congress distinguishes between authorizations and appropriations, but this is a congressional construct.[14] GAO says that "the existence of a statute imposing substantive functions upon an agency that require funding for their performance is itself sufficient legal authorization for the necessary appropriations." For expired authorizations, GAO says that "appropriation of funds for a program whose funding authorization has expired ... provides sufficient legal basis to continue the program."[15]

Mandatory Funding

Programs that rely on mandatory funding are perhaps the most at risk for interruption if the farm bill expires. Most farm bill programs with

[11] See footnote 7. Other nutrition programs, including the Commodity Supplemental Food Program and administrative funds for the Emergency Food Assistance Program, are discretionary. The Special Supplemental Program for Women, Infants, and Children (WIC) also is discretionary, but is not part of the farm bill.

[12] An "authorization of appropriations" is a recommendation from an authorizing committee to the appropriations committee via a law. It is not binding and has no bearing on budget enforcement for an authorizing bill. Appropriators may choose not to fund a program, or may choose to exceed the authorization. Authorization amounts may be specific or indefinite ("such sums as necessary").

[13] Government Accountability Office, *Principles of Federal Appropriations Law* (also known as the *GAO Red Book*), Chapter 2, "The Legal Framework" (4th ed. 2016 rev.), p. 2-55, at https://www.gao.gov/legal/appropriations-lawdecisions/red-book.

[14] CRS Report R42098, *Authorization of Appropriations: Procedural and Legal Issues*, by James V. Saturno and Brian T. Yeh.

[15] *GAO Red Book*, Chapter 2, p. 2-80.

mandatory funding have an expiration date either on their program authority or their funding authority. These include farm commodity programs, some conservation programs, agricultural trade programs, and international food aid programs. For the most part, without reauthorization or an extension, these programs would cease to operate or undertake new activities in an expiration. Exceptions are noted above.

Among the mandatory-funded programs that are usually the focus of the farm bill, there are two subcategories that may affect congressional action—some have baseline beyond FY2018 and some do not have baseline after FY2018.[16] In an expiration, both categories of mandatory programs face similar disruption when their authorizations expire. But the difference in having or not having a baseline is important as Congress writes a farm bill or if Congress considers an extension to deal with an expiration.[17]

For example, when Congress enacted a one-year extension of the 2008 farm bill for 2013, the extension act was budget-neutral. The major programs that had baseline were extended at no additional budgetary cost. However, the subset of programs without baseline did not continue in the 2013 extension because they would have needed budgetary offsets to provide continuing funding and not increase the deficit. Providing funding for those programs without baseline would have made the extension more difficult.

Historical Examples of Expiration

The current, partial expiration of the 2014 farm bill has precedent in the two most recent farm bills—the 2002 and 2008 farm bills. As the 2014 farm bill was being developed, there were two periods of expiration of the 2008 farm bill. The first was from October 1, 2012, through January 1, 2013, and

---

[16] See CRS In Focus IF10780, Farm Bill Primer: Programs Without Baseline Beyond FY2018, by Jim Monke, and CRS Report R44758, Farm Bill Programs Without a Budget Baseline Beyond FY2018, by Jim Monke.

[17] The group of programs without baseline includes certain conservation programs; most of the bioenergy, rural development, and research title programs; various nutrition title pilot programs and studies; organic and farmers' market programs; trade promotion programs; and outreach to socially disadvantaged and military veteran farmers.

the second dated from October 1, 2013, through February 6, 2014. Some programs ceased new operations, while others were able to continue. However, neither expiration lasted long enough for the farm commodity programs to revert to a "permanent law" that would have raised support prices and increased federal outlays. On the first occasion, the 2008 farm bill was extended for one year; all provisions that were in effect on September 30, 2012, were extended through FY2013 or for the 2013 crop year as applicable. Programs without baseline did not continue in FY2013 because no additional mandatory funding was provided in the extension.[18] On the second occasion, no extension was enacted since a conference agreement was expected. The Agricultural Act of 2014 (2014 farm bill; P.L. 113-79) was enacted on February 7, 2014, to cover the 2014-2018 crop years and other programs through September 30, 2018. As the 2008 farm bill was being developed, the 2002 farm bill expired and portions of it were extended six times for less than a year in total. The first of those extensions continued authority for many expiring programs for about three months. Because final agreement was pending, five more extensions each covered a week to a month. With a few exceptions, these extensions continued the 2002 farm bill provisions—including the dairy and sugar programs, but not the direct, counter-cyclical, and marketing loan programs for the other supported commodities. Programs without baseline did not continue during the first part of the fiscal year because no additional mandatory funding was provided in the short term extensions.

FARM COMMODITY SUPPORT PROGRAMS

The last year for the 2014 farm bill's commodity programs is the 2018 crop year—that is, crops harvested during 2018 and marketed during the

[18] While the extension did add authorizations of appropriation for FY2013 for some of the programs without baseline, those authorizations went unfunded because the omnibus appropriations act did not allocate any one-time funding to such programs.

twelve months following harvest.[19] The dairy margin protection program is the first such program that would expire, on December 31, 2018.

The farm commodity income support programs raise farm income by making payments and reducing financial risks from uncertain weather and market conditions. Government-set reference prices offer payments when market prices fall below support levels. These programs collectively are known as "Title I" programs, based on where they have been placed in recent farm bills.[20]

Possible Reversion to Permanent Law

Farm commodity support policy has evolved since the first farm bill in 1933 via successive farm bills that update and supersede prior policies. However, a set of nonexpiring provisions remain in statute and are known as "permanent law." These provisions were enacted primarily in the Agriculture Adjustment Act of 1938 and the Agricultural Act of 1949, as amended by subsequent farm bills.

As more modern farm bills moved away from using the permanent law provisions, they have suspended permanent law, but only for the duration of each farm bill.[21] If the suspension of permanent law were to expire, the commodity programs authorized by permanent law could be reactivated. The first commodity to be affected by the expiration of the 2014 farm bill would be dairy, which has a 2018 crop year that ends on December 31, 2018.

---

[19] A crop year is the calendar year during which the crop is harvested, and determines which law covers that production. Implementation of marketing benefits depends on harvest of the actual commodity based on its marketing year, which is the 12-month period after a new harvest and may extend into a new calendar year. For example, for wool, mohair, and sugarcane, the marketing year is January 1-December 31; for honey, it is April 1-March 31; for wheat, barley, and oats, it is June 1-May 31; for flue-cured tobacco, it is July 1-June 30; for cotton, peanuts, and rice, it is August 1-July 31; for sugar beets, it is September 1-August 31; for corn, sorghum, soybeans, mainland sugarcane, all tobacco but flue-cured, and milk, it is October 1-September 30.

[20] For more background, see CRS In Focus IF10718, *Farm Bill Primer: Title I Commodity Programs*, by Randy Schnepf.

[21] For example, in the 2014 farm bill (P.L. 113-79), see §1602: "(a) The following provisions of the Agricultural Adjustment Act of 1938 ... [and] the Agricultural Act of 1949 shall not be applicable to the 2014 through 2018 crops..."

Some see the existence of permanent law—and the policy and budget consequences that could result—as an assurance that the farm commodity programs will be revisited every time a farm bill expires. In general, recent farm bills have retained permanent law and continued to suspend it, though some bills over the past three decades have proposed to repeal it (see *Table 1*).

Description of Permanent Law

Permanent Law and the "Dairy Cliff"

Dairy is often discussed extensively when farm bill expiration arises, not only because it would be the first commodity to revert to permanent law, but also because it is an example of the scale of market effects and costs of intervention that could result.

Permanent law compels the U.S. Department of Agriculture (USDA) to purchase manufactured dairy products (nonfat dry milk, cheddar cheese, and butter) in sufficient quantities to raise demand in order to raise the farm price of milk to the desired support level. Under permanent law, those mandated purchase prices ($39.08 per hundredweight (cwt., or100 pounds), based on August 2018 data) are more than double current market prices ($15.40/cwt. for all milk in July 2018; Table 1).

The high purchase price under permanent law could result in the government outbidding commercial markets for a sizeable share of output, and that could subsequently raise the retail price of milk. In December 2012, the possibility that milk prices might eventually double became known as the "dairy cliff," named after the concurrent "fiscal cliff"

The commodity support provisions of the 1938 and 1949 permanent laws are commonly viewed as being so fundamentally different from current policy and potentially costly to the federal government—and inconsistent with today's farming practices, marketing system, and international trade agreements—that Congress is unlikely to let permanent law take effect. Permanent law provides mandatory support for basic crops through nonrecourse loans.[22] It does not authorize more modern support approaches such as loan deficiency payments, payments based on prices or revenue but not to actual production (decoupled), or dairy margin protection.

Government Costs under Permanent Law

Official budget estimates of reverting to permanent law have been rare. In 1979, the Congressional Budget Office studied the effect on dairy policy.[23] In 1985, USDA analyzed more comprehensively the possible economic consequences of permanent law. It found that significant market intervention and increased government expenditures could occur.[24] In 2013, the White House indicated that permanent law for dairy could cost $12 billion per year and result in milk prices doubling.[25] This was consistent with an extrapolation of the 1985 USDA report by substituting modern prices and production levels, which estimated outlays between $10 billion and $12.5

---

[22] Under permanent law, commodity support prices would be based on a portion of a "parity price" derived from a 1910 to 1914 prices paid index, but inflated to current values. This is described further in the "Parity Price Support Levels and Production Controls" section.

[23] CBO, *Consequences of Dairy Price Support Policy*, March 1979, at https://www.cbo.gov/sites/default/files/96thcongress-1979-1980/reports/79doc637.pdf.

[24] USDA Economic Research Service, *Possible Economic Consequences of Reverting to Permanent Legislation or Eliminating Price and Income Supports*, AER-526, January 1985, pp. 65-67 and pp. 21-35, at https://www.ers.usda.gov/publications/pub-details/?pubid=40555.

[25] White House, *The Economic Importance of Passing a Comprehensive Food, Farm, And Jobs Bill*, Nov. 2013, pp. 24, 27, at https://obamawhitehouse.archives.gov/ sites/default/files/docs/farm_bill_report_211.pdf. See also, *New York Times*, "With Farm Bill Stalled, Consumers May Face Soaring Milk Prices," December 20, 2012, at http://www.nytimes.com/2012/12/21/us/milk-prices-could-double-as-farm-bill-stalls.html.

billion per year for dairy.[26] At that time, projected outlays for dairy in the 2008 farm bill were about $100 million per year.[27]

Implementing Permanent Law

If the suspension of permanent law expires, USDA would be required to implement the permanent law statutes. When the farm bill faced expiration in 2012, USDA outlined how it would implement permanent law.[28] To achieve implementation, however, USDA might need to write new regulations, which could take additional time. In 2013, USDA indicated that it could take at least a month to implement permanent law.[29] The market effects of implementing permanent law may be more gradual and the effect could take weeks or months.[30]

Implementation of permanent law is based on crop years and tied to the harvest and marketing of a crop (effectively, the marketing year for the corresponding crop year), and thus would be separated from a single, fixed expiration date. For example, the 2014 farm bill covers farm production through the 2018 crop year—including 2014 farm bill payments that might occur after the 2018 crop's marketing year ends in October 2019 for corn

---

[26] The 1985 USDA-ERS report estimated that USDA would need to remove (that is, purchase) 13%-17% of milk production to raise market prices to support levels mandated under permanent law (p. 33). Milk prices nearly would have doubled from a market price about $13/cwt. in 1985 to a support price of $24/cwt. in 1990. The report estimated that by 1990, removing 270 million cwt. from a market production of 154 billion pounds of milk (17.5% of production) would cost about $6.5 billion per year (p. 34). An extrapolation of these amounts to 2013 levels indicated a possible, albeit unofficial, cost range. Using the same elasticity (responsiveness of the quantities demanded and produced to price changes) and purchase ratios needed to achieve a near doubling of prices, and using the midpoint of the removal ratio from the 1985 study (15%), removing 300 million cwt. out of about 200 billion pounds of 2013 production at a then-prospective $37/cwt. support price could cost over $11 billion per year for dairy.

[27] CBO, "USDA Mandatory Farm Programs—May 2013 Baseline," at http://cbo.gov/publication/44202.

[28] USDA, "The Effects of Failure to Enact a New Farm Bill: Permanent Law Support for Commodities and Authorization Lapse of Other USDA Programs," memorandum, 2012, at https://www.agri-pulse.com/ext/resources/pdfs/p/e/r/m/o/Permanent_Law_Authorization_memo.pdf.

[29] Agri-Pulse, "Secretary Vilsack Reacts to No Farm Bill," audio, December 12, 2013.

[30] Andrew M. Novakovic, "Is Reverting to the 1949 Agricultural Act Really a Possibility for Dairy Price Supports?," Cornell Information Letter 13-04, December 2013, available at https://hoards.com/article-11129-is-reverting-to-the1949-agricultural-act-really-a-possibility-for-dairy-price-supports.html.

and soybeans. The 2019 crop year would be the first year potentially covered by permanent law, and the first commodity to be affected would be dairy (on January 1, 2019), followed by wheat, barley, and oats, whose marketing year starts in June 2019.

Parity Price Support Levels and Production Controls

Price support under permanent law uses the concept of "parity prices." Parity refers to the relationship between prices that farmers receive for their products and prices they pay for inputs. Permanent law determines parity using the period of 1910-1914 as a benchmark.[31] Support prices would be set to guarantee producers between 50% to 90% of the parity price, based on the commodity.[32]

Under permanent law, nonrecourse loan rates for wheat, rice, cotton, corn, and other feed grains function as farm price supports. A nonrecourse loan allows the producer to forfeit the crop to the government and keep the principal amount if market prices are below the loan rate.[33] Unless commercial markets pay more than the nonrecourse loan prices, farmers could put their crops under loan and forfeit the commodities to USDA when the nine-month loans mature. However, to avoid forfeiture problems, USDA has permanent authority allowing farmers to repay nonrecourse loans for less than the principal (loan rate) plus interest, similar to marketing loans in the modern commodity program.[34]

Productivity gains and technological advances over the past 100 years have made ratios of parity prices out of touch with—and possibly irrelevant to—modern farming practices.[35]

---

[31] Parity prices are computed under the provisions of Title III §301(a) of the Agricultural Adjustment Act of 1938, as amended by the Agricultural Acts of 1948, 1949, and 1956. Permanent law requires USDA to estimate and publish parity prices regularly. See USDA National Agricultural Statistics Service, *Agricultural Prices*, published monthly at http://usda.mannlib.cornell.edu/MannUsda/viewDocumentInfo.do?documentID=1002.

[32] 7 U.S.C. 1441; 7 U.S.C. 1444; 7 U.S.C. 1444b; 7 U.S.C. 1445; 7 U.S.C. 1446.

[33] For additional information, see CRS In Focus IF10714, *Farm Bill Primer: The Marketing Assistance Loan Program*, by Randy Schnepf.

[34] Added to permanent law in Section 1009 of the Food Security Act of 1985 (7 U.S.C. 1308a).

[35] USDA-ERS, AER-526 (1985), at pp. 1-2.

Additional production controls exist for wheat and cotton. Permanent law would require USDA to announce acreage allotments and marketing quotas during the prior crop year, and to hold producer referenda on implementing marketing quotas. A two-thirds affirmative vote for marketing quotas results in the highest levels of support, with mandatory restrictions on acreage (and the quantity eligible for support).

Even if support levels were set at the lower end of the range in permanent law (e.g., 50%-75% of parity prices), permanent law supports would be above 2018 market prices for all supported commodities and result in greater federal outlays than under the 2008 farm bill (*Figure 1*, *Table 1*).

For example, in July 2018, the national average "all milk" farm price received was $15.40 per hundredweight (cwt.). This is less than half the permanent law support price ($39.08/cwt. at a minimum support level of 75% of parity; *Table 1*).[36] USDA would be compelled to purchase manufactured dairy products in sufficient quantities to raise demand in order to raise the farm price of milk. By contrast, the 2014 farm bill's dairy margin protection program has generally not been making many payments at current prices and margins.[37]

Moreover, as implied by the list of commodities in *Table 1*, not all commodities that are part of the 2014 farm bill would receive federal support under permanent law.

---

[36] The parity support level correlates to a lower grade of milk (Class III or IV) than the "all milk" price, which includes higher grades of fluid milk. The corresponding and higher "all milk" price associated with a $39/cwt. support price likely would be over $40/cwt. (based on Novakovic, p. 4).

[37] See CRS In Focus IF10750, *Farm Bill Primer: Dairy Safety Net*, by Joel L. Greene, and CRS In Focus IF10833, *Dairy Provisions in the Bipartisan Budget Act (P.L. 115-123)*, by Joel L. Greene.

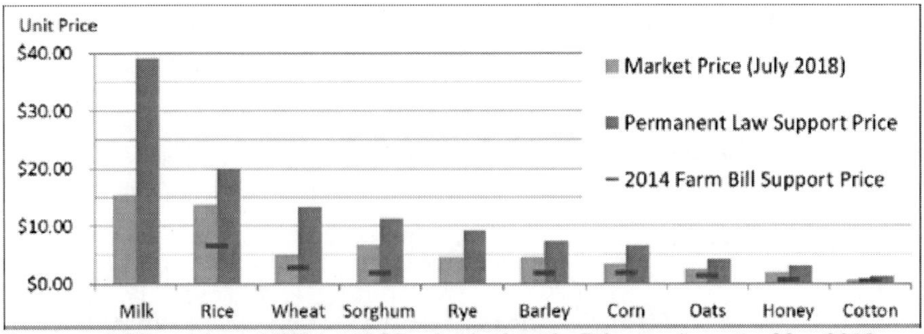

Source: CRS, using USDA-NASS Agricultural Prices, August 29, 2018, at http://usda.mannlib.cornell.edu/MannUsda/viewDocumentInfo.do?documentID=1002, and P.L. 113-79. See Table 1.

Note: The 2014 farm bill support prices identified in this chart are marketing loan rates (rather than the reference price for Price Loss Coverage, another form of income support that is decoupled from production).

Figure 1. Permanent Law Supports Higher Than 2014 Farm Bill and Market Prices.

The commodities that would lose mandatory support include soybeans and other oilseeds, peanuts, wool, mohair, sugar beets and sugar cane, dry peas, lentils, and small and large chickpeas. Parity-based supports once existed for wool, mohair, and peanuts, but were repealed. Parity support is not allowed for oilseeds or sugar. A different set of commodities could receive support under discretionary authority given to the Secretary of Agriculture in the Agricultural Act of 1949 and the Commodity Credit Corporation Charter Act. But for budgetary and other reasons, such discretionary authority has rarely been used.[38]

Crop Insurance

The federal crop insurance program protects producers against losses in crop revenue or yield through federally subsidized policies that are purchased by producers. The program is permanently authorized by the

[38] See CRS Report R44606, *The Commodity Credit Corporation: In Brief*, by Megan Stubbs.

Federal Crop Insurance Act, as amended (7 U.S.C. 1501 et seq.). A reauthorization of the program is not needed in the farm bill.[39]

Table 1. Parity Prices and Supports for Farm Products Under Permanent Law

Commodity[a]	Permanent Law Provisions			Farm Prices Received (July 2018)	2014 Farm Bill Support[b]
	Description	Parity Price	Minimum Support Price		
Milk, All, Cwt.	Purchase milk and butterfat products at	$52.10	75% of parity = $39.08	$15.40	Margin-based[c]
	75%-90% of parity.				
Wheat, Bu.	Nonrecourse loans and direct purchases.	$17.60	75% of parity = $13.20	$5.00	$2.94
	Acreage allotments. If quotas approved:				
	loan rate=65%-90% of parity. If quotas not approved: loan rate=50% parity.				
	Quotas not announced: loan=75%-90% parity.				
Upland cotton, Lb.	Nonrecourse loans and direct purchases.	$2.00	65% of parity = $1.30	$0.741	$0.52
	Acreage allotments. If quotas approved:				
	loan rate=65%-90% of parity. If quotas not approved: loan rate=50% parity. If quotas not announced: loan rate=65%-90% of parity.				
Rice, Cwt.	Permanent authority repealed by 1981 farm bill,	$40.00	50% of parity = $20.00	$13.70	$6.50

[39] CRS Report R45193, *Federal Crop Insurance: Program Overview for the 115th Congress*, by Isabel Rosa.

	but restored by 1996 farm bill.				
	Loan rate=50%-90% of parity.				
Corn, Bu.	Nonrecourse loans and direct purchases.	$13.20	50% of parity = $6.50	$3.47	$1.95
	Acreage allotments are not authorized.				
	Loan rate=50%-90% of parity.				
Sorghum, Bu.	Support for sorghum, barley, oats, and rye is set based on the feeding value of	$22.40	50% of parity = $11.20	$6.79	$1.95
Barley, Bu.	each in relation to corn.	$14.90	50% of parity = $7.45	$4.52	$1.95
Oats, Bu.		$8.59	50% of parity = $4.30	$2.61	$1.39
Rye, Bu.		$18.50	50% of parity = $9.25	$4.50d	none
Honey, Lb.	Purchases of honey at 60%-90% of parity.	$5.15	60% of parity = $3.09	$2.06e	$0.69

Source: Compiled by CRS, using USDA-NASS Agricultural Prices, August 29, 2018, at https://usda.mannlib.cornell. edu/MannUsda/viewDocumentInfo.do?document ID=1002; the Agricultural Act of 2014 (P.L. 113-79), and based on USDA, "The Effects of Failure to Enact a New Farm Bill: Permanent Law Support for Commodities and Authorization Lapse of Other USDA Programs," memorandum, 2012, at https://www.agri-pulse.com/ext/resources/pdfs/ p/e/r/m/o/Permanent_ Law_Authorization_memo.pdf.

Note: Cwt. = Hundredweight, Bu. = Bushel, and Lb. = Pound.

[a] Permanent law mandates support for the commodities listed in the table. Wool, mohair, and peanuts were formerly included, but supports were repealed. Parity support is not allowed for oilseeds or sugar.

[b] The 2014 farm bill support prices listed in this table are the marketing loan rates (rather than the reference price for Price Loss Coverage, another form of income support that is decoupled from production).

[c] The 2014 farm bill does not specify a support price for milk, but rather is a program to make payments if the margin of the milk market price minus feed costs falls below certain guaranteed levels. See CRS In Focus IF10750, Farm Bill Primer: Dairy Safety Net, by Joel L. Greene.

[d] The most recent market price for rye is for the 2017 marketing year (Agricultural Prices, August 2018).

[e] The market price for honey is implied from the "price as a percent of parity" published in Agricultural Prices.

Producers who grow a crop that is ineligible for crop insurance may be eligible for a direct payment under USDA's Noninsured Crop Disaster Assistance Program (NAP). Like crop insurance, NAP has permanent authority under Section 196 of the Federal Agriculture Improvement and Reform Act of 1996 (7 U.S.C. 7333).[40]

CONSERVATION PROGRAMS

USDA administers close to 20 agricultural conservation programs that are directly or indirectly available to assist producers and landowners who wish to practice conservation on agricultural lands.[41] These programs address natural resource concerns on private agricultural and forested lands through technical and financial assistance. Many conservation programs have different expiration dates for program and funding authority. Therefore, they may be affected differently by expiration or extension of the 2014 farm bill. *Table 2* separates the conservation programs by type of funding authority—mandatory and discretionary.

For many conservation programs, program authority is permanent under the Food Security Act of 1985, as amended, but the authority to receive mandatory funding expires. An extension of the 2014 farm bill would allow programs with expired mandatory funding authority to continue, if the program has baseline beyond FY2018. For example, the Conservation Reserve Program's (CRP's) funding and program authority expired at the end of FY2018. Because CRP has baseline beyond FY2018, an extension would allow the program to continue for a period of time at the authorized rate of enrollment—up to 24 million acres at any one time. Without reauthorization or a further extension of mandatory funding and program authority, CRP is unable to sign new contracts or enroll additional acres after September 30, 2018. All existing contracts and agreements stay in force for the contract period, and payments continue to be made.

Some mandatory conservation programs have no baseline beyond FY2018 and therefore would require offsets from other funding in order to

---

[40] See CRS In Focus IF10698, *Farm Bill Primer: Disaster Assistance Programs*, by Megan Stubbs.

[41] For additional information on agricultural conservation programs, see CRS Report R40763, *Agricultural Conservation: A Guide to Programs*, by Megan Stubbs.

Table 2. Conservation Program Expiration in the 2014 Farm Bill, as Amended

Programs Authorized to Receive Mandatory Funding[a]	Expiration of Funding Authority
Agricultural Conservation Easement Program	September 30, 2018
Agricultural Management Assistance	No expiration date
Conservation Reserve Program	September 30, 2018
Conservation Stewardship Program	September 30, 2018
Environmental Quality Incentives Program	September 30, 2019[b]
EQIP Conservation Innovation Grants	September 30, 2018
Grassroots Source Water Protection Program	One-time authority[c,e]
Regional Conservation Partnership Program	September 30, 2018
Terminal Lakes	September 30, 2014d[e]
Voluntary Public Access and Habitat Incentive Program	September 30, 2018[e]
Watershed Rehabilitation Program	September 30, 2014d[e]
Wetlands Mitigation Banking	One-time authority[c,e]
Programs Authorized for Discretionary Appropriations Error! Reference source not found.	Expiration of Appropriations Authority
Conservation of Private Grazing Land	September 30, 2018
Emergency Conservation Program	No expiration date
Emergency Watershed Protection	No expiration date
Grassroots Source Water Protection Program	September 30, 2018
Healthy Forests Reserve Program	September 30, 2018
Water Bank Program	No expiration date
Watershed and Flood Prevention Operations	No expiration date
Watershed Rehabilitation Program	September 30, 2018

Source: CRS using the Agricultural Act of 2014 (P.L. 113-79), as amended.

[a] All of these programs were either reauthorized or created in Title II of the 2014 farm bill. Many were initially authorized by the Food Security Act of 1985 (P.L. 99-198), as amended, or in subsequent farm bills.

[b] Mandatory funding authority was extended through FY2019 in the Bipartisan Budget Act of 2018 (P.L. 115- 123). While funding is available in FY2019, some program provisions expired September 30, 2018.

[c] Some mandatory farm bill conservation programs were authorized to receive a specific amount of mandatory funding, but no fiscal year is specified. Funds are to remain available until expended.

[d] Some mandatory farm bill conservation programs have limited or no baseline funding beyond FY2018. These programs require offset funding or appropriated funding to operate.

[e] Some mandatory farm bill conservation programs were authorized to receive mandatory funding in FY2014, to remain available until expended.

[f] Though some discretionary programs have expired authority to receive appropriations, they are not prohibited from receiving annual appropriations. See “Discretionary Funding” section for additional explanation.

continue (e.g., Voluntary Public Access and Habitat Incentives Program and Wetlands Mitigation Banking). In some cases, provisions within a program do not have baseline, while the parent program does (e.g., Transition Incentives Program within CRP). In these cases, the individual provisions would require offset funding in order to continue.

One mandatory conservation program—the Environmental Quality Incentives Program (EQIP)— was extended in the Bipartisan Budget Act of 2018 (P.L. 115-123) to September 30, 2019. While EQIP has funding authority through the end of FY2019, select program provisions expired September 30, 2018 (see text box below).

Several conservation programs also have permanent program authority, but are authorized to receive discretionary appropriations only through FY2018. Funding for these programs varies and is based on appropriated levels. Similar to other discretionary programs with expired authority, the program can continue as long as it receives appropriated funding.

Select Expired EQIP Provisions (16 U.S. C. §3839aa et seq.)

Livestock funding – requires 60% of funding be used for payments related to livestock practices.

Wildlife habitat funding – requires 5% of funding be used for payments related to wildlife habitat.

Payment limits – limits total EQIP payments to $450,000 for the duration of the farm bill.

Air quality funding – requires $25 million be used for payments for air quality concern practices.

SNAP and the Other Nutrition Programs

As discussed earlier, expiration and extension of SNAP (and most of the related nutrition programs in the farm bill) particularly hinge on whether funding is provided in an explicit extension or in an appropriations act, including a continuing appropriations act (commonly referred to as a continuing resolution or CR). In the case of the 2014 farm bill, certain provisions of law include a September 30, 2018, expiration date; these are primarily authorizations of appropriations but some are program authorizations. The impact on operations is based on factors related to programs' authorizing statutes, appropriations actions, and the terms of a farm bill extension (if applicable).[42]

The 2014 farm bill reauthorized a number of domestic food assistance programs, including SNAP (formerly food stamps), the Emergency Food Assistance Program (TEFAP), the Commodity Supplemental Food Program (CSFP), the Food Distribution Program on Indian Reservations (FDPIR), the Senior Farmers' Market Nutrition Program, the Bill Emerson Hunger Fellowship Program, Community Food Projects, and nutrition assistance block grants for American Samoa and Puerto Rico.[43] The law also created a new program, the Food Insecurity Nutrition Incentive (FINI) grants. With regard to expiration or extension, these programs fall into one of three categories:

1. Programs that are permanently authorized and funded,
2. Programs that can be continued by the enactment of further funding, or

---

[42] For example, the extension in P.L. 112-240 for the most part continued the current law policies for SNAP and the other programs in the SNAP account that had existed on or before September 30, 2012. The exception was that the farm bill extension contained a change to the mandatory funding of the SNAP-related program, the Nutrition Education and Obesity Prevention Grant Program, reducing the program's FY2013 funding by $110 million. Also, the extension continued the FY2012 SNAP Employment and Training (E&T) mandatory funding, which was reduced from $90 million to $79 million. Such funding has been used, in previous appropriations acts, to offset additional discretionary appropriations (i.e., as a so-called CHIMPS, or changes in mandatory program spending).

[43] Note that the National School Lunch Program (NSLP), School Breakfast Program (SBP), Child and Adult Care Food Program (CACFP), Summer Food Service Program (SFSP), Special Milk Program, and Special Supplemental Program for Women, Infants, and Children (WIC) programs are generally not reauthorized in a farm bill. These programs are authorized by the Russell National School Lunch Act and Child Nutrition Act statutes; these statutes were most recently reauthorized by P.L. 111-296 (Healthy, Hunger-Free Kids Act of 2010). See CRS In Focus IF10266, *An Introduction to Child Nutrition Reauthorization*.

3. Programs or authorities which would expire unless extended by statute or explicit appropriations for such purposes.

These categories are elaborated upon below. The majority of farm bill nutrition programs (and the majority of nutrition spending) falls into the second category.

Permanently Authorized and Funded Programs

The 2008 farm bill included an expansion of the Fresh Fruit and Vegetable Program (FFVP, "snack" program), and provided permanent funding through Section 32.[44] FFVP's operations were not impacted by periods of expiration after the 2008 farm bill and would not be affected by expiration after September 30, 2018.[45]

Programs Continued by the Enactment of Further Funding[46]

Appropriations can allow a program to continue even if the underlying authorization or authorization of appropriations has not been extended.

---

[44] Section 32 (of the act of August 24, 1935; 7 U.S.C. 612c) refers to a permanent appropriation of 30% of customs receipts. Section 32 receives about $8 billion annually, though most of it supports the child nutrition programs. About $1 billion is available annually to support mostly commodities typically not covered by price support programs (such as meats, poultry, fruits, vegetables, and fish). USDA often donates these surplus commodities to various nutrition assistance programs. See CRS Report RL34081, *Farm and Food Support Under USDA's Section 32 Program*, coordinated by Jim Monke.

[45] The 2014 farm bill included authority and funding for a one-time pilot project for canned, frozen, or dried fruits and vegetables. The pilot and evaluation have been completed. See Mathematica Policy Research for USDA-FNS, *Evaluation of the Pilot Project for Canned, Frozen, or Dried Fruits and Vegetables in the Fresh Fruit and Vegetable Program (FFVP-CFD)*, January 2017, available at https://www.fns.usda.gov/evaluation-elementary-schools-pilotproject-canned-frozen-or-dried-fruits-and-vegetables-fresh.

[46] This section discusses FY2014, after the farm bill extension expired and the FY2014 CR was enacted. Note that the same continuity of operations was true for FY2013, i.e., the SNAP account and CSFP continued operations based on the provision of funding through the FY2013 continuing resolution (P.L. 112-175) and the subsequent full-year appropriation (P.L. 113-6).

Because many of the nutrition programs are funded by the SNAP account, appropriated funds for this account would allow continued operations for most of the programs in the Food and Nutrition Act of 2008 (most recently amended by the 2014 farm bill).[47]

After September 30, 2018, the farm bill programs listed below could continue to operate if funding for the SNAP account is provided in appropriations acts, including continuing appropriations

- SNAP and related grant programs;
- Purchase and distribution of TEFAP commodities (administrative funds could continue with appropriations in the Commodity Assistance Program account);
- FDPIR;
- Nutrition assistance funding for Puerto Rico, American Samoa, and Commonwealth of Northern Mariana Islands; and
- Community Food Projects (administered by the National Institute of Food and Agriculture).

For CSFP, in the Commodity Assistance Program account, the authority to make commodity purchases and fund administrative costs can continue with funding.

During the periods of expiration before enactment of the 2014 farm bill, for example, when funding was provided, these programs continued to operate.[48] In addition, during a partial government shutdown in October 2013, there was a period where some Commodity Assistance Program account operations were affected, but SNAP continued (discussed in text box below).

---

[47] Because of changes made in the 2014 farm bill, many of the programs that would have expired at the end of the 2008 farm bill do not have the same status at the close of FY2018. More of those expiring provisions could now be continued with a SNAP appropriation.

[48] Funding was provided by the CR (P.L. 113-46) and the full-year appropriation (P.L. 113-76).

Programs that Would Require Extension or Specific Appropriations Language

Two farm bill provisions contain both the authorization of the program and the mandatory funding for the operation of the program. These programs, to continue operations, would require either (a) an extension of the authority and mandatory funding or (b) specific (or explicit) reference in appropriations acts.

The *Senior Farmers' Market Nutrition Program's* (SFMNP's) authorizing law (most recently amended by the 2014 farm bill) contains both the program's authority and mandatory funding (a transfer from the Commodity Credit Corporation). Therefore, operations may be affected after September 30, 2018, without an extension or specific additional funding provided. In parts of FY2013 and parts of 2014, expiration temporarily affected program operations.[49]

The 2014 farm bill created the *Food Insecurity Nutrition Incentive* (FINI) grant program. The 2014 farm bill provided mandatory funding (a transfer from the Commodity Credit Corporation) for FINI to operate from FY2014 through FY2018. Without enactment of an extension of such provisions or specific reference in appropriations acts, a sixth year of FINI grants (FY2019) would not be available.

A third 2014 farm bill authority, *SNAP Employment & Training (E&T) Pilot Projects*, expired after September 30, 2018.[50] USDA obligated the mandatory funding by the law's September 30, 2018, deadline, so even in a period of farm bill expiration, pilot project operations continue through the states' grant project periods. However, after September 30, 2018,

---

[49] This program expired after September 30, 2012. Once P.L. 112-240 was enacted, the funding and authority to operate the SFMNP was extended through September 30, 2013. However, it expired again when that extension ended. Due to the seasonal nature of the SFMNP, it is possible that expiration of the farm bill during the fall and/or winter months may not significantly affect this program. When the 2014 farm bill was enacted in February 2014, the SFMNP provision was backdated to October 1, 2013.

[50] In the law (Section 4022 of P.L. 113-79), these grants were titled, "Pilot projects to reduce dependency and increase work requirements and work effort under [SNAP]." See USDA-FNS website, *2014 Farm Bill Pilot Projects*, https://www.fns.usda.gov/2014-ET-Pilots.

without extension or specific appropriation, USDA does not have authority to award additional SNAP E&T pilot grants.

SNAP and the October 2013 Government Shutdown

The 2013 government shutdown sheds light on how SNAP is affected without certain congressional action; however, an authority available in 2013 is no longer available.

At the start of FY2014 (i.e., October 2013), there was a period when both the farm bill extension (P.L. 112-240) had expired, and Congress had not provided FY2014 appropriations.[51] SNAP operations did continue during this lapse. This continuity of operations was possible due to USDA's reliance on authority and funds provided in the American Recovery and Reinvestment Act of 2009 (ARRA, P.L. 111-5), cited in the Food and Nutrition Service's contingency plan.[52] Regular operations resumed once appropriations were provided in a continuing resolution (P.L. 113-46, enacted October 17, 2013). This ARRA authority ended after October 31, 2013, and, under current law, it would not now be available if there were a lapse in SNAP appropriations.[53]

TRADE AND FOREIGN FOOD AID PROGRAMS

Agricultural trade programs with mandatory funding that are affected by fiscal year expiration include export credit guarantees, facilities credit guarantees, export market promotion (the Market Access Program and the Foreign Market Development Program), and technical assistance for specialty crops. Without new mandatory program authority, the Commodity Credit Corporation would not be able to undertake new activities in these programs.

Several international emergency and nonemergency food assistance programs are authorized in the farm bill to receive annual appropriations and

---

[51] CRS Report RS20348, *Federal Funding Gaps: A Brief Overview*, by James V. Saturno.

[52] USDA Food and Nutrition Service, Contingency Plan, October 1, 2013, http://www.usda.gov/documents/usda-fnsshutdown-plan.pdf, p. 2.

[53] See CRS Report R43257, *Background on the Scheduled Reduction to Supplemental Nutrition Assistance Program (SNAP) Benefits*, by Randy Alison Aussenberg and Gene Falk.

have 2018 fiscal year expiration dates.[54] The Food for Peace Title II, Farmer-to-Farmer, and McGovern Dole International Food for Education and Child Nutrition programs rely on discretionary funding. Therefore, these programs can continue to operate after a farm bill expires as long as the programs receive funding in annual appropriations bills. In contrast, the Bill Emerson Humanitarian Trust and the Food for Progress program rely on mandatory funding; therefore they cannot be reauthorized and continued through an annual appropriation. Their authorization to operate expires without a new or extended farm bill.[55]

APPENDIX. LEGISLATIVE OPTIONS UNDER PERMANENT LAW

Some see the existence of permanent law as an assurance for farm bill supporters that the farm commodity programs will be revisited every time a farm bill expires. Given the problematic consequences of permanent law, Congress is not likely to let a farm bill remain expired without taking some action eventually. Permanent law, however badly it may be widely perceived, has remained in statute, and each recent farm bill has suspended it for the duration of the farm bill.

Several legislative options relative to permanent law exist as a farm bill approaches expiration:

1. Retain permanent law, and then do one of the following:
   a. Do nothing (revert to permanent law)
   b. Pass an extension (with its suspension of permanent law)
   c. Pass a new farm bill (and reinstate the suspension of permanent law)
   d. Suspend permanent law (without a new farm bill or extension)
2. Repeal permanent law, and then do one of the following:

[54] Alyssa Casey, Analyst in Agricultural Policy, contributed to this section.

[55] The Food for Progress program authority terminates on December 31, 2018, but the authority for certain amounts and administrative expenses expired at the end of FY2018.

a. Do nothing (no new farm bill)
b. Pass an extension of the current farm bill
c. Pass a new farm bill (with or without a new permanent law provision).

The existence of an outdated permanent law likely encourages Congress to take action, because, to most people, inaction is perceived to have unacceptable consequences. If Congress cannot reach agreement on a new farm bill, then a path of least resistance may be extending the current farm bill with its suspension of permanent law—but this, too, requires legislative action, which may pose political and budgetary challenges.

For those who oppose the farm commodity programs, repealing permanent law would allow Congress to debate farm supports without the looming consequences of reverting to permanent law. But repealing permanent law also requires legislative action. Some believe that it is easier to negotiate and pass a new farm bill, with compromises and reforms, than to deal with the question of repealing permanent law.

Suspension of Permanent Law

Throughout the 1950s and 1960s, farm bills generally used and amended the 1938 and/or 1949 acts. Amendments were sometimes made permanent and sometimes applied only to specific years. As farm commodity policy continued to evolve, farm bills in the 1970s gradually began to move away from using the permanent law provisions with their parity-based price supports and quotas.

As recently as the 1970 and 1973 farm bills, the farm commodity programs were generally written into the 1938 and/or 1949 farm bills, as a form of suspension, with provisions that were applicable only for the new period of the farm bill.[56] Thus, while those farm bills might not have directly

[56] For example, a form of suspension that occurs within the permanent law itself is in the 1970 farm bill (P.L. 91-524), where §501 reads, "Effective only with respect to the 1971, 1972, and 1973 crops of feed grains, section 105 of the Agricultural Act of 1949, as amended, is

suspended permanent law in the same way as more modern farm bills, they nonetheless supplanted some portion of the permanent law parity-based support system for the life of the farm bill, albeit from within the body of the permanent law itself.

Beginning with the 1977 farm bill and continuing through the 2014 farm bill, direct suspension or nonapplicability language began to be used regarding the permanent laws.[57] The current statute that suspends permanent law is the following: Suspension of Permanent Price Support Authority (7 USC 9092; P.L. 113-79, Sec. 1602)

(a) *Agricultural Adjustment Act of 1938.* The following provisions of the Agricultural Adjustment Act of 1938 shall not be applicable to the 2014 through 2018 crops of covered commodities (as defined in section 1111), cotton, and sugar and shall not be applicable to milk during the period beginning on the date of enactment of this Act through December 31, 2018: (1) Parts II through V of subtitle B of title III (7 U.S.C. 1326 et seq.). (2) In the case of upland cotton, section 377 (7 U.S.C. 1377). 3) Subtitle D of title III (7 U.S.C. 1379a et seq.). (4) Title IV (7 U.S.C. 1401 et seq.).

(b) *Agricultural Act of 1949.* The following provisions of the Agricultural Act of 1949 shall not be applicable to the 2014 through 2018 crops of covered commodities (as defined in section 1111), cotton, and sugar and shall not be applicable to milk during the period beginning on the date of enactment of this Act and through December 31, 2018: (1) Section 101 (7 U.S.C. 1441); (2) Section 103(a) (7 U.S.C. 1444(a)); (3) Section 105 (7 U.S.C. 1444b); (4) Section 107 (7 U.S.C. 1445a); (5) Section 110 (7 U.S.C. 1445e); (6)

further amended to read as follows: 'Sec. 105. Notwithstanding any other provision of law—(a)(1) The Secretary shall make available to producers loans and purchases on each crop of corn at such level, not less than $1.00 per bushel nor in excess of 90 per centum of the parity price ... "

[57] For example, direct suspension of permanent law can be found in the 1977 farm bill (P.L. 95-113) in §§409-410, 503-504, 601, and 703; in the 1981 farm bill (P.L. 97-98) in §§304-305, 402, and 501; in the 1985 farm bill (P.L. 99- 198) in §§312, 402, and 502; in the 1990 farm bill (P.L. 101-624) in §§302-305, 402, 502, and 801; in the 1996 farm bill (P.L. 104-127) in §171; in the 2002 farm bill (P.L. 107-171) in §1602; in the 2008 farm bill (P.L. 110-246) in §1602; and in the 2014 farm bill (P.L. 113-79) in §1602.

Section 112 (7 U.S.C. 1445g); (7) Section 115 (7 U.S.C. 1445k); (8) Section 201 (7 U.S.C. 1446); (9) Title III (7 U.S.C. 1447 et seq.); (10) Title IV (7 U.S.C. 1421 et seq.), other than sections 404, 412, and 416 (7 U.S.C. 1424, 1429, and 1431); (11) Title V (7 U.S.C. 1461 et seq.); and (12) Title VI (7 U.S.C. 1471 et seq.).

(c) *Suspension of Certain Quota Provisions.* The joint resolution, "A joint resolution relating to corn and wheat marketing quotas under the Agricultural Adjustment Act of 1938, as amended," approved May 26, 1941 (7 U.S.C. 1330 and 1340), shall not be applicable to the crops of wheat planted for harvest in the calendar years 2014-2018.

Proposals to Repeal Permanent Law

Proposals to repeal permanent law have been somewhat rare, though some have advanced as far as passing either chamber.[58] For example, a proposal to repeal permanent law advanced perhaps the farthest during the development of the 1996 farm bill. Repeal provisions may have had more saliency then because of a perceived intent that the "Freedom to Farm" plan was to end in 2002 at the end of the farm bill. The existence of permanent law could have been an obstacle. Whether or not repeal was a condition of the plan during its development, repeal was dropped in favor of continued suspension during conference negotiations in 1996.

More specifically regarding the 1995-1996 developments, the initial bill considered by the House Agriculture Committee in 1995 would have continued to suspend permanent law (H.R. 2195, Title IV). After not passing in committee, the text of that bill, including the suspension provision, was incorporated into a broader House-passed budget reconciliation package (H.R. 2491, §1105). However, the Senate-passed version of the 1995 reconciliation package included a provision to repeal permanent law (S. 1357, §1101). The conference agreement for the reconciliation package

[58] The listing of bills discussed here to repeal permanent law is not necessarily exhaustive. It is based on a full-text search of bills since 1989 for the word "repeal" within 20 words of "Agricultural Adjustment Act of 1938" or "Agricultural Act of 1949."

adopted the Senate approach for repeal (H.R. 2491, §1109). The conference agreement passed both the House and Senate, but was vetoed, albeit not because of the farm bill provisions.[59]

The next year, a stand-alone 1996 farm bill was introduced and passed in the House with the provision to repeal permanent law (H.R. 2854, §109). The repeal provision was also in the Senate-reported bill (S. 1541, §19). However, the Senate-passed version (S. 1541, §109) did not repeal permanent law but continued to suspend permanent law. The conference agreement for the 1996 farm bill (H.R. 2854, §171) followed the Senate-passed version and continued the suspension of permanent law.

Other bills besides the farm bill from 1995 to 2001 proposed repealing permanent law, but were not formally considered. In 1995, several bills were introduced to restructure government agencies. A bill was introduced to abolish USDA, eliminate all price support authorities including those of permanent law, and transfer certain powers to the Department of Commerce (H.R. 1354, S. 586). A broader government-wide restructuring bill would have repealed permanent law (H.R. 1923). A separate agricultural reform bill would have phased down agricultural supports and eventually repealed permanent law (H.R. 2010). Two other bills to repeal permanent law were introduced in 1995 (H.R. 2523 and H.R. 2787). In 1997-1998, H.R. 502 and S. 2573 would have repealed permanent law. Other bills to repeal permanent law were H.R. 328 in 1999 and S. 1571 in 2001. None of these bills advanced beyond being introduced and referred to committee.

Other bills in various Congresses have been introduced with targeted repeal provisions for certain commodities, but not comprehensive repeal. These bills are not discussed here.

In the 112th Congress during consideration of the 2012 farm bill, a Senate amendment was submitted, but not actually introduced on the floor, to replace the suspension of permanent law with the repeal of those provisions (S.Amdt. 2379 to S. 3420).

In 2013, the House-passed farm bill (H.R. 2642) would have repealed the 1938 and 1949 permanent laws (§1602). In their place, the House-

---

59 CRS Report R45210, *Farm Bills: Major Legislative Actions, 1965-2018*, by Jim Monke.

proposed farm commodity program would have become the permanent law since it would have applied to "the 2014 crop year and each succeeding crop year" (§§1107, 1202, 1204, 1205, 1206, 1301). The Senate bill (S. 954) continued the long-standing suspension of permanent law, as did the initial House-rejected bill (H.R. 1947). The enacted 2014 farm bill continues to suspend permanent law.

INDEX

A

D

E

F

G

H

T

U

V

W